TERRORISM AND MILITANCY IN CENTRAL ASIA

TERRORISM AND MILITANCY IN CENTRAL ASIA

Dr. Jatin Kumar Mohanty

Publications

KALPAZ PUBLICATIONS

Delhi-110052

Terrorism and Militancy in Central Asia

Rs. 750

ISBN: 81-7835-322-9

Published in 2006 in India by
Kalpaz Publications,
C-30, Satyawati Nagar, Delhi-110052
E-mail : Kalpaz@hotmail.com

Laser Typesetting at : Shiva Infosystem, Delhi
Printed at : Salasar Imaging System, Delhi

Contents

Preface

Terrorism is a global concern today. Despite its long history, it became a global phenomenon only in the last decade, affecting almost all the countries in the world. Even though etymologically the term is not a complex one for anybody's comprehension, for more than half a century it has been a matter of extensive and inconclusive debate in different international forums including the United Nations. During the Cold War period the entire phenomenon was seen in the light of the superpower rivalry which resulted in tacit endorsement of it by the erstwhile power blocks in some cases. It is only after the end of Cold War and the attacks on American establishments both in US and worldwide that there is a global awareness about the challenge it poses to mankind as a whole.

The fall of the Soviet Union in 1991 resulted in the creation of five Central Asian republics - Uzbekistan, Kazakhstan, Tajikistan, Kyrgyzstan and Turkmenistan - all geo-strategically poised in an enviable position. The nascent republics which did not witness any arduous freedom struggle to secede from the Soviet Union faced intractable challenges with their diverse ethnic composition, economic overdependence on Russia and poor political and institutional infrastructure.

Seven decades of communist rule had left immense impact on the social, political and economic life of the region. With the introduction of *Glasnost* and *Perestroika* there was a sudden loosening of the control on the socio-religious life of the people in the region. As a result, religious practices mostly Islamic, which were banned earlier, found massive enthusiastic followers. Money and material flowed in from other Islamic countries to these republics. But along with that there flowed in another dangerous stream of Islamic radicals. Flanked by Afghanistan - a war devastated country on one side and Islamic dominated north of China on the other, coupled with the weak state structures and political leadership the region became a safe playground for the Islamists to realise their dream of an Islamic caliphate. These Islamists with cross-border support tried to weaken the states through terrorist activities and extensive anti-state and religious propaganda.

Despite being Islamic countries with Sunni Islam ruling the go of life, these subversive forces with their religious appeal could be able to garner sizeable local support for their activities the reasons for which are wide and varied. It would be apt to mention here that this part of the globe is historically considered as the place of origin of "Sufism"- a mystical movement within Islam that seeks to find divine love and knowledge through direct personal experience of God. It arose as an organized movement after the death of Prophet Muhammad (AD 632). The importance of Sufism in the history of Islam is incalculable. Sufi literature, especially love poetry, represents a golden age in Arabic, Persian, Turkish and Urdu languages.

In spite of its glorious history, social structure (most of the Central Asians are sedentary settlers except Kazakhs and Kyrgyzs) and lack of an obvious cultural faultline these countries have actually presented a unique case for understanding the growth and spread of terrorism in the region. The present study is an earnest endeavour in this direction.

My research on the subject deals with various aspects of the issue of terrorism in Central Asia. Besides the basic question of the causes for the growth of terrorism, the question of the public perception, the support base it enjoys, the sources for sustenance of terrorist activities, the response of the government and international interventions have also been discussed with supporting documents and elaborations.

This book is primarily based on my seven long years of research on the developments in the region. The history of the pre-independent Central Asia and the sources of the social and political developments in the region are hardly available and whatever is available their authenticity is doubtful. Therefore, this book mainly deals with the period starting from 1992 to 2002, the year in which US intervention in Afghanistan changed the scenario altogether.

The first chapter of the book deals extensively with the concept of terrorism and its different variations. This chapter, to me, is an effort to summarise an ongoing debate on the definition, types, methods and objectives of terrorism. I feel this chapter will benefit general readers who may like to develop an interest as well as those working on Central Asia to carry forward the debate on terrorism that exists in this region.

Writing a book, for me, is an act of bringing out a particular aspect of the concerned subject. It can not be and should not be perceived as the final word on it. Therefore, I would like the readers to take the views expressed in my book which is based on facts and sources from many other experts on the subject as one of the many opinions and try to carry forward the debate with true academic spirit.

A book again is usually a collective enterprise. Even though I alone am listed as an author; I am indebted to the support and guidance of many without which this book would not have been possible. While the shortcomings here are exclusively mine, they all deserve a credit for its merits.

I am grateful to my teachers who have been so generous with their time and advice and have played a significant role in my intellectual development. I am indebted to Prof. Ajay Patnaik, my Supervisor, under whom I completed my Ph.D. His inspiration and motivations have made this work possible.

I am also indebted a lot to my friends Saam, Nalin, Maxew, Chaitanya Prakash, B. Sanjay, Vandana Mishra, Atul Kothari, Shri Rudra Narayan Pani, MP (Rajya Sabha) and Shri Dharmendra Pradhan, MP (Lok Sabha) for keeping my morale up through this arduous journey. Dr. Braj Bihari Singh and Mrs. Pallavi Singh need a special mention for their love and best wishes which made me resolute enough to finish this work. The book of course would not have seen the light of the day without the prayer and sacrifices of my parents, my elder brother and my sister-in-law and my beloved wife Ranjana. Words are simply insufficient to express my feelings for them.

Last but not the least, I express my deep sense of gratitude to my publisher for his patience and cooperation.

New Delhi

Jatin Kumar Mohanty

Abbreviations

CAEC	:	Central Asian Economic Community
CICA	:	Conference on Interaction Confidence–building measures in Asia
CIS	:	Commonwealth of Independent States
CPTJ	:	Communist Party of Tajikistan
CPU	:	Communist Party of Uzbekistan.
FSD	:	Forum for Security Dialogue
FSU	:	Former Soviet Union
HT	:	Hizb-ut-Tahrir
IDU	:	Islam and Democracy in Uzbekistan
IMU	:	Islamic Movement of Uzbekistan
IRP	:	Islamic Renaissance Party
ISI	:	Inter Services Intelligence
JUI	:	Jamiat-i-Ulema-Islami
NATO	:	North Atlantic Treaty Organisation
NGO	:	Non-Governmental Organisation
NSCD	:	National Security Committee Development
ODCCP	:	Office for Drug Control and Crime Prevention
OIC	:	Organisation of Islamic Conference
OSCE	:	Organisation of Security and Cooperation in Europe
RCP	:	Revolutionary Communist Party
SAM	:	Surface to Air Missile
SCO	:	Shanghai Cooperation Organisation
UNMOT	:	United Nations Mission for Tajikistan
UTO	:	United Tajik Opposition

Introduction

The problem of militancy and terrorism and its impact on the social, economic and political structure of a state and on the humankind as a whole has assumed prominence in the writings of social scientists in the post-World War II period. Just from being treated as simple criminal activity it became a phenomenon. There are reasons for this change of emphasis and increased attention on this phenomenon. First, the end of World War-II saw the emergence of a number of new independent nations in Asia and African continents. These countries underwent massive political turbulence due to lack of experienced leadership and competing interests within their societies. This competition instead of settling down in the course of time, aggravated in many cases and widened the social hiatus which later turned violent.The case of India-Pakistan rift (over Kashmir), the Middle-east crisis are few of the examples. Second, the endorsement of terrorism as a foreign policy by several countries in the absense of proper global condemnation and rejection encouraged the states to carry forward their designs without really declaring a war on their opponent. Hence, terrorism also came to be known as "proxy war". Third, the end of the war saw the begining of "cold war" between two super power blocks led by America on one side and USSR on the other. Their quest for power and global dominance, prompted them to tacitly encourage and fuel these forces against each other. For example, in Afghanistan, in order to depose an USSRinstalled government led by Dr. Najibullah, USA supported, funded and guided Taliban forces which in the later period became a major reason of worry for itself. Four, the two world wars made the competing nations realise the difficulty and the massive economic implications of a conventional warfare. Therefore, many found it easy to indulge in "proxy wars" rather than on a direct confrontations. Fifth, the rapid progress of technology and dissemination of information in the post World War-II period made terrorism a viable option for rival nations. Greater flow of information also psychologically hardened the ethnic and religious identities and intensified their urge to assert itself. Sixth, some theorists also opine that terrorism is a direct fall out of the fierce competition between societies for possesion of scare resources available in different forms. For example, today oil is considered as a major source of conflict world wide.

With the disintegration of Soviet Union in 1991, five countries in Central Asia namely- Kazakhstan, Uzbekistan, Tajikistan, Turkmenistan and Kirgyzstan became independent republics. These five republics since their occupation by the Russian forces in 1920's had formed an integral part of Russian empire without any resistance, mostly due to the attempts by the Soviet rule at breaking down any sense of national identity that had emeged over several hunderd years. These efforts, directed by the central authorities in Moscow, were collectively known as the National Delimitation. Under this programme, new boundaries which tended to cut across the region's most important defining parameters-clan and tribe-were established, which resulted in the somewhat artificial national structures that exist today. With the introduction of collectivisation and mass education, Central Asia was assimilated into the Soviet state. Secondly, the population being a mix of indegenous and migratory groups-sedentary and nomadic types-due largely to several centuries of imperial conquest, nomadic movement and periodic migration, either voluntary or by force, as during the Stalin period, the region never developed a strong and assertive nationalism. In the absense of it, there never was a political movement for freedom even to the extent that in the referendum held on 17th March 1991on the future of the Soviet Union, over 90 per cent of the Central Asians (98 per cent in Turkmenistan) voted to remain within the union.

Post-independence, it was but natural for the newly born republics to face tumults. Their transition from merely being a constituent of the Soviet Union to full fledged sovereign states with independent economy, multi-ethnic society, poor democratic tradition, no readymade security set up and above all an over administered cultural and religious lifestyle was bound to be ardous and difficult. One of the problems they faced after their independence is the growing influence of radical and fundamentalist Islam. This problem has become a menace in the newly independent Central Asian states, mainly because of their fragile social systems, economic chaos and underdeveloped political structures, all of which have failed to fulfil the needs and aspirations of the people. At the most basic level, it has come to signify, as it did in Tsarist times, a yardstick for differentiation between "them" and "us." Many Central Asians feel deeply betrayed by the way the Slav republics have treated them. They are determined now to stress the gulf that separates them, where previously they had preferred to emphasise their common Soviet culture. There is also a pride and excitement at rediscovering an important part of their heritage in Islam.To a considereable extent, this serves to fill the vacuume created by the evaporation of the Soviet ideological framework.

During the entire Soviet rule, an anti-religious policy was followed ferociously by the Soviet leaders. The region which was dominated by Islam and was considered another epicentre of Islamic religious thought faced the worst from the Soviet leaders. At the same time, the pace of economic and social development in the region was abysmal with the agriculture mainly dependent on cotton cultivation. Industrial development-considered as the basis of economic development was lagging behind in this region, which was primarily considered a raw material base for the industries in Russia.

After the Soviet disintegration, the governments which took over the reigns of power in the Central Asian republics were headed by ex-Communists with a strong propensity towards single party rule. In the absence of democratic progress and plethora of problems facing the society, centrifugal forces emerged mostly aided and abetted by external actors. Developments in different parts of the globe-prominent among them, the Iranian Revolution of 1979, the Afghan crisis, the military and religious coup in Pakistan and the Middle East crisis gave them the much needed inspiration and motivation to carry out their agenda. Saturated with religious indoctrination and inspired by these events, the Islamist forces extended their grand designs of an Islamic *umma* to the Central Asian region.

With this, a clash of interest emerged with the incumbent governments desiring to preserve the previously forced upon secular, atheistic traditions of the region, eliminate political rivals and the radical Islamists seeking to establish Islamic governments on the basis of *sharia* and *hadith*, the ultimate canons of Islamic faith.

This clash of interests created a vicious circle when the governments reacted to fundamentalism through repressive measures that in some cases resulted in greater legitimacy to these forces and made them martyrs before the people and increased their support base and capability to strike again, inviting greater repression by the state.This violent tactics, adopted by the fundamentalist Islamists largely tantamounts to terrorism, as these are largely low intensity proxy conflicts.

Terrorism in Central Asia has many points which are shrouded with controversy. Its operation is extremely complicated and it does not have any recognisable leadership. Its popularity is doubtful and objectives not very clear. In that respect, the present study attempts to put the different dynamics working behind the phenomenon of terrorism in the region into a comparative perspective. It should be pointed out that while there has been a general consensus on a set of conceptual parameters believed to be capable of having a definite qualitative impact on Central Asian terrorism, very few observers seem to agree on the relative weight and significance of these parameters vis-à-vis one another and in relation to the subject under study. Some scholars have, however, emphasised internal economic factors as the primary force behind the growth of terrorism in the region. Interestingly enough, the continuing economic decline in the region has strengthened the diehard Communists and ultra-nationalists rather than Islamic forces. Others, focussing on the role of Iran and Afghanistan in Tajik affairs in recent years, assign considerable importance to external pressures exerted from the Middle East. The present study will focus both external and internal factors which are considered more critical in shaping militancy and terrorism in the region.

Another very significant aspect of terrorism in Central Asia is its area of operation. In the present study, it has been generally referred to as terrorism and militancy. But looking at their area of operation, one thing that becomes clear is that all the terrorist groups who operate in the region are basically regional groups with cross-border linkages. Secondly, they have also been operating across the border mainly aided and abetted by Afghanistan. Therefore, terrorism in Central Asia can comfortably be classified as cross-border terrorism.

The third important aspect associated with terrorism in Central Asia is that it is intricately intertwined with the growth of Islamic radicalism in the region. In fact, it is one of the immediate causes of the growth of militancy and terrorism. Therefore, it is basically religious in nature and has been aggravated with the revival of Islamism in Central Asia.

The Islamic revival in Central Asia has been characterised by two sets of factors. One, the regional proclivity towards Islam depends on the type of the society prevalent in the particular region - sedentary or tribal. The nature of the dominant Islamic proclivity is influenced, in turn, by the organisational reach and the mobilisation capacities of the Islamic forces operating in the region. The general factors that are equally significant are the weaknesses of the nascent democratic forces and their ability to institute genuine political reforms and also the ethnic make up and orientation of each republic.

Islam, which has been basically peaceful and moderate in Central Asia unlike in Arab and Pakistan, is due to historical factors like the method of spread of Islam there, the geographical and occupational life style and the nature of the population settlements. Islam developed culturally in

Central Asia and was enriched intellectually and spiritually by the Central Asian traditions.

But, during the Tsarist rule Islam did not find the patronage it needed to develop further both culturally and spatially. Again, with the advent of the Communist rule, the scenario turned upside down. Islam was banned only to be revived with the coming of *Glasnost* and *Perestroika* and more vigorously after independence in 1991.

The Islamic revivalist forces since independence have to a great extent been successful in influencing the orientation of Islam through their organisational reach and the mobilisation capacity. Through the rapidly increasing numbers of mosques and madrassahs, they have been well organised and capable of reaching to the public.

The Central Asian governments' general political orientations as well as their attitude towards Islam constitute another reason of the Islamic revival in Central Asia. The reluctance of the incumbent governments to carry out political reforms by including the newly emerging democratic and Islamic forces in the political discourse made the latter rebels and role models for others.

The problems of cross-border terrorism, militancy and radical Islamic revivalism aggravated in the post-Soviet period due to their close nexus with drug trafficking and arms trade. The Central Asian republics in tandem with other neighbouring states have formed several forums and have entered into bilateral and multi-lateral treaties, to counter these threats.

The *First Chapter* provides an in-depth study of the definition, types, tactics and philosophy of terrorism as well as the difference between various similar concepts which are very often used interchangeably. For example, terrorism, militancy and insurgency find their use interchangeably in similar contexts in spite of their latent and theoretical differences. To avoid such overlappings, these have been discussed taking the help of the opinions of various experts and authorities in this field. Several organisational and official definitions have also been examined to draw a clear picture. Among the definitions, those of UN and CIS have been prominently dealt with and finally all these definitions have been compiled in a diagram forwarded by David Easton's Systems Theory. Besides the complex definitional discrepancy, the philosophy, the methods and tactics, the objectives, types and their strategies have been discussed. In the final portion of the chapter, other related phenomenons in the light of which the Central Asian terrorism can be classified, have been discussed.

The *Second Chapter* addresses the growth of terrorism, militancy and religious fundamentalism in the region. With a brief background of the religious policies in the past, the chapter examines the situation prevailing in the Central Asian states in the present times. Gorbachev's period being a watershed, saw radical departure from the previous eras in dealing with the question of religion. Besides the political developments, other factors which contributed to Islamic revivalism in the post-independence period have been discussed. To substantiate the arguments that terrorism in its violent form exists in Central Asia, several incidences of terrorist attacks have been mentioned in a chronological order beginning from 1992. They further have been substantiated with the official and other organisational opinions. The perpetrators of the terrorism in Central Asia, their organisational structures, leaders and affiliations have also been examined in the chapter. Their overall political orientation and their agenda also have been included in the chapter. A discussion on the quantitative dimensions of Islamic revival with respect to the number of mosques, madrassahs and the observance of the Islamic rituals has been presented.

The *Third Chapter* contains the link that exists between the terrorists, the drug traffickers and small arms dealers. Central Asian terrorism is not purely a product of the local conditions but has also been sponsored by outside forces like Afghanistan and Pakistan. Their financial support and material help including logistical succours have kept terrorism in Central Asia alive even on the face of ferocious crackdown by the governments. How the drugs produced in Afghanistan and Central Asia is trafficked to the outside world and the money gained out of it is utilised to procure arms and weapons for the fight against governments, have been dealt with in the chapter. Figures of the drugs seized by state authorities have been presented, giving an idea of the magnitude of the drug business in the region. Besides this, the various causes behind the spread of drugs have been cited. While the rise of the fundamentalist Islam in Central Asia has provided the motivation for the terrorist activities, it is the money drawn from the illegal drugs trade which has sustained these activities and steady flow of arms and supplies to the terrorists.

The various responses of the Central Asian republics towards this menace of terrorism are the subject matter of *Chapter Four*. This chapter delineates the role the states have played in curbing not only terrorism but also the reasons behind such activities. The governments which looked at the problem initially as a kind of law and order situation, adopted stringent and repressive methods to curb their expansion. Of late, there have been various concerted efforts in that direction. These are bilateral and multilateral agreements between the Central Asian governments, multilateral agreements within CIS and outside CIS for greater coordination of the efforts to fight terrorism and drugs trade. The responses of the states have been discussed in this chapter which also focus some attention on the deleterious effects of the governments' repressive policies towards the Islamic forces. This chapter also specifically deals with the developments which have taken place in the post-11 September 2001 period, the extremely transformed strategic scenario and its repercussions on politics of the region have also been incorporated.

The *Fifth Chapter* exclusively contains the various organisational efforts which have been undertaken by the Central Asian states in fighting terrorism in the region. Various organisations like SCO, OSCE, NATO, OIC, CICA, ECO, EEC and CIS have shown great enthusiasm in the developments in the region. Their role with regard to the anti-terrorism efforts in the region have been analysed in this chapter.

The concluding chapter deals with and assessment of the different views and theories forwarded by different quarters and discussed in the preceding chapters.

The objective of this study is to have a comprehensive analysis of the problems of militancy and terrorism which the Central Asian republics are facing. The impact of these problems on the social and political fabric of the region has been assessed. Secondly, the response of the Central Asian republics to the problems, the measures taken by them to combat terrorism and militancy and to consolidate their own position against this threat has also been deatwith.

This study is based on historico-analytical and comparative methods. Speeches of the heads of governments and state officials of Central Asian republics, Russia, China, Pakistan, Iran, Turkey and others published documents by these governments and daily broadcast reports from Summary of World Broadcasts, Foreign Broadcast Information Services and Press Reports from Current Digest of the post-Soviet press and other major newspapers have been consulted. Several books by distinguished experts in the field, various articles published in different journals have also been consulted to substantiate different arguments forwarded in the research.

1

Militancy and Terrorism A Conceptual Framework

With the end of the World War II, there emerged a new world order. Prior to that, in the post - World War I period, the world had already been divided into two different opposite ideological camps with the emergence of America as a capitalist superpower on the one hand and Russia as a Communist country on the other. The end of World War II brought along with it the independence for several small countries in Asia and Africa and with their emergence the race between the two superpowers for supremacy over them began, adding further woes to their fragile political, economic and social set-up. This period is also known as 'Cold War' period because of the rivalry between the two big powers that permeated horizontally and vertically into the world political and strategic arenas. They tried to bring as many countries as possible to their fold by fomenting the various forces on ethnic, religious and cultural grounds.This encouraged the groups on the lines of different affiliations to struggle for a greater share in the limited resources of the world. In this competition and race for resources, some obviously got more while the others, less. Sometimes, the group which could not get its share in the new political set-up waged armed struggle against the state aided and abetted by co-interest groups from outside. Besides this struggle for resources, groups based on ethnic and religious identity tried to assert themselves and in order to satisfy their political objectives - to grab political power, have resorted to violent actions time and again.

Thus, terrorism has become an instrument for achieving political goals thereby raising a worldwide concern. Today, there is no country in the world whether in Europe, Africa, Asia or in any other place which is either not witnessing the menace of terrorism or is not concerned about this. Currently it has assumed the proportions of a potential threat to the entire mankind.

Terrorism has been a complex phenomenon and continues to be so.

In spite of all academic delves in to it, a commonly acceptabe definition of terrorism is yet to evolve for formulation and adoption of a generally accepted policy on it. However, despite the constraints there have been several seminal and pioneering endeavours in this direction.

Defining Terrorism, Insurgency and Militancy

The word, 'terrorism' is interpreted by scholars in different perspectives. There are innumerable definitions which have come out of the involvement of a cross-section of academicians in this field of study. Every definition forwarded by them appears correct in its own perspective. But due to the multiplicity of definitions the meaning of terrorism has not come out in its correct perspective. Scholars from all over the world are entangled in the labyrinth of terminology and have expressed diverse views on it. It would be apt to cite a few famous definitions for a deeper, proper and logical perception of terrorism and its different connotations.

Martha Crenshaw-a Professor of Government at Wesleyan University and author of many books on the subject has given a detailed account of terrorism and its approaches. She writes, "Two views are expressed to understand terrorism and its implications. The first explanation is based on the assumption that the act of terrorism is a deliberate choice by a potential actor. The organisation as a unit, acts to achieve collective values which involves radical changes of practical and social conditions. Terrorism is interpreted as a response to the external stimuli, particularly government actions. An increase in the cost or a decrease in the reward will make it less likely".[1] She further explains the organisational motives and objectives of terrorists and writes, "Terrorism is explained as an organisation's struggle for survival, usually in a competitive environment. Leaders ensure organisational maintenance by offering varied incentives to followers not all of which involves the pursuit of the group's stated political purposes. Leaders seek to prevent both defection and dissent by developing intense loyalties by group members. The organisation responds to the pressure from outside by the incentives offered, members or through innovation. Terrorist actions do not necessarily or directly reflect ideological values".[2]

Thomas C. Shelling, another authority on the subject suggests, "Terrorism is one form of violent coercion, a bargaining process based on power to hurt and intimidate as a substitute for the use of overt military force".[3] As such, it is similar to other strategies based on the 'power to hurt' rather than conventional military strength. Terrorism is meant to produce a change in government's political position, not the destruction of military potential he opines.[4]

Bard E O'Neill in his book has given a small but lucid definition. He mentions "Terrorism is a form of warfare in which violence is primarily directed against non-combatants (usually unarmed civilians) rather than operational, military and police forces or economic assets (public or private)."[5] Another scholar on the subject, Alex P. Schmid, has gaven a lengthy but partially appropriate definition. He writes "Terrorism is a method of combat in which random or symbolic victims share group or class characteristics which form the basis of their selection for victimisation. Through previous use of violence or the credible use of violence, other members of that group or class are put in a state of chronic fear (terror).... The purpose of this indirect method of combat is either to immobilise the target of terror in order to produce disorientation and/or compliance, or to mobilise secondary targets of demands (e.g. government) or targets of attention to changes of attitude or behaviour favouring the short or the long-term interest of the users of his method".[6]

Schmid's definition gives a considerable attention to the target dimension of terrorism distinguishing victims of violence not only from the actual targets of terror but also from targets of demand and attention.[7] It further focuses on the dimensions of purposes and context and to a lesser extent on the acts that differentiate terrorism from other violent activities. Schmid's approach, however, consciously avoids dealing with motive - a dimension that is often used to separate crusaders from criminals or "crazies", and, as such, one that is closely related to the second ranked citation in his frequency chart i.e. political intent.[8] The definitional effort also says little about the perpetrators of terrorism, thereby implying that there is no unique attribute of the phenomenon linked to those who carry it out. In this sense, it sidesteps the extremely contentious debate over whether direct or indirect terror used as state policy is indistinguishable from insurgency or challenge terrorism that has captured international headlines and attention.[9]

Essentially, terror is a tactic that can be utilised in many contexts, for a broad range of purposes, generated by a wide spectrum of motives. Thus, terror is a component in many activities. The question then is how much within a given activity is occupied by this component. In terrorism, unlike its neighbouring reference categories (from state terror to guerilla warfare), the terror component is the pre-eminent and preponderant component of the whole of which it is a part.

Whatever else is said about terrorism, its almost total concentration on targets of opportunity (i.e. the defenceless) provides it with its distasteful flavour whether or not one seeks to justify its occurrence.

The group or class, whose member's sense of security is purposefully undermined, is the target of terror. The victimisation of the target of violence is considered extra-normal by most observers from the witnessing audience on the basis of its atrocity, the time (e.g. peacetime) or place (not a battlefield) of victimisation, or the disregard for rules of combat accepted in conventional warfare. The norm violation creates an attentive audience beyond the target of terror; sectors of this audience might, in turn, form the main object of manipulation. The purpose of this indirect method of combat is either to immobilise the target of terror in order to produce disorientation and/or compliance, or to mobilise secondary targets of demands (e.g. a government) or targets of attention (e.g. public opinion) to change of attitude or behaviour, favouring the short or long term interests of the users of this method of combat.[10]

R.P. Hoffman defines the concept more or less on similar lines. "Terrorism is a purposeful human political activity which is directly designed to influence the ways designed by the protagonists, other human beings and, through them, same course of events".[11]

These definitions are criticised for a certain vagueness or question whether the climate of fear had to be general. All acts of violence produce fear and alarm as a by-product - it is the objective. Being confronted by a mugger who demands your wallet may be a terrifying experience, but a mugger is not a terrorist; he is interested in your wallet. A terrorist on the other hand, is interested in the psychological effects of his violence on the people watching the event. There is, therefore, an awareness of a difference between the victims of terrorist violence and the target audience of that violence. This distinction between the victims of terrorist violence and the target of that violence sometimes manifests itself in extraordinary ways.

This problem of definition is more evident in international terrorism-terrorist actions in which foreign targets are attacked, borders are crossed, or airlines or other international lines of commerce are attacked. The lack of a generally accepted form of terrorism has been an obstacle to international cooperation against this form of terrorism. Slowly, however, a blurred consensus on the meaning of terrorism seems to be emerging without any international agreement on the precise definition.

Former US Senator Jeremiah Denton, while introducing the Anti-Terrorism Act 1984, provided an example of the type of definition some Americans believe in. He says, "Terrorism means knowing use of force or violence against any person or property in violation of the criminal laws of the US or any state, territory, possessions or district, with the intent to intimidate, coerce, or influence a government or person in furtherance of any political or ideological objective".[12]

The former Senator's definition is condemned by Noam Chomsky and Edward Herman with their strong opinions on the subject. They say, "the words 'terror' and 'terrorism' have become semantic tools of the powerful in the Western world. In their dictionary meaning, these words refer to 'intimidation' by the 'systematic use of violence' as a means of both governing and those opposing the existing governments. But current Western usage has restructured the sense, on purely ideological grounds, to the retail violence of those who oppose the established order".[13]

Ihekwoaba D. Onwudiewe outlined the impact of globalisation on terrorism in his book *The Globalisation of Terrorism.* He has compiled a number of definitions of terrorism which have been suggested by different quarters across the world.[14]

(a) An organised pattern of violent behaviour designed to influence government policy or intimidate the government population for the purpose of influencing government policy.[15]

(b) Terror: violence committed by groups in order to intimidate a population or government into granting their demands.[16]

(c) Terror is a symbolic action designed to influence political behaviour by extra-normal means entailing the use or threat of violence.[17]

(d) Terrorism is a non-governmental public violence or its threat performed by an individual and small group and aimed at achieving social or political goals. That may be sub-national, national or international.[18]

(e) Terrorism is the rise of force, violence, or threat of violence to attain goals through fear, intimidation or coercion.[19]

(f) In general, the word terrorism is used today to define at least all illegal acts of violence committed for political purposes by clandestine groups.[20]

One of the definitions which has relatively wide acceptance in the academic circles is by Yonah Alexander. He defines terrorism as "the rise or threat of violence against random or civilian targets in order to create generalised pervasive fear for the purpose of achieving political goals."[21]

Apart from these scholarly works mostly academic in nature, there are also a few official definitions available. Though most of the official definitions are subjective in nature, hence can not be taken or accepted as final ones; but they are important because they provide an insight into the understanding of this thorny problem. According to the US Department of State, there is no single universally accepted definition of terrorism. Even in US, several law enforcement agencies define terrorism in different ways and in different context. The Federal Bureau of Investigation defines terrorism as "the unlawful use of force or violence against the persons or property to intimidate or coerce a government, the civilian population, or any segment thereof, in furtherance of political or social objectives."[22]

The US Department of State provides the following definitions under Title-22 of the United States Code, Section 265(f)d: "the term terrorism means pre-meditated, politically motivated violence perpetrated against non-combatant targets by sub-national groups or clandestine agents, usually intended to influence an audience; the term international terrorism means terrorism involving citizens of the territory of more than one country; and the term terrorist group means any group practising or that has significant sub-groups that practice, international terrorism."[23]

The US Department of Defence defines terrorism as:

"The unlawful use or threatened use of force or violence against individuals or property to coerce or intimidate governments or societies, often used to achieve political, religious or ideological objectives."[24]

Being influenced by the international character of terrorism, the UN has been trying for decades to find out a suitable definition of terrorism, so that a uniform policy can be adopted against it internationally. In 1972, the UN General Assembly adopted a resolution to establish an ad-hoc committee to initiate, "measures to prevent international terrorism which endangers or takes innocent human lives or jeopardises fundamental freedoms and study of the underlying causes of those forms of terrorism and acts of violence which lie in misery, frustration, grievance and despair, and which cause some people to sacrifice human lives, including their own, in an attempt to effect radical changes".[25] Recalling this resolution, the ad-hoc committee created three sub-committees. The first of these was dedicated to examine the definition of terrorism. Seven draft proposals were submitted by member nations. While the Non-Aligned group defined terrorism as acts of violence committed by a group of individuals, which endanger human lives and jeopardise fundamental freedoms, the effects of which are not confined to one state. The NAM draft proposal, however, excluded the inalienable right to self-determination under colonial and racist regimes from this definition. After examining numerous proposals, the member nations agreed to define all acts of terrorism as "criminal". This is again objectionable on the ground that the link between terrorism and crime could be established, but to identify the two as one would be misgiving. However, if it is analysed for administrative purpose, the UN definition perhaps is the simplest way to deal with international terrorism. Further, the CIS countries have adopted a declaration on the agreement on the cooperation of CIS countries in fighting terrorism. According to the CIS resolution, terrorism is "an illegal and criminally punishable action committed to break public security, influence decision-making by state authorities, and intimidate citizens". This definition is much in line with the one forwarded by the UN. This definition narrows terrorism to ordinary crimes such as robbery, blackmail, extortion and taking hostages.[26]

Despite definitional discrepancies, the definitions mentioned above have several aspects which are more or less common to all of them. They can be presented in the form of a model, based on David Easton's Systems theory.

Definitional Model of Terrorism (Based on David Easton's System's Theory):[27]

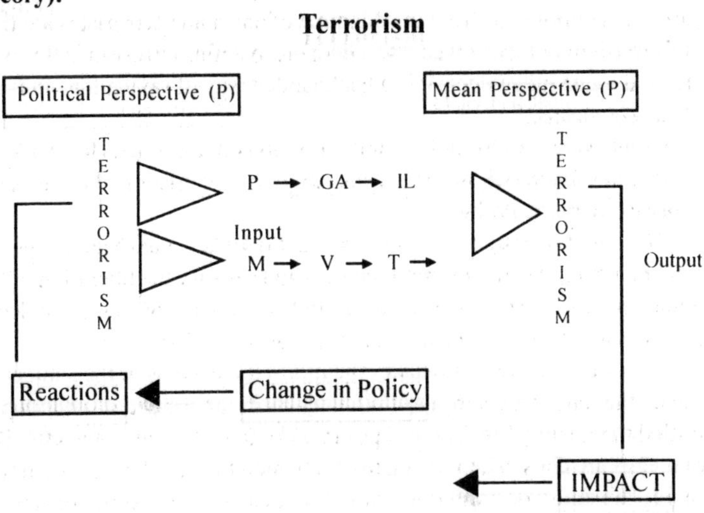

In this model, definition of terrorism is described in two broader perspectives-Politics (P), i.e., terrorism as a political phenomenon and Means (M), i.e., to study terrorism as a means to achieve certain political objectives and not as an end in itself. In the subsequent phase, the model explains that (P) helps actors to form a cohesive whole, which subsequently results into Group Action (GA), and GA heads to International Linkages (IL).

From the point of political perspective, terrorism is defined as a political rather than criminal or psychological phenomenon, as it aims to achieve political power and not accumulation of wealth or personal gain.

In the Means (M) perspective, terrorism is defined as a means to achieve political objectives rather than an end. The model goes further to explain that the means employed are that of Violence (V) and the violence employed is also of specific type, i.e., tactical which needs professional training. A layman cannot operate sophisticated weapons used by terrorists. This aspect also has to be incorporated in the definition of terrorism. A detailed explanation of both the perspectives is given in Model-II.

Reasons Behind the Definitional Discrepancy on Terrorism and its Fallout

To this rider, Michael Jenkins explains that "it is possible to define terrorism objectively as long as we define it in terms of the quality of the act and not in terms of the identity of the perpetrator or the nature of the cause. This removes us from the dilemma of one man's terrorist is another man's freedom fighter." Of course, choosing to define terrorism in this way is itself a value judgement. It is a backhanded way of saying that ends do not justify means.[28]

Grant Wardlaw also holds similar opinion on this issue. He writes, "a major stumbling block to the serious study of terrorism is that, at base, terrorism is a moral problem."[29]

The Palestinian leader Yasser Arafat in his 1974 United Nations speech said, "he who fights for a just cause, he who fights for the liberation of his country, he who fights against invasion and exploitation or single-mindedly against colonialism, can never be defined as a terrorist".[30]

This view, however, mistakes the moral dimensions of the subject. It may be that under a given set of circumstances, an individual or group is entitled to violently break some eggs in order to make a just omelette. But what eggs are chosen and the method in which they are broken are never outside the realm of proper and moral judgements. Just cause or not, he who performs acts of terrorism is a terrorist. And because terrorism violates the norms associated with discriminating and proportional use of violence, it leaves itself open to moral condemnation regardless of its results and its political orientations.[31]

The Philosophy of Terrorism

There are several intellectual postulates that have given respect ability to terrorism in the discipline of political science. And these postulates may be construed as the "philosophy of terrorism."[32]

Sanctified Goals

Terrorism is committed in the name of some popular revolutionary ideology or religious legitimacy. Even the most barbarian group of terror found it necessary to rest their wanton means on some sanctified goals. The first group systematically employing murder for a "cause" it believed to be righteous was probably the famous Muslim sect: 'the Assassins', from whose name the modern word "assassination" is derived. The term is really derived from the Arabic *hashishi* (the consumers of hashish, the well known drug) who represented a sect of fanatics in Palestine in the 13th century, whose chief object was to create a sense of terror by stabbing and murdering the Christian crusaders. The Assassins developed an explicit religious justification for killing the unrighteous and the servants of the unrighteous.[33]

The development of political ideological basis in order to provide a secular justification for revolution, however, originated during the French Revolution period. In the opinion of the ideologues of French Revolution, terror became a legitimate weapon of revolutionary justice and revenge against the absolutist, aristocratic and ecclesiastical systems of the "ancient regime". Their revolutionary theory of popular rights to liberty and justice provided the first ideological justification for revolutionary terrorism.

Intellectual writing on terrorism as an ideology began in the nineteenth century. One of the earliest authors of terrorist thought was Wilhelm Weilting (1808-1871). He was a German Socialist who wrote about the mobilisation of the criminal underworld in a revolutionary struggle.[34] But the concept of systematic terrorism and its use in revolutionary strategy appeared for the first time in the writings of Russian revolution aries Mikhail Bakunin and Sergey Nechayev. Their writings, with an emphasis upon violence as a method for achieving social change, were the inspiration if not the actual source of the doctrine of anarchism and nihilism. They authored rules for revolutionary which often called catechism in view of its doctrine character, is regarded as the greatest text of terrorist literature. It is veritably acknowledged as a treatise on anti-morality and also a programme of action which epitomises the philosophy of personal terror.

Revolutionary catechism has been instrumental in the emergence of philosophy based terrorism. Its predominant theme was the destruction of the existing order. The social world, according to it, has become impotent and sterile. The socialist atmosphere corrupts the people's instincts and wills, contracts their hearts and intelligence. Hence, it is imperative to overthrow the society and purify completely the milieu in which people lived. From such an understanding emanate Mikhail Bakunin's rationalisation of terror. He maintains that the power to think and the desire to rebel represent the essential factor, the negative power in the positive development of human animality and create consequently all that constitutes humanity in man.[35]

He, therefore, recommends the reliance on the "eternally creative source of life.... the urge to destroy" which according to him is also a "creative urge". He substantiates this premise by holding that every forward step in history until now has been achieved only after it has been baptised in blood. Bakunin believed in the total destruction of the legal state and the so-called bourgeois civilisation. The demolition of the state has to come about by a popular revolution, which will be led not by the vanguards of the workers party as Karl Marx envisaged, but by a collective, imperceptible and anonymous dictatorship of the artisans. This collective, Bakunin believed, will be firmly united in a secret society, acting everywhere and always with the same goal and according to the same programme.[36]

The catechism prescribes the same kind of fanaticism that characterises the contemporary terrorist. It states, for instance, that the revolutionary despises all doctrines, rejects the mundane sciences and leaves them to future generations. The revolutionary only knows one science - the science of destruction. "To this end and to this end alone, he will study day and night the living science, people, their character and circumstances. His role and constant object is the immediate destruction of the vile order.[37]

Propaganda by Deed

A cardinal principle in the strategy of the anarchists is a concept called "propaganda by deed". A leading French anti-parliamentarian, Paul Brousse coined the phrase "propaganda by deed".[38] He argued that practical demonstrations are necessary to awaken the consciousness of the masses.

'Propaganda by deed' was also based on several ideological convictions (a) all revolt against oppression was itself progressive; (b) the transformation from blind and spontaneous responses against injustice into conscious and calculated revolt represented significant advances; (c) that decisions to commit specific acts of revolt had to rest with the people.[39] In sum, anarchism attempted to make believe that all those acts which can be considered as terrorism or simply criminal were, in fact, revolutionary deeds heralding the coming socialism.

According to Bakunin, propaganda by deed should be conducted by revolutionary and secret organisations made up of secret cells composed of individuals ready to sacrifice themselves for revolution. He advocated the infiltration of all institutions of the state to undermine them and the stirring up of discontent among the peasantry in order to provoke mass insurrection. Similar ideas were advocated even before Bakunin by Weitling, who contested that the social order had to be deliberately exacerbated through organised theft with the urban lumpen proletariat. The poor he claimed should be given a chance to enjoy the growing disorder just as the soldier enjoyed war.

Anarchism helped to integrate terrorism in the revolutionary strategy to overthrow the established order during the late 19th century. The anarchists' theory came to represent a highly conscious effort to intellectualise, even to rationalise certain social occurrences during that era. The acts of anarchists indicate some of the major contradictions within terrorism. Prominent among them is the lack of any distinction between political violence and ordinary criminal acts. Often, terrorism has degenerated into pure robbery and criminal violence. Besides, the anarchists while vehemently advocating the complete destruction of the bourgeois society, failed to offer concrete ideas for a future society.

Philosophisation of Violence

Although there were many influential apologists for terrorism during the last century,[40] the most elaborate and systematic to create a philosophy or more precisely an ideology of terror can be seen in the works of the twentieth century's prominent thinker, Jean Paul Sartre. His works have succeeded in celebrating violence and amplified the concept of purifying creative crime. Sartre strove to accord a philosophical respectability to the notion that terror, far from being cancer in the body politic, is indeed its very life blood.[41]

Terror is a fraternity and mover of history and hence terrorism should be eternal. In Sartre's perception, man is seen not only as craving and fighting for power and greater power, but as a destroyer impelled to murder his fellow men. Human relations are devoid of any altruism and men only share the "negative reciprocity of mutual and deadly antagonism".[42] In his introduction to Franz Fanon's *The Wretched of the Earth*, Sartre claims that man recreates himself with violence against the oppressor. In essence, terror becomes a condition of freedom and to realise the brotherhood of man it is a dialectical necessity to regard all human life as expenditure.

Another seminal contribution to the philosophy of terrorism came from a neo-Marxist intellectual of Africa, Franz Fanon, who authored The Wretched of the Earth which inflamed the radicals of not only Africa but the entire Western World. Fanon was consumed with hatred for colonialism and racial oppression. Violence, as he saw it, was a cleansing force, liberating the native from his inferiority complex, his despair and inaction. Indulging in brutal forms of violence against the oppressor made the native fearless and restarted his self-respect. He declared that violence alone, violence committed by the people, violence organised and taught by its leaders makes it possible for the masses to understand social truths and gives the key to them. And people who have taken part in the violent struggle for national liberation will be jealous of the results of their action and will refuse to allow their destiny to be placed in the hands of so-called liberators.[43] He further claims that at the level of the community, violence raises national consciousness and mobilises oppressed people and binds them together into a new nation.

Western political analysts believe that Fanon helped to set the stage for international terrorism by justifying the resort to it as a legitimate way of attacking injustice.[44] He instilled among the Western radical movements a sense of guilt and a feeling that the Third World of the ex-colonies had "right" on its side and whatever violence unleashed by them or for them was "just".

Another influential writer was Carlos Mrighella, a Brazilian Communist.[45] He shot into prominence during the 1960s after his Mini-Manual of the Urban Guerrilla was banned in many countries. The book is regarded as the bible of the contemporary terrorist and has greatly influenced the operational art of terrorism. Mrighella's approach is essentially one of provocation, compelling the enemy to "transform the political situation into a military one". He assumed that in the process the government would alienate large sections of the population. Therefore, the people would blame the government for disruption of their lives and would swing its support to the terrorists as against the police and the army.[46]

Mrighella's manual provides strategy as well as movements for the terrorists. The struggle according to him, should proceed on three fronts- the urban guerrilla front, the mass front (meaning a combat front, not agitation) and support network. Mrighella undoubtedly distinguishes himself with his fanatical dedication to revolution.

Ever since the dawn of history, there always existed a spectrum of political thinkers who have glorified the role of violence and terrorism in human society and amplified its indispensability in restructuring the political systems. There is, however, a compelling continuity of irony underlying their intellectual postulates. It relates to their utterly degenerate and vulgar characterisation of human nature. Such a depiction is devoid of historical, sociological or even psychological basis. The fictional understanding of human nature is the cornerstone on which the entire edifice of "terror" philosophy has been erected. And philosophy, ironically, is meant to investigate the most general facts and principles of reality and human nature and conduct. Men, according to the "terror" school of thought, are not capable of experiencing emotions of love, obedience, altruism and compassion but are merely entities impelled to destroy one another. A logical extension of this perception is its utter disregard and disrespect for human life. All or any individual is expendable and can be submerged for the cause of "revolution". There is also among the thinkers, a corresponding scorn for all human institutions and total distrust and cynicism of all existing mechanisms for the achievement of justice and change. It is this intellectual repudiation of human lives and institutions that have instilled in the present day radicals apathy to the life of the individual. Perhaps there is an explanation here for the indifference of the terrorists to the gruesome killing of innocent bystanders who chanced to fall in the way of the revolutionary march.

Invisible Utopia

There is yet another irony in the philosophy of terrorism. There is no dearth of the vocabulary of the philosophers who rationalise violence unlimited for the realisation of revolutionary ends. But none of them could offer any tangible idea of a utopian state which they intend to erect over the debris of death and destruction. Their compulsive obsession with terror as having a cathartic effect on the society led them into a blind alley of "pure nihilism" and prevaricate with the exposition of any viable socio-political and economic theory. Thus, the writings of the thinkers only appealed to the emotions of the masses and not to their rational faculties which could have translated the thesis into positive action. Owing to this factor, the intellectual influence of terrorism has been a contemporary phenomenon and till date, no terrorist movement has been able to bring about a change in the configuration of power.

Finally, there is a particularly disquieting irony in the attitudes of the protagonists of terror among the Western intelligentsia. They have dedicated their links and talents to the repudiation and institutions which have provided the atmosphere of intellectual freedom in which they can espouse their ideas. It is a paradox that the disciples of the terrorist acts and thoughts are not allowed to survive, let alone profess under to talitarian systems and can only thrive in liberal democracies, which they so vehemently denounce. Sartre, for instance, remained conspicuously silent during the Nazi dictatorship in Europe while he conveniently surfaced to provide intellectual support to the terrorist movements during the 1960s and 1970s. History does not record the existence of any philosophers who professed terrorism during Stalin's repression in Soviet Union. May be, philosophers can romanticise and celebrate death, violence and terrorism, but only in a society that accords paramount status to human dignity and not under systems which have come into existence and sustain themselves by celebrating and romanticising violence and terrorism. Herein lies the irony and the philosophy of terror.

Aims and Objectives of Terrorism

Terrorist acts are committed primarily by those, who are not able to fulfil their needs in the existing socio-political structure. The acts are committed deliberately with definite aims in view and cannot be viewed as aberrations. Terrorism is aimed at bringing about "revolutionary changes" in the political system. The most common terrorist objectives include recognition (through publicity), provocation, coercion, insurgency support and intimidation.[47]

Intimidation

By inflicting overwhelming fear on a target audience, a terrorist is able to cripple the movement of its targets, and even society at large. According to David Rappoport, "It is most effective when directed against specific critical groups. In the 20th century, for example, successful terrorist movements following the example of Michael Collins (IRA leader after World War I) paralysed the police early usually by systematic assassination policies".[48] The mere threat of terrorist retaliation can foment fear and cause individuals to completely alter daily routines and habits.

Recognition

This is a critical component of terrorism because it satisfies one of the principles of terrorism. Some associated reasons for seeking recognition include the procurement of funds from outside sources and the recruitment of new members into an organisation. The act could also simply be a demonstration of strength to the world that the group exists and it is able to attack anywhere. Groups that are attempting to gain recognition generally execute spectacular attacks that attract a significant amount of media attention. Other methods to gain recognition include the use of names or labels implying strength or mass of numbers.[49]

Coercion and Provocation

Coercion is an attempt to induce a desired behaviour or action from individuals, groups or governments. This objective calls for a strategy of selective targeting that may cause massive destruction but seldom much loss of life. Examples of this might include the bombing of a corporate headquarters involved in environmental operations or the bombing of abortion clinics.

Provocation is designed to elicit an over-reaction on the part of particular government agency or the military. This strategy normally calls for a terrorist to attack targets symbolic of the government to demonstrate a particular government's vulnerability. The objective is two fold. On the one hand, the terrorist hopes that an attack of this nature will create a sense of uncertainty in the citizens as to their government's ability to protect them. On the other hand, terrorists hope for a heavy-handed response to each compassion and public sympathy for the group. This is one of the cornerstones of Mrighella's revolutionary manual. It notes that "by enraging the establishment to the point that it begins to violently attack the passive population, it is able to garner the support of horrified society, that otherwise may not have sided with the guerrilla".[50]

The people refuse to collaborate with the government and the general sentiment is that this government is unjust, incapable of solving problems, and that it resorts simply to the physical liquidation of its opponents.

Watching the guerrillas, the people now understand that it is a force to vote in any elections which have as their sole objectives guaranteeing the survival of the dictatorship and covering up its crimes. Attacking wholeheartedly this election farce and the so called "political solutions", which is so appealing to the opportunists, the urban guerrillas must become even more aggressive and active, resorting without pause to sabotage, terrorism, expropriations, assault, kidnappings, executions etc.[51]

Insurgency Support

Terrorist action in support of insurgency is likely to include provocation, intimidation, coercion and the quest for recognition. Terrorism can cause the affected government to over-extend itself in attempting to protect all potential terrorist targets. Other users of terrorist skills and organisational relationships in support of insurgency can include the acquisition of funds, coercion of recruits, logistical support and internal group discipline.

Principles of Terrorism

Mao Tse Tung laid down three stages of development to achieve revolution, namely, the organisation stage, the guerrilla warfare and the mobile war stage.[52] This model was followed by individuals such as Ho Chi Minh, and was quite effective during its time. Unfortunately, within a modern context this simple three stage approach is no longer applicable.

The fundamentals are still present, but for contemporary purposes, some adjustments must be made. In order for terrorism to progress from its inception to the ultimate goal of revolution, five general principles of terrorism become apparent. Understanding these principles allows for suitable development of counter-terrorism policies.[53]

1. Grassroot Support: According to Mao, "the guerrilla is the fish and the people are the sea".[54] Mao was quick to recognise the importance of the general public in any terrorist campaign. For terrorists to be truly effective, they must have the support of the general public for their cause and for their tactics. A terrorist group that fails to gain popular support will not be able to progress to the stage of guerrilla warfare, because there will not be enough people to fill its ranks. Such is the case of the right wing militants in America. Likewise, a terrorist group that has popular support, but whose actions are not supported, will most likely not achieve victory. The Algerian Islamic extremists had huge popular support in their campaign against the Algerian government, which they quickly lost after pursuing a campaign of slaughtering entire village.

2. Intelligence: Accurate intelligence is vital for any strategic attack and the same principles apply for terrorism. Terrorists, who accidentally attack a hospital, rather than a military base, will quickly loose support locally and internationally. Accurate, on-time intelligence is vital to carry out any mission effectively.

3. Propaganda: Propaganda is critical for gaining support. A terrorist organisation that does not advertise its cause will find few followers. Propaganda, however, must be focussed both internally and externally. Support from the local population, but condemnation from the international community, will do little to ensure success. Perhaps this is one of the largest failures of the PLO.

Although campaigns such as Intifada have been successful in gaining international sympathy, on the whole, they have been ineffective in gaining support outside of the Arab world. The Jews, in contrast, have been extremely successful in propagating their views to the point that it dominates the Western media.

4. Technology: Technology is rapidly enabling the terrorist communities to carry out their sinister designs effectively. As countries such as the US become more and more reliant on technology, they will be more susceptible to terrorist attack. An inverse relationship exists between the sophistication of technology and the amount of people required to perform a mission. One individual, armed with a laptop or nuclear device can achieve significant results, something that requires large armies.

Most importantly, the technology of the terrorists must be at par with the target's technology. Bare-foot guerrilla fighters attacking a government which is willing to use biological agents will most likely not succeed. Terrorists armed with knives will do little in the face of automatic machine guns. Since terrorist organisations are relatively small, they must have advance technology to outbalance their limited numbers.[55]

5. International Support: The final principle is international support. In the modern world, international support can be a key for the success or failure of a revolution or a terrorist campaign. Although the Russians, after their invasion of Afghanistan, regarded Afghan rebels as terrorists, the Afghans had the support of the Western community and were able to receive arms and training.

In contrast, the Taliban had succeeded in capturing the majority of Afghanistan, but failed to gain international recognition and were therefore, politically and economically isolated. Failure to receive international support and recognition ultimately led to their defeat. International support is a critical component of success. Terrorists who gain internal victory, but neglect to gather international support, may never truly succeed.

Strategies of Terrorism

Strategy is the considered application of means to advance one's ends.[56] Terrorists far from being 'mindless' are disturbingly calculating about the means they use.[57] Military analysts often describe terrorism as less than a strategy and merely as a tactic, but depending upon circumstances and terrorist's intentions, it can be either. In the post-1945 world, terrorism has been a strategic control to a score of revolutionary movements.

At least five terrorist strategies are so common around the globe that they deserve explicit enumeration. They all mould violence and propaganda in some form or other to gain public attention. Normally, these strategies include both, destruction and some forms of construction, that is, the actions yield not just damage to targets but some form of progress for the group in its strive for greater power. The five strategies are: (1) creation of societal dislocation or chaos; (2) discrediting or destroying a particular government; (3) rendering economic and property damages; (4) 'bleeding' state security forces and doing other military damages; (5) spreading fear for international effects.

(1) Creation of Societal Dislocation or Chaos: The first strategy is to create or further a sense of societal dislocation, fear and even anarchy. As the Chinese military thinker Sun Tzu recognised, creating 'disorder' is as useful, or more useful, than the destruction of the enemy forces. This strategy is most commonly used by revolutionaries. It can also work for pro-state terrorists: bombing and other crimes provoke public fears and thus enhance public support for further law enforcement measures, or even dictatorship. Adolph Hitler is believed to have burnt the Reichstag, or the national government building, so that the act could be blamed on German Communists, legitimising a planned crackdown against his opponents.

Carlos Mrighella, the Brazilian terrorist of 1960s, in his manual has delineated the use and effect of this strategy. In that he opines, the more the disaster, the more is the government's repression and it leads to greater alienation of the population from the government, resulting in the increase in the terrorist base.[58]

Of course, not all terrorists aim at such a strange sequence of anarchy, 'crackdown', and then revolution. There are groups with a more direct plan, and there are groups with more limited goals. What does seem nearly universal and yet often ignored by analysts is that the destruction of the terrorist groups is in their minds a necessary part of their own effort at construction of sorts. Terrorists look to positive dimensions of their actions. For example, violence is intended to forcefully draw the polity's attention to a 'neglected' issue. The hope, justified by terrorists' general success, is that a public shocked by a terrorist act or campaign, will give them attention. The public often does respond even if it does not fully believe the propaganda circulated at the time of the action by the terrorists.

(2) Discrediting the Government : The second terrorist strategy is to discredit, diminish or destroy a particular government and replace it with another. Attacks on officials, including tax collectors, judges, policemen, country or village officials, and persons responsible for elections, undermine the prestige or efficiency of government. These can

result in the reduction of the services, or closure of regional or local offices, or implicit acquiescence of 'no go' areas in the country where the government's want no longer counts - 'grey areas' as they are sometimes called.[59]

Government is ordinarily weakened by this process, but if it strikes back with harsh force, making inroads against terrorism, it may also discredit itself among the public. During the mid-1990s, states engaged in rough counter-insurgency efforts, were consequently targeted by influential critics and human rights monitors. A few among them were Peru, Egypt, India, Guatemala, Mexico and Turkey. The 'positive' effects of the political strategies for the terror groups are many and diverse. Political work lends legitimacy to a group or doctrine of which public is suspicious because of its reliance on violence. Political strategies are internally important to the group since it engages or claims to engage in terrorism because of its urgent political programme. The terror group's prestige, size and effectiveness are often enhanced proportionally to how the government is damaged. Each terrorist action creates a platform from which to appeal to the public about its objectives. With time and effort, even an unusual ideology or foreign political conception can gain credibility.[60]

In the struggle with all its sessions of planning, cooperation and physical confrontations with enemies, new leaders with considered ideas about a revolutionary government may emerge. Thus, the long period of covert and overt revolutionary activity became for such leaders as Yasser Arafat and Daniel Ortega, a sort of journeyman's years, in which they exercised authority over an ever growing segment of the nation, gaining experience and credibility at the same time.[61] Some contemporary terror using groups opt not just for a sense of legitimacy but also a direct role in the political power; they use respected and pacific forums of debate, compete in local elections, or consider participation in a national coalition government. Under extreme conditions, a group may abandon violence altogether and choose to fold completely into the political process, as did Cambodia's April 19 Movement and El Salvador's left wing guerrillas once Cuban and Soviet defeat in the Cold War became evident. [62]

(3) Economic and Property Damage: Presently, this strategy has been much neglected by the contemporary political science. General social effects of dislocation are dramatically enhanced by such common terrorist tactics as taking over public highways to tax commercial users; arson campaigns against large corporations; sabotage of oil pipelines, bombings and extortions which increase insurance prices and operating

costs; prolonged efforts to disrupt the export of the manufactured goods or agricultural crops, bank robberies; and campaigns against tourist facilities which garner much of some nations' 'foreign' incomes. Such efforts are intended to directly harm the property owner and perhaps also to harm the government, which immediately experiences losses. Economic strategies yield positive advantages to the terrorists themselves as well. It hurts the government, creates impact, fills the coffers of the terrorists and shoes away the investors.[63]

(4) Military Damage: Military damage is another mechanism by which terrorists advance their overall object. Depending on the group, the rendering of damage to the state's military forces or infrastructure is usually of secondary or tertiary interest; terrorists prefer undefended, non-military targets. In peacetime, the terrorists undermine readiness and spread fear among military ranks; terrorists may thin the ranks of national police forces, which have or can have peace and wartime roles.[64] If events escalate into war, terrorists are in a prime position to act as proxy forces for an external power or an indigenous political organisation. For example, ethnic militants in the north eastern India may or may not wish to serve the interest of China, but they do so by distracting and tying down innumerable Indian national police and military personnel, who are continuously bled with classic 'bite and flee' guerrilla tactic.[65]

The positive effects of the movement using terrorism are many. Military style operations by terrorists provide battle experiences, draw recruits, capture weaponry, develop logistical infrastructure and may lead to foreign support of various types. Depending upon ideology, today's terrorist leaders may anticipate that terrorism can be combined with clandestine organisation and guerrilla combat experience to develop from an underground into a truly national military capability. That is, in fact, the Maoist model of the development of protracted guerrilla war from low level violence and propaganda to a second phase of mixed or 'mobile' warfare featuring formal military units, and ultimately to a third rather conventional phase of operations by regular armies. This was the model generally followed by the Vietnamese Communists.[66]

(5) Terrorism and its International Effects: The act committed by terrorists in recent years is not confined to one particular country. Sometimes terrorist groups commit crime in one country and escape to other country. Due to having close relations with terrorist groups of that country, they find it easy to carry out their objectives.

Most contemporary religious terror groups are 'universalistic' in their appeal; they think internationally by nature. For example, for religious extremists, it is somewhat unnatural to draw a boundary between two states and worry about preserving it when neither regime is 'legitimate'.

The most successful groups calibrate their use of terrorism to suit the political and social environment, and they use multiple means, altering their approach to suit changes caused by the environment, governmental interference, good or bad fortune, and the like. Enough groups and movements using the various strategies of terror do succeed so that observant leaders surely understand there may be prospects for success, not only risks. Such partial and larger successes are keeping terrorism alive long past the time when some have pronounced the waning of state sponsorship.

Freedom Fighter and the Terrorist

In recent years, there has been a huge discrepancy in defining who constitutes a terrorist and who is a freedom fighter. Patric Clauson writes, "one man's terrorist could be other man's freedom fighter".[67] Calling a terrorist, freedom fighter and vice-versa, is an extreme example of dilemma. Terrorism has its own identity and so has freedom fighting. US Senator Henry Jackson dismissed the idea of identifying the two as one and the same in the following words: "It is disgrace that democracies should allow the treasured word 'freedom' to be associated with acts of terrorism".[68]

It is a fact that terrorists are misguided members of society who aim to destabilise an established system and risk their own lives. This is why scholars like Michael Aaronson believe that terrorists are the cruel members of the society, not freedom fighters.[69]

While on one the hand, scholars differ from each other in terminology, rebels and militant groups in the society continue to threaten mankind by adopting terrorism as a means to achieve political goals. It is therefore important to draw a line to distinguish between a terrorist and a freedom fighter. The differences between the two can be analysed in the light of the following determinants:

- Relevance of the UN
- Objectives and means to an objective
- Magnitude of violence
- Colonialism and de-colonialism
- Lack of moral justification
- National versus International

Once a nation is recognised under the UN Charter, no individual or group of individuals of that particular country can be recognised as freedom fighters,[70] as this would promote sub-nationalism within a country and promote disharmony. Civil strife, and ultimately anarchy will prevail upon. Freedom fighting or right to self-determination is well recognised by the UN as an inalienable right of the people. It does not, however, mean that some of the genuine cases of freedom fighting, one like that of India prior to its independence would be allowed as the guiding force for secessionist movement in a country which is already liberated from foreign yoke. It needs to be emphasised that so long as individual or a group of individuals hold the nationality of an independent sovereign nation, as recognised by UN, they have no moral or legal right to claim themselves as freedom fighters. Their acts of violence could be identified as acts of terrorism rather than freedom fighting.

The second distinction between the two lies in their objectives.The main objective of freedom fighter is to acquire independence by any available means, be it moral or immoral, legal or illegal, where as the primary objective of terrorists is violence and intimidation. What they claim to be their political or economic objective is not 'objective' as such but 'a set of demands'. An objective is a well perceived plan, while demands are simple expression of desire of an individual or group of individuals.[71] The freedom fighters never deviate from their demands, i.e., independence or freedom but in case of terrorists, the objective gets diluted when some of their demands are met or considered.

Demands rather than objectives motivate terrorists. This is precisely because the objectives of terrorists are deceptive and ambiguous. It is deceptive because their ulterior motive is succession, but they compromise on partial autonomy or release of their colleagues. As a matter of fact, terrorists resort to violence and terror to get these demands accepted rather than to achieve any broader objective. On the other hand, the freedom fighters are motivated by objectives and to achieve that, unlike terrorists, they sacrifice their trifle demands.

Independence is the goal of the freedom fighter. But terrorism does not have a determined objective and even though the terrorists claim to have some,[72] they are deceptive and fluctuating. They ultimately tend to become victims of self-deception and puppets of their own illusions and disillusions. It is said that terrorism as an objective is a failure,[73] precisely because there is a gap in understanding amongst members of terrorist groups. There are innumerable examples of terrorists renouncing violent course of action, but there is no example of surrender in the history of freedom fighting.

The third significant difference between the two is related to the magnitude of violence. Terrorists are recognised with violence that creates fear psychosis.[74] This is such an important aspect of terrorism that scholars like Brian Jenkins define terrorism in terms of violence and intimidation. He opines that threat of violence, individual acts of violence, or a campaign of violence designed primarily to instil fear, is terrorism.[75]

Unlike this, violence is not a precondition for freedom fighting. It is only under a repressive foreign regime that freedom fighters too resort to violence. Violence is not an essential condition for freedom fighting. Freedom could be achieved through peaceful means too. For instance, Mahatma Gandhi who led the independence movement in India and won it non-violently, was never declared a terrorist by the British government.

Violence, however, is every thing in terrorism. There could be no terrorism without violence. Targeting innocent lives is typical act of terrorism whereas freedom fighters try to protect them. Thus, on the basis of use, magnitude and nature of violence, a terrorist could be seen differently from that of a freedom fighter.

To call a freedom fighter a terrorist is the brainchild of colonialism. After the colonisation of the Afro-Asian countries in the post-Industrial Revolution period by the European powers, there emerged a strong resistance by the colonial natives against the exploitation, basically economic ones, against their colonial masters. This resistance force very often resorted to violence and terrorist activities. These people were branded terrorists by the colonial powers. The natives justified their violence as part of struggle for freedom from foreign yoke. Franz Fanon made it clear that "violence alone, violence committed by the people, violence organised and educated by its leaders make it possible for the masses to understand social truth and gives the key to them. Without that knowledge of practice of action, there is nothing but a fancy dress parade and blare of the trumpets".[76]

But to consider a terrorist as a freedom fighter in a liberated democratic country would mean political destabilisation. In every nook and corner and for any trifle cause, people would organise themselves as freedom fighters bringing about a precarious state of affairs, specifically in a pluralistic society. This would promote sub-nationalism[77] and political chaos. Terrorists are not freedom fighters as such but murderers.[78]

As mentioned, freedom fighters also resort to violence for independence, i.e., to liberate people from exploitation. Their first and foremost objective is to secure civil and political rights for their masses by any available means. It is because of this commitment that freedom fighters are honoured as heroes and their acts of violence are morally justified,[79] whereas terrorist is considered immoral, selfish and criminal because unlike freedom fighter, his objective is not liberation but intimidation and killing.

The basic principle of terrorism hinges around rejection of civilised society. In this account itself, acts of terrorism lack moral justification. Their acts create panic in the socio-political environment of the society. The same is not applicable so far as freedom fighting is concerned. Their target of violence is not crowded places like market places or railway stations where common men become victims. "Freedom fighters are bound by certain rules of behaviour which form cornerstone of our ethics; they draw a sharp distinction between the soldier and the children, between governmental agents and ordinary citizens, between repressive authorities and helpless women, between a military outpost and a common dwelling place. The terrorist, however, knows no such distinctions. He has no moral restraints in the choice of his objectives, as he has none in his methods of warfare. His objective is indeed the whole country on which he concentrates his attacks; his target is its entire population. In these limits, he recognises no innocents, no bystanders, not even strangers. He respects no code of law which was ever established for war or peace. He is above law indeed unto himself", wrote Benjamin Netanyahu.[80]

Another significant difference between a freedom fighter and a terrorist is related to the scope and area of influence. Freedom fighters limit their activities within the national boundary of their country. Their means and ends are confined to a geographical boundary. They do get moral support from foreign countries, but are not dependent on them. They always remain in touch with the people and stay among them. It is difficult for the freedom fighters to achieve their goal without cooperation of the masses, as independence movement is aimed to liberate people from bondage of slavery and without their support, independence would remain a far cry to achieve.[81] Unlike this, terrorism is trans-national by its very nature. It seeks assistance from across the border and uses the international forums to get their demands accepted. They operate in an interwoven organisational structure, which is spread all over the world. Crossing international border to maintain new contacts and to acquire arms is a routine job of a terrorist organisation.

From the above mentioned illustrations, it is clear that there is hardly any similarity between a terrorist and a freedom fighter except for the fact that freedom fighters too use violence at times. The same is not applicable to terrorism. Violence is all that is in terrorism.

Causes of Terrorism

It is hard to find specific causes for terrorism because the factors responsible for this are intertwined and related to each other. Therefore, any analysis of the causes of terrorism has to be studied from a broad macro-framework of social, political and economic causes.

Social Causes

In a society which is fragmented, incoherent and based on hierarchy, a certain section always feels ignored or laid down. They feel frustrated and the social discrimination that they face, creates a sense of revenge or a kind of determination among them to raise their status in an upwardly direction, in order to put themselves at par with others. But the already existing hierarchy and the social order never let them to move up in the social ladder, due to the fear of losing their own opportunities and privileges. This leads to a clash of interests and by getting the minimum spark, it bursts, in most cases quite violently, to create a wide ranging impact. It is a pure case of sociological disorder that causes this kind of terrorism. But as it rarely falls under the gambit of politics, it hardly begets the acronym of terrorism. But in the race for political space in a democratic society, issues of this nature easily take a political colour thereby, leading to greater hatred and violence, creating a fit case for the sobriquet, i.e., terrorism.

In a very strange but interesting development before the onset of the new millennium, government and law enforcement agencies in many countries expressed the concern that one or several groups holding apocalyptic beliefs might stage spectacular actions in connection with the new millennium.[82] But despite the forecasts of a widespread global havoc, only one major incident happened in Japan where a similar cult attacked an underground rail station by posionous gas killing some people. But whether something happened or not, a fear psychosis was created in the public domain of such a possibility and a possible emergence of such a cult. So this may be taken as another social condition in which terrorism finds a space to grow. There is no doubt that apocalyptic perspectives seem to be especially conducive to the legitimisation of violent behaviour, since the "old world" is about to be turned upside down and replaced by a new order. Scholars such as David Rappoport have repeatedly emphasised how eminence, with the setting of deadlines, should be considered as crucial. But most apocalyptic groups do not turn violent.[83] Apocalyptic world view in them apparently plays a role mostly in combination with a variety of other factors.

The other type of violence and terrorism which emanates from the society is a religious one. There are several kinds of religious patronages to terrorism:[84] (a) for the formation of religious doctrines and beliefs, viz. *Jihad* in Islam and *Holy war* in Christianity. Though definition of these concepts are no less lengthy and cumbersome, one can safely say that they all at some point of time or the other justify terrorism, thereby, providing social acceptance to them and in a way promoting them further; (b) to defend itself from state repression and aggressive reaction. There are governments and states whose policies towards a particular religion or religious cult in general encourage terrorism. "The reaction by the authorities or law enforcement agencies just reinforced fears and paranoia and led a group to become more aggressive or to fall into violence".[85] Third kind of terrorism which is largely an offshoot of the social structures is based on ethnic considerations. It is different from violence carried out for ideological, religious or financial motives.[86] Ethnic terrorists often seek to influence their own constituencies more than the country as a whole. They frequently seek to foster communal identity in contrast with the identity proposed by the state. They often target potential intermediaries who might otherwise compromise on identity issues. A secondary goal of the attack is to create a climate of fear among a rival group's population.[87] That kind of terrorism polarises the multi-ethnic societies, increasing communal support for non-violent ethnic political movements of all types. Thus, fear helps alter a nation's demography and politics to the advantage of ethnic radicals.

Economic Causes

Economic condition of a country also plays a significant role in the growth of terrorism. Due to growth of population, urbanisation and out-migration from rural to urban areas, there is a tremendous pressure on the economic system of the country. As resources are scarce, each group tries to obtain these scarce resources, this leads to competition among various groups. Those groups which do not get their share in the economy feel frustrated and neglected which culminates into resentment among them. Finally, the above factors lead to increased isolation of these groups who try to reassert their dominance by waging armed struggle against the authority.

Terrorists believe that they are rightfully entitled to have all the essentials and comforts which they are deprived of but others are enjoying.[88] They consciously reject the fact that total economic equality has never existed in the history of mankind. However, people got swayed by the social awakening under Marx's theory of Communism and began to believe that the wide economic disparity that exists in the society is the handiwork of a few rather than the natural phenomenon that could be accepted as normal living condition. This awareness brought new awakening to overcome economic deprivation by force and violence. This intense desire is also because of the demonstration of wealth by the higher to the lower class in social hierarchy.[89] The economic resources and infra-structure available, yet inaccessible, agitate minds of the deprived class. Besides, there is possibility that regional differences among nations might lead to political violence by people in the less privileged regions.[90] Scholars like Willy Brandt have warned that, "often war is thought of in terms of military conflict, but there is an equal danger from mass anger as caused by economic disaster".[91]

Political Causes

Political issues have equally contributed to the growth of terrorism. Terrorism being one of the means to acquire power is also inspired by the same psycho-dynamics of mankind. The obscure purpose of terrorism is to acquire power through secession, autonomy or revolution. Politicisation of violence is the tactic of terrorists to gain public support.[92] Unless they make a case for a greater common cause, such as liberation, autonomy, secession, and so on, terrorism is unlikely to receive public attention without which the very purpose of terrorism would be defeated. The objective of terrorist group is not only to create fear psychosis but also to prove that terrorism is a viable instrument in politics.

Freedom is the key to democratic society, which is highly prone to terrorism compared to totalitarian, Communist or military government. People have direct access for redressal of their grievances in a democratic set up. However, when they or their fledging political groups fail to get their demands fulfilled, they adopt violence and terror to challenge political will, and morale of the democratic government and its citizens by using various propaganda channels.

Thus, growth of terrorism is not merely due to economic and political deprivations but also out of social disparity, psychological depression, lack of creativity and misinterpretation of different religious codes.

Terrorist Organisations and their Structures

Most of the modern terrorist organisations are like modern corporations. They have established rules and regulations along with worldwide financial investors. The establishment of these organisational structures is an effort by terrorist groups to provide support, training, decision making and other resources that may be required when operating in hostile situation.

Yet in most terrorist organisations, group dynamics, egos and philosophical and ideological differences frequently override attempted organisational structure. Because of international differences, individual members can carry out attacks that are not consistent with group's stated objectives.[93] These internal conflicts within larger organisations often cause smaller groups to splinter into new factions, yet maintain the support of the larger terrorist organisation.

Terrorist-organisations, especially, those with little or no government support generally need to establish clear organisational structures. A typical terrorist organisation is generally at the top of the command and control structure. Its primary role in the organisation is to define policy, set objectives and direct actions. The leadership is intensely committed to the groups' causes and often consists of charismatic individuals who have the ability to motivate others. If a group is state supported or directed, some or all of the leadership is typically trained and educated by the sponsoring state.

Table 1
Typical Terrorist Organisations

Leadership
Active Terrorists
Active Supporters
Passive Supporters

Source: Christopher Kozlow, *op.cit.*, p. 21.

Active Terrorists

The next level within most organisations consists of active terrorists. These are generally men, women and children recruited and trained by the organisation in methods of carrying out attacks. While many terrorists are deeply committed to the group's cause, the general membership may include "professional" terrorists who are generally not ideologically motivated.

Active Supporters

Active supporters are people who do not actually carry out attacks for the organisation. However, they do provide terrorists with money, intelligence, safe houses, forged or stolen documents, legal assistance and/or medical care, but are generally ambivalent regarding use of violence. Most organisations recruit their active members from within this group, since active supporters have proven their loyalty and skills to the organisation and leadership. A certain number of active supporters can be considered thrill-seekers who join predominantly for the excitement of belonging to a forbidden organisation.

Passive Supporters

Passive supporters are more difficult to define and identify.[94] Most are sympathetic to the terrorist cause, but do not assume an active role within the organisation. Some passive supporters become involved in intimidation and extortion operations. Most terrorist organisations depend on passive support for financial banking and logistical operation.

Non-State Sponsored Groups

Non-state sponsored terrorist groups operate autonomously receiving no significant support from any government. Italy's Red Brigades and Spain's Basque Fatherland and Liberty (ETA) are examples of non-state supported group.

State-Supported Groups

A state-supported terrorist group generally operates independently but receives support from one or more governments. The International Hezbollah, a new group formed in June 1996, is an example of a state-supported terrorist group.

State Directed Groups

This category includes the terrorist groups or organisations that operate as agents of a government. The group is provided with intelligence.[95] With increased counter-terrorism initiatives worldwide, newer forms of terrorist organisations and structures are becoming smaller or cellular in nature. These terrorist cells are relatively isolated from others within the terrorist groups thus reducing the risk of potential infiltration or capture from the authorities. In the event of a defection or capture, no member can identify more than a handful of others.[96]

Another lingering confusion about terrorism lies with the similarity and differences it carries with other concepts like insurgency, militancy, fundamentalism and extremism. Though they are used interchangeably in different cases and by scholars, there exist some differences between them. The most frequently used word in place of terrorism is 'insurgency'.

Insurgency is as old as war itself and has been the most prevalent type of armed conflict since the creation of organised political communities.[97] The Encyclopaedia of Social Sciences defines insurgency as use of armed forces against an established government to achieve public purpose, which cannot in the opinion of insurgents be achieved by pacific means. It is also defined as struggle between a non-ruling and the ruling in which the former consciously employs political resources and violence to establish legitimacy for certain issues considered as illegitimate.[98] Bard O'Neill, an expert on the study of insurgency says, insurgency may be defined as a struggle between a non-ruling group and the ruling authorities in which the non-ruling group consciously uses the political resources (i.e. organisational expertise, propaganda and demonstrations) and violence to destroy, reformulate or sustain the basis of the legitimacy of one or more aspects of politics.[99]

Ved Marwah, an Indian expert on the subject holds similar but operationally different opinion. He writes "the terms terrorism and insurgency are frequently used to mean something. Undeniably, the two are very closely interconnected. Both are a form of unconventional war waged to gain political objectives. But there are important points of distinction between the two concepts. Insurgents mostly target the security forces and vital installations. They are more selective in choosing their targets than terrorists, and more discriminating in the use of violence. That's not the ease with terrorism. Insurgents may resort to terrorist methods, but for them creating terror can never be an end in itself. Insurgency and terrorism have been used to soften restricting regimes by hostile foreign governments as well as by secessionist internal movements".[100]

Like the definition of terrorism, there are differences among the scholar academicians on the proper definition of insurgency. But, the common attribute in all the opinions is that terrorism and insurgency are means for violent revolutionary change. But there are differences between the two which could be analysed according to the following model.

Pattern of Vionent Revolutionary Change

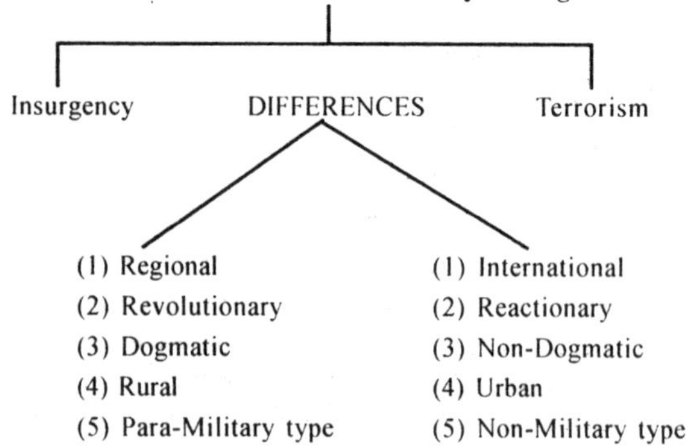

Source: Kshitij Prabha, *op. cit.* p. 28.

Regional and International

The first dividing line between insurgency and terrorism is the fact that, while the former is regional, the latter is international in nature. Insurgency remains confined within a nation or within its neighbourhood. Andrew M. Scott went to the extent of describing the need of appropriate physical and demographic environment as an essential condition for successful application of insurgency.[101] Insurgency needs access to territory and sanctuary which is safe from army attack and close to the border of a nation sympathetic to the rebels. But the same is not applicable to terrorism. Violence inflicted by the terrorist knows no boundary while insurgency remains confined to specific states though there are cases of insurgency funded by foreign land. It is relevant to note that their actions seldom affect international community. The same cannot be said for terrorism. It is perpetrated far and wide all over the world and the international community gets concerned by this phenomenon. Terrorism does not remain confined to one region nor do members belong to any one region, community or race. Terrorist groups recruit people from different parts of the country as their targets are worldwide, whereas insurgency involves local people. Their recruitment is based on commitment to the cause and geographical knowledge of the region, which is not the case so far as terrorism is concerned.

Revolutionary and Reactionary

The second important difference between the two is in their character. While terrorism is reactionary, insurgency is revolutionary in character. Terrorism is an expression of reaction. It is not a planned movement but reaction to certain situations which according to terrorists, is injustice and cannot be tolerated, whereas insurgency on the other hand is well planned and every phase of struggle is chalked out to suit their objectives. Violence perpetrated by the insurgents is not in reaction to any situation but a planned movement to achieve their goal that is revolution. In other words, insurgency is aimed at revolutionary change while the objective of terrorism remains obscure. Terrorists put forward certain demands, which if accepted by the government, they recede and if not, it could be bargained. In brief, there is always a considerable scope for compromise in terrorism but insurgency is committed to its ideology and goal.

Dogmatic and Non-Dogmatic

The third aspect of the distinction between insurgency and terrorism is related to ideology, i.e., while insurgency is dogmatic, terrorism is non-dogmatic. Indonesian Commander Abdul Haris Nasution rightly pointed out that ideological fight is usually the strongest motivation for insurgency and guerrilla warfare.[102] In case of terrorism, the objectives being obscure, it is not supported by any fixed ideology. Their objectives keep changing from one to other as per the response they receive from the government and the people. This flickering tendency is because they lack ideology. This is why terrorists employ 'hit and run tactics' rather than a systematic method to achieve their ambiguous objectives.

Rural and Urban

The fourth significant difference between insurgency and terrorism is related to geographical locations. By virtue of being revolutionary in nature, insurgency depends on rural support for its struggle. Its roots are in the countryside, because it aims to liberate common men from certain bondage. Therefore, support and confidence of the masses are vital to their cause, and second, because the seat of administration is invariably located in urban area which helps the insurgents to escape from marauding eyes of the law enforcement agencies. Simultaneously, by operating in rural side, insurgents enjoy the topographical advantage in their operations against the security forces.

Terrorism, on the contrary, is based in urban society. Urban life is prone to criminal activities. Its socio-economic conditions nurture conflict and dissent.[103] The wide gap between the rich and the poor, mental agony, sufferings, easy availability of weapons, other infrastructure, like communication in the cities make the terrorists mobile and successful in their hit-and-run tactics.

Paramilitary and Non-Paramilitary Type

Finally, difference between insurgency and terrorism could also be analysed in the light of organisational structure of terrorist group. Guerrilla or insurgent groups are organised on military lines.[104] They believe in blind obedience to the command in the same way as regular armed forces demand. The guerrilla insurgency advances according to the command of their authority. Insurgents operate collectively and do not propagate individual heroism. Its organisation and modus operandi is more like a paramilitary organisation rather than a terrorist group.

Unlike insurgency, terrorism is unorganised, and believes in kidnapping, killing innocent masses. Insurgents do not create terror by killing innocents, whereas terrorists bank upon indiscriminate violence and killing. Command is not as important an issue in terrorism as in insurgency. Mode of operation is immaterial in terrorist operation. The goal has to be achieved whether operation is carried by an individual or a group, is not relevant. Therefore, on the basis of modus operandi too, terrorism and insurgency could be evaluated separately. The problem in identifying the two as one is mainly because both belong to the same school of political thought, i.e., violence. To consider them as one would complicate conceptual aspects of terrorism.

Another terminology which is very often used in this context is militancy. Etymologically, 'militancy' according to Oxford Dictionary means 'combative' or 'aggressively supportive'. But generally, this is a term which is more journalistic in nature and application. Militancy is used by the journalists more in place of 'terrorism' and 'insurgency'. But academically, the meaning carries a lesser degree of violence or no violence at all; while carrying forward the cause or the objective aggressively. For example, in Indian struggle for independence, leaders like Tilak were considered militants for their aggressive posturing. But in the modern international relations' parlance, it is more similar to insurgency rather than terrorism for its basically local nature.[105]

George Houghton, in his article "Matter of Militancy", has made some attempt to give militancy a meaningful definition. He says, "It springs from one's values, is expressed as an attitude, and results in certain behaviour. One's values are those things in which one strongly believes. They are what one believes to be fundamentally important and true. From this comes an attitude which is unwilling to tolerate any divergence from these fundamentally important truths and which seeks to defend them. It results in behaviour which speaks up when these truths are attacked or diluted and which refuses to cooperate with any activity which would minimise their importance. The term is a military one and carries the idea of defending, what one believes to be true".[106]

The second frequently used term is 'fundamentalism', which has attracted a lot of literature on it without any commonly accepted definition. Still then, fundamentalism may be defined as a movement that is radical in terms of its goals, extremist in terms of its methods and literalist in terms of sticking to scripture.[107]

Similarly, while analysing other terms like "extremism" and "radicalism", they normally refer to degrees of intensity in commitment to ideologies and willingness to make sacrifices and stick consistently to that which appears to be worth believing in.[108] Some have even argued that extremism, as Barry Goldwater put it in 1964, in the service of liberty is no vice while moderation in the defence of liberty is no merit. By radicalism Karl Marx meant those who would change society by the root, or from the root. But a common understanding of extremism means the commitment and willingness to use a calculus that gives tremendous value to the achievement of the goals and objectives in question, at the expense of other values. Hence, this is a rational movement.[109]

Defining extremism, Peter H. Merki at European Centre for Securities, elaborated detailed aspects of extremism and its subjectivity and the radicalism that causes extremism. In his lecture, he opined that, "extremism simply means identifying far more intensely with a given cause or group than most of its other members or adherents".[110] Such strong identification with the group's interest may lead extremists to plot or take violent action against its presumable antagonists and, not infrequently, moderate leaders of their own group. However, strong belief and violent action do not always go together. There may be many more strong believers than those who take extremist action and at the same time, some violent extremists have long stopped believing in their cause or nihilists to begin with.[111]

Despite their basic differennce terrorism, insurgency, militancy, fundamentalism, extremism and radicalism are of grave concern for the world powers. The newest region to witness the malaise of terrorism is that of Central Asia - the five republics carved out of the erstwhile Soviet Union. The weak political stability coupled with the growing menace of religious fundamentalism has been creating havoc and put the countries in a deep trouble. The region- a seat of Islamic scholarship today has found numerous sponsors from outside who are trying their best to spread their supremacy over the region in the pretext of religious affinity. Though they still have not been able to establish any political supremacy, they have been able to mobilise forces in the name of religion - Islam. But why is it that after 70 years of strictly imposed secularism, these countries are falling pray to religious terrorism? The roots perhaps lie in the pre-Soviet and Soviet handling of religion in the society, in this part of the world.

References

1. Martha Crenshaw, "Theories of Terrorism: Instrumental and Organisational Approaches" in David C. Rappoport (ed.) *Inside Terrorist Organisations*, London, Frank Cass, 2001, p. 12.
2. *Ibid.*
3. Thomas C. Shelling, *Arms and Influence*, New Heaven CT, Yale University Press, 1966, pp. 1-34.
4. *Ibid.*
5. Bard E. O' Neill, *Insurgency and Terrorism*, Washington, Maxwell Macmillan Pergamon Corporation, 1990, p. 24.

6. Alex P. Schmid, *Political Terrorism*, New Brumstick, Transaction Books, 1983, p. 39.
7. Alex P. Schmid's book *Political Terrorism*, pp. 79-96, offers a detailed examination of such distinctions.
8. Frederick Hacker, *Crusaders*, Criminals, Crazies, New York, Bantam Books, 1978, pp. 83-89.
9. See Noam Chomsky and Edward Herman, *The Semantics of Terror in the Washington Connection and Third World Fascism*, Boston, South End Press, 1979, Vol. 1, p. 67, also see, Alex P. Schmid and Jonny de Graff, *Violence As Communication*, New York, Sage Publishers, 1982, p. 2.
10. Alex P. Schmid and Robert J. Jungman, et al., *Political Terrorism*, Amsterdam, North Holland Publishing Company, 1988, p. 24.
11. R. P. Hoffman, as cited in *Political Terrorism*, *op. cit.*, p. 91.
12. Cited in Ray S. Clive and Yonah Alexander, *Terrorism as State Sponsored Covert Warfare*, Fairbox, Virginia, Hero Books, 1986, p. 31.
13. Noam Chomsky and Edward S. Herman, *The Washington Connection and Third World Fascism*, 1979, cited in the *Political Economy of Human Rights*, Vol. 1, Nottingham, Spokesman, 1979, pp. 85-86.
14. Ihekwaba D. Onweidiwe, *The Globalisation of Terrorism*, Ashgate, Burlington, USA, 2001, p. 16.
15. J. Lodge, Terrorism: *A Challenge to the State*, Oxford, Martin Robertson, 1981, cited in *Ibid.*
16. *Webster's Dictionary*, 1983, cited in *Ibid.*
17. P.T. Thorton, "Terror as a Weapon of Political Agitation", in H. Eckeinstein (ed.) *Internal War*, New York, Free Press, 1983, cited in *Ibid.*
18. Krieger, 1977, cited in *Ibid.*
19. A.R. Friedlander, *Terrorism and the Law*, What Price Safety, Gaithersburg, IACP, 1981, cited in *Ibid.*
20. A.L. Sobel, *Political Terrorism*, New York, Facts on File, 1975, p. 84.
21. Yonah Alexander, *International Terrorism*, National, Regional and Global Perspectives, New York, Praeger Publishers, 1976, p. 16.
22. Cited in Christopher Kozlow, *Jane's Counter Terrorism*, USA, Jane's Information Group, 2000, p. 18.
23. *Ibid.*
24. *Ibid.*
25. Cited in Kshitij Prabha, *Terrorism: An Instrument of Foreign Policy*, New Delhi, South Asian Publications, 2000, p. 15.
26. Erean Karin, "Terrorism is Deadly Virus Plaguing Society", *The Times of Central Asia*, 9 May 2002.
27. As cited in Kshitij Prabha, *Terrorism: An Instrument of Foreign Policy*, South Asian Publications, New Delhi, p. 16.
28. Howard Lawrence (ed.), *op. cit*, p. 14.

29. Grant Wardlaw, *Political Terrorism*, Cambridge, Cambridge University Press, 1982, p. 4.
30. Alex P. Schmid, Albert J. Jangman et al., *op. cit.*, p. 100.
31. James Turner, Johnson, *Can Modern War be Just?*, New Heaven, Yale University Press, 1984, pp. 60-63.
32. The literary and philosophical history of terrorism dates back to ancient Greece, if one includes the myth of Electra who helped to avenge her father's murder by her mother or trace Plotonis who seventeen centuries ago said, "Terror in compound is the dread of dissolution".
33. Paul Wilkinson, *Political Terrorism*, London, Macmillan Press, 1974, pp. 45-46.
34. Walter Laqueur, *Terrorism*, Boston, Little Brown, 1977, p. 25.
35. Cited in Marie Fleming, "Propaganda by the Deed: Terrorism and the Anarchist, Theory in Late Nineteenth Century Europe", *Terrorism: An International Journal*, Vol. 14, 1980, p. 6.
36. *Ibid.* p. 7.
37. Sergey Nechayev, Catechism of the Revolutionist (1869), in Machael Confeno (ed.) *Daughter of a Revolutionary: Natalie Herzen and the Bakunin/ Nachayev Circle*, London, Alcove Press, 1974, p. 224.
38. Laqueur, *op.cit.*, p. 229.
39. Flemming, *op. cit.*, pp. 13-14.
40. Terrorist thought also appears in some pamphlets which surfaced in Geneva in 1880. They were authored by two most prominent advocates of terrorist action, Nikolai Maroza and G. Tavnaski who were also members of *Navodnaya Valya* which plotted and killed the Czar in 1881.
41. Paul Wilkinson, *Terrorism and the Liberal State*, London, Macmillan, 1977, p. 72.
42. *Ibid.*, p. 73.
43. Frantz Fanon, *The Wretched of the Earth*, New York, Grove Press, 1966, p. 73.
44. Christopher Dobson and Ronal Payne, *The Terrorists, Their Weapons*, Leaders and Tactics, New York, Facts on File, 1979, p. 29.
45. It would be far too flattering to regard Mrighella as a thinker given the ideological inconsistencies in his writings and his application. In 1966, he regarded terrorism merely as one form of mass resistance and did not expect that it would be a signal for popular uprising. He felt that the centre of gravity should be the country side. His own activities, however, concentrated on the 'complimentary' front and he would frequently refer to the strategic importance of the urban cities.
46. Carlos Mrighella, *For the Liberation of Brazil*, London, Hurmundowarth, 1971, p. 47.
47. Christopher Kozlow, *op.cit.*, 2000, pp. 22-23.
48. David C. Rappoport, *op.cit.*, p. 4.

49. Sean McCormack, Terrorism, Terrorism Conference Course, www.terrorism/Aghai/TCC/US/html, downloaded on 8.8.2001.
50. Cited in *Ibid.*
51. *Ibid.*
52. Sean McCormack, *op.cit.*
53. *Ibid.*, p. 31.
54. *Ibid.*, p. 25.
55. *Ibid.*
56. Martha Crenshaw, "Theories of Terrorism: Instrumental Organisational Approach", *Journal of Strategic Studies*, Vol. 10, No. 4, December 1987, p. 13.
57. Christorpher C. Harmon, "Five Strategies of Terrorism", *Small Wars and Insurgencies*, Vol. 12, No. 3, Autumn, 2001, p. 39.
58. Carlos Mrighella, 'Mini Manual of the Urban Guerrilla', undated, reprinted in *Adelphi Papers*, No. 79, August 1971, p. 40.
59. Cristopher C. Harmon, *op.cit.*, p. 41.
60. Christ Ryan, "Tourism, Terrorism and Violence", *Conflict Studies*, No. 244, September 1991, pp. 1-2.
61. Leonard Weinberg (ed.) *Political Parties and Terrorist Groups*, London, Frankcass, 1992, p. 122.
62. Peter Taylor, *States of Terror: Democracy and Political Violence*, London, BBC Books, 1993, p. 114.
63. Cristopher C. Harmon, *op.cit.*, p. 42.
64. US Department of State, *Pattern of Global Terrorism*, Washington DC, 1997, p. 15.
65. *Bite and Flee* was the slogan of the Italian Red Brigade as well as other terrorist groups.
66. Truong Nhu Tang, and David Chanoff et al., *A Vietcong Memoir*, New York, Vintage Books, 1986, p. 92.
67. Patrick Clawson, "Terrorism in Decline", Orbis, Vol. 52, No. 2, Spring 1988, p. 273.
68. Michael Aaronson, "Terrorism and Freedom Fighting", *International Relations*, Vol. 8, No. 6 November 1986, p. 619.
69. Paul Johnson, *The Age of Terrorism*, New York, New Statesman, 1974, p. 763.
70. A terrorist group normally aims to achieve autonomy or creation of a separate state, which does not come easily unless based on certain valid grounds. Their object remains far-fetched and thus they shift towards violence and intimidation as their goal, which does not draw attention of masses, an essential condition for liberation movement.
71. Kshitij Prabha, *op. cit.*, p. 23.
72. Martha Crenshaw, Theories of Terrorism, *op. cit.*, pp. 13-15.
73. J. Bowyere, Bell, *The Secret Army*: A History of IRA, Massachusetts, Cambridge, MIT, 1974, p. 13.

74. Brian M. Jenkins, *New Modes of Conflict*, Santa Monica, Rand Corporation, 5th year, p.a. 90406.
75. Franz Fanon, *The Wretched of Earth*, London, Penguin Books, 1965, p. 118.
76. D. M. Sehlagheck, *International Terrorism: An Introduction to Concepts and Actors* Massachusetts, D. C. Healths Co., 1988, p. 61.
77. Michael Aranson, "Terrorism as Freedom Fighting", *International Relations*, Vol. 8, No. 6, London, 1986, p. 619.
78. D. J. C. Carmichael, "Of Beasts, God and Civilised Man: The Justification for Terrorism and Counter-Terrorism Measures", *Terrorism: An International Journal*, Vol. 6, No. 1, New York, 1982, pp. 72-79.
79. Frederick Schuman, *Encyclopedia of Social Sciences*, Vol. 17, New York, Macmillan and Co., 1932, p. 117.
80. Benjamin Netanyahu, "*Opening Remarks, International Terrorism: Challenge and Response*", London, Transaction Books, 1981, p. 5.
81. Donna M. Sehlagheck, *International Terrorism: An Introduction to Concepts and Actors*, Massachusetts, D. C. Healths Co., 1988, p. 61.
82. Jean Francois Mayer, "*Cults, Violence and Religious Terrorism: An International Perspective*", Studies in Conflict and Terrorism, 24 January 2001, p. 361.
83. As Rappoport reminds us, millennium groups have been characterized "either by an extraordinary militancy which drives some to 'force the end'", which may lead to terror or "by a refusal to participate in the existing political order" leading to pacifism. David Rappoport, "Some General Observations on Religion and Violence", *Terrorism and Political Violence*, 3 (3), Autumn 1991, p. 132.
84. Steve Bruce, *Fundamentalism*, UK, Polity Press, 2000, p. 4.
85. J.F. Mayer, *op.cit.*, p. 367.
86. Daniel Byman, "The Logic of Ethnic Terrorism", *Studies in Conflict and Terrorism*, Vol. 21, No. 4, September-October 1998, p. 149.
87. Walter Laqueur, *The Age of Terrorism*, Boston, Little Brown and Company, 1987, p. 203.
88. Ted Robert Guerr, *Why Men Rebel*, New Jersey, Princeton University Press, 1970, p. 24.
89. Richard H. Schultz, "The Low Intensity Conflict Environment of the 1990s", *Annals of the American Association of Political Science*, 517, September 1991, p. 125.
90. Willy Brandt, *North-South Dialogue*, London, Pan Book Ltd., 1980, p. 13.
91. Paul Wilkinson, *op.cit.*, p. 80.
92. Richard Clutterback, *Living With Terrorism*, New York, Arlingdon House Publishers, 1975, p. 42.
93. Christopher Kozlow, *op.cit.*, p. 20.
94. *Ibid*, p. 21.

95. Samuel P. Huntington, 'Guerrilla Warfare in Theory and Policy', in Franklin Mark Osanka (ed.) *Modern Guerrilla Warfare*, New York, The Free Press of Glaucae, 1962, p. XVI.
96. Christopher Kozlow, *op.cit.*, p. 22.
97. Bard, E.O' Neil, *op.cit.*, p. 4.
98. Andrew M. Scott & Others, *Insurgency*, Carolina, University of North Carolina Press, 1970, p. 8
99. The definition of insurgency is similar to that characterising civil war in J. K. Zawadny, "Civil War" in *International Encyclopaedia of the Social Sciences*, New York, Macmillan, 1968, p. 499 as cited in Sam C. Sarkesian (ed.) *Revolutionary Guerrilla Warfare: An Introduction*, Chicago, Precedent Publishing Inc., 1975, p. 4. The use of violence by the opponents of the government distinguishes insurgencies from socio-political protest movements, such as those led by Gandhi in India, Khomeini in Iran and Solidarity Movement in Poland.
100. Ved Marwah, *op.cit.*, pp. 30-31.
101. Brian Cozier, *The Rebels*, London, Chetto and Windus, 1960, pp. 37-45.
102. P. N. Gobosky, "The Urban Context of Political Terrorism" in Michael Stohl (ed.), *The Politics of Terrorism*, New York, Marcel Dekker Inc., 1979, p. 53.
103. Julien Paget, *Counter Insurgency Campaign*, London, Faber and Faber, 1967, p. 22.
104. Brian Cozier, *op.cit.*, p. 15.
105. Sean McCormack, *op.cit.*
106. George Houghton, *The Matter of Militancy*, http.//www.faith.edu/pulpits/94_05.HTM
107. Gabriel Ben-Dar, "Uniqueness of Islamic Fundamentalism", *International Journal of Middle East Studies*, Vol. 8, 1977, p. 43.
108. *Ibid*, p. 241.
109. Gabriel A. Almond, 'Rational Choice Theory and the 'Social Sciences" in Gabriel A. Almond (ed.), *A discipline Divided*, New Berry Park ,California , Sage Publishers, 1990, pp. 87-97.
110. Peter H. Merki, *Elements of Extremism*, presented at the Conference on "Enhancing Security of States in a Multi-Polar World: Focus on Extremism", George C. Marshall European Centre for Securities Studies, Garmisch-Partenkirschen Germany, 18-22 September 2000.
111. Peter H. Merki, *The Making of a Storm Trooper*, Princeton, Princeton University Press, 1980, pp. 226-228, 231.

2

Militancy, Cross-Border Terrorism and Crime: An Unholy Nexus

The end of Cold War following the disintegration of Soviet Union has led to a considerable decrease in the international conflicts involving superpowers. But at the regional level, the scenario is quite different. There has been an unprecedented increase in militancy and terrorism promoted by external and internal forces and fuelled by factors like religious fundamentalism and ethno-nationalist chauvinism. The end of the ideological warfare between the two superpowers has created a political vacuum on both the international and regional fronts. The entire South-west Asian region, which has been destabilised and again time in the past by major events like the Iranian Revolution, the Iran-Iraq war is also facing renewed upheavals of different nature. Similarly, the independence of the Central Asian republics from the Soviet orbit is another most dramatic developments of the last decade. In the post-independence period, the newly independent countries of the Central Asian region have encountered a myriad of new problems on their road to democracy and free market economy.[1] The emergence of terrorism in its criminal and political forms is one of these problems. Criminal and political terrorism were not the major security concerns for the Soviet Union, as the authoritarian nature of the political and social systems made it difficult for such activities to surface.[2] Moreover, due to the strict government control over the media and travel restrictions on the foreigners, public knowledge on the existence of such groups or incidents was severely limited. Not only were there few reported political terrorist incidents carried out in the Soviet Union, there were also a few terrorist incidents directed at Soviet targets outside USSR.[3]

With the disintegration of the Soviet Union, the security environment in the region, especially related to criminal and political terrorist activities changed. The resultant poor economic situation in many of the newly independent states contributed to deterioration of the law enforcement and border situation, general unemployment and social malaise. Controls over weapons and explosives weakened.Criminal gangs which previously operated in a non-lethal mode and out of the public eye came out of the closet and quickly engaged in lethal operations.[4]

Here it is necessary to keep in mind the fact that analysis of the former Soviet Union is hampered by certain problems that make reading the extent of terrorism in the region, difficult. In this context, Sir Winston Churchill once, in his first speech as the Lord of Admiralty on October 1939, stated in a BBC Radio broadcast that he could not forecast the actions of the Soviet Union because it is "a riddle, wrapped in a mystery, inside an enigma". Therefore, any discussion on terrorism in erstwhile Soviet Union carries with it the problem of verifiability of facts and biasness of reporting.

The first ever incident of terrorism in an organised form that took place in former Soviet Union and mostly in the Central Asian region was the famous *Basmachi* revolt, which some even call as *Basmachi* movement. Soon after the dissolution of the Kokand 'Autonomous' government, there arose in Fergana, the *Basmachi* movement. The Great Soviet Encyclopaedia simply describes the *Basmachi* movement as "an armed counter-revolutionary nationalist movement in Middle Asia from 1917-1926".[5] It was a form of class struggle of the feudal lords, beys, kulaks, mullahs and nationalist bourgeois against Soviet government. They were supported and directed by British and American internationalists, reactionary circles of Turkey, China and Afghanistan and the Russian White Guards. As it had no broad base among the working masses, it depended largely on support from foreign imperialists.[6] Its followers were mainly drawn from ex-officials of the Tsarist administration such as the *aksakals, mirabs* and *volost* administrators and from the Muslim clergy. Almost conspicuous by their absence in the ranks of the *Basmachi* were the poor peasants and artisans with the exception of some, who either on account of their extreme backwardness, or through fear, remained with them temporarily.[7]

The ideological bases of the *Basmachi* revolt were pan-Islamism, pan-Turkism, and bourgeois nationalism. Among the direct leaders of the *Basmachi* revolt were the counter-revolutionary organisations such as Shura-i-Islam, Shura-i-Ulema and Alash. After the creation of the counter-revolutionary "Kokand Autonomous Government" in 1917, these governments formed bands of *Basmachi* and initiated armed struggle against the Soviet government with the intention of separating Turkestan from the Soviet Russia and establishing a government of the nationalist bourgeoisie and feudal lords under the protection of foreign governments.[8] F. Baily, the chief of the British government's military diplomatic mission, and R. Tredwell, the American Consul, took part in the organisation and arming of the *Basmachi* bands in the summer of 1918. The *Basmachi* employed tactics such as surprise raids on Soviet military units, industrial installations, railroad stations, depots and popular areas, accompanied by mass murders, arsons, and destruction. The *Basmachis* dealt cruelly particularly with the party and Soviet workers and also women who had given up the *Yashmak* (veil).[9] The first *Basmachi* detachments appeared in Kokand at the end of 1917 under the leadership of Irgash. In the spring of 1918, the *Basmachi* extended their active operations to the region of the city of Osh. In the autumn of 1918, a group of *Basmachi* headed by Madomin-bek, the ring leader of the "Turkestan Muslim White Guard" concluded a military and political agreement for combined operations against the Soviet government with K. Monstrov, who led the Kulak army (Southern Kirghizia). The *Basmachi* achieved their greatest development in September and October 1919, when the joint armed forces of the Fergana *Basmachi* and the Kulak army seized Osh and Jalalabad, blockaded Andijan, and began to threaten Fergana. Soviet forces on the Turkestan front (commanded by M.V. Frunze) defeated the Kulak-*Basmachi* army in early March 1920. The Turkestan Commission of the All-Russian Central Executive Committee and the Council of People's Commissars of the RSFSR formed in October 1919 rendered a great assistance to the people of Central Asia in the struggle for Soviet power and liquidation of the *Basmachi*.[10] The frequency of *Basmachi* raids in Fergana increased in the summer and autumn of 1920. By the end of 1920, the valley portion of Fergana had been cleared of *Basmachis*. By April 1926, up to 7000 *Basmachis* remained in Fergana, approximately 7000 in Bukhara, and 1000 in Khiva. Enver Pasha, the former Minister of War of Turkey, arrived in Bukhara in October 1921. He succeeded in consolidating separate uncoordinated bands of Basmachis into an army (approximately16,000 men), which seized a considerable amount of territory in the Bukhara People's Soviet Republic in the spring of 1922.[11] The Soviet government and the Central Committee of the RCP (Bolsheviks) adopted decisive measures for the liquidation of Enver Pasha's *Basmachi* army. In June 1922, Enver's bands were dealt with a lethal blow and in the middle of July, Dushanbe was liberated; Enver was killed in one of the skirmishes during August. By the end of 1922, the main forces of *Basmachi* in Fergana and Khorezm were defeated. However, the reactionary circle of Afghanistan, China and Iran permitted the shattered remnants of the *Basmachi* gangs to take shelter in the territories of their states, and helped them to reinforce their troops, rearm themselves, and to continue attacks on Soviet territories of Central Asia.[12] The *Basmachi* bands of Ibrahim Bek in Bukhara and Junaid Khan in Khorezm managed to hold out for some more time. The band of Junaid

Khan was liquidated early in 1924; the gangs of Ibrahim Bek (approximately 4000 men) were routed in 1926. In 1929 and early 1930s, *Basmachi* detachments again penetrated from abroad and attempted to ruin the collectivisation of farming in Central Asia, but they were liquidated.

The *Basmachi* caused enormous damage to the national economy of Central Asia. Thousands of *Dekhkans* (peasants) supporting the Soviet government were wiped out by the *Basmachis*. From 1917 to 1923, the population was reduced by one-third in Fergana oblast alone.[13] The leaders of the *Basmachi* taking the advantage of the complex military and political situation in Central Asia and the ignorance and the religious fanaticism of the *Dekhkan* masses attracted some of the working population to their side. The imperialists of many countries supplied the Basmachi with all the necessities (weapons, food and money).

In the struggle with the *Basmachi*, the Soviet government combined military actions with economic measures and political efforts. The implementation of the Leninist principles of national policy and party measures for the development of the *Dekhkan* labour economy (favourable taxation, commercial development, water and land reform and so on) played a large role in the liquidation of the *Basmachi*.[14]

Thus, the earliest organised case of terrorism was led by the *Basmachis* that finally lost to the formidable strength of the Soviet power. But what is important in the whole of the *Basmachi* episode is that, it was basically a pan-Islamic movement, wherein, religion, i.e., Islam played an important role of being a rallying point. Since then, the Soviet Union had been affected by religious fundamentalism, terrorist onslaughts from time to time.

The Muslims of Central Asia also revolted several times against the regime which came to power through Bolshevik Revolution in 1917. The main areas where the conflicts occurred were Bashkiria, Kirghizia, Khiva (1918-20), Fergana (1918-26), Bukhara, the Crimea and Azerbaijan.[15] The Red Army crushed most of the revolts in the Muslim areas with great ferocity. On the other hand, in order to neutralise their brutalisation, an attempt was made by the Soviets to deal with the question politically by setting up a Central Muslim Commission in Moscow.

Soviets divided the region on the basis of 'nationalities' that continued until 1991. However, the militant Islamic movements broke out against the Bolsheviks in several parts of the Soviet Union. The Red Army took several years to crush these forces in Central Asia. '*Basmachi*' revolt was also one of them. Eventually, the Bolsheviks with the help of influential Muslim radical nationalists crippled the revolt, but the movement left an indelible psychological and political heritage which remains alive even today.[16]

Besides these measures, the Soviet official Islamic establishment signed a number of agreements-approximately fifty in number-most of which related to cultural exchanges agreements that were signed between the Islamic countries and the Soviet Union.[17]

The Soviet intervention in Afghanistan in December 1979 caused a significant setback to the gains made by the Soviet Union in the previous decade. It is estimated that the Central Asian soldiers formed nearly 30 to 40 percent of the Soviet forces sent to Afghanistan and a large number of Uzbeks and Tajiks were sent to run the administration. However, within a few months it was decided to replace them with the forces from European republics of the Soviet Union. This action was taken because the Soviet authorities were afraid that these Muslim soldiers would identify themselves with local population. Furthermore, the 'iron curtain' created between the Soviet Muslims and the Muslims of the adjoining countries began to crumble and the authorities in Moscow became fearful of a backlash.[18]

Militancy and Terrorism in Central Asia since Independence

After the *Basmachi* revolt was suppressed and liquidated by the Soviet forces, no organised terrorist or militant activity could take place due to a strong vigilance by the Soviet law enforcement authorities and the government. But after independence, the situation changed totally and the Pandora's Box of militancy and terrorism opened up once again, taking advantage of the political confusion and uncertainty that engulfed the region initially. One such incident which influenced the politics of the region tremendously for nearly five years was the Tajik civil war. It was a militant and violent struggle that took the lives of 50,000 people and injured as many as 2,00,000.

Tajikistan which lies to the north of Afghanistan, just across the Panj River was a relatively underdeveloped corner of the former Soviet Union. It rapidly dropped from a low-income republic of USSR to one of the world's poorest states.[19] Tajikistan would have probably moved towards post-Communist reform sooner if it had not succumbed to an internal contest for power in the first year of independence. The contest plunged the country into five years of civil war (1992-97).[20]

The events that precipitated the Tajikistan war, took place in April and May 1992, but the underlying causes of the conflict were lodged in territorial and ethnic identities that go back to the Soviet period. Before the Soviet takeover, no single authority had ruled the people of Tajikistan's rugged mountains and fertile agricultural valleys. The Soviet government brought unified rule but never displaced traditional regional and clan-based loyalties. The territorial division of Central Asia during the Soviet period had long enduring implications.[21] Democratisation and economic reform in the core regions of the Soviet Union in the late 1980s brought greater self-rule to the outlying regions. In Tajikistan, this was manifested primarily in a resurgence of local territorialism rather than Tajik national self-determination.

In the chaotic changes following the disintegration of Soviet power, a former First Secretary of the Tajik Communist Party, Rakhmon Nabiyev, assumed political control in 1991. The country was swept up by the waves of exalting tension that resulted in armed groups vying for control in the streets of capital. In September 1992, Nabiyev, a native of the northern Leningrad region, was forced to resign at gunpoint. Dushanbe then fell under the control of a coalition led by Tajikistan's Islamic Renaissance Party.[22] Civil war ensued and Tajikistan was briefly divided into north and south.

Then aided by the military assistance from Russia and Uzbekistan, a coalition of forces from the southern region of Kurgan Tyube and the northern industrial Leningrad *oblast* collaborated to recapture the capital and reunite the country. These combined forces attacked Dushanbe on 24 October 1992. Thousands of civilians and soldiers were killed while thousands more fled the capital. This early violent phase of the civil war was resolved in favour of a coalition based in the valley region centred in the city of Kulyab. The coalition selected as its leader, a former Kulyab district Communist Party official, Emamali Rahmanov.

During the fighting in Tajikistan, the Russian 201st Motorised Rifle Division, already deployed in the country to guard the Soviet Union's southern border, was given a new domestic peacekeeping mission. Russia assumed primary responsibility for Tajik military operations, and its military presence gradually transformed the country into what Lena Johnson characterises as a "Russian Protectorate".[23]

The fighters displaced by the recapture of the Tajik capital - the groups that eventually comprised the United Tajikistan Opposition were scattered in the mountain areas to the north and east of the capital.[24] Large parts of the country remained under military control, because commanders who were victorious in the war divided the country among themselves. In the wake of the war, normal governmental and political activities were suspended. The civil war divided Tajikistan into several dimensions simultaneously, splitting region against region, clan against clan, religion against religion, and internationalists against nationalists.[25] Significantly, the conflict divided the country into victor and the vanquished. Many of the vanquished retained their weapons.

After the intense fighting in the autumn of 1992, Tajikistan followed a tortuous path of gradual normalisation. Some vanquished fighters fled to Afghanistan, Uzbekistan or Iran. Others continued the conflict from small pockets in Tajikistan. Rebel groups continued to control certain regions of the countryside, particularly the Garm Valley. The country's urban areas were subject to continuous harassment and conflict. Hostage taking became an important mechanism for setting outstanding wartime disputes. Assassinations and contract killings became common.[26]

At the insistence of the international organisations, the government and the leaders of the opposition entered into a dialogue on national reconciliation. On 27 June 1997, President Rahmanov and Sayid Abdullo Nuri, the leader of the United Tajikistan Opposition, signed the general agreement on the "Establishment of Peace and National Accord in Tajikistan".[27]

The signing of the agreement and the subsequent convening of the Commission on National Reconciliation launched a period of transition. According to the terms of the agreement, refugees were to return to their homes, UTO fighters were to be demobilised and their leaders were to be reintegrated into the governmental structures, the armed forces, police and security service were to be reformed and the democratic processes in the country were to be reinvigorated. Despite numerous setbacks, the peace process moved forward.[28] During 1999, more than 6000 ex-fighters were registered and granted amnesty. A September 1999 referendum provided a positive mandate for Rahmanov government. The final peace agreement provided a model for other Central Asian states. For the first time in Central Asia, a coalition government was established between two warring factions that included an avowedly Islamist party. The most powerful reason, which was in fact the propelling force for this early and smooth settlement of the crisis, was the simultaneous rise and conquest of Afghanistan by Taliban.[29]

Tajikistan witnessed several hostage crises during and after the civil war. In February 1997, 15 people were taken hostage in Central Tajikistan by northern warlord Bakhram Sadirov. The captives included four UN military observers, two employees of the International Committee of Red Cross, four UN refugee workers, four Russian journalists and Maj. Gen. Saidamir Zuhurov. Sadirov seized the hostages demanding that his brother Rizvan Sadirov be allowed to return to Tajikistan with a group of rebel guerrillas from neighbouring Afghanistan. Rizvan Sadirov had reportedly been fighting the Afghan Taliban forces alongside former Afghan Defence Minister Ahmad Shah Masud. The crisis ended when President Imamali Rahmanov agreed to Sadirov's demand.[30]

Another important incident of terrorism was the grenade attack on Tajik President Imamali Rahmanov. On 30 April 1997, the President was injured when a man threw a grenade at him in the city of Khojand (the administrative centre of Leninabad province in northern Tajikistan). Two people were killed in the attack and 49 injured. Rahmanov sustained injury in his leg. The man, who threw the grenade, Firdaus Dustboboyev, is rumoured to have been one of the organisers of the May 1996 anti-government demonstrations in Khojand.[31] This incident was followed by another attack on the barracks of the Presidential guards in October, killing 14 service men. There were several cases of bombing in Tajikistan and its capital Dushanbe as well. On July 17 and 26, two bombs exploded in the capital city. While the first caused little damage, the second injured four children.[32] Similarly, on September 9 and 25, a series of bomb explosions took place in Dushanbe, injuring more than 28 people.[33] While these kinds of attacks continued, Dushanbe also witnessed several cases of kidnappings and abductions. On 3 October 1997, a meat dealer and his son were abducted. In the same year, several UN aid workers were also abducted.[34]

In 1997, there was a peace accord in Tajikistan, which for all theoretical purposes ended the civil war, but the acts of terrorism and militancy (which was rampant and extremely gory in nature) continued, though on a smaller magnitude in 1998 and thereafter. Surprisingly, the other four Central Asian republics, which had not witnessed such incidents, now started facing the brunt of the problem.

In the Namangan region, on 30 December 1997, a series of killings occurred in which several policemen were killed.[35] Soon after this incident, President Islam Karimov adopted a plan to fight against "organised crime".

On 16 February,. a powerful bomb explosion occurred in Tashkent, killing 15 people and injuring 100 others. Zakir Almatov, head of Uzbekistan's Ministry of Internal Affairs declared that it was "terrorism perpetrated by religious extremists". At 11.55 a.m., a car bomb exploded as a result of a police shoot-out with one of the assailants. The first blast ignited the second and within an hour or so, there were a series of explosions in other central areas of Tashkent, in front of Internal Affairs Ministry building.[36] President Karimov announced that it was carried out by Hezbollah,[37] but later said that most of those arrested in connection with the incident had undergone training in Chechnya, Afghanistan and Tajikistan.[38] He also said that they all belonged to various terrorist religious extremist groups.[39] Later, a report by the Russian Republic TV said that the attack in Tashkent was originally aimed at President Karimov who reached on the spot within minutes after the blast occurred. The investigators suspected that it was a provocation by the religious extremists. It was also underlined that the terrorist acts were thoroughly prepared and not without help from abroad.[40]

Kyrgyzstan witnessed a major terrorist incident in August 1999. A reconnaissance unit of the Kyrgyz government troops, numbering about 20 men, was taken hostage in the village of Karamyk.[41] Further, on 25 August, militants seized four Tajikistan-controlled villages in southern Kyrgyzstan. According to Interior Minister Omurbek Kutuyev, the militants, on 24 August, seized the village of Darley, where two schools were blown up.[42] In the same month, four Japanese nationals were taken as hostages by Kyrgyz fundamentalist extremists.[43]

In the month of August another incident, which shook the entire region and brought into light the clear vulnerability of the republics, was the 'Batken incursion'.

A silent invasion of the Islamists into Kyrgyzstan began from the Garm area in Tajikistan in 1999, which is also known as the Karategin Valley. This sub-region has been a traditional base of the Islamic radicals as the message of national reconciliation was not well received there. The presence of Uzbeks in Karategin was well known to the government in Dushanbe, but other countries were also informed that a large number of so-called refugees were actually from a group of terrorists headed by Juma Namangani. They took part in the Tajik civil war on the side of the Islamic opposition. About 1,500 members of these terrorist groups who had intruded into Kyrgyzstan formed the main force.[44]

While the negotiations continued with the terrorists for the release of the hostages, the government took measures to locate the terrorists and mounted an army operation to destroy their base. On 13 August, after a negotiated settlement for a ransom of US $ 50, 000 and free passage to Uzbekistan, the hostages were released.[45]

On 15 August, Uzbek Air Force bombed the terrorist's sites and the Kyrgyz troops began the second stage of their operation for liquidation of the terrorist groups. The Secretary of the Council of Security of Kyrgyzstan, Esen Topaex, declared that as the terrorists had violated the laws of Kyrgyzstan, they should be punished according to the laws of the republic.[46]

On 22 August, a group of 30 terrorists occupied the villages of Zardaly and Khalja-Achkan, the camp site of the Japanese geologists' exploration. The terrorists took the Kyrgyz General Shamkeev, one soldier and four Japanese geologists along with their interpreter as hostages. Leaders of the Kyrgyz law enforcement agency believed that it was the same terrorist group, which had entered into Kyrgyzstan from Tajikistan in 31 July. Other sources revealed that another group of 200 insurgents had entered

Kyrgyzstan from Tajikistan to support the terrorists at Zardaly.[47]

On the night of 23-24 August, as the fight began east of village Kan, terrorists retreated by moving into deep gorges without suffering casualties, but there was no information about the hostages. The confrontation continued for two months, during which Kyrgyz troops appeared powerless to expel the insurgents from several villages.[48] On the night of 24 August, terrorists blew up the bridge across the Sokh River, which connects the Canyon with Batken. The terrorists successfully evaded the government troops. On 28 August, Kyrgyzstan, Kazakhstan, Tajikistan and Uzbekistan confirmed that joint operations were being conducted against the terrorist groups in south Kyrgyzstan.

The joint manifesto issued in the city of Osh at the meeting of the ministers of foreign affairs and defence, along with the chiefs of the national security services of the four Central Asian countries confirmed that the terrorists were supported by external forces.[49] At this meeting, modalities of the joint action and the situation in south Kyrgyzstan were discussed. The meeting declared that the terrorist groups included not only people from Central Asian countries, but also nationals from many other foreign countries,[50] which is exactly indicative of the the pan-Islamic character of terrorism and extremist organisations posing a common threat to all the republics in the region.[51]

The participants of the meeting were convinced that the objective of the international Islamic terrorist groups was to destabilise the Central Asian countries whose efforts were directed towards building and developing civilised, democratic and secular societies. It was evident that the Islamic terrorists were trying to turn the clock back to the medieval age.[52]

The participants appealed to the people of their respective countries to stand united in giving a decisive rebuff to the provocative actions of the international terrorists. They also declared that the terrorist violation of the state boundaries and violence towards the peaceful population will be countered by hard and resolute actions in accordance with international law.[53] President Akaev said that this activity was just not regional but global and Kyrgyzstan was being confronted with international religious terrorism and extremism.[54] However, the confrontation which continued for two months came to an end when the insurgents withdrew after getting six million US dollars as ransom from the Japanese government to release the Japanese hostages.[55]

As a result of these events, tensions grew sharply even between the three Central Asian states. Uzbekistan criticised Kyrgyzstan for harbouring Uzbekistan's enemies. Tajikistan protested to the unsanctioned over-flight and bombing of its territory by Uzbekistan (which Uzbekistan first denied, but later admitted). Eventually, however, the incursions prompted the security agreements between these states (and with Russia), as they braced for new incursions in the following summer.[56]

The incursions began again in August 2000, this time initially in Uzbekistan's southern province of Surkhan-Darya, a high mountain area on the border with Tajikistan. Within a week, separate incursions began in separate places in southern Kyrgyzstan.[57] According to Osmonakun Ibraimov, the Press Secretary of the Kyrgyz President, on 11 August 1999, 40 rebels invaded the Batken district.[58] The Kyrgyz army was better prepared this time. Therefore, they swiftly reacted to the incursions and a fight continued between the terrorists and the troops.

Immediately after the terrorist incursions had taken place, a group of American mountain climbers entered the area. The insurgents took these climbers hostage, but they escaped by overpowering and killing an armed guard.[59] Though this fortuitous escape avoided the possibility of direct US involvement in the hostilities, the capture of the Americans prompted the US State Department to include the IMU in its official list of terrorist organisations.[60]

Nevertheless over a month passed before the military drove the fighters from the Uzbekistani territory. On 12 August, the ministers of Uzbekistan and Kazakhstan started joint military meetings on the effort to fight the insurgents in Batken. Military representatives of Tajikistan also participated in the meeting being an aggrieved party.[61] Two days later, insurgents withdrew under assault from the Kyrgyz armed forces. The commander of the Southern group of Kyrgyz army troops Colonel Ormakoyev said that among the dead guerrillas on the border were Uzbeks, Tajiks, Arabs, Afghan, Taliban and Chechens fighters. All of them belonged to IMU.[62]

It was reported in the middle of August that up to 800 international terrorists were concentrated in Tajik regions bordering Uzbekistan and Kyrgyzstan and were ready to invade the Uzbek and Kyrgyz territories "at any time". Kyrgyz Security Council Secretary Balot Dzhamuzakov confirmed that the supporters of IMU had combat aircraft supplied by the Afghan Taliban movement. Namangani, who controlled 70 per cent of the drug traffic from Afghanistan to Central Asia, was trying to undermine stability in Kyrgyzstan, Tajikistan, Uzbekistan and Kazakhstan, according to Dzhamuzakov.[63]

Security and the law enforcement agencies of the four countries agreed to set up a Rapid Reaction Group to coordinate efforts to trace and destroy the militant groups. Dzhamuzakov further added that the militants invading Kyrgyz territory were financed by international terrorist Osama bin Laden.

Quoting one report from the Kyrgyz intelligence sources, he said that the leaders of IMU, Taliban, and Osama bin Laden had met in Mazar-e-Sharif, Afghanistan where they discussed the operations to undermine stability in Central Asia, which "means the beginning of hostilities against Tajikistan, Uzbekistan, Kyrgyzstan and possibly Kazakhstan".[64]

There was a pressing need to set up an operational group with the participation of the military from Kazakhstan, Tajikistan and Uzbekistan to hunt down and destroy the gangs of international terrorists who numbered about 700 to 800 in Kyrgyzstan and Tajikistan, split into small groups of 40 to 50 people, and ready to join hostilities against these two states".[65] This news, on the very next day, was contested by the Tajik authorities who denied that there was any such concentration of terrorists on the border with Kyrgyzstan.[66]

In August 2000, some Kyrgyz soldiers had managed to lay their hands on the offensive plans of the extremists; they were confronted on the river Khodjin-Achkan and suffered heavy casualties. On interrogation of the prisoners, it was revealed that they were supporters of Juma Namangani. According to the Chairman of the Council of Security, Balat Dzhamuzakov, extremists like Rustan Adullin, a Bishkir who came from the village of Aznalino Kurgan region of Russia. Apparently, he was trained for three months in a camp run by citizens of Pakistan. After the interrogation, it became clear that in the Tajik Pamirs[67] and in the district of Talimgokh, there were many training camps for the extremists.

Similar theories were also forwarded by Uzbek intelligence, which said that the militants underwent training in camps in Afghanistan. Then in small groups they slipped into Tajikistan's mountains to move on to their final destination, 'Fergana Valley', through Kyrgyzstan.[68]

Terrorist activities, however, continued and deliberate attempts were made to infiltrate into the territory of Kyrgyzstan. Two groups of terrorists (about 50-60 strong) made attempts to attack the Jily-Suu post in Liya-Liyak region in 2000. Simultaneously, attacks were unleashed from three different directions in the areas of Saddle-point Jangiabad, Jily-Suu and Abramov glacier. Kyrgyz Air Force attacked areas of probable concentration of these terrorists. The armed forces of Kyrgyzstan and Uzbekistan acting jointly successfully countered various intruding groups in Tashkent area.[69]

By the end of September 2000, the Kyrgyz army managed to flush out terrorists from the glacier on the Kyrgyz-Tajik frontier. Some terrorist units which stayed in Kyrgyz territory were destroyed. All the passes were closed.[70]

Batken incident was one of the major terrorist incidents which had a tremendous bearing on the psychology and strategic considerations of Central Asian region. Askar Aytmatov, who was the Advisor on International Affairs to President of Kyrgyzstan republic, summed it up very accurately. He wrote, "the 1999, Batken incident in south Kyrgyzstan was a serious test for the whole of our peaceful nation. At that time, Kyrgyzstan was not ready for military action or neutralisation of armed bandit groups of the Islamic Movement of Uzbekistan. They captured hostages including Japanese citizens and demanded that the authorities provide them a hefty amount and a corridor for free access to neighbouring Uzbekistan. Still, at the cost of human lives, we succeeded in displacing the terrorist groups from our territory and released all the hostages they captured. In the autumn of 2000, these events occurred again but with the military technical support of the friendly countries, the Kyrgyz army resisted the efforts of the international terrorists to intervene on our territory again".

"The Batken events of 1999-2000 have again drawn the attention of the world to the strengthening of the 'Islamic factor' in Central Asia. Unfortunately, there is every reason to assume that in the near future, similar events will be repeated. The current military political situation in the south of our country is the result of the intersection of a number of urgent problems, which cover all of Central Asia".[71]

A number of people were arrested in East Kazakhstan oblast on 19 November 1999, who were reported to be ethnic Russians and veterans of the Afghan and Chechen wars. They had allegedly been planning an armed rebellion in the town of Pavdodar in the north Kazakhstan oblast and Oskune and Leningorsk in east, with the aim of setting up an 'Independent Republic of Russian Altai'. It was further alleged that the rebels had secured the support of a number of prominent local residents.[72]

Long after the Tajik civil war, on 16 February 2000, a powerful bomb exploded in Dushanbe which killed the Deputy Security Minister, Shamsullo Dzabirov, who was also a candidate for the legislative elections. The Mayor of Dushanbe, Muhammad Sayed Ubaydulloyav, was travelling in the same car as Dzabirov but escaped unhurt. President Rakhmanov described the attack as an act of terrorism aimed at destabilising the socio-political situation before the parliamentary elections.[73] In the same month, an attack was made on the car of the first Deputy Prime Minister, and UTO member Ali Akbar Turadzhonzada, as it travelled in a motorcade from Dushanbe to his hometown of Kofarnikhon. No one was injured.[74] In Dushanbe, on 7 February, three powerful explosions occurred in the central places. Asia Plus News Agency reported that the first explosion occurred outside a house at 70, Rudoki Avenue, the second between the Avesto Hostel, where the Russian embassy is situated and the Koh-I-Vahdat (Place of

Unity) complex. The explosive was planted in a square. The third explosion occurred between the buildings of Tajikistan's Tax Committee and Pamir Cinema. No one was hurt or killed.[75]

Though Kazakhstan has been the less terrorist prone republic of Central Asia, several incidences there do not rule out the intention of the terrorists to spread their tentacles to Kazakhstan.

A senior official of the south Kazakhstan told the media on 26 October 2000 that in the run-up to the celebrations of the 1500th anniversary of Turkestan (in south Kazakhstan region), Kazakh special services in conjunction with the law enforcement agencies rendered harmless several armed extremists.[76] He further added that after receiving a tip-off, officers from the National Security Committee Department (NSCD) for south Kazakhstan region found a Kalashnikov rifle and two full magazines in a private house in Turkestan on 13 October. Along with the assault rifle, the security personnel seized literature and leaflets calling for a *jihad*, in Kazak, Arabic and Uzbek languages.[77]

The Interfax-Kazakhstan News Agency also reported that several days before the celebrations, leaflets calling for a *jihad* against the 'infidels', the overthrow of the existing state order and the establishment in Central Asian countries of a single Islamic state were found in the Central market, at the railway station and in Turkestan's main mosque.[78] Tulebay Kulbayev, an official, also told that another two local residents were detained in Turkestan, from whom a handmade explosive device, detonator and drugs were seized. According to his information, one of the detained men was a member of Hizb-ut-Tahrir.

Tajik security forces, on 4th October, carried out a special operation to detain a group of terrorists in Karamov Street in Dushanbe. The terrorists put up armed resistance and fired at the security officers. The terrorists intended to carry out a number of terrorist acts on festive days.[79] One terrorist was killed, second was wounded and a third was arrested.[80]

At a conference in Bishkek in March 2001, the Chairman of the Kyrgyz National Security Service, Bolat Dzhamuzakov, told the journalists that about 3000 militants were undergoing training at bases in Afghanistan and that they might try to break into the border at any moment.[81]

As late as on 8 September 2001, terrorist activities went on in its different forms. On that day, the Tajik Minister of Culture, Abdurahim Rahimov, was shot dead outside his residence in Dushanbe by a lone gunman who then escaped.[82] The very next day, a young man identified as Ghaffar Abdughafforov died when a country made bomb exploded as he was carrying it to the Frunze Central Stadium in Dushanbe. The stadium was hosting festivities to mark the 10th anniversary of the country's independence and was attended by the President and other senior officials.[83]

After 11 September 2001, a remarkable turn around took place in the security scenario all over the world with the focus shifting over to Afghanistan, Central Asian countries and Pakistan. The attack on the World Trade Centre and Pentagon headquarters in US by the Al-Qaeda and Taliban forces created a tremendous after-effect, resulting in America supported by UK and other countries in the world taking up cudgels against terrorism, particularly the Taliban and their 'guest' fundamentalist terrorist Osama bin Laden, the chief and founder of Al-Qaeda. In the American effort in stamping out terrorism, the Central Asian republics wholeheartedly extended their support. There was greater action by these republics against their own suspected terrorists and the terrorist organisations after 11 September episode. The American intervention in Afghanistan resulted in the dissipation and collapse of Taliban and at the same time brought the end of the intervention by the other foreign actors in the region. It had its direct impact on Central Asian republics, as a result of which, incidences of terrorism came down heavily in these republics and the republics also found excuses to heavily crackdown on their religious, separatist fundamentalist groups.

Though the incidences of terrorism have lessened, there is still a growing fear of these latent fundamentalist groups reappearing anytime. In fact, the terrorist elements and perpetrators of violence at present have gone underground waiting for the suitable moment to bounce back.

Even though militancy and terrorism in Central Asia has survived on many fundamentals, the primary requirement to sustain such activities is a huge amount of money. In Central Asia, this requirement has been fulfilled basically from the unholy nexus between terrorism and narcotics.

Drug Trade

While the drug trade promotes political, social and economic instability, it is also true that, nation-states, for a variety of reasons, become prone to a flourishing drug business by allowing it to feed on the weakness prevalent within the state system. There are many such factors which have allowed the five newly independent states of Central Asia to become major drug production and trafficking centres, so much so that the area is being referred to as "a new Columbia".[84]

The traditional poppy growing areas in Central Asia were Kyrgyzstan, Afghanistan and Pakistan. Cannabis also grows in Kazakhstan and Kyrgyzstan. Until the early 1970s, Kyrgyzstan produced some 16 per cent of the world's legal opium. When the Soviet Union banned the opium production in 1974, legal cultivation ended in Kyrgyzstan republic.[85] Neither the mountainous terrain of Tajikistan nor Uzbekistan's arid climate provides a hospitable environment for opium or cannabis cultivation nor neither country has ever been a major producer.

Afghanistan has always been an opposite story in this regard. In the 1980s, the Mujahideen fighting against the Soviet occupation were largely financed by drug cultivation and trafficking. In 1998, about 1400 tonnes of opium was produced, accounting for 25 per cent of the world's opium output, legal and illegal.[86] Between 1992 and 1995, 2200-2400 metric tonnes, in 1996, 2250 tonnes, in 1999, 4,600 tonnes of opium were produced by Afghanistan.[87]

Though theoretically anti-Islamic, poppy cultivation continued under Taliban regime due to its financial importance in the Taliban movement. They derived approximately 20 million US dollar or more each year as taxes on poppy crops.[88]

The region's traditional drug routes to lucrative western markets have always been through Iran and Pakistan. In the post-Soviet period, during 1992-97, the routes changed and carried through Kharog-Osh and the Panj and Muscovskii routes in the Central Asian republics.[89] The UNDCP, in its report, estimates that 80 per cent of Europe's heroin flows through Central Asian republics.[90]

In 1991, Tajik Interior Ministry apprehended 10.9 kg of drugs, but in 1995, it went up to 1750 kg. In 1998-99, the total seizure was 1949 kg.[91] In 2000, Tajikistan seized 1883 kg heroin and 4773 kg opium. By 1 September 2001, 3033.5 kg heroin had already been seized. The amount of confiscated narcotics has risen from 113 kg to 1.5 tonnes over the past five years since 1996. In 2001, there was a big surprise as regards the nature of the seized products. While the amount of heroin seized went up sharply, the opium seizure came down drastically.[92] The drop in confiscated opium coupled with the rise of confiscated heroin in Tajikistan indicates that opium is being replaced by heroin as the major drug export from Afghanistan and in turn, points to an increase in heroin processing laboratories in that country.[93]

In Kyrgyzstan also, a large amount of drugs is produced. At the same time, it also acts as a transit for drugs traffic. Here, the militant groups also support narcotics trade. Chu Valley and Issyuk Kul are the two main drug processing centres. Around 40,000 hectares of land are under cultivation of Cannabis in Kyrgyzstan.[94] Osh is emerging as an important transit point. The thriving drug trade in Osh is evident from the flourishing living style of the people.[95] In 1991, only 5 kg of narcotics were seized, but in 1995, it rose to 627 kg. It was revealed by the Bureau of International Trade and Security that in 1997, around 700 tonnes of opium came from Afghanistan to Kyrgyzstan. In 1998, it went up to 3000 tonnes.[96]

In Uzbekistan, the drug menace is as grave as any other Central Asian republic. Due to its strategic location and communication networks with other republics, Uzbekistan is an attractive transit for drugs traffic. Although a small amount of narcotics is produced in Samarkand region, it acts as a major route for transport of drugs. Narcotics transport takes place through a number of routes in Uzbekistan. One is from Afghanistan to Uzbekistan via the Gorno-Badakhasan region of Tajikistan, through Kyrgyzstan's Osh, into Uzbekistan's Andijan region. Another route goes directly from Afghanistan through the Uzbek city of Termez. In addition to the above, the drug producing region of Tajikistan lies just across the Uzbekistan border. All these led to an increase in drug trafficking in Uzbekistan. It has been reported in ITAR-TASS, the Russian News Agency that around 29 tonnes of drugs have been seized and destroyed since 1991.[97]

Kazakhstan occupies a prominent position in narcotics production and transport. In the southern part of Kazakhstan, huge areas of land are under narcotics cultivation. In 1997, around 500 metric tonnes of marijuana were cultivated in the Chu Valley in southern Kazakhstan.[98] Drug cartels use Kazakhstan as a transit for traffic, which originates in Pakistan, China and Afghanistan. According to the Russian Ministry of Internal Affairs, 93 per cent of the marijuana in Russian drug market comes from Kazakhstan and 85 per cent of Russia's hashish and 73 per cent of its opium are either grown in Kazakhstan or pass through it.[99] According to the Interior Ministry, 17,000 drug users were brought to book in 1995. In 1996, their number was 1678.[100] In the first five months of 1997, security forces seized around 17 tonnes of drugs. This indicated a significant rise in drug smuggling to 12 tonnes seized in 1996.[101]

Kazakhstan's Drugs Control Authority noted that about 1, 38,000 hectares of land in the Chu Valley were under drugs cultivation. In 1998, there were 18,579 drug related offences. Similarly, in 1998, the drugs sale increased by around 90 per cent.[102] In 1999, the Interior Ministry (Inter-Regional Department) seized over 1000 kg marijuana and about 40 kg heroin. Over 260 kg drugs were seized from January to May 2000.

Turkmenistan is also plagued by drug trafficking. The smugglers use Turkmenistan route to transport narcotics from Afghanistan to Europe. Not only is the narcotic trafficking on rise, many areas of Turkmenistan are widely used for drug productions. The Ahal Velayat region, where the capital Ashgabat is situated and the custom posts of Lebap are areas where large amount of drugs are cultivated.

However, in recent years in the Karakum desert, poppy cultivation is also going on. In October 1997, the government of Turkmenistan seized around 78.5 kg narcotics.[103] An estimate shows that some 80 tonnes of heroin enter Turkmenistan each year with about 30 per cent staying in the country.[104] In 2000, the National Security Committee of Turkmenistan seized slightly less than 2900 kg of opium and 220 kg of heroin down from the previous year's total of 4,600 kg respectively. The reduction has largely been attributed to drought and bad harvesting.[105]

The amount seized constitutes, of course, only a small fraction of what is believed to transit Turkmenistan, and the country's neighbours, that are undertaking more serious efforts to curb the drug flow. They are critical of Asghabat's uncooperative attitude. Their officials speculate that the transit traffic is facilitated by Turkmenistan's isolationistic foreign policy as well as its links to both the Taliban and Northern Alliance.[106]

Though the drugs trade in Central Asia has emerged largely because of the financial advantages it has for the various guerrilla forces, there are also several other reasons for its growth, prominent among them is the economic reason. The countries have been forced into the drug trade due to their failure to find legitimate means of making a living in their shattered economies. Many peasants cultivate narcotics as few other crops can provide the economic gains that come with narcotics cultivation. Whether the involvement of the low-salaried government law enforcement officers, or the 201st Division of Russian military in illicit drug trade, or the involvement of women in this business, they are all linked to poverty and unemployment, further aggravated by poor agriculture, withdrawal of subsidies, poor governance and porous borders among the states. The importance of the drugs trade lies in the fact that the terrorist organisations and the radical fundamentalist organisations have been able to sustain their activities out of the profits earned from drug trade. The Kyrgyz officials have charged that the Islamic Movement of Uzbekistan is little more than a group of drug runners.[107] Even Taliban, in spite of its strong belief in staunch Islamic way of belief and faith, had to sustain its activities on the basis of the funding received from drug taxes and drug trading. Though towards 2000 AD they were under severe international pressure to curb the drug related activities, they, by then, were flushed with enough money to sustain their campaign.[108] Even during the Tajik civil war, warring factions on both sides were believed to have engaged in the drug trade to support their operations.[109]

Small Arms Proliferations

Besides the illegal narcotics industry, the proliferation of small arms and light weapons have contributed immensely to the growth of terrorism and militancy in the region. The proliferation of arms provides two kinds of support to militancy. One, in their operations, the militants who basically are guerrilla fighters, resort to light weapons and small arms to counter the security forces. Further more, they also use them to create impact on the civilian masses. Secondly, the trade in arms and weapons provide them with the much needed funds they require to sustain their activities. It is much like drugs which is treated as high value commodity with readymade buyers. Drugs and small arms proliferations are both intricately interlinked subjects. Both are complimentary and supplementary to each other.

There is no precise and formal definition of small arms and light weapons. However, according to Peter Chalk, an expert on trans-national terrorism at the Rand Corporation in Washington, they refer to direct fire weapons that can be carried by an individual on a small vehicle and that have a secondary capability to defeat light armour and helicopter.[110] The NATO definition fixes the size power at 50 mm calibre. They include not only rifles and guns, but also shoulder fired anti-tank and anti-aircraft weapons. Today, it is these weapons that form the bulk of the shipment that transit into conflict areas.

Drug trafficking is invariably linked to the spread of small arms in the producing or transit countries. In many areas of the world, non-state actors like insurgent groups, separatist forces, local warlords, and drug cartels have emerged as major users of arms. The availability and use of sophisticated weapons has contributed to the erosion of state authority. There is a growing worldwide incidence of armed violence within and between groups, tribes and communities. The countries of Central Asia are no exception to this. With their porous frontiers, the Central Asian republics are bound to be smuggling routes for large arms shipments as drugs and guns are transported using the same clandestine routes.[111]

Though the history of small arms proliferation in Central Asia is long, the present phenomenon is a continuation of the Soviet intervention in Afghanistan. In order to counter the Soviet forces, the US supplied the Mujahideen with weapons worth 250 million dollars in 1985, 630 million dollars in 1987 with matching contributions from Saudi Arabia.[112] The US, Britain and China supplied weapons ranging from shoulder-launched surface-to-air missiles (SAMs) to rifles. Prior to 1965, the USA supplied Soviet made SA-7 SAMs. After 1985, it supplied FIM-92, Stinger SAMs and large quantities of rifles and Britain supplied Blown Pipe SAMs; China supplied the Mujahideen a range of small arms.[113]

Not only USA, but also China and Saudi Arabia supplied weapons to the Mujahideen. Pakistan also reportedly supplied 40,000 rockets and 700 trucks of ammunitions to its favourite warlord Hekmatyar after August 1990.[114]

After Soviet withdrawal, followed by Nazibullah's deposition and the capture of Afghanistan by Taliban, the weapons fell into the hands of the Afghan militia. More arms procured by the Taliban using of drug money finally found their way into the Central Asian republics through several Islamic fundamentalist organisations like IRP, IMU, HT and others. Their link with the Afghan militia and the aid from Afghanistan in terms of arms, ammunitions and other logistical aspects have already been discussed in this chapter. But a country wise analysis of the degree of the arms proliferation would provide a deeper understanding of its role in promoting militancy in the region.

Tajikistan is worst affected by the arms proliferation in the region. The internal conflict which started in Tajikistan in 1992, led to a large scale use of weapons, fuelled by supplies from Afghanistan. It has been reported that, around 10,000 weapons distributed among government forces came from Moscow and Uzbekistan. On the other hand, Afghanistan was the main weapon source for the Tajik opposition forces.[115]

Even the Russian forces took advantage of the volatile situation by selling their weapons to various opposition warring factions for huge sums of money.[116] Well informed sources in Tashkent commenting on the easy availability of weapons in Tajikistan stated that, "a Kalashnikov sells for just 100 dollars in Dushanbe".[117] In recent years, most of the small arms came from Afghanistan. The Tajik branch of Islamic Renaissance Party maintained very close relationship with the Afghan Mujahideen leaders who trained Islamic militants in their camps. Ahmed Shah Masood was known to have trained some 70,000 Tajik rebels in Kunduz province of Afghanistan. According to KGB officials, Hekmatyar armed 400 IRP militants.[118] This testifies the role of Afghanistan in spreading Islamic fundamentalism and proliferating small arms.

The most important problem for Tajikistan is how to disarm the armed militant groups after the signing of peace accord between the government and the UTO. Both the parties to the conflict believe that the country faces danger from proliferation of small arms and light weapons and it should be controlled. Despite the signing of the General Agreement on Peace and National Reconciliation in Moscow in June 1997 between the government of Tajikistan and UTO, the disarmament process has not succeeded. For example, armed teenaged boys who were brought up during the years of fighting have known nothing but conflict since they were young.[119] Also weapons seem to be so widely spread that many working on the farms in the countryside, are engaged in 'part time' fighting. This makes it impossible to register them and their arms.[120]

According to United Nations Mission for Tajikistan (UNMOT), most of the UTO fighters were not gathered in the designated assembly areas, and even dispersed more than one year, after the peace agreement was signed. The 5,979 fighters handed over only 1,911 weapons, most of them obsolete. The ratio of fighters to weapon was 3:1.[121]

The above figures show that large numbers of weapons are still in the possession of various groups and it may pose a thumping challenge to the security of Tajikistan. The radical wing of Islamic Renaissance Party, heavily armed with AK-47 assault rifles, landmines, explosives and rockets, amassed funds mainly through drug trafficking.[122]

As far back as July 1992, border guards shot down two infiltrators to Tajikistan from whom three assault rifles, a sub-machine gun and 10 hand grenades were recovered. In 1994, "Operation Mak" in northern Tajikistan resulted in the seizure of 200 tonnes of opium and cannabis and in the arrest of dozens of well armed gangs.[123] Officials from Tajikistan continued to note that Afghan opium had been traded for arms and supplies on the Tajik-Afghan border.[124] This is further substantiated with the fact that in 1995, more than 10,000 automatic rifles, rifles, machine guns, grenade launchers, mines, hand grenades and even one anti-aircraft gun with an armoured personnel carrier were seized.[125] One official even said that the Tajik civil war was instigated by the Tajik drug lords who find it easier to fish in troubled waters.[126]

Kazakhstan is also facing a threat from illicit circulation of small arms. In March 1995, a large scale preventive operation named "Law and Order" involving about 45,000 people, many of whom were brought in to assist law enforcement officials, resulted in seizure of a number of weapons and 70 kg narcotics.[127] There is a growing number of firearms in circulation in Kazakhstan and the increasing use of these weapons in criminal activities. In 1995, there were 167 organised criminal groups. The groups comprised 2500 people and possessed over 500 firearms.[128] Apart from organised mafia groups that are involved in trafficking of arms and drugs, the biggest danger that the Kazakh society is facing today is the emergence of radical Islamic fundamentalist groups which possess sophisticated arms and ammunitions.

Uzbekistan, besides Tajikistan is the most terrorism prone republic in the region. In fact, it is presently the principal target of militants operating over there. The presence of many Islamic militant groups like Islamic Movement of Uzbekistan, Hizb-ut-Tahrir, Islamic Renaissance Party, Adolat, Islam Loshkars etc. and their objective of establishing an Islamic state in Uzbekistan through armed struggle has led to increased use of small arms, partly aided by Afghanistan and neighbouring Islamic countries. On 21 November, Interfax News Agency reported that four grenade-like detonators, two TT handguns with cartridges, a silencer and a certain amount of marijuana were recovered from a passenger travelling in Valgograd - Tashkent train.[129] An Uzbek Interior Ministry official said in this context, that the person was taking the arms to the Fergana Valley. In another instance, Osama bin Laden, the Saudi Arabian terrorist had allocated 20 million dollars to destabilise the situation in Fergana region of Uzbekistan.[130] It is understood that this money was transferred in terms of arms and weapons which were to be used for the said purpose. Moreover, the close link between Taliban and the Islamic fundamentalist organisations of Uzbekistan has been quite conducive to the proliferations of arms and weapons aided by drug trafficking.

The problem of small arms is also acute in Turkmenistan. In January-March 1996, national security officers and border guards ran in on members of these armed groups. During these operations, 12 automatic guns were confiscated besides narcotics.[131] Although Turkmenistan is relatively free from the problem of Islamic fundamentalism, its geographical location facilitates an easy transportation of arms and narcotics from Afghanistan to other CIS countries.

Kyrgyzstan is also no different case. According to the Kyrgyz Television report on 19 April 1997, alongside narcotics, the arms trade is also gathering momentum. The report said that the anti-narcotics forces seized two ground-to-air missiles, two anti-tank bombs, an anti-aircraft device, seven hand-grenades, an AK-47 gun with 100 cartridges and a 20-loader "Pechkin".[132] In recent years, some Wahhabi fundamentalist groups have also become active in Kyrgyzstan. In 1998, they exploded two bombs in Osh. It has also been noted that the drug smugglers who are quite active in Kyrgyzstan have equipped themselves with sophisticated weapons, which match with that of security forces. They are able to handle hi-tech small weapons.

In Batken, where a major case of intrusion took place in 1999, the Kyrgyz border guards seized more than 3 tonnes of arms hidden near the village Khadji-Achkhan. The cache included four grenade launchers, several missile launchers, and a large number of anti-personal and anti-tank mines.[133]

So whether in large or small quantities, small arms and weapons have proliferated in all the republics of the Central Asian region. Coupled with the trafficking of narcotic drugs, the arms proliferation has created a dangerous situation in the region and has also encouraged the terrorist and militant activities. Loaded with religious fanaticism, funded profusely by narcotics trade and arms trade, flushed with all kinds of latest arms, operating in an area with huge numbers of followers due to grinding poverty and unemployment, divided hatefully into ethnic and tribal communities and poorly challenged by the weak political authorities, the militants have created a scenario in this region, that is not only critical but also volatile in nature.

Role of External Factors

While all the above factors have largely contributed to the emergence, growth and perpetuation of militancy and terrorism in the region, another factor which has played a crucial role is the involvement of the neighbouring states, in the affairs of the region.

Afghanistan has been the single most important external factor in the the instability in Central Asia. Afghanistan has for long been linked to Central Asia, historically and culturally. Over the centuries, the two regions have been joined by various empires. The ethnic, social, cultural and political ties between Afghanistan and Central Asia are thus deeply rooted, and the give and take between the two regions today can not be seen as an incident in the history of the region but rather as a continuation of the historical process that was briefly interrupted by the seventy four years of the Soviet Union.[134]

In the 1980s, the American CIA funded arms to the Afghan Mujahideen via Pakistan's Interservices Intelligence (ISI), the ISI gave preference to the Islamic radical parties in Afghanistan, which could more easily be turned into an engine of anti-Soviet *jihad*, and pushed aside moderate Afghan nationalist and Islamic parties. The Taliban were the heirs of that war and that favouritism.[135]

The Taliban played host to most of the extremist Islamic groups in the Muslim world. In Afghanistan, these groups fought for Taliban, and in the process they received military training, battle experience, weapons, funding, access to the drug trade, and contacts with the whole world of Islamic radicalism.

Taliban's international Islamic agenda went into high gear after aligning with Osama bin Laden and other non-Afghan Islamic groups following Taliban's capture of Kabul in 1996.[136] Tens of thousands of Pakistani militants and thousands of Central Asians, Arabs, Africans, and the East-Asians joined the Taliban since then. This consolidated the global perspective of Islamic radicalism which the Taliban propounded. It further pushed its goals beyond Afghanistan-into Central Asia.[137] So while the Taliban needed these foreign fighters, especially the Central Asians to expand its ideology, the Central Asian fighters needed Taliban for a suitable sanctuary to organise themselves.[138]

Before the emergence of Taliban, many other Afghani rulers were involved in Central Asian states due to their clan affiliations, narcotic business and consolidation of their bases in Central Asia. Rashid Dostum-an Uzbek, Ahmad Shah Masood-a Tajik and two other warlords operated from their bases in Central Asia. In such situation, the Taliban tried to push through its agenda of Islamism on the basis of its interpretation of Islam by promoting the radical groups. The organizations like IRP, IMU, HT, and Adolat had their plans drafted in Kabul.

Summarily, we can say that more than the Central Asians themselves, Afghanistan has been able to radicalise the Islamic followers there.These radical Islamists have taken recourse to violence and terrorist methods toeing the line of the Taliban to achieve their objectives.

Another country which has been deeply involved with the region's radical groups providing them all kinds of support is Pakistan. Pakistan not only organised Taliban but also made it survive amongst Afghanistan's warring factions. Indeed, fear of Pakistan's influence in the region had been a critical factor in the mobilisation of the Central Asian states (with the exception of Turkmenistan) against the Taliban.[139] Central Asian leaders also believe that the ISI had been supporting the IMU and other radical Islamic groups in their countries. In the 1980s, the military regime of Zia-ul-Haq encouraged the Afghan Mujahideen attack Central Asia and the CIA supplied arms to the Mujahideen for this purpose through the ISI.

Although successive Pakistani governments have repeatedly promised the Central Asian leaders that they would curb the support given by the ISI to Pakistan's Islamic parties, the Taliban and other militant groups in Central Asia and forbid Central Asian militants to study in Pakistani madrassahs, Islamabad has failed to implement these measures out of self-interest and the fear of an Islamic backlash within Pakistan.[140]

After the 1991 collapse of the Soviet Union, Zia-ul-Haq's reference to the need for strategic depth in Central Asia as well as Afghanistan assumed a greater significance. In 1991, again the elected government of Prime Minister Nawaz Sharif sought a new relationship with Central Asia based on economic interests which got undermined by the arrival of Pakistani Islamic parties in Central Asia, who viewed the region as virgin territory, ripe for recruitment to their particular brand of Islam. Qazi Hussain Ahmad, the chief of the Jamiat-i-Islami party, urged Sharif to provide Central Asia Islamic guidance rather than economic aid.[141] At the same time, several Pakistani and Arab groups sympathetic to Wahhabism were being funded by Saudi Arabia to make inroads into Central Asia. The Pakistani extremist groups like Lashkar-i-Jhangvi and Sipah-i-Sahaba initially funded by Saudi

Arabia have had militants fighting for the IMU. In recent years, Central Asian and Uighur militants poured into Pakistan to study in the huge network of Deobandi madrassahs.[142] The IMU, the HT, the Chechen rebels have sent many of their young men to study in Pakistan, while Pakistani Islamic parties continue to present their Central Asian students as proof of their influence in the region. More than the battlefields in Afghanistan, this madrassah education and the culture of *jihad* it inspires have been turning out ideologically committed Islamic radicals for fighting in Central Asia.[143]

By 1994, when the Taliban emerged, Pakistan instead of being constructively engaged with Central Asia opted to support Taliban which was looked at suspiciously by Central Asian powers. Further, it is widely believed that ISI's discreet support of IMU, which included giving refuge to Yuldeshev in 1990s and allowing Namangani's frequent clandestine visits to Pakistan, had fairly remained consistent.[144] Yuldeshev even opened an office in Peshawar from where he operated for quite a long time. The ISI still sees IMU as a force that may not be strong enough to seize power in Uzbekistan but that can nonetheless, be a catalyst in the shake up of Central Asia's leadership.

Despite Pakistan's persistent denials that it supports the IMU, until 11 September 2001, the military regime appeared set on a course where it followed a state policy of friendly relations with the Central Asian governments but at the same time backed dissident groups such as the IMU in order to win more leverage over these regimes. Islamabad believes that the present generation of Central Asian leaders must be replaced by more Islamic oriented leaders who would look to Pakistan, rather than India and Russia, for support.[145]

The non-state actors in Pakistan viz.the extremist Islamic parties, with their madrassah culture and *jihadi* strategy, Arab terrorist groups such as Al-Qaeda, the smuggling mafia and drug traffickers have close links with Taliban and the IMU independent of ISI and its policies. As a result there has been an explosion of self-interest groups in Pakistan, both Islamic and non-Islamic, who have benefited from the Afghan civil war and Islamic insurgency in Central Asia. These groups see no need for peace, for the assertion of the state authority not just in Pakistan but across the entire region would undermine their business interests and Islamic agendas to flourish.

Pakistan, is not only geo-politically interested in the Central Asian region but the historical, cultural, religious links between the two are strong enough factors for Pakistan to get involved there. Besides the political and economic objectives, the need to satisfy its ambition of a security ring to counter the massiveness of its two arch rivals India and Iran made Pakistan see a potential in Central Asia for expanding its technological, strategic and economic influence. The only way it could transform this former Soviet republics those never patronised Pakistan for the later being a theocratic state and a protégé of US, was to encourage the dissident Islamic religious fundamentalist powers in the name of establishing an Islamic *umma* and a secured Islamic society. Operating through the Taliban, Pakistan gave a fillip to the militant and terrorist activities of the region till it got caught in a riddle after 11 September 2001.

The other country which has equally important stakes in Central Asia is Iran. Despite its Islamic rhetoric, Iran has played the most cautious and prudent role in Central Asia. Iran moved swiftly into the region as the Soviet Union hovered on the verge of break up. Iran intervened briefly in the Tajik civil war, siding with the IRP, but quickly realised that it had to stay out of the conflict if it wanted to keep Russia as an ally. Of course, there is a faction within the Iranian leadership that seeks to export its vision of the Islamic revolution and gain new adherents in Central Asia.[146] But the then Iranian President Rafsanjani restrained the hotheads in the radical camp. Though Iran has maintained a low profile as far as interfering in the religious affairs of Central Asian regimes are concerned, it earlier made several such gestures which, though small in magnitude, expressed a desire to participate in the proselytisation race. It allocated 120 million US dollar and sent several hundred mullahs to proselytise in Central Asian region in 1991.[147] Iran has also built new mosques and Islamic educational institutions in Tajikistan, while some of the Tajik intelligentsia have advocated Iran as a "model".[148] In the mid-1990s Iranian intelligence agents met with Yuldeshev with the hope that they could play on IMU's Uzbek ethnic origins to enlist it in Iran's anti-Taliban and anti-Pakistan agenda-perhaps even make IMU a future surrogate for Iran in Central Asia. Although some Uzbekistan officials believe that IMU received financial aid from the Iranian intelligence service, the organisation subsequently linked itself with the Taliban, Sunni extremism and anti-Shiaism.[149]

Iran has not been very successful in propagating its own interpretation of Islam in Central Asian countries. On the other hand, it has harped more on economic relationship and cultural tie-ups. The primary obstacle to Iran's intention of cultural and military influence in the Central Asian region is that while the Central Asians are predominantly Sunnis, Iran is a Shia dominated country. The present day radical Sunnis even refuse to acknowledge Shiaism as a legitimate branch of Islam; they denounce the Shias as *kafirs*, non-believers.[150]

Turkey is another country, interested in the region. Initally, it intervened in Central Asian radical upsurge in a very limited manner. For a brief period of time, the Central Asian leaders seemed to accept Turkey as a model. Thousands of Central Asians arrived in Turkey on Turkish scholarships and training programmes. Turkish Muslim leaders started building state sponsored madrassahs and schools in Central Asia that taught Turkish Islam.[151]

However, Turkey has always played both sides in Central Asia. Turkish intelligence has been in constant touch with the Central Asian opposition movement, giving refuge to leaders who have been driven out of either from Turkmenistan or Uzbekistan. In 1999, the Uzbek government shut down a chain of Turkish schools run by the Sufi cleric Fetullah Gulen, accusing him of supporting Islamic radical groups and the banned opposition party Erk. IMU leaders had, in fact, travelled to Turkey in mid-1990s in search of funding and they had received some. Turkey, simultaneously, was also funding the Afghan Uzbek leader Rashid Dostum in his fight against the Taliban. The IMU appealed in a spirit of pan-Turkism rather than Islamic fundamentalism. Turkey initially supported the IMU both to cover its options and to keep tabs on the IMU activities, but Turkish support stopped after IMU linked itself to the Taliban and Laden.[152] The attitude of Turkey towards Central Asian states have undergone a radical change with the economic and political crisis in Turkey itself, and the unwillingness of the Central Asian leaders to emulate Turkey and the mutual rivalry between the five nations.

One more country which has been intensely in the race to spread its influence in Central Asian countries is Saudi Arabia. Being a seat of Islamic power and wealth as well as the centrestage of the whole Islamic world for having the 'purest' form of Islam, obviously wanted to meddle in the affairs of Central Asian Islamic revivalism after the independence. And on the other hand Central Asia being a largely Muslim dominated country, that too from Sunni school of thought, welcomed the Saudi intervention with tremendous alacrity.

Saudi Arabia neglected the state-to-state relations with Central Asia, instead allowed Saudi Islamic charities and groups that promote Wahhabism to pursue a policy of funding Islamic groups, mosques and madrassahs, and sponsoring people coming to Mecca for the annual *haj* (pilgrimage). Saudi Islamic charities have provided Central Asia with missionaries, scholarships and Islamic literature, including millions of copies of the Koran translated into native languages. But the Saudi generosity has come with an intention-to turn Central Asia in to a region following radical Wahhabism.[153]

Initially, the Saudi mission in Central Asia was to bring back the people of the region to Islam (preferably Wahhabism), rather than cultivating trade, economic or political ties. Such policies have proven short-sighted and dangerous even for Saudi Arabia. The groups the Saudis funded have now linked themselves to Laden, the enemy of the Saudi royal family, whilst the Central Asian governments have become critical of Saudi Arabia, regarding the Saudis as a threat to future stability rather than an ally.[154]

Saudi Arabia has had consistently backed the most extremist Islamic groups in the region, since the 1980s with the funding of Hekmatyar's Hizb-i-Islami party in Afghanistan.[155] They also backed Taliban until 1996, when they fell out over the issue of Osama bin Laden. The Saudis provided funds to the IRP during the civil war in Tajikistan to keep them away from joining with Iran, and the Saudi regime made no attempt to stop the lavish funding of the IMU from the Saudi-Uzbek diaspora in Mecca and Medina. Many of the large wealthy Islamic charities in the forefront of the funds transfers were controlled by the Wahhabi Ulema, and the royal family was reluctant to interfere because of its sensitivity to criticism from that Ulema.[156]

Saudi Arabia as early as 1980s encouraged its own dissidents to go and fight in distant places like Afghanistan and thereby, stay away from stirring up trouble at home. However, the thousands of Saudis fighting for Taliban and IMU pose a grave threat to Saudi national security itself.[157] The Saudis have never developed a clear foreign policy towards Central Asia which is still formulated largely on the basis of the dictations of the Ulemas. Thus, even as the US shapes up Central Asian armies, its most important ally in the Muslim world, Saudi Arabia, continues to allow funds from the Saudi citizens to reach the IMU.

Though the situation has undergone a lot of change after 11 September 2001, Saudi interests in Central Asia is still dictated by religion, rather than any other reason. Wahhabism, the strictest form of fundamentalist Islam, is rooted in Saudi Arabia. As the US is cracking down on the terrorist organisations world wide and trying to dry up their sources of funding it seems that the Saudi government also may have to follow the instruction of US and cut off the funds supply to the IMU, thereby weakening the latter's organisational strength.

The other Arabian states have also tried to boost up radical Islamic groups, allowing private funding to reach them and giving them facilities in their ports and cities. The Taliban, Osama bin Laden and IMU used these cities as hubs for drug trafficking, smuggling of consumer goods, arms trading, and money-laundering centres of Islamic extremist groups from all over the world.[158] Dubai, rather than Peshawar or Karachi was the centre for fund raising and arms purchase by the Taliban and the IMU.[159]

The problem of militancy and terrorism have posed the biggest security challenge to these nascent states, and there are several factors responsible for this situation viz. economic stagnation, religious upheaval, intervention by neighbouring powers to satisfy their objectives, the situation in Afghanistan, the emergence of the Taliban and massive drug trafficking coupled with equally extensive small arms proliferation in the region. The worst affected republics in terms of terrorism are Uzbekistan, Tajikistan, and Kyrgyzstan. The problem of militancy and terrorism in Central Asia has not just affected the security of constituent states of this region, but has also spread its poisonous tentacles to neighbouring Russia, China and also India. The incidences of terrorism in these Central Asian republics may seem to be like their internal problem but they can not be isolated, for, an analysis of these events shows that most of these have been aided, abetted, prompted, financed and executed from outside. Also, the geographical contiguity of the region and porous borders make possible easy movement for the perpetrators of these acts leaving their impact on the whole region. Therefore, one incidence of terrorism can not be seen as an isolated act from the other in another republic of Central Asia. Hence, terrorism in Central Asia can be truely termed as cross-border in nature.

References

1. Dennis A. Pluchinsky, "Terrorism in the Former Soviet Union, a Primer, a Puzzle, a Prognosis", *Studies in Conflict and Terrorism*, No. 21, September 1998, p. 119.
2. *Ibid.*
3. The two most extensive terrorist campaigns carried out against Soviet targets were carried out by Jewish extremist groups in the United States of America such as the Jewish Defence League in the 1970s and 1980s and a group in France that called itself the 'Bakunin-Gdnsk- El- Salvador' and was active in the 1980s.
4. Stephen Handelman, *Comrade Criminal: Russia's New Mafia*, New Heaven, Yale University Press, 1995, p. 95.
5. *Great Soviet Encyclopedia*, New York, Macmillan, Vol. 3, p. 57.
6. Devendra Kaushik, *Central Asia in Modern Times*, Moscow, Progress Publishers, 1970, p. 168.
7. *Ibid.*
8. *Great Soviet Encyclopaedia*, *op.cit.*
9. *Ibid.*
10. *Ibid.*
11. P.T. Etherton, *In the Heart of Asia*, London, Westerly Publishers, 1925, p. 18.

12. F. M. Baily, *Mission to Tashkent*, London, Fountain Inc., 1948, p. 29.
13. *Great Soviet Encyclopaedia*, *op.cit.*, p. 58.
14. *Ibid.*
15. Mutahir Ahmed, "Prospects of Fundamentalism in Central Asia", *Pakistan Horizon*, Vol. 45 (3), July 1992, pp. 71-72.
16. Alexander Bennigsen, *Soviet Strategy and Islam*, London, Macmillan Press, 1989, p. 21.
17. Alexander Bennigsen, *op. cit.*, p. 56.
18. Maqbool Ahmed Bhatti, "Impact of Central Asian changes on South and West Asia", *Regional Studies*, Vol. 10, No. 2, Spring 1992, p. 17.
19. *Republic of Tajikistan: Recent Economic Developments*, International Monetary Fund Staff Country Report, no. 00/27, 6 March 2000. www.imf.org/external/pubs/ft/scr/2000/cr 0027.pdf.
20. Muhammad Reza Djabili, Fredric Grare and Shirin Akiner (eds.), *Tajikistan: The Trials of Independence*, New York, St. Martins Press, 1997, p. 70.
21. Tajiks and Uzbek populations in Central Asia have historically been intertwined. At the time of the territorial division of Central Asia into republics, only about 3, 00,000 of the total population of 1,100,000 ethnic Tajiks in Central Asia found themselves within the newly established state of Tajikistan. The gerrymandering of the border is "explained by the desire of the Uzbeks to have the historically important cities of Bukhara and Samarkand as part of Uzbekistan, despite the fact that for centuries the majority of the cities' population was Tajik. This was a matter of prestige rather than a political necessity, when the Russians conquered Turkestan, replacing the cities of Bukhara and Samarkand, which had been regional centres for centuries". Sergei Gretsky, "Civil War in Tajikistan: Causes, Development and Prospects for Peace", in Roald Z. Sagdeev and Susan Eisenhower (ed.), *Central Asia: Conflict, Resolution and Change, Centre for Political Studies*, Washington DC, 1995, pp. 217-48.
22. Outside military and financial assistance played a role in the consolidation of the opposition forces during this early period, but the newspaper accounts, particularly by Moscow journalists, indicating that Iran and other Islamic states bankrolled the IRP are not well founded. Virtually all the weapon and ordnance in the Tajikistan war was of Soviet manufacture.
23. Lena Johnson, *The Tajik War: A Challenge to Russian Policy*, London, Royal Institute of International Affairs, 1998, p. 113.
24. The UTO comprised of three main groups: The Islamic Renaissance Party of Tajikistan, the Democratic Party of Tajikistan, and the Rastokhez National Revival Movement. These groups were mostly defeated by the Tajik government forces in the spring of 1993, but isolated units continued fighting from bases in Afghanistan and areas in the south-east of the country until 1997, when the UTO became the recognized

opposition in the reconciliation plan. Same UTO figures such as Said Abdullo Nuri, continued to play a significant role in post-war reconstruction politics.

25. Gregory Gleason, "Politics of Counter-Insurgency in Central Asia", *Problems of Post Communism*, Vol. 49, No. 2, March/April, 2002, p. 6.
26. *Ibid.*
27. *Ibid.*
28. Factions like Khujandis led by former Prime Minister Abdermalik Abdullajanov, and a group of Uzbeks led by renegade army officer Col. Makhmud Khudayberdiev repeatedly tried to disrupt the peace process and even attacked Khojand in November 1998.
29. In 1996, the regional equation changed dramatically when the Taliban captured Afghanistan and ousted the Afghan-Tajik government. Central Asian leaders were fearful that the Taliban, drawn from the ethnic Pashtun group, would try to spread their harsh interpretation of Islam into Central Asia Both the government and the UTO realized that it was in their common interest to negotiate and end the civil war.
30. Kessing's Record of World Events (henceforth Keesing's) Vol. 43, No. 2, February 1997.
31. ITAR-TASS News Agency (henceforth ITAR-TASS), Moscow, 30 April 1997, reproduced in (henceforth rep. in) *SWB/SU*/2907/G/1/1 May 1997.
32. Kessing's, Vol. 43, No. 7 July 1997.
33. *Ibid*, September 1997.
34. ITAR-TASS, Moscow, 3 October 1997, rep. in *SWB/SU*/3041/G/2, 4 October 1997.
35. *Narodnoye Slavo*, Tashkent, 31 December 1997, rep. in *SWB/SU*/3117/G/3, 6 January 1998.
36. The Current Digest of the Post-Soviet Press (hence forth CDPSP), Vol. 51, No. 7, 1999, p. 8.
37. ITAR-TASS, Moscow, 18 February 1999, rep. in *SWB/SU*/3464/G/3, 20 February 1999.
38. Russian Public TV, Moscow, 23 February 1999, rep. in *SWB/SU*/3468/G/1, 25 February 1999.
39. *Ibid.*
40. *Ibid*, rep. in *SWB/SU*/3468/G/2, 25 February 1999.
41. ITAR-TASS, Moscow, 26 August 1999, rep. in *SWB/SU*/3624/G/3, 27 August 1999
42. Interfax, Moscow, 25 August 1999, rep. in *SWB/SU*/3626/G/3, 27 August 1999.
43. *Ibid.*
44. Alexander Knyazev, "International Terrorism in Central Asia", *Aakrosh*, Vol. 4, No. 1, April 2001, p. 78.
45 Keesing's, *op.cit.*, Vol. 45, No. 9, August 1999; Central Asia, "Islamist Mobilisation and Regional Security", *ICG Asia Report*, No. 14, 1 March

2001, p. 7, www.crisisweb.org

46. Alexander Kunyazev, *op.cit.*, p. 79.
47. *Ibid.*
48. "Central Asia: Islamist Mobilisation and Regional Security", *ICG Asia* Report, No. 20, p. 13.
49. ITAR-TASS, Moscow, 28 August 1999, rep. in *SWB/SU*/3626/G/1/30 August 1999.
50. *Ibid.*
51. Alexander Knyazev, *op.cit.*, p. 80.
52. ITAR TASS, Moscow, 28 May 1999.
53. ITAR-TASS, Moscow, 28 August 1999, rep. in *SWB/SU*/3626/G/1, 30 August 1999.
54. The Open Media Research Institute's Daily Digest, 7 March 1995.
55. *ICG Asia Report, op.cit.*
56. *Ibid.*
57. *Ibid.*
58. *Interfax*, Moscow, 11 August 2000, rep. in *SWB/SU*/3917/G/2, 12 August 2000.
59. Michael Vig, "The Great Escape: Utah Climber Recalls Six Frightful Days in Kyrgyzstan", *The Salt Lake Tribune*, 26 August 2000.
60. Only 28 groups worldwide have been assigned this designation. The activities attributed to IMU are actually generally more in line with many more militant opposition groups that have not been placed on this select list. Cited in ICG Asia Report, *op. cit.*, for the list of the US State Department Announcement, see http://www.usembassy.org.uk/terror121.html.
61. ITAR-TASS, Moscow, 12 August 2000, rep. in *SWB/SU*/3918/G/4, 14 August 2000
62. Russian Public TV, Moscow, 14 August 2000, rep. in *Ibid.*
63. *Interfax*, Moscow, 15 August 2000, rep. in *Ibid.*
64. *Ibid.*
65. ITAR-TASS, Moscow, 16 August 2000, rep. in *SWB/SU*/3922/G/2, 18 August 2000.
66. *Ibid.*
67. *Ibid.*
68. CDPSP, Vol. 52, No. 32, 2000.
69. Alexander Knyazev, *op.cit*, p. 83.
70. BBC World Service, 16:19 GMT, 13 September 2000.
71. Askar Aytmatov, "The Shade of Extremism Over Central Asia", *Perceptions*, December 2000-February 2001, pp. 116-117.
72. Keesing's Record of World Events, Vol. 45, No. 11, November 1999, p. 43257.
73. Keesing's, *op.cit.*, Vol. 46, No. 2, February 2000, p. 43407.
74. *Ibid.*
75. Asia Plus News Agency, Dushanbe, 8 February 2000, rep. in *SWB/SU/*

3761/G/2, 11 February 2000.

76. *Interfax-Kazakhstan News Agency* (henceforth *Interfax*-Kazakhstan), Almaty, 26 October 2000, rep. in *SWB/SU*/3983/G/1, 28 October 2000.
77. *Ibid.*
78. *Ibid.*
79. 6 November is the Tajik Constitution Day.
80. Tajik Radio First Programme, (henceforth Tajik Radio), Dushanbe, 7 November 2000, rep. in *SWB/SU*/3993/G/3, 9 November 2000.
81. Kyrgyz Radio First Programme (henceforth Kyrgyz Radio), Bishkek, 19 March 2001, rep. in *SWB/SU*/4100/G/1, 21 March 2001.
82. Kessing's, *op.cit.*, September 2001, p. 44344.
83. *Ibid.*
84. Graham H. Turbiville Jr., "Narcotics Trafficking in Central Asia: A New Columbia", *Military Review*, December 1992, p. 55.
85. UN Information Service, Central Asian Republics, UN-launched Sub-regional Drug Control Plan, UN Press Release, SOC/NAR/741, 29 April 1996. A certain amount of opium is legally declared and produced in the world for legitimate medical purposes under strict international legal controls, notably the single Convention on Narcotics Drugs and Associated Agreements.
86. Ramtanu Maitra, "Afghan Drugs: Gold to the Taliban", *Strategic Studies*, EIR, 8 September 2000, p. 36.
87. *Ibid.*
88. Jean Christopher Peuche, "Central Asia: Changes Link Russian Military to Drug Trades", RFE/RL, 8 June 2001.
89. Central Asia: Drugs and Conflict, *ICG Asia Report*, No. 25, 26 November 2001, p. 2, (hereafter *ICG Asia*).
90. Tamara Makarenko, "Seeking Security in Central Asia", *Jane's Intelligence Review*, January 2001, p. 23.
91. Asia Plus, Dushanbe, 12 October 1999, rep. in *SWB/SU*/3665/G/2, 14 October 1999.
92. From January through June 2001, Kyrgyz officials confiscated 58 kg of heroin; Kazakh officials seized 57 kg and Uzbek officials 160 kg during that period, Tajik officials seized 1,745 kg of heroin. At the same time, the amount of opium being impounded fell from close to 5,000 kg in 2000 to a mere 762 kg for the first half of 2001, State Drug Control Agency Report, Republic of Tajikistan, July 2001.
93. One kilogram of heroin brings Central Asia drug smugglers about six times the money that one kg of opium brings. While it takes ten kg of opium to produce one kg of heroin, to which, the cost of the precursor chemicals must be of added, the result is a much more compact as well as valuable commodity for the traffickers, cited in *ICG Asia*, *op.cit.*, p. 3.
94. Narcotics in Central Asia, International Narcotics Control Strategy Report, 1997, *Central Asia Monitor*, No. 2, 1998, p. 20.

95. Bennet Rubin and Nancy Lubin, *Calming the Fergana Valley*, New York, The Century Foundation Press, 1999, pp. 70-71.
96. Mahendra Ved, "When Silk Routes Become Destructive Drug Route", *Asian Eurasian Commentary*, Vol. III, No. 5-7, April-December 2000, p. 52.
97. Irina Andinayeva, "International Drug Trafficking and Central Asia: Forced Involvement", Building Common Future: Indian and Uzbek Perspectives on Security and Economic Issues, IDSA, New Delhi, p. 81.
98. Narcotics in Central Asia, *op.cit.*, p. 19.
99. D. Zviagelskaia and Vitaliv Naumkin, "Non-traditional Threats, Challenges and Risks in former Soviet Union", in Rajan Menon, Yuri E. Fedarov and Ghai Naida (eds.) Russia, *The Caucasus and Central Asia: The 21st Century Security Environment*, London, M.E. Sharpe, 1999, p. 200.
100. Report of the International Narcotic Central Boards, Vienna, 1995, p. 14, cited in Sumita Kumar, *op.cit*, p. 209.
101. *Interfax*, Moscow, 30 June 1997, rep. in *SWB/SU*/3451/G/2, 3 July 1997.
102. *Interfax* - Kazakhstan, Alma Ata, 1 February 1999, rep. in *SWB/SU*/ 3451/G/2, 5 February 1999.
103. Narcotics in Central Asia, *op.cit.*, p. 21.
104. Gulshen Ashiram, "Turkmenistan in the Path of Afghan Drug Expansion", *The Times of Central Asia*, 26 July 2001.
105. "Turkmen Addiction Rising", *Institute for War and Peace Reporting*, RCA No. 64, 10 August 2001.
106. Interview with Segiy Ratushnyy, Chief Technical Advisor for UNDCP in Tajikistan, July 2001, cited in *ICG Asia*, *op.cit.*, p. 6.
107. Central Asia; "Fault Lines in the New Security Map", *ICG Asia Report*, No. 20, 4 July 2001
108. *ICG Asia*, *op. cit.*, p. 12.
109. Bureau of International Narcotics and Law Enforcement Affairs, US Department of State, *International Narcotics Control Strategy Report*, 1999.
110. Peter Chalk, "Light Arms Trading in SE Asia", *Jane's Intelligence Review*, March 2001, p. 42.
111. Sumita Kumar, *op.cit.*, p. 217.
112. Bennett R. Rubin, *The Search for Peace in Afghanistan*, London, Yale University , 1995; cited in Tara Kartha, "Light Weapons Proliferation and Regional Instability in Central Asia", *Strategic Analysis*, December 1996, p. 1279.
113. Cited in Pieter D. Wegeman, Siemon. T. Wegemon and Nicholos Chipperlied, "Transfer of Small Arms and Other Weapons to Armed Conflicts", *SIPRI Year Book*, New York, 2001, p. 411.
114. Bennett. R. Rubin, *op.cit.*, in Tara Kartha, *op.cit*, p. 1280.

115. Karim, Khodjibaev, "Small Arms Proliferation and Social Militarisation in Tajikistan", *Central Asia Monitor*, No. 3, 1999, p. 24.
116. Michael T. Klare, "The Global Trade in Light Weapons and the International System in the post-Cold War Era", in Boutwell Klare and Reed (eds.) Lethal Commerce: *The Global Trade in Small Arms and Light Weapons*, Cambridge, American Academy of Arts and Sciences, 1995, p. 36.
117. *Ibid.*
118. Buckhard Conrad, "Small Arms Transfers and Disarmament. A Security Leit-motif for Tajikistan in the late 1990s, http://www.ppc.pims.org/csrc, p. 2.
119. Nalin Kumar Mohapatra, "Drugs and Small Arms: Its Impact on Regional Security in Central Asia", *The Asian Journal*, Vol. 9, No. 2, June 2002, pp. 47-61.
120. Cited in *Ibid.*
121. Buckhard Conrad, *op.cit.*
122. *Jane's World Insurgency and Terrorism*, September-December 1999, p. 186.
123. *Report of the International Narcotics Control Board*, Vienna, p. 54.
124. *International Narcotics Control Strategy Report*, (Henceforth INCSR), US State Department Publication, 1997, p. 399.
125. Phil Williams, "Drug Trafficking and Organised Crime in Central Asia: The Economic, Social and Political Consequences", 1996, A Report Prepared for the UNDCP Regional Office for Central Asia, p. 29.
126. *Central Asian Post*, 30 January 1997.
127. Sumita Kumar, *op.cit.*, p. 257.
128. Phil Williams, *op.cit.*, pp. 10-11.
129. *Interfax*, Moscow, 21 November 1995, rep. in *SWB/SU*/2468/G/3, 23 November 1995.
130. *Interfax*, Moscow, 17 August 2000, rep. in *SWB/SU*/3923/G/1 and G/2, 19 August 2000.
131. UNDCP Regional Office for Central Asia, Annual Field Report, 1995, p. 21, cited in Sumitha Kumar, *op.cit*, p. 218.
132. Kyrgyz Television First Channel, Bishkek, in Russian, 19 April, 1997. Cited in Sumita Kumar, *op.cit.*, p. 218.
133. *Central Asia Monitor*, No. 4, 2000, p. 33.
134. Ahmed Rashid, *Jihad*, *op.cit.*, p. 209.
135. *Ibid.*
136. *Ibid*, p. 210.
137. For more details see Ahmed Rashid, "First the War", *Far Eastern Economic Review*, 26 July 2001.
138. Ahmed Rashid, *Taliban: Militant Islam, Oil and Fundamentalism in Central Asia*, New Heaven, Yale University Press, 2000, pp. 117-119.
139. Ahmed Rashid, *Jihad*, *op.cit.*, p. 212.
140. *Ibid.*

141. "Central Asian Muslims Looking Towards Umma", *The Nation*, 18 September 1991.
142. *ICG Asia Report*, *op.cit.*, p. 41.
143. Tahir Amin, "Pakistan, Afghanistan and Central Asian States", in Ali Banuazizi and Myron Weiner (eds.) *The New Geopolitics of Central Asia and its Borderland*, London, I. B. Tauris, 1994, pp. 217-220.
144. Ahmed Rashid, *op.cit.*, p. 216.
145. *Ibid.*
146. Hanna Yousif Hreij, "State Interests vs. the Umma: Iranian Policy in Central Asia", *Middle East Journal*, Vol. 50, No. 1, Winter 1996, p. 80.
147. *Wall Street Journal*, 17 December 1991, as cited in *ibid*, p. 81.
148. Theodore Karasik, "Azerbaijan, Central Asia and Future Persian Gulf Security", Santa Monica, CA; The Rand Corporation, N-3579-AF/A, 1993, p. 31.
149. Zeba Moshaver, "Central Asia and Iran's Northern Policy", *The Oxford International Review*, Summer 1994, p. 48.
150. Ahmed Rashid, *Jihad*, *op.cit*, p. 220.
151. Gareth M. Winrow, "Turkey and Former Soviet Central Asia: National and Ethnic Identity", *Central Asian Survey*, Vol. 11, No. 3, 1993, pp. 112-113.
152. Ahmed Rashid, *Jihad*, *op.cit.*, p. 222.
153. Dillip Hiro, *Between Marx and Muhammad: The Changing Face of Central Asia*, London, Harper Collins Publishers, 1994.
154. Ahmed Rashid, *Jihad*, *op.cit.*, p. 224.
155. P. B. Sinha, "Pakistan - The Chief Patron Promoter of Islamic Militancy and Terrorism", *Strategic Analysis*, October 1997, pp. 1021-1022.
156. *Ibid.*
157. Ahmed Rashid, *Jihad*, *op.cit.*, pp. 224-225.
158. Gregory Gleason, *Politics of Counter- Insurgency in Central Asia*, *op.cit.*, p. 8.
159. P.B. Sinha, *op.cit.*, pp. 1021-1022.

3

Growth of Fundamentalism and Radical Groups in Central Asia

The great purges in the Islamic republics under the Soviets, which was to destroy the pre-revolution era Muslim intelligentsia, began in 1928. It started in Crimea with the execution of Veli Ibrahim, First Secretary of the Tatar Communist Party and the liquidation of Milli Firka. In Kazakhstan, the execution of Alash Orda coincided with the forced sedentarisation of the nomads, which was to ruin the country and cost thousands of lives. In Central Asia, all the leading members of young *Bukharan* movement and nearly all the pre-revolutionary intellectuals were eliminated from local Communist parties between 1922-1938.[1]

The "Muslim National Communists" were liquidated by Stalin in the 1930s. With their demise also went the attempt at partnership with the Russians, which was seen by the Muslim leadership as the least painful means of throwing off foreign domination. One final attempt, however, was made to shake off the '*infidel*' yoke, when during the World War II, the conservatives North Caucasian Mountaineers rose in armed revolt. But this attempt too was crushed.[2]

Under Khrushchev, the situation in Central Asian region remained the same. He had an uncompromising hostile attitude towards Islam and other religions. The anti-Islamic propaganda increased massively. He tried to portray the Soviet Union as a centre of the world Communist movement; especially during the Bandung Conference of 1955, the Soviet image makers were successful in portraying Soviet Union as an important Asian power and not just a country with large Muslim components.[3] Until the early 1960s, the Soviet Muslims lived behind an iron curtain.[4]

The period 1964-79 saw a major shift in the policies of the Soviet Union towards its Muslim population. During the 1960s, a new generation of young experts on Islam emerged from the Soviet educational establishment. They were totally different from the dogmatic experts of the Stalin and Khrushchev periods. These scholars were not only better equipped with secular knowledge but also were acquainted with Islamic traditional education. During this period, the activities of the Soviet Islamic establishments received wide media coverage. Several initiatives were taken, including organisation of conferences in Tashkent in 1970 and 1973, another in Samarkand in 1974 to commemorate the 1200th anniversary of Imam Ismail-al- Bukhari. Numerous visits to Muslim countries were arranged to project a favourable image of the status of the Muslims in the Soviet Union.

After 1985, the society in the former USSR diametrically changed. Gorbachev's 'glasnost' and 'perestroika' changed the entire scene. But prior to this, the religious policy of Soviet Russia, its policy towards the Muslims in particular had created a different phenomenon-the phenomenon of "unofficial Islam" that worked clandestinely and became root of the future radicalisation of Islam in Central Asia and in the CIS.

Gorbachev was the only Soviet leader who did not have a well publicised anti-religious agenda as his preoccupation was mainly with the over all planning and economic health of the country. During the first couple of years of his rule he chose to maintain status quo as far as religious matter was concerned.[5] Only after the 27th Party congress held in late February 1986, he reiterated the Brezhnevian anti-religious views saying, "the party will use all forms of ideological influence for the wider propagation for a scientific prejudices without permitting any violation of believer's feelings".[6]

For Gorbachev, however, the battle against Islam in Central Asia was more than a battle against a religion or a reactionary world view. As Olcott then pointed out, "the prevalence of Islam is viewed by (Gorbachev) as troublesome in so far as it undermines the regime's reform programme".[7] This general perception became Gorbachev's driving force in Central Asia.

By 1988, the Soviet policies towards Islam and for that matter other religions, began to show signs of positive change. It was the same period when Gorbachev's reform initiatives, *glasnost* in particular, began to draw response in Central Asia. Groups and associations in informal way appeared with location specific agendas, some of which later evolved into political parties and movements.

The second phase of Gorbachev's rule that roughly extended from 1988-1991 saw again major shifts in Gorbachev's policy orientation. The 1988 defeat of the anti-religious hardliners paved the way for religious reforms, which culminated in a new law on freedom of conscience on 1 October 1990. In the law containing 31 articles, article 3 professed the rights to freedom of conscience, placing "only those restrictions that are necessary for protecting public safety and order, life, health and morality, as well as the rights and liberties of other citizens", article 11 provided for establishment of religious educational institutions, article 13 extended legal status to religious organisations. By early 1989, Islam had joined the ranks of other free religions in the Soviet Union with enthusiastic reopening of old mosques and holy shrines, madrassahs, collective Friday prayers, religious festivals and pilgrimage to holy place in Central Asia.

Radical Islam in the USSR

While the Sufi movement in Central Asia remained buoyant, it by no means represented the whole of 'parallel' or 'underground' Islam in the USSR. A number of other smaller but more militant movements were active in the Soviet Union since the 1930s. The Muslim brotherhood (*Ikhwan al-Moslemeen*) had succeeded in creating a number of secret cells in Dagestan in 1920s.[8] The Wahhabi movement had also established a presence, especially in Turkmenistan, in the 1930s. Wahhabism[9] was brought to Central Asia in 1912 by Sayyed Sharie Muhammad, a native of Medina in Arabia. He created many circles some of which remain active. An important circle in Tashkent was named after Bahauddin Vaisov, a Wahhabi teacher who died in Moscow in 1950s. It is unlikely that the brotherhood was able to survive the period of Stalinist terror in the mid-1930s, but judging by the attacks made on it by the Soviet media during the 1970s and 1980s, the movement had almost certainly managed to retain some influence.

After Iran's Islamic Revolution, however, still more militant Islamic groups began to appear on the Soviet scene. Islamic 'Samizdat' (underground literature), generally known as 'Islamizdat' started from 1982 onwards was part of the initiatives taken by these new groups of Muslim radicals. Judging by their literature the groups were patterned after the *fidayeen* of Islam and Egyptian Taqfir wal-Higrah movements. They were committed to the eventual overthrow of the Soviet system which they described in their literature as 'Shaytani' (satanic) and *taghuti* (*in revolt, against God*). Because they operated in small secret cells often with little or no formal organisational contact with one another, the radical group cannot be described as a single movement. Nor can their exact numerical strength be ascertained. But through the attacks made on them by the official media and a survey of 'Islamizdat' available, it was clear that such groups were active in Kazakhstan, Central Asia, Dagestan and Azerbaijan.

The new radical groups seemed to be specially strong in Tajikistan where over fifty Muslims were reportedly in prison in 1989. Those arrested belonged to five different cells dedicated to the propagation of a militant and combative version of Islam. Unlike 'official' Islam which attracts the older generation and the *tariqats* which have a special place among the middle-aged professionals, the new radical groups appeal to the young and the less favourite.[10]

The leader of one group, Ashghar Shah Jaberov, arrested in a raid on his home in 1986, was born in 1958. A native of Kulyab, he had turned his modest house into a meeting place for fellow Muslims. Another member of the same group, also arrested in Kulyab was Ne'matallah Inayatov, a mullah born in 1950.

A second group of Tajik militants dismantled in the Leningradsky district, was also led by a young mullah Abdul Rahim Karimov. This group included three university students and operated a clandestine press.

A third group discovered in the Vakhsh district of Tajikistan, consisted of the close supporters of Mullah Abdullah Ibn Nureddin Sa'idov who had emerged as a charismatic leader in the region. Another young mullah Rajab-Ali Sha'yev (born in 1955) was arrested in Doshanbe as the head of a group of Muslim militants.

A fourth group headed by Imaduddin Ahmadjanov, a young engineer born in 1962, was dismantled in Doshanbeh in 1982. He was sentenced to nine years imprisonment, including three years in a labour camp.[11]

Between 1982 and 1989, eight Muslim militant groups were broken up by the authorities in Uzbekistan. One group led by Sayyed Karim Khajov, was active in Tashkent and had produced the Smizdat' booklet *Truth about Islam* in 1982. Khajov was in contact with another group of militants led by Piyar Jafarov, active also in Tashkent; Jafarov was arrested in the summer of 1982. A third Islamic militant group functioned under the leadership of Sayyad Karim Azymov in Tashkent, where it operated a clandestine Quranic school.

A fourth group had as its head, Mardan Puladov, a merchant who was arrested with his daughter Jamilah Qamtrova in 1985. They operated an Islamizdat Centre in the city of Samarkand, Abu Zakar Rahimov who led another radical group in Tashkent, was arrested in 1982 and sentenced to seven years detention in a labour camp. In August 1985 another group was discovered in Bukhara, and its leader Sayyad Gafur Usulev, was sentenced to four years hard labour. Two more groups were broken up by the police in Ugrench and Khiva and their leaders, Abel-Qassem Yadagarov and Ashraf Bassirev, were arrested.[12]

In Turkmenistan, two clandestine cells were uncovered in Ashgabat and Charju in the winter of 1987.[13] Their leaders, Arslan Salurbayev and Akbarkhaqaov were sentenced to three years of hard labour each.

In Kazakhstan, a group of militants led by Kelim Qurbanov was broken up by the authorities in Jambul and its clandestine printing press seized in March 1988. This group was also accused of having organised an illegal school.[14]

Similarly, there were Islamic radical groups in northern Caucasus, fighting for an Islamic Dagestan and in Azerbaijan, which were crushed and dismantled by the Soviet authorities. The Soviet authorities had invoked a variety of laws in their campaign against Islamic radicals. Some militants were charged for anti-state activities and thus treated as political prisoners. A majority however, were tried and sentenced under criminal law and treated as ordinary felons.

There are different views forwarded by various scholars regarding the culmination of this radical and fundamentalist development in USSR. Amir Taheri opines that in the 1980s when religious groups were gaining ground, they were a long way from preaching terrorism as a means of achieving their secular goals. Throughout the 1980s, they tried to find ways to achieve a better understanding of the experience of other Muslim countries, especially Iran and Egypt, and to create the minimum of native literature needed for the future growth of the radical Islamic movement in the USSR. In other words, the best part of the energy of the clandestine groups was spent on theoretical work and education. At no point, did they try to take on the Soviet authorities in a direct confrontation and were content to allow official Islam and Muslim intellectuals associated with the Communist Party to recapture from the Soviets as much of the public space as possible. At best, the radicals acted as a pressure group militating for more decisive action by official Islam, student organisations, intellectuals associations and even sections of local party structures. The tactic of 'leading from behind'- successfully tested by Muslim radicals in Egypt, Algeria, Turkey, Iran and Pakistan- seemed to have been copied by many members of the radical Islamic movement in the USSR. The radicals were able to apply a certain degree of pressure, for example, during the Kazakhstan riots in 1986 or throughout the demonstrations leading to the resignation of Mufti Shamsuddin Baba Khan, without exposing themselves to the danger of being arrested.

It is difficult to gauge the effects of the anti-radical crackdown in the 1980s. However, judging from the fact that "Islamizdat" continued to thrive and expand, and that the number of Quranic schools did not diminish, it was possible to suggest that radical Islam had by no means been rooted out from the Soviet Union. As mentioned earlier, with the onset of the decade of 1990s, the scene in USSR and Muslim dominated Central Asia was much more different than the earlier one. The latent forces of radicalism and fundamentalism in the region assumed a force of greater magnitude when combined with violence and terrorism.

By October 1991, all the five Central Asian republics declared their independence. Like many post-colonial societies these republics were also faced with serious political uncertainties that have been brought about by the clash of the old Communist power structure, reorganised under a nationalist disguise, and the emerging new Islamic and democratic forces in each republic. Out of these two the former proved more formidable and lasting. Since 1980s, a number of Islamic parties, organisations, and movements with a variety of ideological orientations entered into the public arena of Central Asian republics. Driven by political objectives, these forces have presented a qualitatively different face of Central Asian Islam, which has been marked with fundamentalist and radical features and some of them even have violently confronted the establishment resorting to terrorist tactics.

Islam and Democracy in Uzbekistan (IDU)

Two types of Islamic organisations have been active on the Central Asian political scene in recent years. The first is the republican parties that have so far exhibited weak to moderate organisational and mobilisation capabilities, encompassing a wide range of ideological tendencies.[15] The most radical of these organisations have either gone underground or have been absorbed by other organisations during the last two years. One such organisation was Islam and democracy of Uzbekistan, which held its founding Congress in Alma-Ata (Almaty), the capital of Kazakhstan, on 28 October 1988. Though at first, it hoped to become an inter-republican party drawing its support from all over Central Asia, it failed to reach beyond Uzbekistan's cities and rural areas. According its Chairman, Almaz Estekov, the basic objective of the organisation was "the spiritual cleansing of people from the immortality and preaching of the Democratic principles of the Koran".[16] The organisation was instrumental in forcing the removal of Mufti Babakhanov (Babakhan), in 1989 subsequent to a series of demonstrations on 3 February. The leading members of the party had apparently produced evidence attesting to the fact that Babakhan drank alcoholic beverage, womanised and lacked the necessary religious board of Central Asia and Kazakhstan. The membership of the party was estimated at 2,500 in 1989, of whom the overwhelming majority came from Uzbekistan's cities of Andijan, Bukhara and Samarkand.[17] Though it is not very clear what actually happened to the party towards 1996 but it is probable that, as a fundamentalist party, Islam and democracy may have been absorbed by larger organisations of the same ideological colourings in 1990.[18]

People's Front of Uzbekistan

The People's Front of Uzbekistan is also a radical organisation operating out of Tashkent. Due to its clandestine nature, little has been publicised about its activities apart from the fact that it supports the establishment of an Islamic republic.[19]

Similarly, the Islamic Democratic Party has been advocating the creation of a theocracy modelled after the Islamic Republic of Iran. In a 1999 interview, one of the party leaders, Dadkhan Hassan, had openly praised the leader of the Islamic Republic of Iran, indicating that "Khomeini was very good for us". In its founding Congress, he called for veiling of women and the imposition of Islamic law on Uzbek society. Hassan, however, pointed out that "we will not attempt to seize power by force.... our strategy first is to unite all our Muslims.... and the then to educate the new generation in the spirit of Islam".[20] Furthermore, the party was to nominate candidates for local offices on an Islamic platform with the aim of replacing the secular Soviet laws with *Sharia law*. The party's objective was nothing short of a non-violent Islamic revolution in the region. The proceedings of the party congress were broadcast live by a local radio station in Namangan without government interference. Yet, the scope of the party's activities has been limited to the city of Namangan in Uzbekistan.

Alash

In Kazakhstan, an Islamic party named "Alash" for the National Independence of Kazakhstan was established in April 1990. Headed by Aron Atabek and Rashid Yutoshev, the party had been pressing for the creation of an Islamic state in Kazakhstan. On 13 December 1991, the Alash party held a meeting during which a decision was to taken to remove the mufti of Kazakhstan, Nysnnbai Uly Ratbek, who had been accused of violating the Islamic *sharia*. Shortly thereafter, seven militant members of the Alash made their entry into the Muftiate in Almaty and demanded his resignation. Subsequently, a fight broke out during which the mufti was beaten and injured.[21] The Muftiate, however, remained under siege until the government militia stormed the building and captured the assailants whose numbers had grown to 200.[22] Forty one members of the Alash were arrested by the government militia. According to Kazakh Attorney General Tukakbayev, this act was designed to raise the confidence of the fundamentalist forces within the republic and strengthen the Alash position in this regard. Faced with dwindled support, the party had moderated its position by dropping its demand for the establishment of an Islamic republic and the expulsion of all Russians from Kazakhstan. But Alash has maintained its pan-Turkic demand that calls for consolidation of the Turkic peoples of the former Soviet Union in a peace loving republic of Great Turkistan.[23] According to one government official, the party in 1997 had a total of 85 members in Almaty.[24] Unconfirmed reports indicate a much larger following most of whom operate out of Chimkent bordering Uzbekistan. As an illegal party its leaders have been forced to exile in Baku, and their newspaper 'Khak' has been banned.[25] In the summer of 1993, the party moved its headquarters to Moscow in order to conduct its affairs without the fear of government reprisal.

Islamic Revival (Renaissance) Party

It emerged out of the inter-republican party of Islamic Revival or Islamic Renaissance - *Partiya Islamskovo Vozrozhdeniya*. In short it is also known as IRP. Islam was a natural way to encourage Tajik nationalism, for an underground political Islam had thrived in Tajikistan more than in any other Central Asian state, during the Soviet period. The most influential underground spiritual leader in the Soviet era was Mullah Muhammad Rustamov Hindustani, who had studied in the Madrasa in Deoband, India, before returning to home to open a clandestine *madrassah* in Dushanbe in the 1970s. Hindustani brought the new ideas shaping the Muslim world and the ideology of Islamic Fundamentalist movements in India, Pakistan and Arab states to Central Asia, spreading his message to both Tajiks and Uzbeks in the Fergana Valley. He died in 1981.[26]

One of Hindustani's students was Abdullah Saidov, known as Syed Abdullah Nuri, who was born in the town Tavildara in 1947. Along with other clans from the valley, Nuri's family was forcibly moved in 1953 by the Soviet authorities to the work in the cotton fields in the Vaksh Valley in the south. By 1974, Nuri had helped to form an illegal Islamic educational organisation, Nahzar-I-Islami (Islamic knowledge), while being trained to become a surveying engineer. In March 1987, at Panj, close to the border with Afghanistan, Nuri led the first public demonstration in support of the Afghan Mujahideen; a few weeks after guerrillas belonging to Gulbuddin Hekmatyar's Hizb-i-Islami (Party of Islam) had launched a rocket attack on the city from the Afghan side of the border. Nuri was arrested along with four others on charges of circulating illegal Islamic literature and organising a protest against the Soviet occupation of Afghanistan. Released in 1988, Nuri continued his clandestine political activities, eventually becoming a founding member and leader of the Islamic Renaissance Party.[27]

Another of Hindustani's students was Muhammad Sharif Himmatzada, who became a leader of the military wing of the IRP. Nuri and Himmatzada helped found the Tajik branch of Islamic Renaissance Party.[28] The IRP held its founding Congress in the city of Astrakhan (Russia) in the Soviet part of the north Caucasus on 10 June 1990. Attended by 150 delegates, the party's initial goals revolved around "the revival of ideals of Islam".[29]

But from the outset, its objectives were political in nature. For instance, the party called for the establishment of *Shariah* courts and the teaching of Islam in secular schools and organise the Muslims within the Soviet Union. Although the creation of Islamic states was not explicitly addressed during the Astrakhan gathering, some members expressed their desire to move in that direction upon their return to their respective republics. Mullah Muhammad Abdullah Mirsaidov of Tajikistan, who later played a significant role as a local opposition leader to the Nabiyev government, had openly entertained such an idea in his sermons. It was also decided to let each Soviet republic set up its own, independent branch of the party.[30] With Glasnost in full swing under President Mikhail Gorbachev, the IRP registered as a political party in Russia, but it was banned in Central Asian republics by their ruling Communist Parties. Tajik representatives on their return faced an immediate ban.[31]

The IRP continued its campaign through its newspaper Al-Wadah since January 1991, in order to shed its negative reputation. By 1992, the party's fortunes had started declining with only 40 members in total attending its conference in Saratov.[32] Leaving aside the declining status of the Central IRP in Moscow, the organisational reach and mobilisation capacities of the IRP branches had been relatively more advanced in Tajikistan and Uzbekistan as compared to the rest of the Central Asian republics.[33]

With support form Nuri's youth organisation, however, as well as from clans in the Karategin Valley and Karategins who had been resettled in the Vaksh Valley around the town of Kurgan Tyube, a clandestine branch of the IRP did emerge in Tajikistan.[34] With the support from the above mentioned quarters, two of the Tajik participants of Astrakhan Congress, Dawlat Usman and I. Gadoev, on 6 October 1990, organised the IRP branch in Tajikistan.[35] The party's founding Congress was held outside the city of Dushanbe at a place called Chartut where 300 delegates participated.[36] A council of Ulema with a membership of 27 was created. Abdussamad Himmatov was elected Chairman.[37]

Since its inception, the party emphasised the primacy of electoral means for achieving its basic political objectives. For instance, the party Secretary in charge of education and propaganda, Abdullah Dadkhuda stated that, "the only way to advertise Islam is to do it through a parliamentary and democratic political system.... We are against forcing people to accept our path but we rely on any means to awaken them".[38] He further indicated that, "by an Islamic government, we mean that a government where the orders of the God, the sacred Quran, the teaching and knowledge of the prophet are the principal elements. We must have a parliament because the Quran encourages collective consultations. Future leaders should be chosen by the people and judged by their world view, their scholarly enlightenment and their knowledge of Islam.[39]

The IRP received official recognition on 26 October 1991 and declared its independence from the all- Union IRP in December 1992 under the name of Nehzat-e-Islami-ye-Tajikistan. S. Tajbakhsh has provided a summary of the basic objectives of the IRP as follows:

- a spiritual revival of the citizens of the republic;
- an independent economic and political system;
- a complete political and legal awakening with the aim of applying to the everyday life of Muslims of the republic the principles of Islam;
- the spread and advertising of Islamic thought among different nationalities of the republic.[40]

Similar opinions were also given by the Chairman of the party, Himmatzada, who in a press conference reassured the country that the party's aim was to establish a democratic state committed to the rule of law rather than an Islamic state.[41]

By 1991, the party had succeeded in developing an elaborate republican wide organisational network, expanding its membership through active involvement in mosques and prayer houses whose numbers had expanded significantly since 1989. Quite expectedly, the bulk of its support came from far regions with strongest Islamic proclivity: Maschah and Ura Tepeh in Khojand *oblast*, Dushanbe and the surrounding areas, Gharm (Gharatakin) and Gharghan Tepeh (Kurghan Tepeh) in Khatlon (Khatlan) *oblast*. Although the extent of the membership of the Tajik IRP had not been determined, a 1990 report in *Izvestiya* put the figure at 10,000. In 1992, it was reported that some 30,000 members had joined the party.[42] Majority of the IRP members seemed to be from rural socio-economic background and much of its urban support came from unemployed youth and elderly men and women. It must be indicated, however, that the IRP, at least publicly, had denied that it was working towards the creation of an Islamic state. Its leaders Muhammad Sharif Himmatzada and Daulat Usman had frequently stated that the creation of an Islamic republic was an unattainable goal in the foreseeable future.[43]

Despite the party's united leadership stance, the Tajik IRP had been plagued by ideological factionalism. There were Wahhabi tendencies, such as those that condemn Muslim celebrating feasting and other costly rites such as Kalym, or bride price, as well as the veneration of the saints and deities.[44] Mullah Abdullah (Mir Saidov) was a strong proponent of this condemnation, arguing that such activities have reduced the purity of Islamic faith. The support for this view had been strengthened by exposure to Wahhabi literature smuggled through Uzbekistan and elsewhere into the republic.[45] This faction was also more adamant about the establishment of an Islamic republic in Tajikistan. The second faction was influenced by the ideology of the Muslim brotherhood which has a strong pan-Islamic orientation. The third faction was a moderate Islamic faction whose ideology was more or less in line with that of Kazi Ali Akbar Turajonzada. This faction that had been advocating the revival of Islam in Tajikistan was effectively absorbed by the IRP subsequent to the Communist takeover in the fall of 1992 that led to the removal of Kazi Turajonzada from his past.

With the beginning of the civil war in Tajikistan, IRP played a crucial role in it. While the party was faction ridden it could not decide exactly the role it should be playing in the ensuing civil war. When the civil war engulfed the whole of Tajikistan, IRP also participated in it on many fronts. It took to violence and later became the lynchpin of the opposition to the government. This was the period when the terrorist activities of IRP came to prominence.

The party had already come out open in February 1990 after the Dushanbe housing riots, which were incited by fears that Armenian refugees, fleeing from the fighting in their region, would be resettled in the capital. Activists for the IRP managed to include Islamic demands amongst those of the masses surrounding headquarters of the Communist Party of Tajikistan (CPTJ). For several days, they staged sit-ins and put up banners demanding that more mosques be opened, that stores selling pork and alcohol be closed, and that Tajik street names replace the Russian ones.[46]

As the political situation deteriorated in late 1991, political infighting broke out within CPTJ, leading to several leadership replacements. Hardline Communists in the Tajik Parliament eventually forced through the election of 62 year-old Rahman Nabiyev as President in September. Mass protests at his election broke out in Dushanbe as tens of thousands of people camped out in Lenin Square- renamed Azadi (freedom) Square- in the centre of the city. This was the time when IRP tried to extend its base among the people.[47]

Meanwhile, an election took place and in a controversial election Rahman Nabiyev won which led to more demonstrations, more riots in March 1992, which were followed by a severe crackdown in which many people were killed, anarchy broke out in Dushanbe, as assassinations, kidnappings and random killings became daily events. By now it was clear that a civil war was imminent and key IRP leaders took to the mountains to set up military bases in the Karategin and Tavildara valleys north of Dushanbe.

In the following events, violence dominated the scene from both government as well as IRP side. IRP launched guerrilla attacks on the government forces and the Kulyabi militants from its bases in Karategin and Tavildara valleys, Kurgan Tyube and Afghanistan, where they were joined by some 80,000 refugees. They established Kunduz and Talaquan in the north east with the support of the Kabul government, then controlled by the Afghan-Tajik leaders. Gradually the Tajik conflict became an international issue and a trans-national war. IRP leaders travelled to Iran, Pakistan and Saudi Arabia seeking military and financial support.

In 1996, the regional equation changed dramatically when the Taliban captured Kabul and ousted the Afghan-Tajik government. Fearing greater isolation and decrease in the popularity of the party due to growing poverty and miserable economic conditions of the Tajik people, IRP and the government finally settled the issue under the mediation of UN that brought the war to an end.[48]

The inter-Tajik negotiations were periodically interrupted by military clashes. IRP was engaged in not only the direct military clashes with the government forces but also in bombing and hostage taking.

By 2000, the IRP had become one of the most powerful political parties in Tajikistan. Its members filled most of the government positions allocated to UTO and it has again become a parliamentary party committed to peaceful and legal political methods.[49] As IRP has become a political party today and as a part of the government running the country, some believe that there has been a total decline of IRP, while some hardliner elements that had refused to join the Tajik army are still carrying on their disruptive activities, this time, under the patronage of IMU, operating from Uzbekistan. A small group of IRP men led by Rakhmov Sanginov, as recently as summer of 2001, was carrying on activities like kidnappings, robberies mostly bank robberies and occasional blasts, before he was killed by the Tajik army in an operation that lasted for more than a month.

Even when the party was at its peak of popularity, the debate over whether further radicalisation of the party should be carried out or stress on education and religious aspect of the organisation should be given, went on. This ideological confusion continued even after the party finally became a part of the government with the settlement of the Tajik civil war that also ended the activities of IRP. But being an inter-republican organisation, its Uzbek branch carried out its work in Uzbekistan to a great extent.

The IRP in Uzbekistan was established on 26 January 1992, in Tashkent, provoking a similar reaction to that of the Tajikistan authorities. The party was denied official recognition and due. Its activities of 1991 were banned under Uzbek law on public associations. Ever since that, the party has been conducting its affairs underground. A review of the party's initial platform which was made public on 16 December 1990, clearly demonstrates its comprehensively religious orientation and its similarities with the Tajik IRP.[50]

- to explain to the people the real meaning of the holy Koran an *hadith* and to call the people to line and act according to *Koran* and *hadith.*
- to call to Islam by all means of mass media.
- to fight national and racial discrimination, impudence, crime, alcoholism , and all other things that are forbidden by *sharia* through understanding and appeal.
- to educate young people on principles of Islam and for this
- purpose to create instruction and training centres and *madrassahs.*
- to ensure that the right of all Muslims are exercised according to the Koran.
- to strengthen Islamic brotherhood to develop religious relations with the Muslim world, and to seek for a relationship of equal rights with representatives of other religions.
- to cooperate with other democratic parties and state organisations in all fields.
- to create philanthropic funds that will support any one in need of help.
- to strengthen the family according to the principles of Islam and to ensure the rights of women and children.

- to ensure the principles of an Islamic economy and regaining ecological purity.
- to ensure the distribution of food according to the *Sharia*.
- to solve the problems of people according to the Holy Koran and *hadith*.

The IRP had its stronghold in the densely populated Fergana Valley in particular the two cities of Namangan and Andijan. The party also enjoyed substantial support among the rural Uzbek population. Due to the government crackdown there are no verifiable sources of information on the membership of IRP. But there may be as many as 40,000 to 50,000 members most of whom operate out of the Fergana region. There are also reports of the IRP activities in Kara Kalpak Autonomous region, in the north western section of Uzbekistan.[51] The organisational reach and mobilisation capacity of the IRP have been severely hampered by the geographical isolation of the Fergana, which can become inaccessible during the winter months and by its predominantly rural constituency.

In Kyrgyzstan, the IRP has had a considerably smaller following. Most of the IRP activities in Kyrgyzstan are limited to the Osh and Jalalabad *oblasts*, particularly among those with Uzbek origin. In Turkmenistan, on the other hand there are no visible signs of the party. One Turkmenistan expert has stated that the party has no organisation in Turkmenistan.[52]

While the IRP branches had become increasingly independent they shared a number of functional and contextual characteristics. First, the most obvious was the overriding objective of creating an Islamic republic. Although in countries like Tajikistan IRP has dropped this objective from the main agenda for tactical reasons. In other countries, there is still a feeling that the party's principles can only be fully realised when such an Islamic state is established. Second, all parties have tried to capitalise on the deteriorating economic conditions, albeit with very limited success, to delegitimise the Central Asian governments.[53]

Going by the foregoing descriptions, one can definitely say that IRP as a party, though theocratically never believed in violence, had participated in the Tajik civil war violently that caused around 50,000 deaths. The methods that it adapted were all that of established terrorist ones including bomb blasts, kidnappings, hostage takings, armed fighting etc. The sole objective behind all this was the creation of an Islamic *Umma*.

Islamic Movement of Uzbekistan (IMU)

Another organisation which like IRP, took up the cause of organising the people of Islamic faith to work for the creation of an Islamic empire starting from Central Asia is the Islamic Movement of Uzbekistan. The relevance of this organisation herein lies the fact that, in its endeavour to establish the principles of Koran and sharia, it gradually took up arms to establish itself. Although their leadership still denies any such involvement, the Central Asian republics where IMU is still very much active, accuse it of indulging and fomenting terrorism in the region.

The revival of Islamic militancy in Uzbekistan began in Namangan, a small agricultural town in the heart of the Fergana Valley in 1991, a few months before the break-up of the Soviet Union.[54] What started as a relatively peaceful attempt to raise Islamic consciousness in the community had already turned violent by December, when a handful of unemployed young men in Namangan seized the building which housed the headquarters of the Communist Party of Uzbekistan (CPU), after the mayor refused to give them land to build a mosque. That incident set in motion, events whose repercussion still reverberates.[55]

The young men were led by Tahir Yuldeshev, 24 years old, a university drop-out and a local underground *mullah* who was a fine orator. At his side was Jumaboi Ahmadzhanovich Khojaev, 22, who later adopted the name of his hometown and became Juma Namangani and Abdul Ahad, 33, trained in Saudi Arabia, a militant Wahhabi. Yuldeshev began to impose strict Islamic practices in Namangan.[56] Yuldeshev then demanded that President Karimov impose *sharia* in Uzbekistan. Karimov finally agreed to talk to him, but the talk turned into a fiery shouting match when Yuldeshev kept some impossible demands, for example, that Karimov declare Uzbekistan an Islamic state and open more *madrassahs* and mosques. Karimov rejected these demands.[57] Yuldeshev and his men attacked the CPU headquarters and set in motion a movement that they claimed was a *jihad* to remove Karimov from the government of Uzbekistan.

All these leaders were the clandestine members of Uzbekistan's IRP but disillusioned with its refusal to confront the authorities, they founded Adolat (justice) and demanded an Islamic revolution. Young men linked to Adolat set up mosques and *madrassah* across the Fergana Valley, in Andijan, Margilan, Kuva, Fergana city and even Osh in Kyrgyzstan, undercutting the influence of the IRP. What differentiated them from the other militant Islamic groups was their disrespect for official Islam, for Central Asia's liberal Islamic traditions, and for the regime.[58] State authority was undecided on how to deal with this new threat, and for several months (1991-92) Adolat had a free hand to spread its message in the Fergana Valley.

Finally, the government cracked down, banning Adolat in March 1992, and arresting 27 of its members. The leaders fled to different neighbouring countries. From 1996-98, Yuldeshev stayed in Kabul and Peshawar where Afghan and Pakistani Islamic militant groups provided him with funding and recruited young men. During this period he also met the Saudi terrorist Osama bin Laden in Afghanistan and got influenced by the extreme Deobandi and Wahhabi teachings on *jihad.*

After visiting countries like Pakistan, Saudi Arabia, UAE and Turkey, he stayed in Peshawar in Pakistan from 1995-98 and 1998 onwards in Kabul. In Peshawar, his Uzbek activists were trained in the madrassah. The students also included few from Kazakhstan, Kyrgyzstan and Uighurs from China.[59]

Yuldeshev finally settled in Taliban controlled Kabul in 1998, where he set up the Islamic Movement of Uzbekistan (IMU). At home, the situation worsened. Namangani who had fled to Tajikistan to escape the government forces was disillusioned by the willingness of the Tajik Islamists to enter into peace talks with the government, but he maintained contacts with the UTO and continued to run his armed camp at Tavildara in the Garm Valley in Tajikistan. He maintained his forces by being involved in the lucrative and expanding heroin trade between Afghanistan and Tajikistan. But Namangani became now a liability to the UTO, as his presence annoyed Uzbekistan and Russia.[60] Fearing that his forces would be forcibly disbanded, Namangani crossed into Kyrgyzstan in early August 1999. After that he got engaged with the Kyrgyz government in the Batken region where a series of hostage takings, incursions and terrorist activities took place.

In an interview with the Voice of America, Yuldeshev set out the IMU's goals, "the goals of IMU activities are firstly fighting against oppression within our own country, against bribery, against inequalities and also the freeing of our Muslim brothers from prison… who will avenge those Muslims who have died in the prison of the regime? Of course, we will. We consider it our obligation to avenge them and nobody can take this right away from us. We do not repent our declarations of *Jihad* against the Uzbek government. God willing, we will carry out this *jihad* to its conclusion".[61]

Yuldeshev pledged to set up an Islamic state: "We declared a *jihad* in order to create a religious system, a religious government. We want to create a *sharia* system, a model of Islam which has remained from The Prophet, not like the Islam in Afghanistan or Iran or Pakistan or Saudi Arabia, these models are nothing like the Islamic model…. before we build an Islamic state we primarily want to get out from under oppression. We are therefore, now shedding blood, and the creation of an Islamic state will be the next problem". Yuldeshev also claimed that "we have a movement of one hundred thousand people. It takes only a spark to burn down a forest, and for that one match is sufficient. We have enough strength to settle the scores with Karimov, and God willing, there are a many more thousands of Mujahideen who share this dream". In the interview Yuldeshev traced the origin of IMU back to the *Basmachis*. Our "roots go back 70-80 years, when our grandfather Mujahideen fought against the communists. We compare ourselves to these ancestors and do not regret that we are continuing their work.... We do not need foreign contacts because our roots are deep and located in our homeland".[62]

On 25 August 1999, the IMU issued an official communiqué declaring *jihad* on the Karimov regime and calling for its overthrow (see appendix). Although the IMU forces never posed a serious military threat to the armies of Central Asia and Russia, their tactics were infinitely superior, and they created terror amongst the Central Asian regimes.

The leadership of the IMU has felt it important to stress their terrorist nature for several reasons. First, given that majority of their members are Islamic militants for hire, espousing an Islamic fundamentalist line keeps the membership relatively complacent. Second, by instilling fear within society in general, the IMU has found it easier to extort money and traffic in illicit narcotics. Third, by deterring public attention from the fact that the primary motivation are criminal in nature, the IMU has won popular support from sections of the Islamic communities within the region who believe that the IMU is fighting to free Muslims from government oppressions.[63]

Though the operation of IMU has been there for quite a long time, the doubt over its effectiveness in its objectives is still in the air. IMU, in the last so many years of its existence, has become a multi-national pan-Islamic force, and although it insists that its only aim is to topple the Karimov government in Uzbekistan, there is little doubt that it also seek an Islamic revolution across Central Asia. Although IMU's ideology i not pure Wahhabi, as Karimov claims, its idea of a universal *jihad* i clearly rooted in Deobandi Wahhabi teachings. However, it remain localised in Fergana and has been unable to overcome the problem o regionalisation that confounds all Islamic movements in Central Asia, nc has it articulated the kind of Islamic state it envisages, which undercuts it appeal to Central Asians, who are unlikely to swap an authoritarian syste they know for one and they know nothing about. The movements' refus to incorporate Uzbekistan's Islamic history and traditions into its militant ideology makes it unlikely that it will gain greater public support beyond the Fergana valley, but its attacks will continue to destabilise the fragile Central Asian regimes. For the most part, the IMU remains an 'outsider' force, and as such it faces competition for the hearts and minds of the people of the region from a much more potent internal force.

IMU is at present a banned organisation by the US Department of State for being a terrorist organisation under its law on 25 September 2000. The Clinton administration referred at that time to armed incursions into Uzbekistan and Kyrgyzstan and taking of hostages including US citizens.[64] In the late November 2001, a report said that the groups' leader, 32-year-old Juma Namangani died from wounds received during US bombing in the Mazar-e-Sharif region of Afghanistan, although accounts varied.[65]

Hizb-ut-Tahrir

Though IMU has been one organisation put under maximum scrutiny in the Central Asian region, another organisation, known as Hizb-ut-Tahrir (Hizb-ut-Tahrir-al-Islami), has become the most popular, widespread underground movement in Uzbekistan, Kyrgyzstan and Tajikistan. The challenge that the Hizb-ut-Tahrir-al-Islami poses to the regimes of these countries can be judged by the fact that there are more HT (Hizb-ut-Tahrir) members in the jails in Central Asia than those of any other movement, including the much better known IMU.[66]

HT has a vision of uniting Central Asia, Xinjiang province in China, and eventually the entire *Umma* (Islamic World community) under a *Khilafat* (Caliphate) that would establish the Khilafat-i-Rashida, which ruled the Arab Muslims for a short time after the Prophet Muhammad's death in 632 AD.[67]

The HT was founded in Saudi Arabia and Jordan in 1953 by diaspora of Palestinians by Sheikh Taquiuddin al-Nabhani Filastyni (the Palestinians). "The point-in hand is not establishing several states, but one single state over the entire Muslim world", he wrote in 1962.[68]

Although the HT believes in *Jihad* as a means to mobilise supporters against non-Muslims it does not advocate a violent overthrow of Muslim regimes as do other extremist groups. HT believes in winning over mass support.

An-Nabhani's concept of the future Islamic state promotes a utopian view of political Islam under which social problems such as corruption and poverty would be banished by the application of the Islamic law and government.

While HT believes in such a society, it strives for a political system in which a caliph elected by an Islamic *shura* (council) would have dictatorial powers in a highly centralised system. The caliph would control the army, the political system, the economy and foreign policy. Sharia (Islamic law) would prevail, Arabic would be the language of the state, and the role of the women would be severely restricted. The Defence Minister, whose title would be the Amir of *Jihad*, would prepare the people for *jihad* against the non-Muslim world. Military conscription and training in preparation for this *jihad* would be mandatory for all Muslim men above 15. Particularly, this is the reason which gives a ground to the local law enforcing organs to declare the HT as a terrorist organisation.[69]

Initially, HT was with Wahhabi but later it separated from them on several issues. As a leader of HT points out "we had a united plan with the Wahhabis but we soon developed differences and split. HT wanted to work with people in each country separately and bring about *sharia* in a peaceful manner, but the Wahhabis were extremists who wanted guerrilla war and the creation of an Islamic army".[70]

HT operates secret, decentralised, five-to-seven-man cells throughout Central Asia, making it extremely difficult for the authorities to penetrate the organisation. The cells called *diara* (circle) are study groups dedicated to the spread of Islam and the HT message.[71] According to the statements of the arrested activists and members, the supporters' strength of HT is now something between fifty to sixty thousand.

Like the Wahhabi, the HT is virulently opposed to Jews and Israel and a lot of HT literature portrays Karimov as a Jew. HT believes that the Jews should leave Central Asia because they do not belong to Central Asia.[72] Also like the Wahhabis, the HT is also anti-Shia even violently it is. The group would expel all Shia Muslim from Central Asia and if it came to power, a stance that would clearly alienate the Shia communities in southern Uzbekistan and eastern Tajikistan. The HT has imparted its beliefs from the Arab world and the debates and the conflicts within the Islamic radical camps there.

Most members of the HT came from the ranks of the young and unemployed given the lack of opportunity, many youths appear attracted to HT because of motivations as simple as boredom and dissatisfaction with their lot in life.[73]

From its cells in Fergana Valley, the HT movement spread rapidly into adjacent areas of Kyrgyzstan and Tajikistan. The appeal of the HT in Kyrgyzstan appears to be growing because of the country's increasing poverty and public criticism that the government is incapable of solving the people's problems- and too corrupt to try.

The HT is also gaining popularity slowly in Kazakhstan where Islamic radicalism has so far not penetrated. In 2001, for the first time, Kazakh police reported the arrest of HT activists in the south of the country. On 6 July 2000, HT leaflets appeared in thousands of mailboxes in Kazakhstan's largest city, Almaty, shocking the security forces and the local population.

The HT is becoming extremely popular in northern Tajikistan, despite the war weariness of the people. In 2000, more than a hundred alleged HT members were arrested in Tajikistan and put on trial.[74]

Though HT leaders deny that they have any formal links with other radical movements like Taliban, Al-Qaeda, or IMU, several hundred HT activists escaped to northern Afghanistan, where they were welcomed by the IMU. The HT leaders lived in IMU camps and received military training from the guerrillas. A Kyrgyz official reported that during the IMU offensive in the summer of 2000, they discovered HT literature on the dead bodies of several IMU militants.[75] Clearly, there are strong links and cooperation between the rank and file of both groups especially when the members come from the same village or town.

Ali, the HT leader who was interviewed by Ahmed Rashid, a Central Asian expert, admitted that HT supported the Taliban movement in Afghanistan and many HT members fled to safety in Afghanistan to escape the crackdown in Central Asia. He also admitted that though HT does not have any relationship with Osama bin Laden, its members are full of admiration for him.[76]

Diplomats in Uzbekistan and Kyrgyzstan strongly dispute these denials, claiming that all the Islamic groups are working closely together. They cite a meeting in Kabul in September 2000 where the Taliban, IMU and the HT, Chechen separatists and bin Laden held lengthy talks about future cooperation.

There still exists a great deal of debate over the nature and type of HT. Some opine that it is a radical religious organisation with terrorist leanings and linkages.[77] There are others who say it is not a political but a social organisation based on religious principles,[78] and there are also opinions which accuse it as it a radical terrorist organisation. Going by the methods adopted by HT to propagate its ideas it seems that the organisation has only adopted methods like pamphleteering, postering, organising discussions and personal contacts etc. modes to spread itself and its beliefs. Therefore, while method wise, it does not seem to be a terrorist organisation, it has definitely contributed to the radicalisation of Islam in the region thereby prompting the latent groups to carry on their agenda in a destructive manner.

Apart from these three main organisations which have been either involved directly in the ongoing militancy and terrorism in the region there are few other small organisations which have again either directly participated in terrorism or have contributed to it indirectly. Some of them are Islam Laskarlary which is a radical Islamic group in Fergana valley, Nahzar-i-Islami, Tauba, Hizb-i-Islami and Hizb-al-Nusra (a splinter group of HT).

The Taliban

Strictly speaking, Taliban never participated in any of the terrorist activity in Central Asia directly. But being a fundamentalist, radical organisation with aims much similar to those of the organisations functioning in Central Asia with terrorist tactics, Taliban during its rule in Afghanistan played the role of a co-operator and host to them. Therefore, it is quite essential to know the role played by Taliban in patronising and fomenting militancy and terrorism in the Central Asian region.

The world first became aware of the Taliban in 1994 when they were appointed by Islamabad to protect a convoy trying to open up a trade route between Pakistan and Central Asia.[79]

The predominantly pushtun Taliban emerged in late 1994 as a messiahnic movement made up of *Taliban* (literally, students), from Islamic *madrassahs* (seminaries) who were living as refugees in Pakistan. They vowed to bring peace to Afghanistan, establish law and order, disarm the population and impose shariah (Islamic law). The group which accompanied the convoy proved effective bodyguards driving off other Mujahideen groups who attacked and looted the convoy. They went on to take the nearby city of Kandahar, beginning a remarkable advance, which led to their capture of the capital, Kabul, in September 1996. Welcomed by war-weary Pushtuns, the Taliban were at first remarkably successful and popular. After the capture of Kabul in 1996 they did not show any desire to rule the country.[80]

But abetted by their Pakistani and Saudi backers and inspired by ideological mentors such as Osama bin Laden, the Taliban committed themselves to conquering the entire country and more.

In 1998, the Taliban overran much of the northern Afghanistan and later almost 90 percent of Afghanistan. Only three nations, Pakistan, Saudi Arabia and UAE recognised Taliban and their leader Mullah Mohammed Omar, as the legitimate government of Afghanistan. US, EU, and UN imposed sanctions on Taliban, mostly as a pressure tactic to have Osama bin Laden, the accused Saudi terrorist.

The *Taliban* claimed that their aim was to set up the world's most pure Islamic state, banning frivolities like television, music, cinema, forbidding women to work and receive education, and forcing to cover themselves from head to toe.[81]

Being situated on the border of Afghanistan, the five Central Asian republics were most affected by the growth of Taliban movement in Afghanistan. During the Afghan civil war, the newly independent Central Asian republics supported their ethnic kin in northern Afghanistan, who provided a buffer against the spread of Pushtun fundamentalism. But with the Taliban occupation of Afghanistan, that buffer vanished away and the Central Asian states started facing a strong wave of Islamic insurgency supported by Taliban.

The IMU militants after undergoing training in the Taliban camps, penetrated into the south of Uzbekistan, across Tajikistan and some of the groups even reached Tashkent.[82] Afghanistan which came under Taliban control was also inhabited by a large number of ethnic Uzbeks. This worked as a factor to improve the ability of the IMU, which largely depended on their logistical support, to recruit new members. The territorial gains also minimised the distance between the IMU sources of support in Afghanistan and their areas of military operation in Central Asia.[83]

The other way in which Taliban promoted militant activities in Central Asia was by providing sanctuaries to dissident movements in countries around Afghanistan which had been under Islamic influence in the past. In this respect, Central Asian region was quite vulnerable to the Taliban influence in its Islamic orientation. In 1999, Tahir Yuldeshev, the leader of the Islamic Movement of Uzbekistan fled to Afghanistan. Yuldeshev is allegedly one of the masterminds behind the assassination attempt against Uzbek President Islam Karimov. In May 1999, the Taliban allowed Yuldeshev to set up a military training camp in northern Afghanistan, just a few miles from the border. Sources point out that he trained several hundred Islamist militants from Uzbekistan, Tajikistan, and Kyrgyzstan as well as Uighurs from Xinjiang province in China.[84]

Though the Taliban officials then denied helping the IMU, in June 1999, the Taliban rejected a request to extradite Yuldeshev to Uzbekistan. Instead in August of the same year, Namangani entered southern Kyrgyzstan with 800 militants. Apart from this, Taliban also provided men and money for the militant movements that were going on in Central Asia till October 2001. Reports say that IMU was largely financed by Osama bin Laden and his host Taliban in Afghanistan.[85]

It has been stated earlier that in September 2000 the Islamic militant leaders of various groups gathered in Kabul under the patronage of Taliban to discuss the future coordination among them in carrying out their activities. Taliban organised the meeting, and according to reports of the Uzbek intelligence, promised to help the militant organisations in its struggle materially and financially.[86]

Thus, from the above illustrations it can be assumed that Taliban though never played any role directly in the Central Asia militancy, it nevertheless helped, cooperated and patronised such activities. In spite of the methodological differences all the organisations, including Taliban, shared a common objective, i.e., the establishment of pure Islamic states on the basis of the Koran and *sharia.*

In the foregoing descriptions it is evident that after 1991 several groups large and small cropped up in the region and almost all, including Taliban resorted to militancy as a method of operation to achieve their objective i.e. establishment of an Islamic state. There are several factors responsible for these organisations to opt for this means. The most important of them is the growth of Islamic fundamentalism in the region especially after the disintegration of the Soviet Union.

After the *Basmachi* revolt, till the collapse of the Soviet Union i.e. end of cold war, as discussed earlier, the ruling dispensation of the USSR had faced challenges from religious, political, ethnic and nationalist groups in many forms but most of them went either unnoticed or unpublished. Very often these groups resorted to terrorist methods to make their point public. But especially after the collapse of the Soviet Union, such incidents have become frequent and most of them reported in different media. The most disturbed region from this point of view is the Central Asian region comprising of Kazakhstan, Kyrgyzstan, Tajikistan, Turkmenistan and Uzbekistan. Due to its geo-strategic importance, ethnic composition, religious diversity and economic backwardness, it has been the worst affected region of terrorism and militancy largely fuelled by religious fundamentalism.

Islamic Revivalism, Fundamentalism and Militancy in the Region

The year 1991 marked the beginning of a new chapter in the history of the Central Asian republics when the dream of national independence was quickly transformed into a political reality. Interestingly enough, the Central Asian population as a whole played a marginal or at best, an indirect role in the realisation of that dream. Rather, it was the breakdown of the Soviet central authority that provided an almost effortless opportunity for independence. Unfortunately, the rapidity with which the independence was brought to bear left these republics ill prepared to fill the ideological void created by the collapse of Marxism, leading to the proliferation of a variety of ideological trends, the roots of which were inadvertently nurtured by Gorbachev's policy of glasnost. Of these, only the Islamic trends seem to have attracted considerable attention. These are, of course, a ground for concern especially when one considers the radical manifestation of Islam in the twentieth century and their practical implications, which have, among other things, given rise to the Islamic Republic of Iran and other forms of Islamic extremism elsewhere in the world. It is the availability of such Islamic doctrines to the Central Asian republics that has contributed to the over all uncertainty with regard to the future political development of these newly emerging states.[87] With initial euphoria that the Islamic revival in the Central Asian republics would be more of cultural and peaceful nature fading away, analysts now feel that the situation in Central Asia has transformed and Islamic radicalism has gained a toehold there. The Tashkent bombing in February 1999 followed by incursions into Kyrgyzstan in 1999 and 2000 and into Uzbekistan in 2000 indicates this transformation.[88]

Another aspect of the ongoing Islamisation is that Islam as a form of cultural, social, political and national identity acquired new scope. A phenomenal increase in the observance of Islamic rites, religious marriages, performance of daily prayers and attendance at mosques in society was noticed more mosques and *madrassah* began to open, more personnel entered into theological training institutes, leading figures got elected into parliamentary bodies and made appearance in the media key religious feasts were turned into public holidays (except Kazakhstan).[89]

Surveys conducted in Central Asia showed increased level of religiosity among Muslims, especially among younger generation and intellectuals.[90] An equally significant dimension of the ongoing Islamisation is that it has not been a monolithic phenomenon with uniform inter-republican socio-political manifestations. Quite to the contrary, proclivity towards Islam varies considerably from republic to republic, with Kazakhstan and Kyrgyzstan having the weakest and Tajikistan and Uzbekistan having the strongest tendencies. Sizeable variations also exist at the intra-republican level.[91]

It is worth mentioning that the degree of involvement in the Islamic faith at the civilisational level varies from place to place, depending on their socio-economic background and the period in which they were converted.[92] Much disparity exists between one state and another. Within a state, disparity in faith prevails between the settled and the formally nomadic people. For example, Uzbekistan has the strongest religious traditions with the Bukhara region having played a vital role in the development of Islamic theology and Sufi mysticism, than Kazakhstan and Kyrgyzstan where Islam has traditionally played a less dominant role.[93] Further, people in the Fergana valley are more Islamic in belief than in the northern and eastern parts near Issyk Kul area in the same state of Kyrgyzstan.

Secondly, at political level, the secular elite of Central Asia were faced with a dilemma. In order to retain Islam as an important component of the Central Asian identity, they showed great deference to Islam (For example, President Islam Karimov of Uzbekistan performed the *haj* and took his oath of office with his hand on Koran. In his speech also he identified Islam as an integral part of Uzbek culture).[94] At the same time, it was made clear that religious institutions could neither aspire to play overt political role nor escape their duty to support state institutions.[95]

Nonetheless, wary of the potency of the religion, the leaders of Central Asia took steps to ensure control over religious institutions and to prevent the politicisation of Islam. Each state has passed laws prohibiting political parties that are based upon religion and each has maintained some degree of state control over religion.[96]

The concerns of the leadership also show that Islam has regained its importance in Central Asia, though popular knowledge of the religion of Islam was minimal and the information on political activism, ideas and debates in the Islamic world beyond Central Asia was almost non-existent.

Since 1989, a 'popular Islam' under the aegis of parallel mullahs re-emerged in Central Asia. The vast majority of the Central Asians are Sunni Muslims of the Hanafi'i school (or *mazhas*), one of the four main branches of Sunni Islam.[97] but as discussed in the previous chapter Russian colonisation in the nineteenth century was driven primarily by geo-political, not religious concerns, and as a result, Russian colonial administrators, who already had centuries of experience accommodating Muslim peoples in the empire, were for the most part willing to allow local people to practice Islam in peace. The Soviets in contrasts launched a full scale assault on the Islamic institutions and practices in the mid-1920s, a campaign that intensified dramatically during Stalin's "revolution from above and the purges of late 1920s and 1930s. The great majority of Mosques were destroyed as a result and most members of the Islamic clergy were imprisoned or shot".[98] The forced collectivisation of both nomads and peasants led to large-scale persecutions and the flight of Muslim population to China and Afghanistan. In 1917, there were some 20,000 mosques in Central Asia but by 1929 fewer than 4000 were working, and by 1935, there were only 60 registered mosques in Uzbekistan.[99]

With the launching of Gorbachev's reforms, the region began to witness an "Islamic revival". The number of Central Asians making the *haj* to Mecca increased dramatically and many new mosques were built, much of it with funding from Islamic governments, charitable organisations and wealthy individuals abroad. Islamic literature and Korans were brought in from Saudi Arabia and Pakistan and itinerant mullahs became overnight leaders. This religious resurgence revealed the depth of the roots of Islam, which had flourished underground in defiance of the repressive Soviet state.[100]

The Islamic revival in Central Asia follows closely the general pattern of Islamic proclivity that existed prior to the communist take over, with Uzbekistan and Tajikistan leading the process. Unfortunately, there is no comprehensive data to present a complete quantifiable picture of Islamic revival in the region. The following is thus an attempt to piece together the available information in order to provide an understanding of the scope of the ongoing revival.

As of 1994, an estimated 7,800 mosques and prayer houses have been opened in Central Asia, of which nearly half are located in Uzbekistan.[101] An overwhelming number of these mosques are located in Fergana and Kara Kalpak regions. Between 1989 and 1991, the Uzbek government returned a number of religious sites to the believers, including the Abu Isha al Termezi Mausoleum in the republic's south, the Kalon mosque, the Ata Walikhai mosque in Namangan, the Imam al Bukhari mausoleum in Bukhara, and the Jami mosque in Kokand. In Tajikistan, 126 mosques and 2,870 prayer houses were established in the 1991-92 period.[102] According to the Kazi of Kyrgyzstan, Kimshanbay Ben Abdurahaman, 1000 mosques have been operating in the republic, more than 60 percent of which are located in the Osh and Jalalabad *oblasts*.[103] In Kazakhstan, 300 mosques had been officially registered by the Kazakh Religious Board, and as many as 200 were under construction in 1993.[104] An estimated 80 mosques have been reopened in Turkmenistan, of which 20 are located in the capital city, Ashgabat. In 1994, the government reported that the construction of 180 mosques had been completed and that another 100 mosques were under construction.[105]

In conjunction with the opening of mosques, Islamic education has been gaining popularity among young Muslims who wish to make a career in religion. An estimated 380 *madrassahs* have been operating in Uzbekistan since independence. The number of students enrolled in Barak Khan and Mir Arab, the two major *madrassahs*, has nearly tripled. In addition, other religious schools have been reopened, including the Kukuldash *madrassahs* which has started functioning since 1991. The enrolment in Al-Bukhari Higher Islamic Institute has doubled since independence. It is reported that as many as 5000 students have been receiving Islamic education in various mosques. In 1990, the second largest Islamic institute for higher education was opened in Dushanbe. One source says that around 1700 students are receiving Islamic training by the mid 1990s.[106]

In addition to these scholars, several students have been despatched to various Middle Eastern countries to receive Islamic training. For instance, Kazakhstan has sent 100 students to Turkey, 40 to Egypt, and 40 to Pakistan. There are also 96 Kyrgyz students in Turkey and 26 students in Egypt. Turkmenistan has also sent some 200 students to Turkey to receive religious training in 1992.[107]

The Central Asian Islamic school curriculum cover courses in Arabic, *shariah* law, Fiqh, Islamic history and civilisation, and Islamic culture. The most comprehensive training is given in Uzbek schools, were Arabic language and literature have been extensively taught. Besides Uzbekistan, shortages in Arabic instructors have been a serious problem in providing an in-depth Islamic education. In Kazakhstan, the mufti has recently translated the Koran into Kazakh, but most Central Asian clerics agree that the meaning of Islamic precepts can only be fully understood in Arabic.

Despite the availability of these institutions, the educational process has been severely hampered by an apparent lack of Islamic literature. In 1990, Saudi Arabia donated 10,00,000 copies of Koran to the religious Board of Uzbekistan for distribution. Egypt, Turkey, Pakistan and Kuwait have also contributed literature, but the quantity of illegal literature that has been smuggled into Central Asia by fundamentalist organisations, which clearly underscores the need to overcome this deficiency if the impact of such radical literature is to be counteracted. The problem is especially serious in Tajikistan and Uzbekistan's Fergana Valley.[108]

The observance of the Islamic rituals has also been steadily on the rise, and on the whole it has followed the general, regional and republican patterns of proclivity discussed earlier. It is interesting that of all Islamic practices, the most widely observed are the rituals of circumcision, marriage, and burial which are in essence, the most marginal aspects of Islamic conduct. Circumcision is practised in almost all Muslim family in Central Asia. A study conducted in 1987 shows that *Kalym* (the bride price) was reported to be widely observed in the region.[109] The Muslim burial practices have also been practised widely. The practice of placing the dead body in a traditional *yurt* for several days in a city street is no longer an unusual sight. Attendance at Muslim burial sites has shown a significant rise in recent years.

Participation in Friday prayers, one of the most significant acts of faith, has been on the rise in Uzbekistan and Tajikistan.[110] Fasting during the month of Ramadan has made a significant comeback especially in Uzbekistan. The Uzbek President issued a decree whereby working Muslims were permitted to miss work on the first day of Ramadan. Most rural Uzbeks and Tajiks fast for the entire month.

Muslim pilgrimage from Central Asia to Mecca has increased steadily since 1990. In 1992, 40 pilgrims made the trip to Mecca from Kazakhstan and in 1993, 300 were sent directly to Saudi Arabia. The Kyrgyz religious authorities in 1993 sent around 1000 pilgrims.[111] The largest group of pilgrims from Central Asia belongs to Uzbekistan. In 1990, 500, in 1991, 1250, in 1993, 3500 pilgrims paid a visit to Mecca.[112]

Other manifestations of the religious zeal and fervour like women using *burqa*, men using white cap and growing beards have also been on rise in all over Central Asia in spite of the possible crackdown by the government authorities. In Fergana valley, this trend is remarkably high.

Although the various manifestations of the religious fervour discussed above show the degree and the extent to which Islam has percolated into the life of the people of this region, the observance of Islamic rituals and other manifestations can be just termed as 'peripheral', with limited contribution to the growth of religious fundamentalism. However, the *madrassahs* and mosques really became a cause of concern especially after the emergence of Taliban in Afghanistan who also were products of madrassahs in Pakistan. The basic spirit behind this kind of education is to create a section of people who would be conservative, radical and work for the spread and consolidation of Islamic values and practices and creation of an Islamic state.

Our discussions and analysis show that there was an upsurge in the religious sentiments of the Islamic people of Central Asia. This fact has been corroborated by several other prominent figures from the ruling dispensation also. One such personality is Islam Karimov, the much discussed President of Uzbekistan. He in his book *Uzbekistan on the Threshold of the 21st Century; Threats to Security and Stability* wrote, "In periods of stagnation, crisis and splits in the society, the populism of the outside Wahhabism demand strict observance of the Islamic ethics, rejection of luxury and greediness. Regretfully, such slogans received support and spread in separate areas of Central Asia recently and now a days. Uzbekistan and other Central Asian states constitute an integral part of the very complicated and multi dimensional Islamic world. It is a well known fact that in the world there exist many formal and informal movements which use Islam for their political purposes, some of them either recognise the exclusiveness of Islam or demonstrate intolerance towards all other regions, and use Islam as a platform to defend narrow-minded national interests. Intentions to involve the newly independent states of Central Asia into their political supporters and allies, to exercise their influence upon them are typical attempts for their ideological purposes, which are shaped and manifested in their definite action."[113]

Karimov further elaborates in his book, the Islamic fundamentalism manifested towards Uzbekistan. He writes, "first, in the attempt to disseminate fundamentalism to undermine the confidence of the faithful Muslims to the state reformer, to destroy stability, national civil and inter-ethnic harmony that are fundamental pre-conditions of the transformation for the better changes, Islamists target to discredit democracy, the secular state, the multi-national and multi-confessional society".

"Second, we must have a clear cut idea, particularly our youth, the younger generation, that those who follow populist attractive but entirely noisy and ungrounded slogans of the fundamentalists about justice turn out to be the hostages of the other's will, that in the end, command not only their brains, but also their fate and destiny."

"Third, in provoking confrontation among social groups an regions of population that is based on 'true' and 'false' principles of religiousness. This sort of activities led to the split of the nation in Algeria, Afghanistan."

"Fourth, the situation of the never ending civil war on the southern borders of Uzbekistan, in neighbouring countries reproduces new generations of terrorists, armed militants who consider themselves to be true Muslims, fighters for faith, and those who are eager to impose their monstrous ideas on our people."

"Fifth, in creating a repulsive image of Uzbekistan among both Muslim and non-Muslim states and their public opinion to which they want to present us either as anti-religious atheists or as the hidden supporters of the state Islamisation."

"Sixth, in shaping a global confrontation between the Islamic and non-Islamic civilisations that has the most negative impact on the integration process within the world community that preserves the backwardness of the newly independent states. And what is worse, people's expectation of the 'civilisation clashes' is based on the religious principles."

"Seventh, in exerting influences on the mass mind, the concept of religion being a universal means to solve all economic political and international problems and contradictions, reflecting upon the Islamic fundamentalism threat, we are constantly compelled to look through its internal Islamic causes, but to the factors that provoke and stimulate it. These factors are well known colonialism and neo-colonialism, great power chauvinism and anti-Muslim dictate in international relationships, the 'divide and rule' policy".[114]

In 1992, the then foreign minister of Uzbekistan Ubaidullah Aburazakov, while signing documents on establishing diplomatic relations between Iran and Uzbekistan, had warned the Iranian diplomats in Uzbekistan not to advocate any Iranian type of religious fundamentalism locally, signifying that even as early as 1992, fundamentalist tendencies had developed in Uzbekistan.[115] In the same year, in a press conference, President Islam Karimov was more straight forward. He said that, the danger of Islamic fundamentalism was existing in the country without any doubt.[116]

During his visit to India in 1995, Imamali Rahmanov, the President of Tajikistan, said that Islamic fundamentalism was one of the main factors responsible for some of the problems being faced by the democratically run Central Asian republics formed after the break up of the erstwhile Soviet Union.[117]

Muslim clerics in the southern Kyrgyz region of Osh, bordering Tajikistan, also expressed similar views in November 1995 when they said in a statement that "propagators of Islamic fundamentalism are not only going to the people with their sermons, but are also opening their own schools, in the south of the republic".[118]

One Kazakh English newspaper *Ekspress-K* on 3 March 2000, reported that the south of Kazakhstan was being affected by Islamic fundamentalism and that many of the missionaries visiting the region are propagating "radical Islamic ideas". The paper said the students who studied in the private religious schools condemned secular society and the official clergy and cherish the idea of establishing an Islamic state. The newspaper also added that Kazakhstan with its ideological vacuum, unemployment and falling living standards was "still perfect testing grounds for Islamic missionaries to kick start the extremist mood".[119]

On 12 September 2000, the foreign minister of Kazakhstan said in his speech at the 55th session of the UN General Assembly in New York, "our young state has to face the challenges like international terrorism, extremism, illegal arms trade, drugs and organised crime, in the prime of its independence. We are seriously worried by the situation in Central Asia and regard the Afghan conflict, the intrusion of guerrilla units into Uzbekistan and Kyrgyzstan as well as the situation in Chechnya as the links in one chain".[120]

From the above analysis, the fact gets established that fundamentalism had gained ground in Central Asia almost immediately after the independence of the five republics. The manifestations, religious in nature, which occurred in the post-1991 period, were neither blank enthusiasm nor mere expression of the long subdued sentiments. They were carefully planned, properly executed, immensely abetted and were logically impregnated. The fundamentalist spirit with due religious sanction in an extremist radical form expressed itself in militants' terrorist methods.

Though, religious fundamentalism is the principal driving force behind the ongoing terrorism in the Central Asia region, it is being accelerated and pushed forward by several other factors such as the poor economic development and the huge narcotics trade along with proliferation and trading of small arms in the region, and the role that is being played by the external actors.

The Economic Factors

After the collapse of the command economic structure in 1991, along with the collapse of the Soviet Union, the economies of the Central Asian economies were in complete disarray, resulting in growth of poverty and unemployment, the two very basic prerequisites for the proliferation of social tension in the form of terrorism, fundamentalism and militancy. A careful analysis of the economic indexes would substantiate the above arguments.

The collapse of the Soviet Union deprived the Central Asian region of huge central subsidies as well as a captive market for their products. Though some of the Central Asian republics are endowed with rich gas and oil reserves, they neither possess the technology nor capital to extract and process these resources. Therefore, all the countries of the region are facing the sharp deterioration in growth performances. During 1992-96, real GDP declined on an average by 37 per cent cumulatively (though it varied from 16 per cent in the case of Uzbekistan to 60 per cent in Tajikistan).[121]

However, positive growth trends have been visible since then, though they are still not out of the red and some of them have incurred heavy foreign debts and some like Kazakhstan and Kyrgyzstan were particularly badly hit by August 1998 financial crisis in Russia and other neighbouring

CIS countries. The total external debt of the Central Asian states between 1992-98 increased nearly seven fold, reaching 10.5 billion US dollars by the end of 1998. This too has from a non-existent basis at the time of their independence since Russia undertook the foreign trade liability of the former USSR. The debt to GDP ratio has grown from 0.67 per cent in 1992 to more than 54 per cent by 1997 in Kyrgyzstan from 74.47 per cent to 109 per cent in Tajikistan from nil to 63.9 per cent in Turkmenistan. Only Kazakhstan brought it down form 43.27 per cent to 20.6 per cent. In the case of Uzbekistan, though it increased from 3.1 per cent to 17.6 per cent it is within reasonable limits.[122] (See Table 3 for additional information)

Table 3
Basic Macroeconomic Indicators (1999)

	GDP Growth	*Inflation*	*Fiscal Balance*	*Current Account Balance*	*Foreign Direct Investment*	*Exchange Rate*
	(%)	(%)	(% of GDP)	(% of GDP)	(Million US $)	(Na.cur/$)
Kazakhstan	2.7	17.8	-5.4	-1.0	1587	109.6
Kyrgyzstan	3.7	35.9	-13.0	-14.8	35	39.0
Tajikistan	3.7	30.1	-3.1	6.2	29	1,237.2
Turkmenistan	14.9	19.5	-1.8	-17.3	80	*5,200
Uzbekistan	4.1	-0.02	29.0	–	-2.6	–

Note: (*) Official exchange rate.
Source: http://www.ecosecretariat.org/

Inflation is still high though it has been brought down from dramatically high levels in 1992 (two digit levels by 1997 form four digit levels in 1992). For example, Kazakhstan whose inflation rate was 29.62 per cent at the end of 1992 had brought it down to 11.3 per cent by the end of 1977. While the economies of the countries of the region have more or less stabilised after near total disruption in the beginning of 1990s, the social sector affected by economic factors is still in a very bad shape. Unemployment, both official and disguised, is at a high level. Real wages plummeted and barring Uzbekistan, where it was more in 1997 compared to the beginning of 1993, and Kyrgyzstan, where it was roughly same, other states registered significant drops and in Tajikistan it was 95 per cent less.[123] The fall in the employment and real wage, combined with declining spending in social sector and removal of subsidies have brought down the general living standard of the masses.[124]

Poverty manifests in a variety of ways that includes the lack of resources necessary to provide for a normal life, and to avoid hunger and malnutrition, weak health, limited access to education and other basic services. Poor are not those who are retired and unemployed but even those who subsist in lower wage conditions. Households try to deal with economic stress by borrowing and reducing consumption to depleting household assets through distress selling and sometimes, attempting to diversify into alternative sources of income generation by using kinship and other social networks. The social networking has become crucial to daily survival.[125]

Further, the privatisation of Central Asia has not produced the expected results, as successful enterprises have been transferred to narrow, powerful elite. Growing disparities of income and wealth have introduced a series of social tensions as the gap between average monthly wages and the minimum living wages continues to widen. Supporting this opinion, Geoffery J. Jukes, Kirill Nourzhanov and Mikhil Alexander have opined, "Poverty, like wealth, is seldom shared out equally between or within ethnic groups, but inequality of poverty is for harder to bear than inequality of wealth, and because Central Asia, like the rest of the FSU, had become accustomed over several decades to a modest but gradually improving or at worst stable standard of living backed by non-cash benefits in the shape of comprehensive health, education and welfare services, the decline which began in Perestroika period and accelerated after independence, has accentuated inter-ethnic and inter-regional tensions".[126]

While all kinds of state subsidies have been withdrawn, the old pattern of command and centrally planned economy is continuing for all practical purposes. The impact of this is acute in the rural areas where the condition is miserable. The collectives there are required to grow crops (cotton and wheat) which they must sell to the government at well below market price. Even these market prices may be paid late and in kind. As a result, in many rural areas, the population has very serious problems maintaining basic sustenance.[127]

Scarce jobs and lands, lack of opportunities and firm social framework coupled with extreme economic difficulties have left the people susceptible to radical influences. When the incursions occurred over the past years, the insurgents found support among the local population of the region.[128]

Individual Freedom and State Repression

Another factor which has greatly contributed to the growth of terrorism in the region is the policies of the governments of the various republics towards the political opposition and against practising Muslims not affiliated with officially recognised Islamic organisations. Though we will be dealing in detail on the various policies of the governments to curb the growth of religious fundamentalism and terrorism, here, the relevance lies in the effects of the policies, which rather than being helpful in curbing the menace, have contributed substantially to its growth and spread due to the reaction they generate among the suffering masses.

The government's treatment of those, whom it identifies as enemies of the state on the basis of their affiliation with un-official Islamic organisations, is so severe that it is polarising a segment of the population in hard opposition to the state. In Uzbekistan and Central Asia as a whole, the general public is politically quite passive and inclined to accept established political authority and to support the status quo. However, since the government of Uzbekistan has resorted to putting pressure on entire families of its perceived opponents, it has succeeded in turning many against the state. When siblings or parents are detained or harassed for the alleged ideological crimes of their family members, the strength of extended family relationships and close knit quality of the communities results in an ever widening circle of individuals identifying themselves against the state. It is not always clear on what basis individuals are targeted for persecution for ideological crimes, but it appears likely that local law enforcement officials are given quotas or plans to fill and rewards for bringing in more people. Consequently, the polarisation process now affects a segment of the population.[129] Yuldeshev's mother, Karamat Asqarova, was forced to denounce her son in 1999, "May Tahir be swallowed up by the earth, may he and his accomplices rot in their graves. I blush before our President and all the people. May this rebellious Tahir, who made me feel like this, die", she proclaimed in a public meeting.[130] Namangani's sister Makhbuba Akhmedov and his brother Nasyr Khojaev also publicly disowned Namangani after constant harassment from the police. Later in March 2000, they travelled to Travildara to urge their brother to lay down his arms. "we went to tell him face to face about the suffering he was causing to his family", explained Akhmadov.[131] Nevertheless, on their return to Tashkent, both were arrested, and in June, Khojaev was sentenced to fourteen years in jail. Although Namangani's sister is no longer in jail, the police regularly called her in for questioning. In August, Namangani's mother was summoned to a public meeting at a school auditorium in Namangan, where her neighbours denounced her, and relatives of the soldiers killed fighting the IMU blackened her face with paint and condemned her for bringing Juma into this world. She broke down, tearfully apologized and cursed her son.[132] The government appeared to have no compunction about targeting innocent relatives of known IMU militants or any one with radical Islamic connection. Karimov urged the young men not to let themselves to be brainwashed by the fundamentalists, warning, "trying to escape the subordination to authority may result in a personal tragedy".[133]

Apart from such cases, the crackdowns on the general support to these fundamentalist groups have been severe. Anyone who exhibits any sign of devotion to radical Islam is the object of official suspicion. This applies especially to those who attend mosques that are not integrated into the government's Islamic administration, though association with the latter is increasingly a serious liability. Private mosques - in an increasing number associated with a particular kind of Islamic orientation - have become the targets of official disapproval and designated illegal. Those who were previously associated with the mosque later designated as illegal were particularly at risk. They may be called to account for their earlier association with an *imam*, who has since been arrested. Given that in most parts of Uzbekistan association with a particular mosque reflects more one's place of residence than ideological orientation, to brand those who attended a particular mosque as subversives is in many cases highly arbitrary.[134]

Virtually any young man who regularly attends mosque or who dresses in a manner which the police perceive as symbol of Islamic fundamentalism can recount repeated incidents of having been detained or brought in for questioning about his Islamic activities. Some have been forcibly shaved off their beards which are perceived as demonstrating an anti-government, Islamic orientation. Young women are likewise under pressure not to dress in an Islamic manner. Female students in high schools and universities are forbidden to wear *hijab* (a headscarf that covers the hair and neck). Officials are generally perceived as having the capacity to act in an arbitrary and dominating manner in all spheres of life. However, this campaign against Islam, with sanction from the central governments, has given license for local police to harass the population in a manner considered particularly intrusive and in conflict with moral and traditional values. The effect is an increasingly sharp polarisation of the population against the government.[135]

Vitaliy Ponomarev, the Director of the Information Centre for Human Rights in Central Asia, has underlined that human rights are being violated most of all, in Uzbekistan and Turkmenistan. According to him, there were more than 7,500 political prisoners in Uzbekistan by the middle of 2001. He further added that the increase in the political repression is only contributing to the destabilising of the situations in the region. The total persecution and destruction of the secular opposition in the early 1990s created a vacuum inside Uzbekistan, which has now been filled with Islamic radicals and According to him it is Karimov himself who is primarily to blame for this.[136] Later, in a press conference he was more categorical when he said that the people of Uzbekistan and Tajikistan published have become extremists against their will because they have no other way of defending their freedom.[137]

Similar views were also voiced by an international observer group. In their report, the International Crisis Group argued that, "the IMU did not spring up in Taliban Afghanistan but in Uzbekistan". It also stated "political oppression frequently serves as the final straw that drives many young Uzbeks to turn to underground Islamic groups in the intensively formed and overcrowded Fergana Valley". The abusive behaviour of the regime of Karimov is fuelling armed Islamic extremism, severe economic dislocation and growing tensions with the neighbouring states."[138]

Similar measures are also being increasingly employed in the neighbouring states as well. In its report the International Helsinki Federation for Human Rights (IHF) recently, has said that in Kazakhstan, Kyrgyzstan, and Uzbekistan the governments have focused on security issues and have failed to properly address democratisation, human rights, economic issues and poverty. This failure ironically leads to more support to Islamic movements and their radicalisation in exile. It is feared that the government's much publicised threat of religious extremism may therefore eventually turn into a self-fulfilling prophecy, as repressive actions creates insecurity in the country, contributing to increasing underground opposition, victims of repression, torture and unfair trials and imprisonment.[139] The state human rights organisations also have reported similar incidences. The independent human rights organisations of Uzbekistan have reported that the number of political prisoners in Uzbekistan prisons and colonies stands at 7,600 men, of whom 7,400 are prisoners of conscience convicted for their membership in outlawed religious organisations.[140] In August 2001, hundreds of women relatives of the political prisoners at a rally in Tashkent issued an appeal saying "we inform you that in prisons, and colonies our relatives are being tortured; both physically and mentally" and asked for amnesty for their relatives from the President.[141] The HRSU in its reaction said, "in absence of at least some amnesties or effective political engagement, a new round of rallies and radicalisation of the affected communities may be on the cards. Religious organisations are well placed to exploit the disaffection to the detriment of the security in the country".[142]

The religious policies of the governments of the Central Asian republics are also to a greater extent fanning the radicalism in the region. For example, government's attempt to draw the clergy in its efforts to control Islam, meanwhile, can have the effect of worsening the situation, by developing a rift between the 'loyal' clergy, who are increasingly discredited in the eyes of the population, and the 'popular' clergy, who resist the government's control. Thus, one Imam Alauddin Mansur, a prominent Islamic scholar regularly preaches that the supporters of Hizb-ut-Tahrir are 'even more dangerous than atheists or communists.... they are not Muslims, the members of this party are like virus, and people should distance form them'.[143] Many local Muslims whether or not they are supporters of Hizb-ut-Tahrir, consider Imam Mansur to be following directives of the Mufti of Uzbekistan when he does not allow Hizb-ut-Tahrir members to pray in his mosque. As the government seeks to co-opt a segment of the clergy, it drives the population away from those who might otherwise be identified simply as moderates, and towards those groups strongly opposed to the government.

Another major motivation for the support to the radical opposition is the question of justice. Many who would be otherwise politically passive in Central Asia can be moved to action when they perceive infringement of justice, and this issue dominates the rhetoric of the Islamists. As the government is perceived as corrupt and abusive of its authority, as especially as people are persecuted for moral and religious convictions, the argument grows increasingly compelling that only a change of government will achieve justice.[144]

References

1. A. Vakabov, *Muslims in the USSR*, Moscow, Novosti Press, USSR, 1980, pp. 111-112.
2. F. Rehman, "Evolution of Soviet Policy towards Muslims in Russia: 1917-1965", *Journal of Institute of Muslim Minority Affairs*, Vol. 1, No. 2, 1980, pp. 28-30.
3. *Ibid.*, p. 30.
4. Mutahir Ahmed, *op.cit.*, p. 73.
5. Paul Steeves, "The June 1983 Plenum and the post-Brezhnev Anti-Religious Campaign" *Journal of Church and the State*, Vol. 26, No. 2, Summer 1986, pp. 349-57.
6. Michael Bordeaux, *Gorbachev, Glasnost, and the Gospel*, London, Hodder and Stoughton, 1990, p. 36.
7. Martha Brill Olcott (ed.), *The Soviet Multinational State: Readings and Documents*, New York, M. E. Sharpe Inc., 1990, p. 375.
8. A. Taheri, *Holy Terror: The Inside Story of Islamic Terrorism*, London, Hutchinson, 1987, p. 388.

9. In the eighteenth century, against a background of general stagnation, a puritanical fundamentalist movement erupted in Arabia under Muhammad-ibn 'Abd al- Wahhab (1703-1792)'. The movement called for a return to the purist Islam of the Quran and the Sunnah and its unadulterated monotheism, uncompromised by the popular cults of saints and their shrines. Ibn 'Abd al Wahhab married into the family of the Sa'ud, a chieftain of Najd, who accepted his teaching and brought all Arabia under his ruling ideology. It is today the state religion of Saudi Arabia. The *Encyclopaedia of Religion*, Vol. 7, New York, Macmillan Publishing Company, p. 318.
10. *Ibid.*, p. 389.
11. *Ibid.*, p. 190.
12. *Ibid.*, p. 390.
13. *Ibid.*, p. 391.
14. *Ibid.*, p. 392.
15. Mehrdad *Haghayeghi, op.cit.*, p. 85.
16. Annette Bohr, "Background to Demonstration of Soviet Muslims in Tashkent", *Radio Liberty Research Report*, 4 February 1989.
17. Mehrdad *Haghayeghi, op.cit.*
18. *Ibid.*
19. *Ibid.*
20. *Los Angeles Times*, 6 August 1990.
21. *The Current Digest of the Soviet Press*, Vol. XLIV, No. 26, 1992, p. 29. For details of the incident see, Vitaly Naumkin, "Islam in the State of the Former Soviet Union", *Annals*, Vol. 524, November 1992, p. 140.
22. *Interfax*, Moscow, 5 October 1992, rep. in *SWB/SU*/1506/B/4, 8 October, 1992.
23. *The Current Digest of the Soviet Press*, Vol. XLIV, No. 26, 1992, p. 29.
24. Interview, Zhounisbek K. Soultanmuratov, Press Service Consultant to the President of the Republic of Kazakhstan, 7 June 1993, cited in Mehrdad *Haghayeghi, op.cit.*, p. 86.
25. *Pravda*, Moscow, 25 August 1992, rep. in *SWB/SU*/1470/C2/2, 27 August 1992.
26. Olivier Roy, *The New Central Asia: The Creation of Nations*, London, Tauris, 2000, p. 57.
27. Kamaluddin Abdullaev and Catherine Barnes, *Politics of Compromise: The Tajikistan Peace Process*, London, Conciliation Resources, 2001, p. 99.
28. Due to difference in the translation, the name of the party has been mentioned differently by different authors. While some write it as Islamic Revival Party, some others write it as Islamic Renaissance Party. Though etymologically 'revival' and 'renaissance' carry different connotations, literally they have been treated equal by these authors. As mentioned earlier the original name of the party was *Partiya Islamskovo Vozrozhdeniya*.

29. *Soviet Muslims Brief*, Vol. 6, No. 3, September-October 1990, pp. 4-5. See also, Mavlon Makamov, "Islam and Politics in Tajikistan after 1985", in Hafiz Malik (ed.), *Central Asia*: *Its Strategic Importance and Future Prospects*, New York, St. Martin Press, 1994, p. 201.
30. According to Allen Hetmanek, Mullah Abdullah has been involved in clandestine activities, since early 1983, when he began creating the creation of an Islamic state. By 1986, he publicized his views in this regard, asking his followers to petition the 27th Congress of USSR Communist Party to permit the formation of such a republic. When his request was denied, he called for a *jihad* or holy war, against the authorities, leading to his arrest and a six years jail sentence. He was, however, released in 1989, subsequent to Gorbachev's reorientation of the Soviet religious policies. For more information, see Allen Hetmanek, "Islamic Revolution comes to the Former Soviet Central Asia: The Case of Tajikistan", *Central Asian Survey*, Vol. 12, No. 3, 1993, pp. 370-371
31. Ahmed Rashid, *Jihad, op. cit.*, p. 98.
32. *Central Asia Brief*, No. 3, 1992, pp. 9-10.
33. Mehrdad *Haghayeghi, op. cit.*, p. 87.
34. Ahmed Rashid, *op.cit.*, p. 99.
35. The spokesperson for the Democratic Party of Tajikistan pointed out that a clandestine Islamic Party had been operating in Tajikistan since 1977 with unofficial clergy conducting underground training of the young. Ahmad Rashid, "Tajikistan: State of Anarchy", *Karachi Herald*, November, 1992, p. 68.
36. Bess Brown, "The Islamic Renaissance Party in Central Asia", *Radio Liberty Research Report*, 26 April 1991, p. 13.
37. Mavlon Makhamov, "Islam and the Political Development after 1985", in Hafeez Malik (ed.), *Asia: Its Strategic Importance and Future Prospects*, New York, St. Martin Press, 1994, p. 202; But Ahmed Rashid in his book "*Jihad: The Rise of Militant Islam in Central Asia*", mentions the name as Muhammad Sharif Himmatzada.
38. Shahrbanou Tadjbakhsh, "The Tajik Spring of 1992", *Central Asia Monitor*, No. 2, 1993, p. 25.
39. *Ibid.*
40. *Ibid.*
41. S. Olimova, "Islam and the Tajik Conflict", in Roald Sagdeev and Susan Eisenhower (eds.), *op.cit.*, p. 33.
42. *Radio Liberty Daily Report*, 23 November 1990; *The Economist*, 19 December 1992.
43. Mauriel Atkin, "Islami Assertiveness and the Waning of the Old Soviet Order", *The Nationalism Papers*, Vol. 20, No. 1, Spring, 1992, p. 64.
44. In the eighteenth century, against a background of general stagnation, a puritanical fundamentalist movement erupted in Arabia under Muhammad-ibn 'Abd al- Wahhab (1703-1792)'. The movement called for a return to the purist Islam of the Quran and the *Sunnah* and its

unadulterated monotheism, uncompromised by the popular cults of saints and their shrines. Ibn 'Abd al Wahhab married into the family of the Sa'ud, a chieftain of Najd, who accepted his teaching and brought all Arabian under his ruling ideology. It is today the state religion of Saudi Arabia.

45. Allen Hetmanek, "The Political Face of Islam in Tajikistan", *Central Asian Survey*, Vol. 9, No. 3, 1990, p. 106.
46. Ahmed Rashid, *op. cit.*, p. 99.
47. *Ibid.*, p. 100.
48. *Ibid.*
49. Saadat Oliman and Muzaffar Olimov, *Islamic Renaissance Party, Accord and Conciliation Resources*, October 2000, p. 37.
50. For a complete list of the items on the platform see, Abdujabar Abduvkhitov, "Islamic Revivalism in Uzbekistan", in Dale Eickelman (ed.), *Russia's Muslim Frontiers*, Bloomington, Indiana University Press, 1993, pp. 96-97.
51. Mehrdad *Haghayeghi*, *op. cit.*, p. 90.
52. M. Zarif Nazar, Director of Turkmen Service, Radio Liberty, 16 July 1993.
53. William Fierman (ed.), *Soviet Central, the Failed Transformation*, Boulder, Westview Press, 1991, pp. 64-66.
54. Ahmed Rashid, *op.cit.*, p. 137.
55. Ahmed Rashid, "The Fires of Faith in Central Asia", *World Policy Journal*, Spring 2001, p. 45.
56. He insisted that people say their prayers regularly; women abandon coloured clothes and veil themselves from head to toe with white veils. He set up neighbourhood watch committees to combat crime; vigilantes patrolled the streets maintaining law and order and ensuring that shopkeepers did not raise their prices.
57. Yuldeshev is reported to have made the following demands: "we set fine conditions which must be fulfilled by the authorities. First, Islam Karimov must come here. Second, he must swear his faithfulness to Islam on the Koran here and now proclaim an Islamic state. Third, visiting mosques must become compulsory for all Muslims including the leaders of the state must pray together with the people. Fourth, Friday should be announced as a day off and fifth to open the religious schools immediately". Cited in Olag Yakubov, *The Pack of Wolves: The Blood Trail of Terror*, Moscow, Veche Publishers, 2000, p. 9.
58. Ahmed Rashid, *Jihad*, *op.cit.*, p. 139.
59. Both Pakistani intelligence officials and Uzbek diplomats claimed that Yuldeshev received funds from a variety of sources, cited in Ahmed Rashid, *Jihad*, *op.cit.*, p. 256.
60. Ahmed Rashid, *World Policy Journal*, *op.cit.*, p. 52.
61. Tohir Yuldeshev, interview on Voice of America, 6 October 2000.
62. Cited in Ahmed Rashid, *Jihad*, *op.cit*, p. 149.

63. Tamara Makarenko, "Crime and Terrorism in Central Asia". *Jane's Intelligence Review*, July 2000, p. 17.
64. The IMU and Hizb-ut-Tahrir: Implications of the Afghanistan Campaign, *ICG Asia Briefing Paper*, 30 January 2002, p. 1.
65. General Tommy Franks, Commander of the US action in Afghanistan told journalists in Uzbekistan that Namangâni was indeed dead although he did not receive the source of this information. "Uzbekistan Gets US Military Pledge", Associated Press, 24 January 2002.
66. Ahmed Rashid, *Jihad, op.cit.*, p. 116.
67. Under the Khilafa-i-Rashida, which lasted until 661AD, the message of Islam spread rapidly across the Middle East and Africa through conquest and conversions. This period is revered by many radical Islamic movements including the Taliban, as the only time in Islamic history when a true Muslim society existed.
68. Taquiuddin an-Nabhani Filastyni, *The Islamic State*, Lahore, HT Publication, 1998, p. 44.
69. Bakhtiyar Babadzhanov, "Radicalisation of Islam in Uzbekistan: A Study of Hizbat-Tahrir-al-Islami", *Contemporary Central Asia*, Vol. 4, No. 12, April-August 2000, p. 15.
70. Interview with Ali, a HT leader with Ahmed Rashid, Cited in Ahmed Rashid, *Jihad, op.cit.*, p. 118.
71. Bakhtiyar Babadzhanov, *op.cit.*, p. 14.
72. Interview with Ali, an activist of HT by Ahmed Rashid, cited in Ahmed Rashid, *Jihad, op.cit.*
73. For example, according to the materials from the Osh city court archives, of thirteen Hizb-ut Tahrir members sentenced in the Osh city courts in 2000, almost all were unemployed and had at most secondly education. Cited in *ICG Asia Briefing Paper*, 30 January 2002.
74. US State Department, Tajikistan: Human rights Practices, Washington DC, February 2000.
75. Igor Rotar, "The Hizb-ut-Tahrir Party in Central Asia: A Fault line?", *Jamestown Monitor*, Vol. 53, No. 6, 1 May 2001.
76. Ahmed Rashid, *Jihad, op.cit.*, p. 144.
77. Kyrgyz lawmaker Tursunbay Bakir Uulu told the *Moscovsky Komsomalets* newspaper that he did not agree that HT was a political party; it was a purely religious party consisting of underground groups. Cited in *The Times of Central Asia*, 11 October 2001.
78. Sanya Sagnayeva in Alexy Sukhov, Hizb-ut-Tahrir in Kyrgyzstan, *Central Asia Times, op. cit.*
79. Verinder Grover (ed.), *Encyclopaedia of International Terrorism*, Vol. 1, New Delhi, Deep and Deep Publications Pvt. Ltd., p. 15.
80. Ahmed Rashid, "The Taliban: Exporting Terrorism", *Foreign Affairs*, Vol. 78, No. 6, November-December 1999, p. 24.
81. *Ibid.*

82. Poonam Mann, "Taliban at the Doorstep of Central Asia", *Strategic Analysis*, Vol. XXV, No. 1, April 2001, p. 139.
83. *Ibid.*
84. Ahmed Rashid, The Taliban: Exporting Extremism, *op.cit.*, p. 30.
85. *The Times of Central Asia*, 11 October 2001.
86. *Ibid.*
87. Mehrdad *Haghayeghi*, *op. cit.*, p. 72.
88. Poonam Mann, "Central Asia: From Islamic Revivalism to Extremism", *World Focus*, 265, Vol. 23, No. 1, January 2002, p. 14.
89. The Search for identity: Nation Building and the Islamic Factor, in John Anderson, *The International Politics of Central Asia*, Manchester, Manchester University Press, 1997, pp. 154-159.
90. K. Warikoo, "Soviet Central Asia in Ferment", in K. Warikoo, Dawa Norbu (ed.), *Ethnicity and Politics in Central Asia*, New Delhi, South Asia Publishers, 1992, pp. 6-20.
91. Mehrdad *Haghayeghi*, *op.cit.*, p. 72.
92. Poonam Mann, *op.cit.*
93. John Anderson, *op.cit.*
94. William Fierman, "Political Devèlopment of Uzbekistan: Democratisation", in Karen Dawisha and Bruce Parrott (eds.), *Conflict, Cleavage and Change in Central Asia and the Caucasus*, Cambridge, Cambridge University Press, 1997, p. 394.
95. John Anderson, *op.cit.*
96. *Ibid.*
97. The three others are Shafi, Hanbali'i and Malini'i *mazhas*.
98. Edward W. Walker, "Roots of Rage: Militant Islam in Central Asia", Presentation from "Central Asia and Russia: Responses to the War on Terrorism", a panel discussion held at the University of California, Berkeley, on 29 October 2001, available at http://socrates.berkeley.edu/~issues/, downloaded on 8 December 2001.
99. *Ibid.*
100. Ahmed Rashid, *The fires of Faith in Central Asia*, *op.cit*, p. 3.
101. According to the Deputy Mufti, Shamsuddin Babakhan, an estimated 5,000 mosques and prayer houses have been opened in recent years. The numbers, however, seems to be exaggerated, as cited in Mehrdad *Haghayeghi*, *op. cit*, p. 227.
102. *Far Eastern Economic Review*, 9 January 1992; also see *SWB/SU*/1213/B/15, 26 October 1991
103. Interview, Kimshabbay ben Abdurahman, Kazi of the Religious Board of Kyrgyzstan, 18 June 1993, cited in Haghayeghi, *op. cit*, p. 96.
104. Interview, Nysanbai Ulyratbek, President, Clerical Administration of Kazakhstan Muslims, 6 June 1993, cited in Haghayeghi, *op. cit.*, p. 96.
105. Interview, Zarif Nazar, Director of Turkmen Service, *Radio Liberty*, 16 July 1993, cited in Haghayeghi, *op. cit.*, p. 96.

106. Kamal Siddiqui, "The Call of the Taliban", *The Indian Express*, New Delhi, 2 June 1997.
107. M. Haghayeghi, *op.cit.*, p. 97.
108. Mavlon Makhamov, "Islam and Politics in Tajikistan after 1985", in Hafeez Malik (ed.) *Central Asia: Its Strategic Importance and Future Prospects*, New York, St. Martin's Press, 1994, p. 201.
109. Alexander Bennigsen, "Islam in Retrospect", *Central Asian Survey*, Vol. 8, No. 1, January 1989, p. 95.
110. Interview, M. Zarif Nazar, Director of Turkmen Service, *Radio Liberty*, 16 July 1993, cited in M. Haghayeghi, *op.cit.*, p. 98.
111. Interview, Himsanbay ben Abdurahaman, Kazi of the Religious Board of Kyrgyzstan, 18 June 1993, cited in Haghayeghi, *op.cit.*
112. Interview with Samsuddin Babakhan, Deputy Mufti, 24 December 1993, by M. Haghayeghi, *op.cit.*, p. 99.
113. Islam Karimov, "Uzbekistan on the Threshold of the 21st Century; Threats to Security and Stability", *Himalayan and Central Asian Studies*, Vol. 1, No. 3, October-December 1997, p. 47.
114. *Ibid.*
115. *Interfax*, Moscow, 30 August 1992, rep. in *SWB/SU*/1475/B/6, 2 September 1992.
116. Mayak Radio, Moscow, 1 September 1992, rep. in *SWB/SU*/1476/B/9, 3 September 1992.
117. *PTI News Agency* (henceforth PTI), New Delhi, 11 December 1995, rep. in *SWB/SU*/2485/G/1, 13 December 1995.
118. *Kabar News Agency* (henceforth Kabar), Bishkek, 2 Oct. 1995, rep. in *SWB/SU*/2461/G/2, 15 November 1995.
119. *Ekspress-K*, Almaty, 3 Mar. 2000, p. 2, rep. in *SWB/SU*/3789/G/3, 15 March 2000.
120. *ITAR-TASS*, Moscow, 14 September 2000, rep. in *SWB/SU*/3946/G/3, 15 September 2000.
121. Ajay Patnaik, "Central Asia since Soviet Disintegration", *World Focus*, August 2000, p. 4.
122. Economic Reforms in Kazakhstan, Kyrgyz republic, Tajikistan, Turkmenistan and Uzbekistan, International Monetary Fund, Occasional Papers, Washington DC, 1999.
123. *Ibid.*
124. *Ibid.*
125. Ajay Patnaik, "Central Asia since Soviet Disintegration", *World Focus*, August 2000, p. 4.
126. Jeoffery J. Jukes, Kirill Nourhanov and Mikhail Alexandrov, "Race, Religion, Ethnicity and Economics in Central Asia", Slavic Research Centre, 1998, available at http://www.src-h.slav.hokudai.ac.jp/sympo/97summer/jukes.html
127. Abdumannob Polat, "The Islamic Revival in Uzbekistan: A Threat to Stability?", in Roald Sagdeev and Susan Eisenhower (eds.), *Islam and*

Central Asia; An Enduring Legacy or an Evolving Threat?, Centre for Political and Strategic Studies, Washington DC, 2000, pp. 53-54.

128. Poonam Mann, "Religious Extremism in Central Asia", *Strategic Analysis*, December 2000, p. 1041.
129. Central Asia: Islamist Mobilisation and Regional Security, *ICG Asia Report, op.cit.*, p. 13.
130. Quoted in Ahmed Rashid, *Jihad, op.cit.*, pp. 146-147.
131. *Ibid.*
132. *Ibid.*, p. 147.
133. G. Bukharvaeva, "Uzbek Terror Suspects Targetted", Institute of War and Peace Reporting, 7 July 2000; Islam Karimov, *Uzbekistan on the Threshold of the Twenty First Century*, Tashkent, Uzbek Government Press, 1997, p. 44.
134. *ICG Asia Report, op.cit.*
135. *Ibid.*
136. Quoted in "State Terror in Uzbekistan", *The Times of Central Asia*, 28 June 2001.
137. *Ibid.*
138. Quoted in "Autocratic Uzbek Regime Fuels Instability a Decade after Independence", *The Times of Central Asia*, 13 September 2001.
139. Quoted in "Human Rights Violation in Central Asia: Dramatic Deterioration in HR Situation", *The Times of Central Asia*, (hereafter TCA), Vol. 3, No. 30 (126), 26 July 2001.
140. Quoted in "Uzbek Women Plead for Religious Prisoners", *TCA*, Vol. 3, No, 33 (129), 23 August 2001.
141. *Ibid.*
142. Quoted in *Ibid.*
143. These quotes derive from Imam Mansur's teachings on Islam, which are distributed free on audio tape. Cited in *ICG Asia Report*, No. 14, *op.cit.*, p. 17.
144. *ICG Asia Report, Ibid.*

4

Response of the Central Asian States to Militancy and Cross-border Terrorism

As discussed in the previous chapters, the independence of the Central Asian states from USSR came almost as a surprise for the leaders of the republics. The process of political transition which should have preceded the independence of the republics was not experienced, for which immediately after the independence, political confusion, economic chaos and social upheaval in the form of ethnic and regional clashes marked the scenario in the region. The situation there was suitably used to their advantage by the extremists to carry out their ulterior designs.The years of Soviet forced atheism got an immediate shock with an unrestricted exposure to the religious assertions outside the region. To make the matter worse, consolidation on ethnic lines added fuel to the fire. The hostility among different ethnic groups (for example, Tajik civil war) created suitable atmosphere, by weakening state authority, for the militant groups to spread their terror network. But as the time moved on and the republics settled their authority over their respective regions, they tried to strengthen their grip by adopting required measures to control the situation. One primary measure they adopted immediately is the provisions in the constitution.

Kazakhstan

The Kazakh constitution was adopted in 1994. While drafting the constitution, the framers ostensibly had in mind the various problems facing the country as far as the religious and ethnic aspects are concerned. Hence, the constitution in articles contains provisions which deal with the ethno-religious aspects as well as making clear the position of the government on these issues. In the clause-I of the article-1 in section-I (General Provisions), the constitution declares itself a democratic, secular, legal and social state and highest values of the state are individual, his life, rights and freedoms.[1] Thus, in the opening article itself, the constitution clearly spells out the position of the government as far as the role of religion in the public life is concerned. While proclaiming itself as a democratic country, the word 'secular' has also been added in order to give equal status to all religions, not just any particular religion. It makes mandatory for the government constitutionally to provide equal opportunity for all the religions and not to declare any particular religion a state religion.

The article also outlays the various aspects of the human life and their needs. It says the primary duty of any government always is to look after the welfare of its population by ensuring their rights and freedoms.

In Article 5, part-I, the Constitution says, "The Republic of Kazakhstan shall recognise ideological and political diversity. The merging of public and state institutions and the formation of political party organisations in state bodies shall not be permitted".[2] This article is an important one from the point of view that in the erstwhile Soviet Union ideological and political diversities were never recognised and any effort in that direction was ruthlessly crushed. Hence, the article indicates the growing spirit of accommodation in the politics of the republic.When political and ideological diversities are not recognised it leads to unitary and autocratic form of government, giving radical dissidence legitimacy among the masses. On the other hand by allowing diverse ideologies and political opinions the government has created a 'safety valve' to minimise the effects of radical opinion and bring the opponent to the constitutional fold.

In the Clause-2 of the Article 5, of theSection-1, the constitution says, "public associations shall be equal before the law. Illegal interference of the state in the affairs of the public associations and financing of public associations by the state shall not be permitted".[3] This article clearly states that public association of any kind would not be allowed to have a say in the matters of governance. Even the financing of public associations by the state is illegal according to the provision, thereby putting a check on the government sponsored radical associations.

The clause-3 of the Article-5 is quite explicit and important from the point of view of dealing with radical and militant organisations. It says, "formation and functioning of public associations pursuing the goals or actions directed towards a violent change of the constitutional system, violation of the integrity of the republic, undermining the security of the state, inciting social, racial, national, religious, class and tribal enmity, as well as the formation of unauthorised paramilitary units shall be prohibited".[4]

This article aims at curbing the threat and inception of terrorism. It prohibits formation of public associations with the aim to use violence as an integral tool of terrorism for changing the constitution, the system or harming the unity and integrity of the republic. It also provides that no public association will be allowed to indulge in activities that would potentially threaten the security of the state and "incite social, racial, national, religious, class and tribal enmity". Terrorism theoretically rests upon group activities. Without proper grouping, terrorism can hardly sustain for a long time. At the same time, mutual hatred and enmity works as a fuel for the sustenance of terrorism and gun (weapon) works as the means to achieve the goal (creating terror aimed at achieving political objectives). In view of the basic nature, scope, methodology and means of terrorism, the article exactly intends to deal with them.

Another major requirement of terrorism is the constant flow of money in order to sustain its activities. It is a common phenomenon world over that terrorist organisations functioning in different parts are all flooded with abundant amount of money from different sources; one important source being the finances from across another country. For example, the terrorist outfits like Lashkar-i-Tayyeba (Taiba) generate funds through several sources in Pakistan to fund its activities in India. It runs offices all over the country (Pakistan) and collects funds. Moreover, all Jehadi organisations have rich support all over the world.[5] Similarly, the main financier of the terrorist outfits in Central Asia has had been the Taliban. In this context Askar Aytmatov has said, "Afghanistan is one of the largest drug producers and a huge amount of money circulates around it.... to some extent, the increase of drug trafficking from Afghanistan through Central Asia, to Russia and Europe may account for this. According to current data, around 30 per cent of world's drug production is concentrated in Afghanistan, from where 65 per cent of heroine and hashish is delivered to Europe. This is a financial support for the Taliban in realising their far-reaching strategic targets, i.e., the establishment of political influence in Islamic countries and regions. Since Central Asia has been undergoing broader and internal problems for a long time now, the region is quite suitable for a possible attack of Islamic extremism".[6]

The funding across the border takes place mainly in illegal ways and sometimes in the name of charity and aid. To put an effective control on such of transaction, Clause-4 of Article 5, Section-I of Kazakhstan's constitution says, "activities of political parties and trade unions of other states, religious parties as well as financing of political parties and trade unions by foreign legal entities and citizens, foreign states and international organisations shall not be permitted in the Republic".[7] While aiming at any kind of illegal flow of money for wrong purposes the article even targets the legal money supply for any kind of anti-government purpose.

Terrorism propped up by religious bigotry constitutes the majority in the terrorist activites of the present world. In this regard, Prof. Jean Francois Mayer from University of Fribourg, Switzerland, has some interesting and justifying views. He writes "when religious beliefs are used for justifying violence, violent actions tend to become endowed with cosmic dimensions, and there is nothing left to restrain them".[8] In most of the cases of terrorist activities, the actions are always made out to be endowed with cosmic dimensions - religious approval. For example, 'Jihad' in Afghanistan which has been exhorted by the Taliban as the ultimate wish of the God which so far, has been the most important factor for the promotion of fundamentalism and terrorism in the Central Asian states. The Kazakh constitution has dealt with this possibility in some ways. It says "activities of foreign religious associations on the territory of the republic as well as appointment of heads of religious associations in the republics by foreign religious centres shall be carried out in coordination with the respective state institutions of the republic."[9]

The constitution further provides that, "the state shall promote conditions for the study and development of the language of the people of Kazakhstan".[10] Before the independence, Russian was the recognised official language of all the Central Asian republics, though Kazakh language was the common language among its people. The imposition of Russian language as the compulsory official medium had created a lot of resentment among the people of this region. So, when they got their independence they adopted their own language as the official language. This step has also to a large extent prevented the encashment of the linguistic dissidence for furthering terrorist objectives. Like religion, language has been a key factor for common bonding, unity among sections of people and an indicator of national identity. In anysort of betrayal of this sentiment lies the possibility of violent uprisings against the state and authorities. Therefore, this article of Kazakh constitution addresses this problem to an extent.

In another clause the constitutuion says, "no one shall have the right to arbitrarily deprive a person of life. The law shall establish death penalty as an extra-ordinary measure of punishment for especially grave crimes and grant the sentenced person the right to appeal for pardon".[11] Though this is a law, practiced worldwide and a part of natural justice, the very mention of this reassuringly expresses the resolve of the state in protecting the lives of its own citizens. It also acts as a deterrent for curtailing violence as a method for achieving objectives. The same clause also contains the provision for the "right to appeal for pardon" which is a rational and reformative step, though placed at the discretion and satisfaction of the authorities. This article is a powerful weapon in the hands of the government to deal with the terrorists by awarding capital punishment and create a sense of fear among the potential ones.

In the subsequent article in the same section, the constitution says, "everyone shall have the right to confidentiality of personal deposits and savings, correspondence, telephone conversations, postal, telegraph and other messages. Limitations of this right shall be permitted only in the cases and according to the procedures directly established by law".[12] This article empowers the state security agencies to monitor and scritinise the information of suspected persons and finances, if any.

In article-19, the constitution provides that, "everyone shall have the right to determine and indicate, not to indicate his national, party and religious affiliations".[13] This article is a clear deviation from the old Soviet practice when atheism was forcefully imposed by the state. The article gives the individual the ultimate choice in the matters as important as party and religion. In the succeeding clause of the same article the constitution further says, "everyone shall have the right to use his native language and culture, to freely choose the language of communication, education, instruction and creative activities".[14] Like 'religion', language has been one of the most powerful unifying factor in the society and has the capacity to make well knit groups and associations. When this group or association feels alienated, suppressed, deceived or ignored on linguistic lines there is a possibility of them turning violent. It becomes a divisive force creating inter-linguistic group rivalry and violence. Therefore, in order to overcome this possibility equal treatment to all the linguistic groups and the freedom to adopt, pursue and propagate besides the state language has been granted by the constitutution. This not only creates a harmonious atmosphere but also discourages terrorist elements to take advantage of ethnic hostility and propagate their ideology and agenda. Secondly, this freedom caps all possible ethnic dissidence againt the state.

While the next article, in the constitution categorically expresses the 'freedom of speech', the subsequent clause deals with the right to information. Clause-I says, "The freedom of speech and creative activities shall be guaranteed. Censorship shall be prohibited". Clause-2 writes, "Everyone shall have the right to receive and disseminate information by any means not prohibited by law. The list of the items constituting the state secrets of the Republic of Kazakhstan shall be determined by law".[15] The first clause allows each and every citizen to express his or her opinion or feelings without being restricted by law. This is a measure that goes a long way in building a bridge of trust and mutuality between the ruler and the ruled through the establishment of a dialogue process. The second clause is a straight and sharp one. It allows everybody to receive and disseminate accurate and sensitive information. Terrorists thriving on rumour- mongering are the basic targets of this law.

The last clause of article-20 is in fact, the most forthright and most important clause that directly targets the terrorist methods of functioning declaring them illegal. It mentions "propaganda of or agitation for the forcible change of the constitutional system, violation of the integrity of the republic, undermining of state security, and advocating war, social racial, national, religious, class and clannish superiority as well as the cult of cruelty and violence shall not be allowed".[16] Terrorist activities are aimed at changing the constitutional system through violent methods because terrorists do not believe in democracy and function according to constitutions which they formulate and change according to their suitability. Terrorists always want to engage in violent activities for quick and sharp reaction from the political side. Therefore, they always engage in intra-community, inter-community, inter-state clashes to further their agenda. It always aims at taking on the government by surreptiously instigating racial, clan, religious, class etc. superiority. Their basic intention is to create a sense of hatred towards the other community or the government and increase friction in order to draw the attention of the world community. Today all over the world, several such activities are going on. In Kashmir, Middle East, Britain, China, US such type of hatred mongering has been continuing by terrorist groups to flare up passion and generate clashes. The Kazakh constitution through this provision out-rightly rejects similar as illegal.

In another provision, the constitution differentiates between illegal disruptive organisations from legal associations. It says, "citizens of Kazakhstan shall have the right of freedom of forming associations. The activities of the public associations shall be regulated by law".[17] This provision in the constitution of Kazakhstan is important in the sense that it legally allows the citizens to lawfully carryout their activities through public associations. It is a fact in the current times that militant organisations begin their operations under the guise of charity and public welfare organisations to avoid the penalties of the law. Also, there are organisations which work in close coordination with terrorist groups based outside the particular country. They facilitate the operation of the group logistically and financially. Therefore, close scrutiny of public associations and monitoring of their activities and flow of finances to them is an important part of the administration. The Kazakh Constitution has carefully addressed this through the above mentioned provision.

Constitutional Provisions in Tajikistan

The preamble of the Tajik constitution carries a socially powerful message- "the equality of rights and friendship of all nationalities and peoples of Tajikistan seeking to build a just society".[18] This commitment of constitution tries to win the confidence of different nationalities. Normally, discontent is brewed when the share in the government of the different stake-holders in the society is ignored, which snowballs in to inter-community clashes and gives a suitable opportunity to the terrrist elements to spread their network.

Article-1 of the same constitution can be seen as an appendage to the preamble. It says, "The republic of Tajikistan is a sovereign, democratic, law-governed, secular and unitary state".[19] This is more like the opening provision of Kazakh constitution. The secular, democratic and law-governed aspects define the position of the government as far as religion and the governing principle of the government is concerned. The importance of this article lies in the fact that it resolves not to discriminate on the basis of religion, race, creed or any other criterion thereby, not leaving any section of the society feeling left out in enjoying the equal rights on the resources of the country. Similarly, Article- 5 of the constitution provides that 'the life, honour, dignity and other rights of the individuals are sacred". Recognition, observance and protection of human and civil rights and freedoms are the obligation of the state.[20] Though this article does not have any specific relevance to the efforts of curbing violence and terrorism, it has certain indirect bearing on that. By ensuring that the life, dignity, honour and rights of the individuals be protected by the state, the constitution makes it mandatory for the government to take all necessary action in this regard.

Next article of the constitution has specific bearing on the problem. One part of it says, "no social association, group of people, or individual has the right to seize power. The seizure of power is the gravest crime".[21] As it appears, the article expresses the stand of the government on illegal capture of power other than specified constitutional and democratic methods. As capture of power is the ultimate objective of the terrorists this provision in the constitution declares them illegal and unconstitutional.

Article-8 of the constitution is highly comprehensive and illustrates the secular aspect of the state, "In Tajikistan, public life is to develop on the basis of political and ideological diversity. No ideology including religious ideology is granted the status of the state ideology. Social associations are established and will function within the framework of the constitution and laws. The state provides equal opportunity for their activities. Religious organisations are separate from the state and cannot interfere, with state affairs. The establishment and functioning of the social and religious enmity and hatred as well as advocating the forcible overthrow of the constitutional structures and the formation of armed groups is prohibited".[22] This is the most elaborate and pointed article in the whole constitution, which without the use of the words like terrorism or militancy aims exactly to that. It outrightly rejects imposition of any single ideology and speaks clearly about pluralism and co-existence of ideological diversity. The concept of state ideology has been rejected. Like Kazakh constitution, this constitution also provides for the public associations to functin within the framework of the law of the land. One special thing about this article is that it specifically and objectively says that religion and state should function separately without interfering in each other's affairs. Like Kazakh constitution, Tajik constitution also prohibits formation of armed groups, forcible overthrow of the government and flaring up of passion of any kind on the basis of religion, creed, nationality, race etc. This article in its spirit declares any kind of militant or terrorist activity as illegal and unconstitutional.

Article-17 of this constitution is much similar to that of Kazakh constitutional provision which guarantees the equality of all the individuals irrespective of their religion, race, sex, political persuasions, social status, knowledge and property, before the law. It also guarantees rights and freedoms to all the individuals irrespective of all the above mentioned considerations. It assures the citizens about their positions and status in the state, hence dissuades them to take recourse to constitutional methods rather than violent means for grievance redressed. It says, "All are equal before the law and the courts. The state guarantees the rights and freedoms of every person regardless of nationality, race, sex, language, religious beliefs, political persuasions, social status, knowledge and property. Men and women have the same rights".[23]

Again similar to Kazakh constitution, Tajik constitution also provides the right to freedom of religion. In categorical and unambiguous terms, it specifies that, "every person has the right to freely determine his position towards religion, to profess any religion individually or together with others or not to profess any, and to take part in religious customs and ceremonies".[24] By allowing the co-existence of all religions and equal legal protection to all of them, this article attempts to create a sense of security among the minority community and dissuading them to live under pressure of any kind. A fear psychosis always helps in breeding terrorism and militant activities. In that case this constitutional provision is a real help.

Article-30 of the same chapter II prohibits the state censorship and prosecution for criticism. It grants the freedom of speech to its citizens. It is a fact that sometimes genuine grievances, when forcibly suppressed, gives rise to frustration forcing people to take up the matter on to themselves. To avoid such a situation, the article provides that "every person is guaranteed freedom of speech, publishing and the right to use means of mass information. State censorship and prosecution for criticism is prohibited".[25]

These constitutional provisions are someway an attempt to deal with the problem of terrorism and militancy in Tajikistan.

Provisions in Uzbekistan's Constitution

Article-4 of the constitution of Uzbekistan forthrightly says, "The state language of the republic of Uzbekistan shall be Uzbek. The republic of Uzbekistan shall ensure a respectful attitude towards the languages, customs and the traditions of all nationalities and ethnic groups living on its territory and create the conditions necessary for their development".[26] As elaborated earlier, this provision in the constitution of Uzbekistan is an important one in the sense that it reiterates the government's commitment and assurance of equal treatment to all the communities - religious, nationalities, ethnic etc. This is basically helpful in creating a sense of confidence in their minds and so that they can be a part of the national mainstream, rather than opposing rebels.

In the next chapter of article-7, the constitution declares the illegal seizure of power of any kind as unconstitutional. It says, "Any seizure of power belonging to the state authority, suspension or termination of activity of the bodies of the state authority contrary to the procedure prescribed by the constitution, as well as the formation of any new or parallel bodies of state authority shall be regarded as unconstitutional and punishable by law."[27] With this, the constitution declares the primary objective of terrorists as illegal and punishable.

Similar to article-5 of Kazakh constitution and article-8 in Tajik constitution, article-12 of Uzbek constitution declares that "in the republic of Uzbekistan, public life shall develop on the basis of a diversity of political institutions, ideologies and opinions. No ideology shall be granted the state ideology".[28] Though terminologically different, the spirit and intention of this article is samillar to the constitutions of Kazakh and Tajikistan. By declaring the neutrality of the state in promoting any particular ideology and reorganising the pluralism in the matter of ideology, the constitution assumes a secular, impartial role.

Article-13 says, "Democracy in the Republic of Uzbekistan shall rest on the principles common to all mankind, according to which the ultimate value is the human being, his life, freedom, honour, dignity and other inalienable rights. Democratic rights and freedoms shall be protected by the constitution and the laws".[29] As it has been made clear in the lines of the article itself, the article aims at satisfying certain common principles of the society. The constitution, through this, values the life of the human being as the ultimate goal of the state and constitution. The specific relevance of this article in reference to military and terrorism lies in the interpretation that when democracy succeeds, and human concerns are addressed within it, the terrorist tendencies find it difficult to influence the people.

Article -8, is similar in spirit. It says "all citizens of the Republic of Uzbekistan shall have equal rights and freedoms and shall be equal before the law, without distinction by sex, race, nationality, language, religion, social origin, convictions, individuals and social status. Any privilege may be granted solely by the law and shall conform to the principles of social justice".[30]

This article's importance lies in the fact that every citizen of the country is promised to be treated equally before the eyes of the law. Inequality in the state policy worldwide has always been a major reason for dissent - a favourable field for the germination of militancy and terrorist activities.

Article-19 of the constitution strictly declares any infringement into the rights and freedoms of the citizens illegal , "....no one shall have the power to deny a citizen his rights and freedoms, or to infringe on them except by the sentence of a court".[31] The purpose of quoting the article here is to mention the guarantee that the government provides for the protection of the rights and freedom of the citizens.

Article-24 of the same constitution is very lucid in the explanation when it says, "the right to existence is the inalienable right of every human being. Attempts on everyone's life shall be regarded as the gravest crime".[32] Under this article, any kind of militant or terrorist activity that threatens the life of the individuals becomes illegal. Basically, terror as a tactics is perpetrated through violence. This article specifically deals with that of possibility.

Article-25, at the same time, guarantees the rights of the innocents and law abiding citizens. Sometimes, the state sponsored excesses result in creation of widespread protest that prepares the ground for the terrorist and militant operations. So, it is absolutely necessary to protect the rights and life of the innocents. "Every one shall have the right to freedom and inviolability of the person. No one may be arrested or taken into custody except on lawful grounds".[33] Some other articles also support this article and basically aim at the objectives specified above. These are: everyone shall be entitled to protection against encroachments on his honour, dignity and interference in his private life, and shall be guaranteed inviolability of the home. No one may enter a home, carry out a search or an examination or violate the privacy of the correspondence and telephone conversations, except on lawful grounds and in accordance with the procedures specified by law.[34]

"Any citizen of the Republic of Uzbekistan shall have the right to freedom of movement in the territory of the republic as well as a free entry to and exit from it, except in the events specified by law".[35]

"Everyone shall be guaranteed freedom of thought, speech and convictions. Everyone shall have the right to seek, obtain and disseminate any information, except that which is directed against the existing constitutional system and in some other instance, specified by law. Freedom of opinion and their expression may be restricted by law if any state or other secret is involved".[36]

Like other constitutions discussed earlier, the Uzbek constitution also is quite categorical about religion in the state structure. In real secular spirit it allows the existence of any religion without any interference from the state and imposition of any kind in this matter. Realising that a theocratic mode of state policy always fans the disruptive groups to 'fish' in troubled waters, the constitution prefers to be secular and neutral. It says "freedom of conscience is guaranteed to all. Everyone shall have the right to profess or not to profess any religion. Any compulsory religion shall be impermissible".[37]

Article-33 directly deals with the democratic expression of public views, opinions and perceptions. It says "citizens shall have the right to engage in public life by holding rallies, meetings, and demonstrations in accordance with the legislation of the Republic of Uzbekistan. The bodies of authority shall have the right to suspend or ban such undertakings, activities exclusively on the grounds of security".[38]

Some other articles which are relevant as far as dealing with militancy and terrorism is concerned are, "every one shall be entitled to legally defend his rights and freedoms, and shall have the right to appeal any lawful action of the state bodies, officials and public associations".[39]

"The formation and the functioning of political parties and public associations aiming to do the following shall be prohibited: changing the existing constitutional system by force; coming out against the sovereignty, territorial integrity and security of the republic as well as the constitutional rights and freedoms of its citizens; advocating war and social, national, racial and religious hostility and encroaching upon the health and morality of the people as well as of any armed associations and political parties based on the national or religious principles, all secret societies and associations shall be banned".[40] The article, as the text speaks, directly deals with the possibility of the menace of militancy and terrorism. Terrorists and militant outfits, most of the time, operate in formal and informal groups - NGOs, charitable and humanitarian organisation. In such cases, dealing with them legally becomes all the more difficult. Secondly, some organisations of equal nature also function secretly and as underground outfits. The article declares them as illegal, facilitating action against them.

Article -58 of the constitution is also of similar in nature. It says, "the state shall safeguard rights and lawful interests of public associations and provide them with equal legal opportunities for participating in public life. Interference by state bodies and officials in the activity of the public associations, as well as interference by public associations in the activity of the state bodies and officials is impermissible".[41]

In the same chapter on "Public Associations", article-61 is one of the most important articles from the point of view of restricting militancy and terrorist activities. It says "religious organisations and associations shall be separated from the state and equal before the law. The state shall not interfere with the activity of the religious associations".[42] It reiterates the secular objectives of the constitution and the state and expresses the commitment of the government of not meddling in the religious affairs of the people.

The article-62 is a supporting article of the article-58. This article brings the public associations, organisations etc. under the purview of the law of the land, court and judiciary to punish them whenever found guilty. It largely puts a rein on the public organisations and acts as a monitoring method for regulating the activities of the public associations. The text says, "Public associations may be dissolved or banned or subject to restricted actively solely by the sentence of a court".[43] These are some articles which directly or indirectly deal in curbing the menace of terrorism and militancy in the region.

Constitution of the Kyrgyz Republic

The constitution of Kyrgyzstan also contains several provisions which directly or indirectly aim at discouraging terrorist and militant activities. In chapter-I of the constitution, the opening article declares, "the Kyrgyz republic (Kyrgyzstan) is a sovereign, unitary, secular state".[44] Here, the two connotations- secular and unitary should be emphasised.

The other article which works in the similar perception is the clause-2 of article-2. It says "no separate group of people, no associations, or any individual person shall have the right to usurp power in the government.

The usurpation of government power shall be the gravest crime".[45] The content is very clear, straight and lucid. It declares any attempt to topple the government and assume power, illegal.

Like the previously discussed constitutions, the Kyrgyz constitution also declares the Kyrgyz language as the language of the Republic. It says, "The state language of the Kyrgyz Republic shall be the Kyrgyz language."[46] This provision caters to the aspirations of the majority of the population and settles the question of ethnic supremacy in the state. In the following clause, the constitution again categorically says "the Kyrgyz Republic guarantees the preservation, equal and free development and functioning of the Russian language and all other languages, used by the population of the republic".[47] This clause is a unique one and is not so unambiguously mentioned in the constitutions analysed earlier. It not only spells out the attitude of the state towards other languages and groups but also strengthens the preceding clause to a great extent.

Clause-1 of the article-8 says, "Political parties, trade unions and other public associations may be organised in the Kyrgyz republic on the basis of free will and unity of interests. The state shall guarantee the rights and lawful interests of public associations".[48] This provision, like similar provisions in other constitutions, makes the legal associations permissible while keeping a check on the illegal ones. Clause-3 in the same article is another provision which boldely declares that "religious and all other cults shall be separated from the state".[49] This is an important provision from the point of view of the separation of religion from politics. Terrorism and militancy always survive on the diet of religion and religious sentiments. By separating religion from state, the constitution envisages to cap the growth of militancy and terrorism. In Clause-4 of the same article, the constitution further provides that the following shall not be allowed in Kyrgyzstan for formation of political parties on religious grounds. Religious organisations must not pursue political goals and objectives, "interference by members of religious organisations and cults with the activity of the state bodies, activities of political parties of the foreign countries".[50] This is a related provision of its earlier one. In this provision, the constitution prohibits the involvement of religion in politics and the use of religion as an instrument to capture and run the state power or links of any religious, political party with any foreign country.

".... Actions aimed at disturbing the peaceful coexistence of people, propaganda and encouragement of ethnic clashes shall be deemed unconstitutional".[51] Terrorists always intend to disturb the peace and harmony. They create and promote hatred among the sections of the society. To speak plainly, they aim at disturbing peace and coexistence to attain their objectives. Therefore, the Constitution declares such activities as unconstitutional, illegal and punishable.

In article-15, clause-3 guarantees the equality of every citizen before the law of the land. This attitude of the government towards its own citizens helps curbing the popularity of the militants and terrorists by subliming dissent. It says, "All persons in the Kyrgyz republic shall be equal before the law and the court. No one may be exposed to any discrimination, infringement of rights and freedoms, on the motives of origin, sex, race, nationality, language, and creed, political and religious convictions or by any other public or personal conditions or circumstances".[52]

Article-16 of the Kyrgyz constitution consists of a list of various individual rights of the citizens and human rights that the government promises to protect and ensure to its citizens. Among them, the right to "freedom of creed, spirit and worship",[53] the right to free expression and dissemination of one's thoughts, ideas, opinions, freedom of literary, artistic, scientific and technical creative work, freedom of the press, transmission and dissemination of information,[54] right to freedom of movement,[55] right to association,[56] right to assemble peacefully and without weapons, to free meetings and demonstrations[57] are the important ones, which give the citizens of Kyrgyzstan an opportunity to express themselves without resorting to any kind of violent or illegal methods.

Clause -4 of the Article-18 is an important and supporting provision of the earlier provision. It is a kind of safeguard rather, to the earlier provisions. It says "no one may be arrested and detained on the basis other than the law. Any action aimed at imposing a liability on a person before the sentence has been passed by the court, shall not be allowed, and shall be grounds for the material and moral indemnification to the victim by the court".[58] The relevance of this particular piece of the provision lies in the fact that sometimes the misuse of police power and certain rules result in harassment of innocents who fall prey to the terrorists. Secondly, this provision aims at strengthening the faith of the common citizens in the efficacy of law and justice.

Article-30 of the constitution says the citizens of Kyrgyzstan shall have the right to strike.[59] Though this article is intricately related to the 'right to freedom of expression', its importance again lies in the fact that it allows the citizens to democratically express their grievances and seek their redressal without being lured by violence and terrorism.

Though it is difficult to ascertain the efficacy of the above mentioned constitutional provisions in fighting terrorism and militancy, one thing is certain that because of these provisions the fight with the terrorists has been facilitated and several provisions have acted as ventilating channels, discouraging the emergence of terrorism.

The Constitution of Turkmenistan

Like the other previously discussed constitutions, Turkmenistan's constitution also contains certain provisions with direct or indirect implications on terrorism as an instrument of achieving political goal or expression of public opinion.

Article-3 in section-I says, "The human beings shall be the highest value of the society and the state in Turkmenistan".[60]

Th provision sends out a message that welfare of the human being is the primary aim of the government. Their development is the sole reason for existence of the government. This wipes out the sense of alienation among the people which induces people to adopt violence to make their voice heard.

Similarly, article-11 of the same section holds that "the state shall guarantee the freedom of religions and confessions and their equality before the law. Religious organisations shall be separate from the state and may not fulfil state functions. The state educational system shall be separate from religion and shall be of a secular nature".

Every one shall have the right independently to define his attitude towards religion, to profess and disseminate beliefs associated with his attitude to religion; and to participate in the practice of religious cults, rituals and rites.[61]

This article is one of the most important articles which has several aspects clubbed into one. It speaks about religious freedom, public and religious associations, freedom of choice and the position before the law. The constitution in this article proclaims it as secular by allowing all the religions to co-exist without any one of them enjoying any state patronage. The importance of this article lies in the fact that it discourages any religious discrimination, thereby, not hurting any one's religious sentiments. By providing freedom to profess and propagate one's own religious belief, the state gives the people a sense of security as far as religion is concerned. Religion is one of the most important factors for the survival of terrorism. The peaceful co-existence of religious and mutual accommodation does not provide any fertile ground to it to survive.

The language issue is also addressed in the same section. The provision says, "The state language for Turkmenistan shall be the Turkmen language".[62] Like other Central Asian states, this provision in the Turkmeni constitution settles the language question once for all. This not only satisfies the majority sentiment in the country but also caps any possibility of future rivalry.

In the next section, the constitution further says, "human rights shall be inviolable and inalienable. No one shall have the right to deprive a person of any rights or freedom what so ever or to restrict his rights except in accordance with the constitution and the law...."[63] This article goes much in justifying the opening article of the constitution that upholds the interest of the human being as sacred and uncompromising.

Article-17 of the same section says, "Turkmenistan shall guarantee the equality of the rights and freedoms of citizens, as well as equality of citizens before the law irrespective of nationality, origin, property status or official position, place of residence, language attitude towards religion, political beliefs or party membership".[64] The article by guaranteeing the equality of the citizens irrespective of their diversities reiterates the secular and non-discriminatory approach.

In the article-26 of the same section, the constitution guarantees the right to freedom of thought, expression and information. All these are the primary indicators of a free and democratic society. Arbitrary and undemocratic governments and societies are by and large prone to disturbances as it does not provide any space for its citizens to express their opinions and thoughts.

Constitutional provisions are like the foundations on which the efforts of the republics to fight terrorism and violence is based. It provides the guiding principles to move ahead in that direction without harming the basic fundamental rights of the people. But like any other provisions in the constitution the above discussed constitutional provisions of the Central Asian republics are inadequate in themselves to root out terrorism. Moreover, the constitutional provisions are all subject to proper and correct interpretation. They have also their limitations in dealing with terrorism.

Legal Procedures

Keeping in view of the inadequacy of the constitutional provisions, the governments have also taken several legal measures to counter the menace of terrorism they are facing viz. specific laws in this regard. Some republics like Kyrgyzstan have their anti-terrorism laws, arms laws, language laws, anti-drugs laws, which specifically addresses the problem, its causes and perpetrators. The Kyrgyz Parliament passed a law regulating the legal production of narcotics in the republic for medical and scientific purposes on 24 April. The head of the State Commission for Narcotics Control, Asker Maumeyev, said that the law not only regulates production, but also envisages measures against illegal drug trafficking.

The law was drafted to ensure Kyrgyzstan's compliance with three UN Anti-Drug Conventions to which the republic signed up in 1994. Countries like Uzbekistan and Kazakhstan have recently passed anti-terrorism laws specifically dealing with the threat. After 29 September 2001, all the member nations of UN have resolved to pass their anti-terrorism laws as required by the UN resolution. An analysis of a few of the provisions of some laws in different countries would show how the countries are specifically trying to deal with the problem through legal measures.

The Religious Practices Act in Uzbekistan prohibits or severely restricts activities such as proselytising, imparting and disseminating religious literature and offering religious instruction.[66]

The law also requires all the religious groups and congregations to register and provides strict and burdensome criteria for their registration. Among its requirements, the law stipulates that each group must present a list of at least hundred Uzbek citizens (compared with the previous minimum of 10) to the local branches of the Ministry of Justice.[67] This provision enables the government to ban any group simply by denying its registration petition. The government officials designed the law to target the Muslims who worship outside the system of state organised mosques. A special commission created in 1998 may grant exemptions to the religious laws strict requirements and register groups that have not been registered by the local officials. As of 24 May 2001, the government had registered 2008 religious congregations and organisations.[68]

The Uzbek parliament passed two laws in May 1998 that restrict religious activities. The Law on Freedom of Conscience and Religious Organisations provides for freedom of worship, freedom from the religious persecution, separation of Church and state and the right to establish schools and train clergy. At the same time the law also severely restricts the religious activities. It restricts the religious rights that are judged to be in conflict with national security, prohibits proselytisation, bans religious subjects in the schools, prohibits private teaching of religious principles, forbids the wearing of religious clothing in the public by anyone other than the clerics, and requires the religious groups to obtain a license to publish or distribute materials.[69]

The second legislative change in May 1998 consisted of a series of revisions to Criminal and Civil Codes that stiffened the penalties for violating the religion law and other statutes on religious activities. It provided for punishments for activities such as organising a banned religious group, pursuing others to join such a group and drawing minors into religious organisations without the permission of their parents. The criminal code was amended again in 1999 with two changes that affected religious freedom. The changes draw a distinction between the 'illegal' groups- those that are not registered properly, and 'prohibited' groups, which are banned altogether. The first measure makes it a criminal offence punishable with up to 5 years in prison to organise an illegal religious group or to resume activities of such a group (presumably after being denied registration or ordered to disband). Furthermore, the measure punishes any participation in such a group by up to 3 years in prison. The second measure sets out penalties of up to 20 years in prison and confiscation of property for 'organising or participating' in the activities of religious extremists, fundamentalists, separatists, or other prohibited groups.[70] In practice, the courts ignore the theoretical distinction between illegal and prohibited groups and frequently convict members of disapproved Muslim groups under both statutes.

The Uzbek Supreme Soviet also banned foreign aid to political parties through legislation on 16 April 1992. It not only banned foreign government sources but also any individual or organisational sources of funding. The aim was clearly to set up the funding for any kind of illegal and banned activities. As most of the terrorist organisations work either as religious or political organisations with foreign sources of funding this law aimed at cutting off the source of funds for such activities.[71]

Uzbekistan passed the law on political parties on 6 January 1997. In this law, provisions were made prohibiting parties based on ethnic or religious lines, and parties advocating war or subversion of the constitutional order.[72] It has made mandatory for prospective parties to submit full details of 5000 members spread over at least eight of Uzbekistan's 14 regional level administrative territories along with constituent documents and a registration fee, to the Justice Ministry, which would decide on whether to register them or not. Over and above, the Uzbek Supreme Court also has been empowered to suspend registered parties for up to six months and eventually ban them if they persist in violating the legislation.

It has also asked for transparent party funding and ban on parties from using foreign bank accounts and accepting donations from state, foreign, religious or anonymous sources.[73]

The Supreme Court of Uzbekistan on 27 February 1996 decided to introduce tougher punishments for people found guilty of illegally possessing arms and associated with smuggling drugs and weapons. The two resolutions adopted by the plenum of republic's Supreme Court has also envisaged stricter measures against persons who violate legislation related to the right to possess arms, tougher measures against those indulging in smuggling of drugs, arms, ammunitions and other items; the import and export of which is banned-that poses a serious threat to the public and the state.[74] Though draconian, the government of Uzbekistan has this way is trying to contain the proliferation of religious resurgence, particularly the Islamic fundamentalism in the region.

Like Uzbekistan, another country which is immensely affected by the menace of terrorism and militancy is Tajikistan. Therefore, the government of Tajikistan has also made certain laws to counteract the spread of terrorism in the region. On 21 April 1997, the President of Tajikistan issued a decree regarding the anti-terrorism measures. The decree among other things also instructs the government to draft an anti-terrorism programme for the period 1998-2000 and has ordered the Security Ministry to create an anti-terrorism department, including special units, to be staffed with elite troops.[75] Besides this, the Criminal Code of the Republic of Tajikistan also contains several stringent measures that aim to check any violent activity.

The code in article 179, Part-IV provides for capital punishment for acts of terrorism, illegal trafficking of narcotics (article -200, Part-III), illegal cultivation of plants containing narcotic substance (article 306), encroachment on the life of a statesman of the republic of Tajikistan (article 310), intentional violation of the norms of the international humanitarian law committed in the course of an armed conflict (article 403, Part -II). It also declares that, "in case of a pardon, death penalty may be changed to deprivation of freedom for a period of 25 years".[76]

In 1992, the then President of Tajikistan Rakhmanov Nabiyev strongly defending the secular character of the state, said in an interview to "Pravda" that it was necessary to create 'the own legal, secular, democratic state based on richest experience of human civilisation'. He also opined, "as far the transformation of the republic of Tajikistan in the near future into an Islamic state, I must say that Tajikistan will maintain the secular character of the state".[77]

On 4 August 1992, the President passed another decree on disbanding illegal armed formations. Under it, the executive committees of the Soviet People's Deputies of all levels, which created all sorts of self-defence headquarters and detachments not provided for by the law, were instructed to take all measures to have them surrender weapons.[78] Though, these are the few instances of the legislative measures taken by Tajikistan's government there are several other laws which indirectly or directly aim at curbing terrorism in the state viz. language law, the anti-narcotics law, the arms laws etc.

Other republics have also enacted similar laws to counter terrorism in their respective countries. Kyrgyzstan, on 5 February 1992, adopted a law called "Law on Freedom of Confessions". It encompasses provisions on religious practices as well as on religious organisations. The law has imposed restrictions on activities related to protection of public safety, order, life, health, morals and the rights and liberties of other citizens.[79]

Turkmen government led by Niyazov passed an anti-terrorism law in the country's parliament in 1992 along with an arms law and new language law.

Kazakhstan has also passed an anti-terrorism law to counter the menace of terrorism effectively. During his visit to New Delhi in 1992, Nazarbayev told that Kazakhstan will remain a secular state. He said, "The government of Kazakhstan rejects any form of extremism, including religious extremism. Islamic fundamentalism would put us back several centuries".[80]

On 20 July 1995, the Deputy Prime Minister of Kazakhstan instructed his officials to draw up a document to regulate the activities of the religious groups and sects operating in Kazakhstan after concerns were expressed over the way some of them were behaving. In the meeting, he also said "some of the embassies of Islamic states are sending young men and women from our country to their countries without obtaining the approval of the Muslim spiritual leadership of Kazakhstan".[81] Among all the sects and religious groups, the main concern of the government is the proliferation of Islamic fundamentalism for which they have been under the close watch of the Kazakhstan's government.

The Kazakh President Nazarbayev has also been actively trying to counteract the spread of Islamic extremism. He therefore, on 22 September 1999, set up an Inter-Departmental Commission of the Security Council to oversee the job. The then aide to the President on national security issues and Secretary of the Security Council of the republic, Marat Tazhin, was appointed to head the commission.[82]

The Kazakh government's National Security Council on 9 November 1999 approved a security strategy up to 2005. The council did not discuss the case of Islamic fundamentalism especially but adopted plans on the control of the hot spots which were facing armed conflicts. It especially focussed on aviation security. The meeting and the security strategy adopted there focussed especially on the problems of drug trafficking and drug abuse in Kazakhstan. The security strategy also confirmed the setting up of a special authorised body to counter the spread of drugs in the republic.[83]

Despite being a country less affected by terrorism, Kazakhstan has been very cautious in this regard. It still has not attracted the kind of terrorism the others are facing but being situated on the borders of the much more volatile countries like Tajikistan and Uzbekistan, Kazakhstan has no other option but to be on alert and take necessary steps time to time.

Though Turkmenistan is least affected by militancy and terrorist activities, it is largely a transit route for Afghan and Central Asian drugs to the European countries and the sanctuary for the fleeing Afghan and other Central Asian radical Islamic leaders. Keeping this fact in view, the Turkmenistan government has, of late, started taking suitable legislative measures to check the fundamentalist activities and drugs trading.

Turkmenistan's Foreign Minister Avdi Kuliyev on his way back to home from Tehran in February 1992 said , "our goal is not to Islamise our state" indicating that the cooperation with the other Islamic countries in the region would not transform Turkmenistan into an Islamic state. He added that, "we are not going to elevate someone's ideology to the state level, even Islamic, which has its roots in our country. Turkmenistan is neither Islamic, nor Soviet, but a secular and democratic state".[84]

Other than this, Turkmenistan has also passed several laws to counter the problem of fundamentalism, radicalism and the trafficking of drugs.

In another set of measures initiated by President Nursultan Nazarbayev in Kazakhstan to counteract the growth of Islamic fundamentalism he severed Kazakhstan's religious ties with the Muslim Religious Boards and created a separate Muftiate in 1990, in an attempt to reduce the spillover effect of the perceived Islamic fundamentalist activities in neighbouring Uzbekistan.[85]

Tajikistan became the second Central Asian republic to create its own separate Muftiate in the aftermath of the civil war in 1992, essentially to curtail the influence of the Islamic forces operating within Tajik territory, particularly in Fergana Valley and sympathetic to the Islamic Renaissance Party. Turkmenistan and Kyrgyzstan have not yet separated their Muftiate officially because, Turkmenistan is not facing the problem of terrorism like others are and Kyrgyzstan's local mufti is strongly in favour of Tashkent Muftiate and does not want to separate.[86]

In addition to these legal measures, these countries are members of different international organisations like UN, OSCE, OEC and also part of the CIS Collective Security Agreement. Therefore, the anti-terrorism resolutions of these organisations like UN are binding on these states to take necessary steps to clamp down on it whenever necessary.

Legal measures always provide the strength and instrument for the enforcement authorities to act against the culprits to keep up the law and order in the society. But it is no end in itself nor can it solely fight out the menace successfully. Therefore, the counter terrorism moves of the republics are being adequately supplemented by other operational measures.

Co-option, Appeasement and Coercion

In their endeavour to stave off the threat of Islamic fundamentalism, the Central Asian governments have resorted to the policies of assimilation of the Islamic forces and appeasement to religious sentiment in general. In both Kazakhstan and Uzbekistan, the official clerical structures have made numerous attempts to co-opt the members of the Islamic opposition to prevent further radicalisation of their activities. Mufti Ratbek, for instance, extended an invitation to the unofficial clergy- particularly from Chimkent and Jambul - sympathetic to the IRP to join the official clerical establishment. In Uzbekistan, the former Mufti Muhammad Sadiq Muhammad Yusuf had met with IRP and unofficial clergy on numerous occasions to assimilate them into the Muftiate,[87] but to no avail. One such meeting was publicised during the fifth Kurultay of the Muslim Religious Board of Central Asia on 26 February 1992. Reportedly the, Mufti Muhammad Yusuf met with Islamic opposition representatives, including the Mufti of Tashkent, Abduraziz Mansur, an IRP supporter. The meeting was mediated by the Uzbek presidential adviser, Bakhtiyar Nazarov, during which IRP members were offered posts of deputy muftis, but the Muftiate's proposal was turned down.[88] The basic objection of the Islamic opposition has been the government's constant monitoring of and interference with, the affairs of the religious establishment. The Central Asian governments have also been active in placating the public in an effort to reduce the appeals of the Islamic opposition forces which includes financial assistance for the construction and renovation of mosques, which has been done sometimes quietly and indirectly through the official clerical structures, or with fanfare and propaganda, to boost the image of the republican leaders in Uzbekistan and Kazakhstan, as well as in Kyrgyzstan and Turkmenistan. Karimov has, for instance, organised and refurbished many Islamic holy sites including the Islamic complex at the shrine of the Sufi leader, Khoja Bahauddin Naqsband. In addition, local television and radio stations have incorporated limited Islamic and language programmes designed to reach the more traditional segment of the population in Kazakhstan and Kyrgyzstan. On 25 February 1994, Tajikistan banned the broadcast of all programmes "that might offend national traditions and generally accepted moral standards".[89] The state media has also been prohibited from carrying advertisements for alcoholic beverages and tobacco products.

Another important policy to combat fundamentalism has taken the form of repression and crackdown on the religious opposition, which has been carried out systematically in Uzbekistan and Tajikistan and to a lesser extent in Turkmenistan and Kazakhstan.

Governments have declared the prominent groups like IRP, HT, IMU, and Adolat as banned groups. In Tajikistan, presently IRP is a constituent of the government as per the post-civil war settlement. In 1993, at least 20 high ranking members of the outlawed IRP in Uzbekistan, including its Chairman, Abdullah Utaev, were jailed.[90] Members of Adolat who exercised considerable power in Fergana Valley in 1992 were arrested and tried. In Tajikistan, criminal charges were brought against the Chairman and the Deputy Chairman of the IRP as well as former Kazi Turazanjoda and a leading IRP member, Mullah Abdullah Nuri (Mir Saidov). Since July 1993, a host of other IRP leaders including Ajik Aliyev were tried and sentenced to death by the government of Imamoli Rahmonov.[91] Several hundred sympathisers of IRP have also been captured and executed without trial since 1992 in the Kulyab and elsewhere in southern Tajikistan. In Kazakhstan, members of the Religious Nationalist Party Alash, have been tried and given jail sentences, forcing its leaders to go into exile.

Prior to this, the Uzbek President on 17 and 18 March ordered the mass arrest of the Muslim leaders in Namangan as a part of his severe crackdown. The police arrested 19 members out of originally listed 71 people. The religious affairs buildings were ransacked and the city was brought under the administration of Ministry of Internal Affairs units.[92]

During the Tajik civil war, the government took all possible military steps to suppress the armed groups. There were also several cases where massive killings of the armed gangs were carried on, for example, on 11 January 1993, in the Pamir region, the Tajik government forces surrounded, killed and disarmed a large group of militants.[93]

Karimov came heavily on the armed groups and terrorists, who in February 1993, declared a 'war' against organised crime and ordered 'tough measures' by the national security service and Ministry of Internal Affairs.[94] The Uzbek government also took strict steps to control the proliferation of arms and in this regard heavy punishments were awarded. In 1995, when the condition was 'stable', according to an officer in the army, Uzbek police seized a big quantity of arms and other contrabands from him.[95]

Karimov in a strong statement condemning 'Political Islam' in 1998 said that he would never allow the religious extremism to take root in Uzbekistan. On 17 April same year, he told the press conference that "we in Uzbekistan will never give the go ahead to those who are today trying by any means to introduce political Islam, religious extremism and fanaticism". He, in the same conference, also said that one way to avoid religious fanaticism was to 'integrate with European structures'.[96]

In the strongest ever gesture and statement, President Karimov in May 1998, told the parliament that he was ready to shoot the leaders of an Islamic fundamentalist movement himself if MPs lack the courage to do so. He said, "such people must be shot on the forehead! If necessary, I will shoot them myself, if you lack the resoluteness!"[97] In the same speech, he said that Islamic warriors were trained in Tajikistan in order to 'blow up their homeland'. Explaining why the law put new restrictions on the registration of religious groups, he further said that if the society did not take strict measures against fundamentalism then, "Uzbekisthan will become Tajikisthan, tomorrow". In another bizarre declaration, he announced that there was to be a public trial on 2 May 1998 of 'bandits' accused of planning to blow up dairies, water reservoirs, power stations and official buildings in the Fergana towns of Namangan and Andizhan, and that the trial would eventually be broadcast on state television.[98] The above description shows the extent of desperation of the President to suppress extremists.

A public trial began the next day in which members of an Islamic fundamentalist group whose alleged aim was to set up an Islamic state in the country, Vali Egamberdiyev and Mukhtar Mannonov were shown behind the bars admitting to their connection to the groups and their crimes.[99]

In another instance of his harsh attitude, Uzbekistan's Supreme Court on 5 June 1998 sentenced seven men to terms of imprisonment ranging from seven to ten years for attempting to destabilise the country and establish an Islamic state. In the previous month, a court in Namangan had sentenced 12 people to prison terms of five to eight years on similar charges.[100] Cases of trial and awarding punishment to the suspected Islamic extremists continued in the following months also. There were several cases of capital punishment, which were awarded for charges like attempting to undermine the constitutional system, igniting the ethnic and religious animosity, illegal possession of arms and drugs and terrorism.[101] These were the common charges under which most of the cases were tried and persons prosecuted. According to one source, while one person was sentenced to death on these charges, another 26 received long prison sentences in 1998.[102]

The Uzbek crackdown on the Islamic militants went up by leaps and bounds especially after the Tashkent bombing of 16 February 1999, in which an attempt was made on the life of the President himself. On 23 February 1999, the President declared that 30 persons were arrested on charges of bombing.

The Supreme Court of Uzbekistan handed down severe punishment to 22 people in June 1999, who were suspected of involvement in Tashkent bombing. Out of 22, six persons were sentenced death penalty, eight were awarded 20 year jail terms and other eight were sentenced to terms between 10-18 years in high security prisons with confiscation of property.[103]

Besides closing down the mosques, the Uzbek government in the fear that religious extremism might spill over to Uzbekistan from neighbouring Afghanistan and Tajikistan, intensified the crackdown, with arrests being made for merely wearing beards as a sign of their faith.[104]

The Fergana Valley is not the only problematic region in Uzbekistan. But while international attention has been fixed on the alleged fierce fighting against terrorism in the Fergana Valley, serious repressive measures have been undertaken in other regions, such as that of Surkhan Darya. In August, some 4000 inhabitants were forcibly evacuated from their homes by the military as a result of collective punishment to the villages on suspicion of some inhabitant's alleged sympathy with and assistance to the IMU. Their villages were burnt.[105]

In June 2001, 73 men were tried on charges of terrorism and anti-constitutional activities, for "establishing links" with IMU and related acts. All of the 73 men were found guilty and sentenced to between three to eighteen years of imprisonment.

In the post-September 11 attack on World Trade Centre in US and the subsequent American engagement in Afghanistan with a broad slogan "fight against terror", the anti-terrorism efforts have undergone a substantial change. It is now being viewed by President Karimov as a justification for the repressive measures of the pervious years and for the crackdown to follow in the future on the Islamic fundamentalists.

A well known poet and activist of 'Birlik' movement, Yusuf Jumaev, was arrested on 23 October 2001. He was accused of publicly calling for an "unconstitutional change of the existing order".[106]

Simultaneously along with the crackdown on the fundamentalist religious forces, the Uzbek government is also attacking the major source of sustenance of the terrorism, i.e., the drug and arms trade. Strong punishments have been recommended in the country's anti-narcotics laws.

Uzbekistan, from the very beginning, has been dealing with the problems of militancy and terrorism with an 'iron hand'. Realisation of the importance of having a secular, multi-ethnic government and the experience of Afghanistan and Iran in the neighbourhood having an Islamic state, prompted the Central Asian leaders to discourage religious and political extremism through all possible means. Coming from a background with communist set up in the erstwhile Soviet Union, they had all experienced

Stalin's purges in dealing with the opposition and the methods he adopted to deal with the religious sentiment during his period.

Another country which has been in the vortex of terrorism and religious fundamentalism is Tajikistan. As discussed in the previous chapter, the civil war in the immediate aftermath of independence created a scenario wherein, the state machinery was negated and militarily challenged. In this troubled water, the fundamentalist militant organisations, like IRP, found a suitable opportunity to further their own agenda of establishing an Islamic state. But the situation improved gradually with the intervention of the international powers and the government came out heavily on the Islamists.

The Tajik government, in May 1992, ordered the border guards to strongly check any kind of border crossing from the other side. In another measure in July 1992, the Tajik government created a department for disarming illegal formations operating on the republic's territory. It was expected that the sub-units of this department would employ professionals with a lot of experience in combating organised crime. The department also included snatch groups and motorised units.[107] On 12 October 1992, the Tajik National Security Committee set up a General Security Directorate. The directorate was divided into five departments for handling the campaign against illegal armed gangs, protecting constitutional order preventing mass disturbances, fighting corruption and organised crime in the economy and finally fighting organised crime involving smuggling and drugs.[108]

The government also resorted to rampant and strict prosecution of the leaders of the opposition groups as well as the suspected militants. In January 1993, judicial prosecutions were initiated against Haj Akbar Turanjudzoda, the then spiritual head of Tajik Muslims, Shadmon Yusuf, the leader of the Democratic Party of Tajikistan and former Deputy Prime Minister Davlat Usmon, Deputy Chairman of the Islamic Rebirth Party. These leaders were accused of entering into a criminal collusion in May 1992 for the purpose of seizing power and overthrowing the lawfully elected leadership of the republic. They were also charged of creating unlawful armed groups and masterminding combat actions that led to the fratricidal war and entailed thousand casualties and multi billion dollar damage to the national economy of Tajikistan.[109]

The Tajikistani leaders also from time to time by their statements, have tried to express their firmness and stringency as far as militancy is concerned. After the murder of the Deputy Prime Minister, the Tajik President almost declared a 'war' on crime in his statement on 7 August 1995.[110] Further, in his Ramadan address to the nation, President Rahmanov categorically rejected religious extremism. In 1998 address, he said, "we will not let an extremist and separatist outlook regardless of how it is dressed up, to be imposed by force on our people because an extremist outlook has not led to peace, tranquillity and calm in any Muslim country". He also said that it was disrespectful "to the true religion of Islam to put it to the political ends".[111]

President Rahmanov, in an address to the Tajik intelligentsia said that the roots of religious extremism and fanaticism were still very much alive in the country and he called upon everybody to eliminate these roots. From the same stage, he decried the then Taliban leadership of Afghanistan for its extremist and ignorant attitude. He accused Taliban of destroying the country's historical and cultural heritage, in an apparent reference to the destruction of the Buddha statue in Bamiyan. He described the extremist attitude as unislamic and 'ignorance'.[112]

Tajikistan's crackdown also extended to the very sources of support to militancy and extremism. On 12 April 1996, President Imamoli Rahmonov issued a decree spelling out "urgent measures" to tackle the growing drugs problems in the republic. The decree is designed to curtail drug smuggling and tighten up on the production and marketing of drugs in Tajikistan.[113]

In another attempt, the Tajik government set up a national headquarter to coordinate the poppy-96 anti-drugs campaign under the leadership of Deputy Prime Minister Jamalidelin Mansurov, the government also through a resolution made it mandatory for all the local authorities to set up similar bodies, and special groups to seek out illegal plantations.[114] Tajikistan also took tough judicial measures to curb the drug trafficking. Tajikistan's penalties for drug traffickers are also stringent. Under article 200 of the Criminal Code, the death penalty may be employed, and fifteen to twenty years sentences are not uncommon.[115] The death penalty depends upon the quantity of drugs caught on a person, rather than whether it is a repeated offence. Technically, the penalty can be imposed for anything beyond one kilogram, but it is rarely applied for that quantity.[116]

The anti-terrorism effort in Tajikistan also has undergone a sea change after the opposition alliance UTO, joined the government which is the first instance of any Islamic organisation joining the government. Now the efforts are basically concentrated on those organisations which are not members of UTO and are carrying out their operations, like Hizb-ut-Tahrir.

The second most important factor which has brought a change is the September 11 attack on US and the subsequent American intervention in Afghanistan. Due to its strategic importance, the international community has widely focussed on the Tajik-Afghan border. In spite of the initial hiccups and internal protests, at a press conference in Dushanbe on 7 November 2001, President Rahmonov confirmed that the country will provide an air-corridor for conducting military rescue and search actions.[117]

Tajikistan has also engaged in serious combat against international terrorism. Following UN Security Resolution No. 1373, the Tajik President signed a decree on 13 November that provides, for example, for the national bank and the commercial banks are to freeze bank accounts and other financial assets belonging to the persons and organsiations who directly or indirectly are connected to the execution of or attempts of terrorist acts. The Ministry of Justice was ordered to submit within one month, suggestions on how to bring all legislations into line with the decree.[118]

From the above discussions, we can succinctly make out that Tajikistan, next to Uzbekistan, is the most targeted state in Central Asia, by the fundamentalist forces. But after the Tajik civil war, the Tajik authorities have also come down heavily on these forces and are in control of the situation though human rights, democracy and the civil society have been affected to some extent.

The next in Central Asia to have experienced the impact of militancy and terrorism is Kyrgyzstan. Being a bordering state of China, Kyrgyzstan has also been witnessing the activities of the Uighur separatists of the Xinjiang region in China. Besides that, it being a transit republic from Tajikistan to Uzbekistan's Fergana Valley, Kyrgyzstan has been affected by the terrorism in the region. More than that, it has become the latest hub of the region's drug trade and the Afghan drug finds its route through Kyrgyzstan to Russia and Europe.

The relatively less militancy affected republic of Kyrgyzstan became the hot spot of Central Asia after the post-Batken incident of 1999. Not only incursions and armed attacks but also the hostage taking of several foreigners including few Japanese geologists drew the attention of the international community towards it, thereby putting tremendous pressure on the administration to toe the line of the other republics in dealing with the terrorists. Equipped with suitable constitutional provisions, anti-terrorism laws, arms laws, language laws, and religious practices laws, Kyrgyzstan has of late, come down heavily, militarily on the Islamic fundamentalist forces who are trying to take over the state.

Fearing the heavy crackdown by the Karimov administration, the Islamic fundamentalists of Uzbekistan started fleeing to Kyrgyzstan which has been relatively liberal in dealing with organisations like Hizb-ut-Tahrir and IRP.[119] Whereas, in Tajikistan members are sentenced to an average of eight to twelve years in prison for "anti-governmental activities", they receive an average of two to four years of imprisonment in Kyrgyzstan, and are more often fined than imprisoned.[120]

The head of the National Security Services in Osh oblast, Marat Imankulov has said that he does not favour strong arm methods and believes that the local Imams should be at the forefront of the educational work among believers.[121]

But under pressure from Uzbekistan, Kyrgyzstan has become harsher in its policy towards all kinds of Islamic forces. In one of the initial measures to curb the spread of radicalism, Kyrgyzstan on 2 October 1995 banned religious and aesthetic teaching in the republic's educational institutions.[122] One of the Bishkek newspapers 'Svobodnyye Gory' published a government resolution in August announcing the creation of a body to monitor religious affairs and instructing the justice and security services to put a stop to "unconstitutional activities carried out by foreign Kyrgyz citizens under the guise of religion". The resolution said that the religious climate in the republic as a whole was "cause for concern".[123]

Acting on the alleged separatist activities of the Uighurs, Kyrgyz Justice Ministry issued a resolution suspending the activities of the Ittipak (Union) Society of Ethnic Uighurs for three months for their failure to hold earlier official warnings, on 4 April 1996.[124] The resolution said the Ittipak society has "continued to carry out separatist activities or to be more precise, a policy contradicting the interests of the Chinese people, despite recent warnings of the Ministry of Justice and special resolution of the Prosecutor General". The activities of the society violated the article in the Kyrgyz constitution, covering public associations and also the Kyrgyz - China communiqué, signed on 16 May 1992, on non-interference in each other's internal affairs.[125] The ban debarred the society from campaigning in the press and media, from organising any meetings, demonstrations or other mass activities in Kyrgyzstan for three months.

In another case of harsh crackdown, the Kyrgyz security forces uncovered an illegal 'group of foreigners' sending minors to neighbouring states where they were trained as religious militants in May 1998. The police confiscated hundreds of audio and video cassettes calling for a sacred war against the unfaithful and large quantities of religious literature, with some openly sadistic and extremist publications.[126] Messir Ashirkulov, the Interior Minister said, "Extremism whenever it may come from is a threat to the national security of Kyrgyzstan". He also added that there were religious leaders in Kyrgyzstan propagating 'Wahhabism'. He promised that the National Security Ministry would continue taking resolute steps to stop its spread in Kyrgyzstan.

The Kyrgyz government had become more stringent in its approach to the Islamic extremism in the beginning of 2000. The presidential spokesman Kanibek Imanalyev told Interfax news agency on 12 May 1998 that Kyrgyzstan would act to stop any expression of religious extremism and terrorism in the republic as it poses a threat to national security.[127] Same day in another press briefing, he told that the public was concerned about the religious extremism, particularly the appearance of Wahhabi missionaries, who, according to him were discrediting Islam. He also passed a warning saying that "any movement aimed at personal or other interests under the cover of Islam would be identified and strict action would be taken against them".[128]

In another interesting step, the intellectuals of Kyrgyzstan in August 1998 decided to set up a centre to help end religious extremism, wild outburst of amorality, social cataclysms and nationalist tendencies, which, as they described, are extremely dangerous for "every sensible person and for the whole world public".[129]

The President of Kyrgyzstan Askar Akayev in March 2000, expressed apprehension that international terrorist formations might attempt to penetrate Kyrgyzstan from the neighbouring republics. Akayev, at the same time, instructed the law enforcement agencies to beef up the security of important and strategic installations. He also reiterated the strong preparedness of Kyrgyzstan for any kind of terrorist strike.[130]

Cracking down on the terrorist group can not be successful without cutting down their source of supply in terms of men, money and arms. Therefore, the Kyrgyz government has also taken several operational measures to control drugs trafficking as well as arms proliferation. Tough laws have been enacted to control the drug traffickers and arms proliferators.

In April 1998, Kyrgyzstan was the first country in Central Asia to pass a comprehensive law. Its new criminal code includes the death penalty for large scale drug trafficking. According to the Interior Ministry sources, the law was drafted in compliance with three anti-drug conventions to which the republic signed up in 1994.[131]

Though Kyrgyzstan is relatively less affected by terrorism and has a strong legal system as far as fighting terrorism is concerned, it is bowing to the pressures of the neighbouring powers as well as other international forces and has therefore adopted strong arm measures against the militants of several banned groups. There have been several cases of human rights violations but due to weak political opposition the issue has not come much into limelight.

Being the largest among all the Central Asian republics, Kazakhstan has been the natural leader of the region. The sheer size of the country and its geographical location makes it very important as far as approaching Russia is concerned. Therefore, Kazakhstan has also been widely used by the militants Islamists and drug traders in their northward expansion.

Equipped with an anti-terrorism law and other relevant laws, Kazakhstan as far as cracking down on the militants is concerned, also has adopted an aggressive policy. A closer examination of the actions taken over the last few years would give a proper understanding of the nature of the policy, the republic of Kazakhstan has adopted in this regard.

In April 1998, the Kazakh Interior Ministry set up a special unit in Almaty to protect foreign residents from the kidnappers and to investigate crimes committed against them. The step was taken after several cases of hostage taking and extortion were reported last year.[132]

In the same year, the Kazakh government cracked down on several missionary groups for propagating radical Islamic religious teaching. The law enforcement agencies also took note of the fact that a number of Kazakh residents were studying at foreign clerical centres preaching Islamic radicalism.[133]

Few months later, authorities in Kazakhstan instituted criminal proceedings against members of a radical Islamic sect in the oil rich Atyrau region in Western Kazakhstan in October 1998. About 30 members of this Wahhabi religious sect aged 10 to 40 were arrested and another 100 were put under watch.[134] The Prosecutor's office said these "Wahhabi" followers were inciting the people to disobey the authorities and follow the sect's rules. Further, it alleged that the leaders of the sect used as a means of propaganda, audio and video cassettes with recordings of call for 'jihad' or 'holy war', manuscripts magazines and photocopies of type written texts brought into Kazakhstan from Moscow and Makhachkala (capital city of Russian republic of Dagestan).[135]

In another important incident, seven suspects in Tashkent bombing were arrested and extradited to Uzbekistan in March 1999 by Kazakhstan. For this purpose, the Kazakh authorities checked 50 secret addresses and had questioned 30 witnesses.[136] All of them were Wahhabis from the IMU. Investigations found that Almaty was a refuge and safe-haven for them, from where they were sent to other countries. Recruits had been taught how to wage subversive activities and commit acts of terrorism.[137] The above example is an expression of the seriousness of the Kazakh authorities not to let their country become a hub of Islamic radical activities. Through the above incident the Kazakhs either wanted to send a message to the other groups that their country can not be used for narrow religious objectives or fearful of Uzbek hostility which it could least afford. On 30 October 1999, Mazhit Isabekov, the Deputy Head of Regional Department of the National Security Committee urged for the tighter supervision of the Islamic groups.

In another very interesting and far reaching step, the Interior Minister of Kazakhstan, Kairbek Suleimanov declared the year 2000 as the "Year of Fighting Organised Crime" in the parliament in March 2000.[138]

The then newly formed eastern military district of Kazakh armed forces held its first ever exercises in August to thwart any terrorist attack and waging war in mountainous region.[139] This was a step which was unprecedented at that time. It expressed Kazakhstan's urge and concerns to fight the menace of terrorism.

Acting in line with a recommendation from Kazakh President Nursultan Nazarbayev on 7 September, the Kazakh authorities decided to recall the Kazakh students studying at Islamic academic institutions abroad.[140] The Director of the Kazakh Higher Education Department, Abdumutalib Abzhapparov said that the uncontrolled training of Kazakh citizens at Islamic academic institutions threatened the national security of Kazakhstan.[141] He further added that most of these people had gone there with the assistance of the mosques, embassies or through private agreements and without the involvement of the Ministry and he was not aware of what they were doing there.

Under the coordination of the National Security Council of Kazakhstan, the President of Kazakhstan approved a programme on fighting terrorism and extremism for the year 2000-2003 on 9 November 2000.[142]

Kazakhstan also increased its military preparedness in the year 2000. The southern military stationed in the town of Tanaz, the administrative centre of Zambyl region was set up. The detached 5th Motor Rifle Company specialising in military actions in mountainous and desert terrain was trained in the units protecting the border. In addition, active training of the sniper groups was undertaken; people with the background of chasseurs and professional hunters were recruited for military service; the citizens from the local population were also recruited to work as guides.[143] Through border guards, detachments were set up on the southern front, 25 new customs checkpoints were set up and a rapid reaction patrol company was stationed in Saryagash district of south Kazakhstan.

In addition to this, Kazakhstan's special services created a data bank on all terrorist bands active in the region and on their leaders and members.

On the basis of the information available, urgent search raids were carried out and the 'activities of the radical Hizb-ut-Tahrir religious grouping were strictly stopped'.

On religious front, intensive works were carried out to prevent and stop radical views. Councils for liaison with religious associations under the government and akims (heads of the regions) were set up to this end.[144]

Illegal migrations were also strictly prevented to combat terrorism. The regulations for issuing visas to citizens of Tajikistan, Pakistan and a number of other countries were considerably tightened and illegal migrants were also deported on a large scale. Around 1,446 citizens of foreign states were deported from the republic in the first nine months of 2000.

Special watch was also kept on the terrorists who had links with national or foreign terrorist organisations. A data bank in this regard was also created. Migration control cards were introduced for the inter-regional travellers.[145]

Confirming these steps taken by Kazakh authorities, the Kazakh Security Council Secretary on 27 November said that Kazakhstan's armed forces were fully prepared to take part in the Central Asian region.[146]

In order to curb terrorists activities, Kazakh authorities also have taken some measures to weaken them financially. As discussed earlier, the main sources of the extremists' finances are drugs and arms trafficking. Therefore, Kazakh government drafted required strategy to curb them.

First of all, Kazakhstan revived the criminal code to ensure law enforcement agencies go after the drug dealers rather then users.[147] Recently, however, drug trafficking has become so serious that some officials have proposed introducing the death penalty for trafficking.[148] That measure has not yet been passed,[149] but officials are taking steps to tighten the borders. In 2000, US$9,00,000 was allocated for this purpose, a figure that rose to US$1 million in 2001 and doubled in 2002.[150]

The anti-terrorism measures have received a tremendous fillip after the recent American intervention in Afghanistan. On 8 November 2001, Allyubek Sarsenbaevm, the Security Advisor to the President Nazarbayev said that his country had plans to step up its assistance to the US-led campaign against terrorism. On the same day, President Nazarbayev said during a meeting with the head of diplomatic missions in Almaty that his country was prepared to campaign against terrorism with all means at its disposal. Kazakhstan offered the US to use its airspace and bases.[151]

Since the 11 September, and the launch of war in Afghanistan, there has been a notable increase in security controls at the borders of

Kazakhstan. Also, an increasing number of people who are (who are believed to be) members or supporters of Hizb-ut-Tahrir have been arrested in recent months.[152]

Ethnic Tajiks and Kyrgyz men have been deported from the country. Kazakhstan has unilaterally posed restrictions on Tajik citizen's entry in to Kazakhstan. Kazakhstan, though facing low intensity militancy has drastically stepped up its crackdown on religious fundamentalists. The state crackdown increased after 1998 in the post-Tajik civil war period. A possible reason for this could be that in the post-Tajik civil war period the activists of the armed opposition either joined the army or scattered to other countries in search of greener pastures with Kazakhstan receiving a chunk of it. Also, Kazakhstan being a country with little democratic development and faced with the fear of religious radicalism has opted for the path of suppression by force rather than addressing the situation more democratically. Moreover, the US fight against terrorism in Afghanistan has given a certain amount of legitimacy to the Kazakh crackdown on the Islamic radical forces.

As far as the growth of Islamic radicalism and terrorism is concerned, Turkmenistan poses a different picture. It is the only Central Asian republic which maintained a cordial relationship with Taliban through out its existence. It allowed certain amount of religious activity in the country. But Turkmenistan has responded, though in a lesser degree to the activities of the radical forces.

As early as 19 April 1994, the President of Turkmenistan Samparmurat Niyazov addressed a gathering of the religious leaders in the country where he said that, "any attempt to intervene in state affairs will be decisively stopped".[153]

In the same meeting, the President further emphasised that Turkmenistan is a "secular democratic state, laws of which give everybody right to freedom of religion". In a constructive approach to the religious establishments, he appealed for use of their authority to wage a war against drug addiction. He also announced the creation of a Council of Religious Affairs under the President of Turkmenistan which would consist of Muslim qazis together with the workers of the Russian Orthodox Church.[154]

In Turkmenistan, only Muslim communities loyal to the officially sanctioned Muslim Board and some parishes of the Russian Orthodox Church have been allowed to register as legal religious communities. Other religious groups and other minority religions face continuing harassment. Numerous non-registered mosques and Qoranic schools have been closed down.[155] Hundreds of foreign religious activists have been expelled in recent years.[156]

Though the media coverage of the September 11 terrorist attack was minimal in Turkmenistan, it could not keep itself aloof despite its desire to do so. President Niyazov did not allow the US to use the country's territory for military purposes. Turkmenistan had agreed only to act as a base for humanitarian aid.[157]

According to Vitaly Ponomarov of the 'Memorial'- the Moscow based human rights organisation- in the post-September 11 incidents, the members of the suspected supporters of the former political opposition have been increasingly monitored. In 2000, restrictions had already been imposed on the freedom of movement within Turkmenistan, as well as the foreigners visiting the country and many were deported. Since 1988, there have been limitations on Islamic activities.[158]

Suppression of religious minorities has also been adopted by Turkmenistan as a policy to counter any kind of religious radical upsurge. In 1999, the authorities in Ashgabat spent a week destroying the newly built Adventist Church with bulldozers.[159] As mentioned before, the authorities also expelled a large number of religious minority people in 1999. Besides, they carried on their second agenda of crushing the religious minorities. But this strong repression has been directed towards all non-Islamic sects, while Islamic sects-particularly those belonging to Sunni sect has been patronised. Officials at all level, whether in KNB, the police local administrators or the Council of Religious Affairs- have repeatedly declared that only Islam and Orthodox Churches are allowed in the country, despite the fact that nowhere is this stated in the law.[160] Through these actions, the Turkmen authorities are trying to show a reconciliatory attitude towards the Islamic community and win its confidence. Niyazov is fully aware that suppression of Islamic resurgence might be a step but can never be the only step. Therefore, other methods like appeasement have been tried.

Turkmenistan's crackdown on the drug trafficking and production is also equally emphatic. Being a country used as a transit point for drug trafficking to the CIS and Europe from Afghanistan, Turkmenistan in the recent years has been cracking down on the on this business.

President Niyazov, in May 1998, approved a state programme to control illegal drug trafficking, through the year 2000. The programme was scheduled to be carried out by the government commission in charge of the fight against drug trafficking. At the same time, funds for the programme's implementation were allocated.

Besides burning down the seized drugs, Turkmenistan, in February

1998, set up a special anti-drug department. Later, in another decree the banks were prevented from laundering the proceeds from the illegal drug deals, as well as annual exercises for anti-drug units were provisioned.[161]

Regional Cooperation as a Measure to Fight Militancy

The unrest in Central Asia has forged a consensus among the countries of the region and the great regional powers based on recognition that they are all threatened by a syndrome of lawlessness that involves political opposition, radical religious doctrines, gun running and narcotics trafficking. As Kyrgyzstan's President Askar Akayev, put it, the traffic in drugs and weapons has become "problem number one" for his country.[162] Similarly, Kazakhstan's President, Nazarbayev warned that drugs, terrorism and competition over the country's scarce water resources were the threats to stability in Central Asia.[163] During a visit to Kazakh capital, Astana, in March 2000, Defence Minister Igor Sergeev informed his Central Asian colleagues that "the military political situation in this region suggests that the Central Asian states are in the vanguard of the struggle against international terrorism and religious extremism".[164]

The consensus on the seriousness of the threat has brought forth a new spirit of cooperation among the states of the region. Therefore, in order to fight the menace of terrorism and militancy, the Central Asian nations have entered into cooperation and agreements of different kinds. They can be classified into categories such as:

- Bilateral agreements on mutual cooperation against terrorism and drug related crimes.
- Multilateral agreements with more than three countries of Central Asia and CIS countries and
- Bilateral agreements between Central Asian states and other foreign powers.

Bilateral Agreements

Since 1992, the Central Asian republics have began efforts for cooperation to thwart the emergence of militancy and terrorism, often called in politico-legal language as 'organised crime'. Though all the treaties and cooperation declarations do not directly deal with the subject, some of them indirectly aim at it.

Abdumalik Abdullozhonov, the then Tajik Premier, met the Uzbek officials on the Tajik-Uzbek border. During the meeting, Uzbek side offered "all round assistance" to stabilise the situation in Tajikistan.[165] On the agreed condition, Uzbekistan set up 40 militia posts on the border with Tajikistan.

An agreement on cooperation or interaction was signed between delegations from the National Security Committee of Kazakhstan and the National Security Service of Uzbekistán in January 1993. The agreement was to enable the two respective security bodies to use the available potential for cooperation, and interaction in the fields of intelligence and counter-intelligence, combating terrorism, drug trafficking, organised crime and corruption more actively on a legal basis.[166]

Though the above agreement was in the security services level, there are a series of agreements at the government level. Uzbekistan and Kazakhstan governments signed a number of cooperation agreements following talks in Almaty on 2 June 1997. The documents included a protocol on further deepening of the cooperation and friendly relations between the two countries and agreements on legal assistance in civil, family and criminal cases and the setting up of a joint inter-governmental commission on bilateral cooperation.[167]

Tajik President Rahmonov visited Uzbekistan in 1998. On 4 January, the same year, the Presidents signed a joint communiqué in Tashkent in which they undertook to oppose political and religious extremism. The both sides also condemned ethnic, racial, and religious intolerance.[168]

During the same meeting, both Uzbek and Tajik Presidents announced plans for joint action to fight the drugs trade which, as Karimov said, was "destabilising the region". Another agreement was signed between the foreign ministers of both the countries in this regard.[169]

An Uzbek delegation of the heads of the Ministry of Foreign Affairs, the National Security Service and Ministry of Internal Affairs visited Tajikistan. Among a wide range of issues of bilateral relations, the Uzbek and Tajik foreign Ministers signed an inter-governmental agreement in fighting terrorism, religious and other forms of extremism and drugs trafficking. The agreement envisaged close cooperation between the law enforcement agencies, including on the territories of both the countries.[170]

In another example of bilateral cooperation, Kyrgyz President Askar Akayev and his Tajik counterpart Rahmonov signed 14 agreements including joint declarations on deepening and developing relations between the two countries on 6 May 1998. Among others, they signed an agreement on cooperation between the Kyrgyz Ministry of Internal Affairs and the Tajik Ministry of National Security on controlling narcotics and the raw materials from which they are produced.[171] The custom agencies of Kyrgyzstan and Tajikistan signed an agreement on cooperation to prevent smuggling and trafficking of arms and drugs.

The Kyrgyz Prime Minister Amangeldi Muraliyev visited Uzbekistan on 9 July 1999. On the same day, the first meeting of the Uzbek-Tajik inter-governmental joint commission took place for discussion on broadening mutual cooperation between the two countries. The meeting concluded with the signing up of the inter-governmental and inter-ministerial documents between the republic of Uzbekistan and the Kyrgyzstan. Uzbek Prime Minister Utkir Sultonov and his Kyrgyz counterpart signed two agreements between the governments of both the republics on cooperation in fighting illegal drugs trafficking and on cooperation in fighting crime.[172] A protocol of the inter-governmental joint commission on bilateral cooperation was signed by Deputy Prime Minister of Uzbekistan Rustom Yunusov and his Kyrgyz counterpart Esengul Omuradiyev during the same visit.

In the wake of the armed incursion in August 1999 in the Batken region in south Kyrgyzstan, the then Kazakh acting Defence Minister Bakhtyzhov Yertoyev announced on 30 August 1999 to send ammunitions and the first detachment of Kazakh reservists to Kyrgyzstan. He further disclosed that a group of Kazakh military experts was currently working in Osh region.[173]

In a joint statement issued by the President of Kazakhstan and Uzbekistan, both the countries on 21 April 2000, on the sidelines of the Central Asian summit in the Uzbek capital Tashkent, pledged to intensify interaction in fighting against the international terrorism, religious and political extremism, smuggling of drugs, psychotropic substances, precursor chemicals and arms and against organised trans-border crime.

They also declared that the sides could perceive any action directed against one of the states as a common threat and would take all measures to counter them. If necessary, joint and coordinated measures would be carried out.[174]

The Kazakhastan President of Nazarbayev visited Tajikistan on 13 June 2000, where he signed nine important documents. Besides exchanging views with his Tajik counterpart on bilateral security, political and religious extremism, drug trade and organised crime, both the leaders signed a declaration on further expansion of relations between Kazakhstan and Tajikistan and inter-governmental agreements on cooperation in the fight against illegal drug trafficking, special official posts on security, arms smuggling etc.[175] The very next day, both the heads of the states decided to create an anti-drug security belt around Afghanistan.

As a quid pro quo of the unprecedented support of the Kyrgyz government to Uzbekistan in August 2000 in the fight against the international terrorists, on 20 August, Uzbek President declared whole-hearted support and approval for the Kyrgyz action on the militants in the south of the country. In a strongly worded statement he said, "I approve of the Kyrgyz army's action and I want to say that we are ready to support the Kyrgyz at any time so as to give the bandit formations a real rebuff so that it teaches not only them, but also their children, not to intrude into the territory not only of Kyrgyzstan but of all Central Asian states".[176] The joint military operation of Kyrgyzstan and Uzbekistan managed to halt the progress of gunmen sponsored by IMU. The gunmen were surrounded and most of them were killed.

Kyrgyz Defence Minister, who visited Kazakhstan on 1 March 2001, signed a defence cooperation protocol on further cooperation with his Kazakhstan counterpart. After the ceremony, Kazakh Defence Minister Tokpakbayev said that the protocol provided for the country's cooperation in the military and technical sectors. Both sides agreed to regularly exchange operational information especially the tactics that the terrorists used in the military clashes in 1999 and 2000 in Batken. They also agreed for a joint military exercise later in 2001.[177]

During the same visit, Kazakhstan's Defence Minister strongly committed his country's support to Kyrgyzstan in case of a fresh incursion by the Islamists into the country.[178]

The bilateral ties among the Central Asian republics have gone a long way in containing militancy and terrorism in the region and cutting down the magnitude of the drugs and arms trade, as in the case of Uzbek-Kyrgyz relations, wherein the cooperation in the military field has contributed tremendously towards meeting the challenges of the militants. Besides this one-to-one joint efforts and tie-ups, there are many multilateral efforts and agreements which have taken place among the Central Asian republics and other CIS countries. They have also contributed to their anti-terrorism endeavour.

Multilateral Cooperation within CIS Republics

Besides the bilateral cooperation endeavours discussed above to combat terrorism, there were also several similar efforts on part of Central Asian states involving members of the CIS countries to form a cooperative mechanism which can help them in curbing the menace of terrorism within the CIS framework. They signed several agreements, treaties and declarations expressing their commitment to the cause even though all of them are not affected by this menace the way the five Central Asian countries are.

Though the Central Asian republics are the worst affected ones as far as terrorism is concerned, there are other CIS countries which are facing the growing challenge of these forces, for example, Armenia and Azerbaijan. Therefore, in the Central Asian efforts to curb the tendency, the other republics are participating in growing numbers.

On the occasion of the birth anniversary of three Kazakh national figures (Talebi, Kazbeki and Aytekebi), Presidents of Kazakhstan, Kyrgyzstan and Uzbekistan signed a joint declaration on 28 May 1993 calling upon the three nations to strengthen friendship and mutual situation in Central Asia.[179] This declaration was the first in the series of following multilateral declarations and treaties within CIS.

An agreement signed between Kazakh, Kyrgyz and Uzbek security forces provided for cooperation between the security forces of these republics. At the same time, Kazakhstan and Kyrgyzstan signed an agreement for cooperation in the field of militancy counter-intelligence.[180]

Russian commander of its border troops, Andrey Ackolayev, signed an agreement in Tashkent on 2 November 1994, on the joint control of the border with Afghanistan with his Uzbek and Tajik counterparts. During the same occasion, a separate ten-year bilateral agreement on regional border security issues was signed between the Russian military head and Uzbekistan's President. This agreement provided for joint efforts against terrorism, arms and drugs smuggling, as well as for social and legal guarantees for troops and families stationed there.[181]

Uzbek and Belarusian leaders also on 22 December 1994 signed twenty agreements including one on mutual cooperation in military intelligence, thus bringing countries like Belarussia to the regional security net.[182] In July 1993, in the field of narcotics control also, the department of narcotics representatives from Kazakh, Kyrgyz, Turkmen, and Uzbek interior ministers met in Kazakhstan to discuss the ways of cooperating in the fight against drug related crime. They signed a protocol which was to form the basis of future action by the interior ministers.[183]

During the last ten years, several treaties and agreements have been signed among the CIS republics which have provided a counter-force to end militancy and terrorism in the Central Asian region. The council of the heads of CIS border troops meeting in Tajik capital in Dushanbe on 22 December 1995 signed 26 documents coordinating border policy throughout the member states and along the Tajik-Afghan frontier. The documents included the Russian -Turkmen Agreements on the presence of up to 1,000 border guards and Russian military advisors in Turkmenistan and an agreement between Kyrgyzstan, Tajikistan and Russia on cooperation to combat drug trafficking on the Tajik-Afghan border to stem the flow of narcotics from Afghanistan to Russia.[184]

In another far-reaching agreement, the presidents of Kazakhstan, Kyrgyzstan and Uzbekistan signed a treaty on "eternal friendship" on 10 January 1997 in Bishkek. Under the terms of the treaty initiated by Kazakhstan, the three Central Asian states undertook not to allow their territory to be used for armed aggression or any other activities hostile to their cosignatories. "Karimov described this effort as another milestone in the development of good neighbourly relations".[185]

Aga Khan Development Foundation, Russia and five Central Asian republics signed a Memorandum of Understanding on cooperation in the illegal production of drugs, drug trafficking and abuse on 15 January 1998. The sides agreed that the drug problem should be solved through well coordinated concerted action and in cooperation with international organisations like Interpol.[186]

The heads of the member states of the Central Asian Economic Community (CAEC), Republic of Kazakhstan, Kyrgyzstan, Tajikistan and Uzbekistan met on 24 June 1999 in Bishkek in 'an atmosphere of mutual understanding and confidence'. In the meeting, among other things, the sides noted the supreme urgency and importance of joint action against terrorism, religious and political extremism, and the illegal trafficking of drugs, arms and explosives. In this connection, the need was affirmed to adopt joint programmes between foreign ministry departments, special services and other structures to combat these factors. This was the first reaction from CACE on this crucial topic.[187]

In another very important gesture of mutual cooperation against terrorism, the foreign and defence ministers and heads of the national security of the four Central Asian republics, except Turkmenistan, adopted a joint declaration at the meeting in the town of Osh in southern Kyrgyzstan on 28 August 1999. The declaration confirmed their common position relating to the criminal activities of the militant groups in the south of Kyrgyzstan. They called this an act of terrorism carried out by foreign organisations not recognised by the international community. It also mentioned a joint plan for measures to eliminate the terrorist groups. The declaration asked the citizens of the region to combine efforts to give a good rebuff to the rude assault by the bandits. It also warned that terrorist action involving illegal crossing of a state border and violence against a peaceful population would be halted using the most severe and decisive measures in accordance with international law. The document which was signed by the foreign ministers of these countries also expressed confidence on the support of the international community.[188] This declaration was basically prompted by the seasonal incursion by armed militants into the southern provinces of Kyrgyzstan, especially Batken region. The August 1999, Batken armed incursion was the most prolonged and dangerous terrorists (mis)adventure in Central Asia.

But as the summer unfolded, the south Kyrgyz region of Batken became again the hot spot with remarkable armed incursions. In order to effectively counter that and keeping up the spirit of cooperation against terrorism, Kyrgyz President Askar Akayev and Secretary General of CIS Collective Security Council Vladimir Zemskiy signed an agreement on military assistance to Kyrgyzstan on 2 October in Bishkek. According to the agreement, the six member states of the CIS Collective Security Treaty were to provide weapons and ammunitions for combat action in Kyrgyz mountainous region and Central Asian and Russian military experts were to set up an operations group. The agreement envisioned cooperation of the special services and foreign ministries among the CIS treaty signatories.[189]

The presidents of all the Central Asian republics except Turkmenistan, the respective foreign ministers of the republics along with their Security Council heads met in Tashkent on 20 April 1999 to discuss the terrorist threat to the region. The next day, the Presidents signed an agreement on joint actions in fighting terrorism, political, religious and other kinds of extremism and international organised crime. In implementation of the clauses of this agreement, the central competent bodies of the sides were to cooperate in carrying out special operations and measures involving armed forces contingents and special divisions of law enforcement structures, exchanging information on crimes, being planned or committed and on those people and organisations involved in them and on carrying out joint operational searches and investigations and searches for those who are hiding from criminal prosecution and imprisonment. The other important aspect of the agreement was that the sides confirmed that they would refuse to grant asylum or concessions to terrorists and extremists and also would endeavour to prosecute them and extradite them to the country concerned on the basis of international extradition agreements.[190] A summit meeting hosted by Kazakhstan, was held in Alma Ata on 3 July 1998 and attended by Russian Prime Minister, the Presidents of Kyrgyzstan, Kazakhstan and Tajikistan. Among other things, they expressed concern on the large number of weapons which was being smuggled from Afghanistan to CIS.[191] Later in a joint statement issued by all the participating countries, it was stressed that they were unanimous that any form of national splitism, ethnic exclusion and religious extremism was unacceptable. The parties would take steps to fight against international terrorism, organised crimes, arms smuggling, the trafficking of drugs and narcotics and other trans-national criminal activities and would not allow their territory to be used for activities undermining the national sovereignty, security and social order of any of the five countries.[192] Though this declaration was almost a reiteration of the stands taken by the member states earlier, it expressed their determination further in that direction.

All the CIS member states signed nine agreements on joint fight against all types of organised crime at a regular meeting of the Council of Interior Ministers of CIS countries, on 8 September 2000, at Cholpan-Ala, Kyrgyzstan. Among the agreements, the most important was their joint fight against international terrorism.[193]

As per a report, there were around 200 agreements, treaties, declarations and MoUs regarding bilateral and multilateral cooperation among the Central Asian and among the CIS countries till 1999. They covered almost all the fields of cooperation including terrorism, drugs trafficking and small arms proliferation.[194] The affected countries have also made a plethora of efforts to draw the cooperation of various countries outside the CIS. In their effort to internationalise their cause and garner the support of the world community, they have signed documents and declarations with countries from Europe, Africa and Asia.

After the Batken incursion in August 1999, President of Kyrgyzstan and the Secretary General of CIS Collective Security Council signed an agreement on military assistance to Kyrgyzstan on 2 October 1999 in Bishkek. According to the agreement, six member states of the CIS collective treaty and Uzbekistan were to provide weapons and ammunition for combat action in Kyrgyzstan. The agreement envisioned cooperation of the special services and foreign ministries among the CIS treaty signatories.[195] The CIS treaty which was initially aimed at defending CIS countries against an external threat through such agreements had shifted its focus to combating international terrorism.

In another important step towards the cooperation among the CIS states, the secretaries of the security councils of member states of the CIS Collective Security met in a working session in Bishkek on 5 November 1999. It discussed the issues of fighting terrorism, drug trafficking and arms smuggling. In this regard, the secretaries also adopted a statement of intent.[196]

Following the Central Asian Security Summit in Bishkek, on 20 August

2000, the presidents of all the Central Asian republics except Turkmenistan and the special envoy of Russia adopted a joint statement declaring that international terrorism was "encroaching upon the constitutional and democratic foundations of our societies". Pledging to crush terrorism and wipe out terrorists "where there are located", the statement called for urgent measures to tackle the situation, including strengthening the Tajik-Afghan border, as the southern flank of the CIS (see Appendix).[197]

In a major development, Uzbek Foreign Minister Abdulaziz Kamilov visited Pakistan on 25 January during which both the countries signed an important agreement in the form of an extradition treaty under which both the countries agreed to detain and hand over criminals wanted by the other side.[198] This was an important step from the point that Pakistan has been a major player in the Central Asian politics. Secondly, Pakistan being an Islamic state was the main promoter of Taliban, the mainstay of Central Asian terrorism and extremism. Therefore, an extradition treaty with Pakistan have made it no longer a safe haven for perpetrators of extremist violence in Uzbekistan. During the Tajik civil war and later, many of the members of IRP and IMU like Haji Turazonjada and Abdulla Nuri took shelter in Pakistan to escape the 'hot pursuit' followed by Uzbekistan and Tajikistan.

In the post-September 11 period, the Central Asian republics became highly focussed from the international strategic point of view. The anti-terrorism efforts of the Central Asian republics received international support and attention. As a result, several efforts for coordination were also made through agreements, declarations and treaties. One such effort was made on 22 January 2002, when General Tommy Franks, the commander of the anti-terrorist operations in Afghanistan, visited Tashkent and signed an agreement which outlined future cooperation and more frequent contact between the two countries.[199]

On the same line, the US government on 9 January announced that restrictions on the transfer of military equipment to Tajikistan imposed in 1993 would be lifted following the country's close cooperation with the international anti-terrorism coalition.[200]

The Kazakh legislature made an amendment to the laws on terrorism and religion on 1 February 2002. The law on terrorism made any attempt on life a state official punishable by a death sentence or a term of 20 years imprisonment and the law on religion permitted the prohibition of any unregistered religious group; required all missionaries to be registered with the authorities; and forbade the legal registration of Muslim organisations except within the framework of the spiritual administration of Muslims of Kazakhstan.[201]

The attack on World Trade Centre and Pentagon on 11 September 2001, by Islamic terrorists, linked with Al-Qaeda movement led by Saudi terrorist Osama bin Laden brought a major shift in the security scenario in Central Asia. The anti-terrorism endeavour of the affected states in the region found a new ally in US and its other friendly states from Europe and Asia. The US-led coalition against terrorism had to depend on the Central Asian republics for logistical and strategic reasons, whereas the Central Asian Republics for the first time had an opportunity at their hands to bring to the international community the menace of the religious fundamentalism and terrorism, and to get rid of the constant accusations of human rights violations by the western human rights organisations including the US. Another reason they thought it appropriate to support the coalition in their engagement with Afghanistan was the fact that most of the terrorists in Central Asia were the products of the situation in Afghanistan and were constantly aided and abetted by Afghanistan's Taliban administration.

The Central Asian republics quickly condemned the attacks in America and offered their help and also supported the retaliatory attacks by America on the Taliban and the Al-Qaeda.

Of all the Central Asian republics Uzbek government emerged as the key ally in terms of US military strategy in October 2001. By an agreement, it gave the US the extended use of Khanabad base in the Karshi province, the biggest airbase in Central Asia.[202]

While Karimov said the agreement covered the mutual responsibilities and guarantees, the Americans confined themselves to only consultation. However, on 12 October 2001, a US-Uzbek joint statement was issued stating that the US had extended security guarantees to President Islam Karimov's regime. Subsequently, Uzbekistan which had previously insisted that the US could only use Uzbek facilities for humanitarian and search and rescue missions now sanctioned the use of its military facilities by the US armed forces for offensive military operations against Afghanistan.[203]

Kyrgyzstan was the next Central Asian republic to grant US military access to its territory. The Kyrgyz parliament agreed to allow the US to set up a military base at Manas International Airport, some 30 kilometres from the Kyrgyz capital Bishkek.[204]

President Karimov of Uzbekistan visited US in March 2002 where he signed a Declaration on Strategic Partnership between the US and the Republic of Uzbekistan. It incorporated almost all the suggestions from the Uzbek side.[205]

Tajikistan, which along with Russia, Iran and India played a significant role in helping the fight of the Northern Alliance against the Taliban regime, also offered its help to the US by offering three of its airfields namely Kulyab, Khojand and Kurgan-Tyube. "Being in solidarity with the US people, we at the same time, express our willingness to cooperate with international community including US government, in the fight against international terrorism and extremism", the Tajik President said after the attack in America.[206]

Kazakhstan which has no common border with Afghanistan and did not face any serious threat to its security from the Taliban-supported religious extremism, gave support to the US-led struggle against international terrorism in Afghanistan in the form of over flight clearances. It also offered Washington use of its bases. In his talks with the US Secretary of State Colin Powell in December 2001, President Nazarbayev stated that "from the very first day, Kazakhstan declared that it should be in a coalition fighting terrorism and would help with all the forces it has at its disposal."[207] Later, during his visit to the US, President Nazarbaev reiterated Kazakhstan's intention to cooperate in the war against terrorism to its conclusion within the framework of international coalition.[208]

Since the disintegration of the Soviet Union, Turkmenistan has launched itself on a foreign policy course of permanent neutrality. After rejecting all offers of cooperation from several countries including the US and Germany, Turkmenistan agreed to participate in the international efforts in Afghanistan only in terms of humanitarian assistance[209] after meeting Russian Foreign Minister Igor Ivanov.

Through all these show of concern and cooperation to the US-led war on terrorism, the Central Asian countries aimed at the destruction of the radical, extremist terrorist organisations in the region and their bases in Afghanistan and cut off their supplies from Taliban and Pakistan. In appreciation of these gestures, the US government also gave assurances to the regimes of these republics to target IMU as well. US government had included IMU in its list of terrorist organisations in the year 2000.[210] In his national address on 20 September 2001, US President George W. Bush linked the IMU to Osama bin Laden suggesting, the IMU may be a target of the US counter-terrorism efforts in the wake of the 11 September attacks.[211] Further, the executive order on the terrorist financing of the US government to freeze terrorist assets abroad, also included IMU, thereby attacking the roots of its existence.

Though the foregoing illustrations show the urge of the Central Asian republics to ensure national security through cooperation, they have not been fully successful in this regard. Their mutual differences are manifested in the accusations they make against each other from time to time. For example, President of Uzbekistan accused Tajikistan of harbouring and training terrorists. Kyrgyzstan strongly denounced the unilateral action of the Uzbek security forces in its own territory in violation of the standard international norms, and Uzbekistan bombarding southern regions of Kyrgyzstan on the pretext of terrorist movement. To add to this, the constant rivalry between Kazakhstan and Uzbekistan for supremacy in the region is jeopardising the spirit of cooperation. Nevertheless, the efforts made by the countries in the region since 1992 are massive in spite of their shortcomings. The few points which can be generalised in this context are:

- The neutrality maintained by Turkmenistan by staying away from the regional cooperation initiatives has had its adverse impact on the anti-terrorism and anti-drug trafficking efforts.
- In spite of all the republics coming together except Turkmenistan, all are still dependent on Russia for the final nod as the guarantor of regional security.
- Kyrgyzstan and Turkmenistan have befriended more with China and Iran, which has maintained their involvement in the region in some pretext or the other.
- Except a single extradition treaty, very few efforts have been madeto rope in Pakistan and ensure its involvement in anti-terrorism drive. This, if achieved, would have put the latter in a position, that would have probably diverted its attention from Afghanistan and Taliban.
- China has been more concerned with its own problem of terrorism and separatism in the Xinjiang province, where the Uighur separatists are demanding secession from the Chinese mainland. It is for this reason that China has been showing greater concern for Kyrgyzstan and Turkmenistan rather than Kazakhstan and Uzbekistan.
- Iran is playing the most difficult role. Though it has craving for promoting Islamic groups, it differs from them on the ground that majority of them are 'Sunnis' belonging to Hanafi School of Islamic thought. Secondly, as the groups in Central Asia are being supported by Pakistan, Iran is averse to the idea of Pakistan playing greater role in Central Asian politics.
- Another very important factor that draws the far-off countries like

Germany is the huge economic potential of the region in the form of Caspian oil and gas.

- Israel being a country facing the problem of Islamic terrorism has befriended with the Central Asian countries and promised to exchange its anti-terrorism expertise with them.
- Russia's involvement in Chechnya and Dagestan forced it to support and cooperate with the Central Asian republics and their dealing of the problem of terrorism.
- Finally, US after the 11 September, has learnt that it can not just keep it confined to the issue of non-proliferation by Kazakhstan as far as its policy towards Central Asia is concerned. Secondly, Islamic terrorism and religious fundamentalism is not the problem of the region only, but sooner or later would endanger the security of the world as a whole, including America. Therefore, it has extended its cooperation towards the countries in the region as far as dealing with terrorism is concerned and at the same time, taking interests in rescuing the sagging economies of the Central Asian republics.[212]

As mentioned before, the Central Asian republics in spite of their cooperative efforts have not been able to eliminate the menace of militancy and terrorism in the region. In simple words, the cooperative efforts have not worked out as desired by the participating countries. This results out of both conflicting views of security interests and from a range of other incompatible aspects of political regimes.

Problems of Cooperation

(A) Incompatible Threat Perception

Uzbekistan is often responsible for the lack of security cooperation between Tashkent, Bishkek and Dushanbe.[213] Kyrgyzstan has a considerable number of serious points of contention with Uzbekistan, apart from the problems with Tashkent over its bombing of Kyrgyz villages and its politics which are perceived as radicalising the Islamist underground throughout the region. In February 2001, a newly printed map of Uzbekistan drew that country's borders into Kyrgyzstan's territory and even showed a land corridor from Uzbekistan to its enclave Sokh in Kyrgyzstan although no such links had been agreed. A secret meeting had given Tashkent reasons to hope that they would get territorial concessions but Uzbekistan's highhandedness antagonised the Kyrgyz parliament which had to ratify an agreement which heightened public distrust between the neighbours.[214]

While the map drew criticism in Bishkek, Tashkent almost arm twisted Kyrgyzstan by linking the border dispute to the cutting off of gas supplies to Kyrgyzstan.[215] It demanded that if Bishkek agreed to cede the corridor to Sokh, then Uzbekistan would resume gas deliveries.

Meanwhile, Kyrgyzstan claimed Uzbekistan owed it US $180 million for rent on its territory and exploitation of its gas fields.[216] Kyrgyzstan has also sought to link the issue of gas with water supplies, as Uzbekistan depends on its neighbour for free irrigation. Uzbekistan has resisted any linkage between gas and water provisions despite international support for the countries to trade.[217]

In August 2000, Tashkent introduced a visa regime for Kyrgyzstan's citizens. People living in border areas can still travel to Uzbekistan without visas as long as they do not stay in the country longer than three days. Those needing to stay longer now must present a fee and present justification for their visit. The general consequence of Uzbekistan's tightening of border controls has been a bourgeoning of corruption by border control officials who take bribes from those attempting to violate the border control regime and equally from those who attempt to adhere to the rules. In Kyrgyzstan, there is a perception that terrorists and drug traffickers can find ways across the borders more readily than law-abiding citizens.[218]

Tajikistan's internal strife made the country a problematic strategic partner for its neighbours and it did not develop close relations with any of its neighbours after independence. Tajikistan has been very inwardly oriented, preoccupied with problems of regional disputes over power and the building of integrated institutions in the aftermath of civil war. Indeed, Tajikistan has been a conduit for destabilising influence to its neighbours. There have been some concerns in China that the Uighur separatists might use the country as a route into Xinjiang.

Relations between Tajikistan and Uzbekistan in the post-Soviet period have been marked by nearly continuous tensions. Uzbekistan has been seen as sponsoring the aspirations of the northern province of Sughd (formerly Leninabad) to regain the dominance of Tajikistan's political and economic structures that it had during Soviet times. This issue became prominent after the incursions into northern Tajikistan by Khudaiberdiyev, which Rahmanov attributed directly to Uzbekistan's sponsorship and to the northern political figure then in exile in Uzbekistan, Abdumallik

Abdullajanov. In Tajikistan, a further proof of Uzbekistan's meddling in the affairs is proved from the fact that Khudaiberdiyev reportedly fled to Uzbekistan and yet neither Abdullajanov nor Khudaiberdiyev has been turned over to Tajikistan to stand trial.[219] Some observers claim that the incursions conducted by Namangani were a direct answer by authorities in Tajikistan to the Khudaiberdiyev incursion.[220]

For much of the post-Soviet period, Tajikistan has felt itself under siege by Uzbekistan, which has maintained a blockade of sorts to contain the perceived threat of spreading instability. Tajikistan is almost exclusively dependent on Uzbekistan for transport links to the outside world, and yet in crossing into Uzbekistan, citizens of Tajikistan are often humiliated and forced to pay bribes. Similarly, in Kyrgyzstan and Kazakhstan, it is often impossible to get across the country without having all of their assets confiscated. Though these are undoubtedly, not out of any specific state policy, it is supported by the general system of corruption existing in the region and in Uzbekistan; it is combined with a tacit endorsement by the official policies whereby containment of instability translated into an ethos of domination by the stronger neighbour.[221]

There have also been serious differences between Kazakhstan and Uzbekistan. Though a self-contended state and largely loyal to Russia, Kazakhstan in January 2000, discovered that border guards from Uzbekistan were marking out their border allegedly deep into the territory of Kazakhstan. Kazakhstan responded with protest.[222] Moreover, Uzbek border guards were frequently caught carrying out unilateral demarcations.[223]

Meanwhile, Kazakhstan has occasionally adopted a dominant stance, particularly in relations with Kyrgyzstan. For example, when Kyrgyzstan became the only Central Asian state to be admitted to the World Trade Organisation, Kazakhstan responded by imposing severe restrictions on trade with its weaker neighbour.

From the very beginning, Turkmenistan's policy was to insulate itself from regional conflicts rather than to cooperate in any regional security system. Relations between Turkmenistan and Uzbekistan have often been tense and there have been shooting incidents on their common border. President Niyazov called for the construction of border fortifications in the problem areas and reinforced the border guards with an additional 500 servicemen. These incidents led Ashgabat to view its relationship with Tashkent as potentially more volatile than its relations with Kabul.[224]

All attempts at regional cooperation run up against problems of resources and priorities. While it is evidently a high priority to be perceived as promoting cooperation, as expressed through high profile summits, the practical work of cooperation is often not covered in budgets. For example, though all three countries entered into the regional anti-terrorist centre established in Bishkek in December 2000, as of June 2001, none of them followed through on their financial commitments.[225]

Cooperation is also hindered by different perceptions about the proper role for outside powers, with Russia and the US sometimes undermining regional cooperation by encouraging bilateral relations and discouraging participation in regional structures. The US appears satisfied , for example, that Uzbekistan has left the CIS Collective Security Treaty and joined GUUAM. Washington has been sceptical about the participation in the Shanghai Cooperation Organisation (SCO), which increasingly appears oriented against the US and the West. Russia has sought to play a dominant role in the regional groupings in which it participates, such as the CST and the Eurasian Economic Community (EEC). The Central Asian States themselves have prioritised bilateral relations over regional structures, and there have not been any attempts, for example, to employ regional institutions to address border delimitation issues, as the Shanghai Cooperation Organisation was used to resolve China's border issues with former Soviet states.[226]

(B) Incomplete Political Systems and Domestic Environments

Cooperation among the Central Asian states is not only difficult because of their divergent security concerns, there is also difference on the ways three states are governed that makes effective cooperation elusive. In Uzbekistan, the media and dissemination of information are tightly controlled and there is little political pluralism. Political parties are illusory having been set up by the regime to give the appearance of democracy. President Karimov has sought to gain legitimacy by appearing strong, and sometimes this has resulted in belittling his neighbours. In a February 1999 radio interview, he accused Akayev of being unable to "do much of anything apart from smile".[227] This had predictable effects on the public opinion in Kyrgyzstan, where parliamentary deputies demanded that cooperation with Uzbekistan be reduced and measures be taken to defend the dignity of the country. President Karimov also frequently broadcast invectives aimed at Tajikistan and its President, reducing further the already dim prospects for friendly relations.

There has also been a widespread outcry in response to Uzbekistan's efforts to seek territorial concessions. The sharp difference between the media cultures and political cultures of the two countries make cooperation often difficult.

The more open societies in Kyrgyzstan and Kazakhstan present a challenge to Karimov who feels that he must discredit his neighbours in order to validate his own authoritarian style of rule.[228] The presence of a legitimised Islamist party in Tajikistan presents a particular problem since the approach in Uzbekistan is diametrically opposite. Uzbekistan severely restricts the free flow of information but many issues that it considers sensitive are openly discussed in broadcasts from Kyrgyzstan, Kazakhstan and to a lesser extent Tajikistan.[229]

Turkmenistan not only maintains astute neutrality but its administrative pattern has created certain doubts in the minds of the neighbouring countries. Niyazov has declared himself endorsed by the parliament as the President for life. It has come as an irritant for others and following the same pattern, Kazakhstan also tried to perpetuate the rule of Nazarbayev. Other important point of difference is the attitude of Turkmenistan towards Islamic radicals and the problem of drugs. Turkmenistan has never been harsh in dealing with the Islamic forces and it had also allegedly harboured several Islamist leaders who were hounded by Uzbekistan and facilitated their entry into Iran. Turkmenistan never cracked down heavily on the drug traffickers much to the irritation of its neighbours.

The economic differences present additional challenges. Uzbekistan due to its non-convertible currency erects barrier to trade with its neighbours, driving most commerce underground. In Kyrgyzstan, there is a relative free market and high corruption and drug trafficking. Because of these factors, the security services are also given the task of imposing restrictions on the flow of goods and populations across the borders, further inhibiting regional cooperation.

The present leaders, who are any way ex-Communists, are desperate enough to crush the forces more through military intervention than other diplomatic and non-military measures. Being landlocked and long stretches of common borders it has been difficult to man and guarded the republics totally from all sides due to which greater cooperation is necessary to meet the challenges of terrorism and drug trafficking. Although it can not be said that the measures have proved successful, but so far they have kept the groups from taking over. In the post-September 11 period, the world attention to this specific problem in the Central Asian region has increased tremendously giving further legitimacy and strength to the efforts of the republics in dealing with terrorism and extremist fundamentalism in the region.

References

1. The Constitution of the Republic of Kazakhstan, Section I, General Provisions, Section-I, Article 1, http://www.geocities.com/capitolhill/lobby/2171/kzconst.html-7k
2. Section-I, Article- 5, Clause-I, General Provisions, Constitution of the Republic of Kazakhstan.
3. Constitution of the Republic of Kazakhstan, Clause-2, Article 5, Section I.
4. *Ibid*, Clause-3, Article- 5, Section- I.
5. Zaigham Khan, "Inside the Mind of the Holy Warrior", *The Herald*, July 1999, p. 43.
6. Askar Aytmatov, "The Shade of Extremism over Central Asia", *Perceptions*, December 2000- February 2001, p. 118.
7. *Op.cit.*, Clause- 4, Article 5, Section- I.
8. J.F. Mayor, "Cults, Violence and Religious Terrorism", *Studies in Conflict and Terrorism*, Vol. 24, 2001, p. 367.
9. The Constitution of the Republic of Kazakhstan, Clause-5, Article 5, Section-I.
10. *Ibid.*, Article 7, Clause-5, Section-I.
11. *Ibid.*, Section- II, Article 15, Clause-2.
12. *Ibid.*, Section- II, Article 18, Clause-2.
13. *Ibid.*, Section- II, Article 19, Clause-1.
14. *Ibid.*, Section- II, Article 19, Clause-2.
15. *Ibid.*, Section-II, Article 20, Clause 1 and 2.
16. *Ibid.*, Section- II, Article 20, Clause 3.
17. *Ibid.*, Section-II, Article 23, Clause-I.
18. Constitution of Tajikistan, Preamble, www.geocities.com/paris/9305/Constitution.html-43k
19. *Ibid.*, Article 1, Chapter-I.
20. *Ibid.*, Article 5, Chapter-I.
21. *Ibid.*, Article 6, Chapter I.
22. *Ibid.*, Article 8, Chapter I.
23. *Ibid.*, Article 17, Chapter II.
24. *Ibid.*, Article 26, Chapter II.
25. *Ibid.*, Article 30, Chapter II.
26. Constitution of the Republic of Uzbekistan, Article 4, Chapter II, www.ecostan.org/laws/uzb/Uzbekistan.html
27. *Ibid.*, Article 7, Chapter 2.
28. *Ibid.*, Article 12, Chapter 2.
29. *Ibid.*, Article 13, Chapter 2.

30. *Ibid.*, Article 18, Chapter 5.
31. *Ibid.*, Article 19, Chapter 8.
32. *Ibid.*, Article 24, Chapter 5.
33. *Ibid.*, Article 25, Chapter 5.
34. *Ibid.*, Article 27, Chapter 5.
35. *Ibid.*, Article 28, Chapter 5.
36. *Ibid.*, Article 27, Chapter 5.
37. *Ibid.*, Article 31, Chapter 5.
38. *Ibid.*, Article 33, Chapter 8.
39. *Ibid.*, Article 44, Chapter 10.
40. *Ibid.*, Article 57, Chapter 13.
41. *Ibid.*, Article 58, Chapter 13.
42. *Ibid.*, Article 62, Chapter 13.
43. *Ibid.*
44. Constitution of Kyrgyz Republic, Clause I, Section One, Chapter I, www.Kyrgyzstan.org/law/Constitution.htm downloaded on 15 February 2002.
45. *Ibid.*, Clause 2, Article 2.
46. *Ibid.*, Clause 2, Article 5, Section 1.
47. *Ibid.*, Clause 2, Article 5, Section 1.
48. *Ibid.*, Clause 1, Article 8, Section 2.
49. *Ibid.*, Clause 3, Article 8, Section 2.
50. *Ibid.*, Clause 4, Article 8, Section 2.
51. *Ibid.*, Clause 4, Article 10, Section 2.
52. *Ibid.*, Clause 3, Article 15, Section I, Chapter 2.
53. *Ibid.*, Clause 2, Article 16, Section I, Chapter 2.
54. *Ibid.*
55. *Ibid.*
56. *Ibid.*
57. *Ibid.*
58. *Ibid.*, Clause 3, Article 18, Section 2, Chapter 2.
59. *Ibid.*, Article 30, Section 3.
60. The Constitution of Turkmenistan, Article 3, Section I, www.uta.edu/pols/psees/turkcon.htm downloaded on 12.12.2001.
61. *Ibid.*, Article 11, Section I.
62. *Ibid.*, Article 13, Section I.
63. *Ibid.*, Article 16, Section II.
64. *Ibid.*, Article 17, Section II.
65. *Ibid.*, Article 24, Section II.
66. Section I, http://www.state.gov./g/drl/rls/inf/2000/5724.htm downloaded on 15.12.2001.

67. Section II, *Ibid.*
68. *Ibid.*
69. *Ibid.*
70. *Ibid.*
71. *Izvestia*, 17 April 1992, rep. in *SWB/SU*/1363/B/3, 24 April 1992.
72. *Interfax*, Moscow, 6 January 1997, rep. in SWB/SU/2811/G/2, 8 January 1997.
73. *Ibid.*
74. *Narodnoye Slovo*, Tashkent, 28 February 1996, rep. in *SWB/SU*/2548/G/2, 29 February 1996.
75. *Interfax,* Moscow, 21 April 1997, rep. in *SWB/SU*/2900/G/1, 23 April 1997.
76. Criminal Code of the Republic of Tajikistan, http:// preventgenocide.org/law/domestic/Tajikistan.htm
77. *ITAR-TASS*, 9 April 1992 rep. in *SWB/SU*/1352/B/2, 10 April 1992.
78. Russia's Radio, Moscow, 3 August 1992, rep. in *SWB/SU*/1451/B/4, 5 August 1992.
79. Mayak Radio, Moscow, 30 January 1992, rep. in *SWB/SU*/1297/B/18, 6 February 1992.
80. *Izvestiya*, Moscow, 25 February 1992, rep. in *SWB/SU*/1314/B/7, 26 February 1992.
81. *Kazakhstanskaya Pravda*, Alma-Ata, 21 July 1995, rep. in *SWB/SU*/2364/G/3, 25 July 1995.
82. *Interfax*-Kazakhstan, Almaty, 23 September 1999, rep. in *SWB/SU*/3650/G/3, 27 September 1999.
83. *Interfax*-Kazakhstan, Almaty, 9 November 1999, rep. in *SWB/SU*/3689/G/3, 11 November 1999.
84. *ITAR-TASS*, 25 February 1992, rep. in *SWB/SU*/1314/B/9, 26 February 1992.
85. Mehrdad Haghayeghi, *Islam and Politics in Central Asia*, London, Macmillan Press, 1995, p. 158.
86. *Ibid.*
87. *Ibid.*, p. 160.
88. *Interfax*, Moscow, 26 February 1992 rep. in *SWB/SU*/1316/B/6, 28 February 1992.
89. *Radio Liberty Daily Report*, No. 40, 28 February 1994.
90. *New York Times*, 13 February 1993.
91. Tajik Radio, Dushanbe, 20 July 1993, rep. in *SWB/SU*/1753/B/3, 29 July 1993.
92. *Nezavisimaya Gazeta*, Moscow, 21 March 1992, rep. in *SWB/SU*/

1342/B/2, 30 March 1992.

93. *ITAR-TASS*, Moscow, 11 January 1993, rep. in *SWB/SU*/1584/B/7, 12 January 1993.
94. *APN Uzbekistan News Agency*, Tashkent, 1 February 1993, rep. in *SWB/SU*/1604/B/2, 4 February 1993.
95. *Interfax*, Moscow, 21 November 1995, rep. in *SWB/SU*/2468/G/3, 23 November 1995.
96. *Interfax*, Moscow, 18 April 1998, rep. in *SWB/SU*/3206/G/3, 21 April 1998.
97. Uzbek Radio, Tashkent, 1 May 1998, rep. in *SWB/SU*/3218/G/3, 5 May 1998.
98. *Ibid.*
99. Uzbek TV First Channel, Tashkent, 1 May 1998, rep. in *SWB/SU*/3218/G/4, 5 May 1998.
100. *Interfax*, Moscow, 5 June 1998, rep. in *SWB/SU*/5248/G/5, 9 June 1998.
101. Voice of Islamic Republic of Iran (henceforth VOIRI), Tehran, 8 July 1998, rep. in *SWB/SU*/3274/G/2, 9 July 1998.
102. *Interfax*, Moscow, 15 October 1998, rep. in *SWB/SU*/3360/G/3, 17 October 1998.
103. *ITAR-TASS*, Moscow, 28 June 1999, rep. in *SWB/SU*/3573/G/1, 29 June 1999.
104. A.P. Burt Herman, "Uzbekistan Government Keeps Close Watch on Religion", cited in *ibid.*
105. *Ibid.*, p. 22.
106. *Ibid.*, p. 23.
107. Russia's Radio, Moscow, 12 July 1992, rep. in *SWB/SU*/1435/B/11, 17 July 1992.
108. Tajik Radio, Dushanbe, 19 October 1992, rep. in *SWB/SU*/1517/G/4, 21 October 1992.
109. *ITAR-TASS*, Moscow, 11January 1993, rep. in *SWB/SU*/1584/B/8, 12 January 1993.
110. *ITAR-TASS*, Moscow, 4 August 1995, rep. in *SWB/SU*/2375/G/2, 7 August 1995.
111. Tajik Radio, Dushanbe, 28 January 1998, rep. in *SWB/SU*/3138/G/1, 30 January 1998.
112. Tajik Radio, Dushanbe, 21 March 2001, rep. in *SWB/SU*/4103/G/3, 24 March 2001.
113. *ITAR-TASS*, Moscow, 12 April 1996, rep. in *SWB/SU*/2586/G/3, 15 April 1996.
114. Khovar News Agency (henceforth Khovar), Dushanbe, 11 June

1996, rep. in *SWB/SU*/2637/G/2, 13 June 1996.

115. Interview with Prosecutor General for Tajik Customs Department, Sharief Zhuraev, July 2001, cited in ICG Report No. 25, 26 November 2001.
116. Interview with Deputy Prosecutor in Kharag, July 2001, cited in *ibid.*
117. IHF Report, *op. cit.*, p. 18.
118. *Ibid.*
119. The IMU and the Hizb-ut-Tahrir: Implications of the Afghanistan Campaign, ICG Asia Briefing Paper, 30 January 2002, p. 11.
120. *Ibid.*, p. 12.
121. Oibek Khamidov, Evening Bishkek, 28 January 2002, cited in *ibid*, p. 11.
122. Kabar News Agency (henceforth Kabar), Bishkek, 2 October 1995, rep. in *SWB/SU*/2425/G/2, 4 October 1995.
123. *Svododnyye Gory*, Bishkek, in Russian, 23 August 1995, p. 10, cited in ibid.
124. Kyrgyz Radio, Bishkek, 4 April 1996, rep. in *SWB/SU*/2581/G/5, 9 April 1996.
125. *Ibid.*
126. *Interfax*, Moscow, 11 May 1998, rep. in *SWB/SU*/3225/G/2, 13 May 1998.
127. *Interfax*, Moscow, 13 May 1998, rep. in *SWB/SU*/3227/G/1, 15 May 1998.
128. *Ibid.*
129. Kyrgyz Radio, Bishkek, 12 August 1998, rep. in *SWB/SU*/3306/G/2, 15 August 1998.
130. *Interfax*, Moscow, 25 March 2000, rep. in *SWB/SU*/3800/G/3, 28 March 2000.
131. UNODCP, Kyrgyzstan: Country Profile, available at http://www.undcp.org/Uzbekistan/country-profilekyr.html and *SWB/SU*/3212/G/2/2, 28 April 1998.
132. *ITAR-TASS*, Moscow, 24 April 1998, rep. in *SWB/SU*/3212/G/1, 28 April 1998.
133. *Ibid.*
134. *Interfax-Kazakhstan*, Alma-Ata, 27 October 1998, rep. in *SWB/SU*/3370/G/1, 29 October 1998.
135. *Ibid.*
136. *ITAR-TASS*, Moscow, 18 March 1999, rep. in *SWB/SU*/3490/G/2, 23 March 1999.

137. *Ibid.*
138. 'Panorama', Almaty, 25 February 2000, p. 3, rep. in *SWB/SU*/3779/ G/3, 3 March 2000.
139. Kazakh Khabar TV, Almaty, 19 August 2000, rep. in *SWB/SU*/ 3924/G/3, 21 August 2000.
140. Kazakh Commercial TV, Almaty, 7 September 2000, rep. in *SWB/ SU*/3941/G/1, 9 September 2000.
141. *Ibid.*
142. *Interfax*-Kazakhstan, Almaty, 24 November 2000, rep. in *SWB/ SU*/4008/G/1, 27 November 2000.
143. *Ibid.*
144. *Ibid.*
145. *Ibid.*
146. *Interfax*-Kazakhstan, Almaty, 27 November 2000, rep. in *SWB/ SU*/4012/G/3, 1 December 2000.
147. "Summary of Fact Finding Mission to Kazakhstan", Eurasianet.
148. "Ministers argue about Introducing Death Penalty for Drug Trafficking in Kazakhstan", *The Times of Central Asia*, 21 December 2001.
149. Until 26 November 2001.
150. Interview with the Deputy Minister of Justice of Kazakhstan, Nurian Mazhcdevich in Astana, August 2001, cited in *ICG Asia Report*, No. 25, 26 November 2001.
151. *RFL/RL*, *Weekday Magazine*, "Kazakhstan: Country Pledges More Anti-Terror Assistance", 8 November 2001.
152. Interview with Amnesty International, 5 December 2001, cited in IHF Report, *op.cit.*, p. 10.
153. ITAR-TASS, Moscow, 19 April 1994, rep. in *SWB/SU*/1980/G/3, 25 April 1994.
154. *Ibid.*
155. *Ibid.*
156. Felix Corley, "Turkmenistan: Every Believer is Controlled", says former Foreign Minister, Keston Institute, www.keston.org, 6 November 2001.
157. Nazik Ataeva, "Turkmenistan: Niyazov Ponders War Options", Institute of War and Peace, RCA No. 72, 1 October 2001, http:// www.iwpr.net/index.pl.?archive/rca/rca-200/09-72-2-eng.tat
158. Report Vitaly Ponomarov, Memorial, Moscow, 28 November 2001.
159. *Central Asia Monitor*, No. 1, 2001, pp. 29-31.
160. *Ibid.*
161. *Interfax*, Moscow, 11 June 1998, rep. in *SWB/SU*/3254/G/4, 16

June 1998.

162. *RFE/RL*, *Newsline*, 15 December 1998.
163. *Reuters*, 25 February 2000, cited in Gregory Gleason, "Politics of Counter Insurgency in Central Asia", *Problems of Post-Communism*, Vol. 29, No. 2, March-April 2002, p. 8.
164. *Interfax*, Moscow, 29 March 2000, rep. in *SWB/SU*/3801/G/1, 29 March 2000.
165. *ITAR-TASS*, Moscow, 30 October 1992, rep. in *SWB/SU*/1527/B/4, 2 November 1992.
166. *ITAR-TASS*, Moscow, 5 January 1993, rep. in *SWB/SU*/1579/B/2, 6 January 1992.
167. Uzbek Television, First Channel, Tashkent, 2 June 1997, rep. in *SWB/SU*/2937/G/1, 5 June 1997.
168. *RIA News Agency*, Moscow, 4 January 1998, rep. in *SWB/SU/*3117/G/4, 6 January 1998.
169. *Interfax*, Moscow, 5 January 1998, rep. in *ibid.*
170. Uzbek Television, First Channel, Tashkent, 27 May 1999, rep. in *SWB/SU*/3547/G/2, 29 May 1999.
171. Russian TV Channel, Moscow, 6 May 1998, rep. in *SWB/SU/*3222/G/3, 9 May 1998.
172. Ibid., 9 July 1999, rep. in *SWB/SU*/3584/G/4, 16 July 1999.
173. Khabar TV, Almaty, 30 August 1999, rep. in *SWB/SU*/3628/ G/2, 1 September 1999.
174. Published in *Narodnaya Slavo*, 22 April 2000, rep. in *SWB/SU/*3822/G/3, 24 April 2000.
175. Kazakh Television First Channel, Astana, 13 June 2000, rep. in *SWB/SU*/3867/G/1, 15 June 2000.
176. Kyrgyz Radio, Bishkek, 20 August 2000, rep. in *SWB/SU*/3925/G/2, 22 August 2000.
177. *Interfax*-Kazakhstan, Almaty, 1 March 2001, rep. in *SWB/SU*/4085/G/1, 3 March 2001.
178. *Ibid.*
179. Kazakh Radio, 28 May 1993, rep. in *SWB/SU*/1702/B/13, 31 May 1993.
180. *ITAR-TASS*, Moscow, 12 May 1994, rep. in *SWB/SU*/1997/G/1, 14 May 1994.
181. Ostankino Radio Mayak, Moscow, 2 November 1994, rep. in *SWB/SU*/2144/G/1, 4 November 1994.
182. Belarus Radio, 22 December 1994, rep. in *SWB/SU*/2188/G/6, 29 December 1994.

183. Kyrgyz Radio, Bishkek, 9 July 1993, rep. in *SWB/SU*/1743/B/4, 17 July 1993.
184. Interfax, Moscow, 22 December 1995, rep. in *SWB/SU*/2495/G/1, 28 December 1995.
185. *RIA News Agency*, Moscow, 10 January 1997, rep. in *SWB/SU*/ 2816/G/1, 14 January 1997.
186. *Interfax*-Kazakhstan, Alma Ata, 16 January 1998, rep. in *SWB/ SU*/3128/G/1, 19 January 1998.
187. Tajik News Agency, Khobar, 25 June 1999, rep. in *SWB/SU*/3574/ G/1, 30 June 1999.
188. ITAR-TASS, Moscow, 28 August 1999, rep. in SWB/SU/3626/G/ 1, 30 August 1999.
189. *Interfax*, Moscow, 2 October 1999 (henceforth *Interfax* Moscow), rep. in SWB/SU/3657/G/1, 5 October 1999
190. Tajikistan Television First Channel, (henceforth Tajik Tv.1), Dushanbe, 21 April 2000, rep. in SWB/SU/3822/G/3, 24 April 2000.
191. ITAR-TASS, Moscow, 3 July 1998, rep. in SWB/SU/3272/G/1, 7 July 1998.
192. Xinhua, Beijing, 3 July 1998, rep. in SWB/SU/3272/G/3, 7 July 1998.
193. *ITAR-TASS*, Moscow, 8 September 2000, rep. in SWB/SU3941/G/ 1, 9 September 2000.
194. *ITAR-TASS*, Moscow, 28 August 1999, rep. in SWB/SU/3626/G/ 1, 30 August 1999.
195. *Interfax*, Moscow, 2 October 1999, rep. in SWB/SU/3657/G/2, 5 October 1999.
196. Kyrgyz Radio, Bishkek, 5 November 1999, rep. in SWB/SU/3686/ G/1, 8 November 1999.
197. Kyrgyz Radio, Bishkek, 20 August 2000, rep. in SWB/SU/3925/G/ 1, 22 August 2000.
198. Uzbek Radio, Tashkent, 26 January 2001, rep. in SWB/SU/4057/ G/2, 30 January 2001.
199. Keesing's Record of World Events (henceforth Keesing's), Vol. 48, No. 1, 1 January 2002, p. 44555.
200. Ibid.
201. Keesing's Record of World Events, Vol. 48, No. 2, February 2002, p. 44617.
202. Devendra Kaushik, "Central Asia: Changing Geo-Political Alignment in the Aftermath of 11 September", *Dialogue*, Vol. 3, No. 4, p. 44.

203. Anthony Baird, "New Alliance Brings US-Uzbekistan into Long Term Embrace", posted on *TOL Wires*, 19 October 2001, rep. in Poonam Mann, "Religious Extremism in Central Asia", *Strategic Analysis*, Vol. XXXV, No. 9, December 2001, p. 1039.
204. *Ibid.*
205. Yurri Cherngaev, Kommersant, Moscow, 14 March 2002, rep. in Devendra Kaushik, *Dialogue, op. cit.*, pp. 45-46.
206. Quoted in Poonam Mann, *World Focus*, Vol. 23, No. 6, June 2002, p. 18.
207. *The Times of Central Asia*, 20 December 2001.
208. Devendra Kaushik, *Dialogue, op. cit.*, p. 47.
209. *News from Russia*, Vol. V, No. 12, 22 March 2002, p. 1.
210. Poonam Mann, *World Focus, op. cit.*, p. 18.
211. *Ibid.*
212. US has announced aid worth $ 408 million to these republics in 2002 out of which $81.6 million to Kazakhstan, $49 million to Kyrgyzstan, $85.3 million to Tajikistan, $ 16.4 million to Turkmenistan and 161.8 million to Uzbekistan. In the year 2001, US provided aid worth $244.2 million including $71.5 million to Kazakhstan, $40.6 million to Kyrgyzstan, $56.4 million to Tajikistan and $12.2 million to Turkmenistan and 55.9 million to Uzbekistan. Cited in Poonam Mann, *World Focus, op.cit.*, p. 19.
213. "Unichtozhat Terroristov budut poka no kartakh", *Nazavisimaia Gazeta*, 21 March 2001, rep. in ICG Asia, No. 20, *op. cit.*, p. 13.
214. ICG Asia, No. 20, *op.cit.*, p. 13.
215. Arslan Kaichiev, "Kyrgyzstan and Uzbekistan Map Out their Differences", *Eurasia Insight*, 5 March 2001, http://www.eurasianet.org/departments/insight/articles/eav030501.shtml.
216. Zamir Osorov, "Kyrgyzstan-Uzbekistan: Border Disputes", *The Times of Central Asia*, 3 August 2000.
217. USAID has been pushing for a solution which links water and energy, which Tashkent has found unacceptable. A high level OSCE initiative to resolve regional water disputes, led by Britain foreign and commonwealth office in 1999, encountered by intransigence from the leadership of Uzbekistan and Turkmenistan which apparently felt that there was no need to compromise their own position by involving international actors which could give negotiating strength to weaker countries from whom they currently receive summer water releases for their agriculture at no cost. Rep. in ICG Asia, No. 20, *op.cit.*, p. 14.

218. *Ibid.*
219. *Segodnia*, 1 November 1998, rep. in *ibid.*
220. Arkadi Dubnov, "Uzbekskii dzhikhad", Vremia MN, Moscow, 30 September 1999, p. 1 and 6, reprinted at www.fergana.ru/news/kirghiz46.html.
221. *Ibid*, p. 15.
222. *Panorama*, 14 July 2000.
223. Granitsa na Grani, *Express-K*, 7 September 2000, rep. in ICG Asia, No. 20, *op.cit.*, p. 16.
224. Nikolai Mitrokhin, "Turkmenistan's Open Surveillance of Foreigners Cops Policy of Isolation", Eurasia Insight, 6 March 2001, available at http://www.eurasianet.org/departments/insight/article/eavo71000.
225. "CIS Anti-Terrorism Centre not Operational", *Monitor* (Jamestown Foundation), Vol. 7, No. 108, 3 June 2001.
226. *ICG Asia*, No. 20, *op. cit.*, p. 15.
227. Nick Megeran, "The Borders of Eternal Friendship", *Eurasia Insight*, 19 November 2001, available at http://www.eurasianet.org/departments/insight/articles/eav120899.shtml.
228. *ICG Asia*, 20, *op.cit.*, p. 16.
229. *Ibid.*

5

Cooperation Against Terrorism through International Organisations

The end of Cold War marked a spectacular change in the world order. This led to better cooperation among the states in tackling common problems. Trade, tourism, communication and relations in general, on the whole, have increased. There has also been a growing awareness among the states that as a matter of practical necessity, there has to be a greater cooperation in the utilisation of resources, in the protection of environment and in other fields.[1].

Another essential feature of international relations, after the end of Cold War, has been the growing tendency among the states to cooperate with each other, to tackle problems, which are common to them like combating drug trafficking, checking illegal cross-border trade, cross-border terrorism etc. Since no single state has total resources to tackle these problems, they have to cooperate with the other states.This necessity has led to the growth of regional cooperation in international politics.

Regional cooperation is facilitated and strengthened by certain basic elements. First, the sharing of some problems on historical·basis. Second, close linkages of between those countries and societies, in other words, recognition of a boundary of the region within which interaction would be more intense than that with the outside world-regionalisation. Finally, the emergence of an organisation giving shape to the region in a legal and institutional sense, and providing some rules of the game within the region-the elements of a conscious policy which is central to regionalism.[2]

The Central Asian republics which attained their independence faced numerous challenges during their initial years of independence. The unstable political system, transitional nature of Central Asian economy fragile social structure etc. created some sort of structural imbalances in the political system. In addition to that cross-border terrorism, drug trafficking and growth of Islamic militancy posed new challenges for them. All these problems created a chaotic situation in the Central Asian

Republics. As these states were weak politically, economically and militarily, they prefered to enter in to cooperation among themselves and with other powers to solve their problems. In this context, the current chapter will try to assess the extent of the regional cooperation mechanisms that the Central Asian states have developed to meet the growing challenges of militancy, drug cartels, cross-border terrorism and arms trade.

Commonwealth of Independent States

The formation of Commonwealth of Independent States was a landmark step in the direction of establishment of a regional security mechanism. Soon after the disintegration of Soviet Union, all the 11 countries which initially formed the CIS realised that Russia should play a pivotal role in managing the security of their respective countries. Keeping this objective in mind, CIS came into existence in December 1991. Soon after its formation, all the five Central Asian countries decided to join the CIS when they signed the treaty on 12 December 1991.

Soon after its formation, the first thing the members of the CIS did was to sign the CIS Treaty on Collective Security. The basic objectives-as outlined by CIS in the treaty are as follows: Article-1 states that the participating states confirm their commitment to refrain from the use of threat of force in inter-state relations. They pledged to resolve all disagreements among themselves and with other state by peaceful means; Article-2 of the treaty mentions that states will consult with each other on all important question of international security affecting their interests and will coordinate their position on those questions. Under the provision of the Article, the members will activate the mechanism of joint consultations for the purpose of coordinating their positions and taking measures to eliminate the threat that has emerged.[3] Under this provision, the member states of Central Asia invoked Collective Security Treaty to combat drug trades, Islamic militancy and other security related problems.

Subsequently, in order to strengthen the Collective Security Treaty, the member countries in their meetings in Tashkent on 6 July 1992, and on 16 July 1992, decided to create a common unified military system, 'CIS Blue Helmet Force' for rapid deployment in those areas, which were affected by regional conflict. In Tashkent Conference, Russia announced the allocation of additional military force to protect the border with Iran and Afghanistan. This additional military force was to get support from military force of the respective Central Asian countries.[4]

During meetings of the heads of the CIS in Moscow, an agreement was signed on forming coalition defence forces on the territory of republic of Tajikistan. The entire Tajik-Afghan border was divided into zones of responsibility between Russia, Tajikistan, Uzbekistan, Kyrgyzstan and Kazakhstan.[5]

At the Minsk Summit of 22 January 1993, a charter for closer political, economic integration and defence alliance among the CIS countries was prepared. Russia, despite its own domestic crisis, maintained that it would continue to guarantee security and stability of the CIS states.[6]

In October 1993, Kazakhstan, Kyrgyzstan, Uzbekistan and Tajikistan signed an agreement on the concept of Military Security of the CIS member states in Bishkek. The document considered; "the instability of the social, economic, military and political situation in a number of regions, the existence of potent military potential in certain states which exceed their defence needs, the proliferation of nuclear and other weapons of mass destruction", as a major sources of potential military threat for member states of the CIS. [7]

On February 1995, at a CIS meeting, a declaration of member states on Collective Security Agreement was adopted. The declaration defined major sources of military danger and factors which contribute to military dangers evolving into a direct military threat. It defined it in the following way:

- The build up of military capabilities in the region's neighbouring member states to limits which disturb the existing balance of forces.
- The formation and training on the territory of other states of armed forces intended for use against member states.
- Inflammable border conflicts and armed provocations from the territory of bordering states.
- The transfer of foreign troops onto territories neighbouring member states.[8]

The security environment around Central Asia underwent a marked change after Taliban assumed power in Afghanistan. Immediately after taking over Afghanistan they encouraged businessmen for trafficking of narcotics and small arms to the neighbouring countries and Central Asia became a conduit for trafficking of small arms and narcotics. Not only the then Taliban government encouraged trafficking of narcotics and weapons, but also many radical Islamic groups of Central Asia, took shelter in Afghanistan and tried to destabilise the whole of Central Asian region in the hope of establishing a theocratic Islamic state. This raised anxiety among Central Asian leaders, who felt threatened. It was in this background that the CIS under the leadership of Russia took some active measures to combat these radical elements.

In October 1995, the tenth Conference of International Ministers of the CIS member states was held which ended with the signing of a series of protocols, agreements and documents. The representatives of the 12 states of the member states put their signature to a draft treaty on the procedure for the stationing of, and interaction between, members of the law enforcement bodies of the CIS on the territory of commonwealth member states and to a document on amendments and addenda to the CIS's Minsk convention of 1993 on legal aid and legal relations on civil, domestic and criminal cases. Describing the significance of these documents, Maj. Gen. Saidaimir Zhukhurov, the Tajik Minister of Internal Affairs said that Yeravan documents would in future help to impose significantly the operational and procedural activities with the framework of the Ministry of Internal Affairs. The minister further said that the criminals were not biding time but moving ahead of the law enforcement bodies. He summed up the objective of the meeting that it would enable better coordinated work on major direction of operational activities.[9]

The Council of the head of CIS Border Troops meeting in the Tajik capital, Dushanbe on 22 December 1995 signed 26 documents coordinating border policy through out the member states and along the Tajik-Afghan frontier. The Deputy Director of the Russian Federal Border Services, identified as Lt. Gen. Alexander Manilov told a news conference that the documents included the Russian-Turkmen agreement on the presence of up to 1000 border guards and Russian military advisers in Turkmenistan and an agreement between Kyrgyzstan, Tajikistan and Russia on cooperation to combat drug trafficking on the Tajik-Afghan border to stem the flow of narcotics from Afghanistan to Russia.[10]

On 4 September 1996, in Almaty, a CIS Summit on Afghanistan was held in which Russia and four leaders of Central Asian republics, except Turkmenistan, participated. Those leaders, after the Summit declared that UN Security Council should take urgent steps to end the protracted armed conflicts, which were going on in Afghanistan. These leaders also pointed out that conflict in Afghanistan pose a grave threat to regional security and stability of Central Asia and the whole region.[11] However, CST as a mechanism of regional security received a serious jolt when Uzbek President Islam Karimov criticised the dominant role played by Moscow and criticised it as a failure.

The five Central Asian states in a joint statement issued on 6 January 1998, following two days of talks in Ashgabat agreed that CIS is "an acceptable model for cooperation at the transitional stage." However, "each member of the commonwealth should determine its participation independently on the basis of the domestic priorities and international commitments." Uzbek President Islam Karimov told a news conference after the talks that "CIS cannot act as an international legal entity, nor can exist as a military and political bloc".[12]

This statement of the President, for the first time, showed the fissure that was developing among the CIS states in their cooperation. This mindset continued even after the talks were over and was the impediment for the success of the CIS efforts in curbing terrorism and militancy.

Notwithstanding Uzbekistan's withdrawal from CIS Collective Security Treaty on 2 April 1999, CIS guidelines on development came into force. The Head of the states who participated in the conference took a stand that "armed conflicts in the CIS regions should be settled by peaceful means and by invoking UN principles to settle armed conflicts".

On 2 October, Kyrgyz President Akaev and Secretary General of CIS Collective Security Council Vladimir Zemskiy signed an agreement on military assistance to Kyrgyzstan in Bishkek. Six months of the CIS Collective Security Treaty and Uzbekistan were to provide weapons and ammunitions for combat action in Kyrgyz mountainous region, according to the treaty. Further, the Central Asian and Russian military experts were to set up an operation group.

The agreements envisioned cooperation of the special services and foreign ministers among the CIS treaty signatories after the agreement was signed Zeniskiy pointed out that "the recent events in southern Kyrgyzstan go beyond the Central Asian region and fall under the category of international terrorism". He further said that "the same forces are fuelling wars in Chechnya and Dagestan, wanting to destabilise the situation in CIS and throughout the world". Describing the shift in the focus of CIS he added that "the collective security treaty was initially aimed at defending CIS countries against an external threat, but its focus has been shifted to combating international terrorism".[13]

A working session of the secretaries of the security councils of member states of the CIS was held at Ala-Archa state residence in Bishkek on 5 November 1999. Issues concerning the implementation of a resolution of heads of states of Armenia, Belarus, Kazakhstan, Kyrgyzstan, Russia and the republic of Uzbekistan on the situation in the Central Asian region were discussed at the session. The resolution places special emphasis on the need to unite efforts to fight international terrorism.[14]

A joint-military exercise named "Commonwealth Shield 2000" was held in Central Asia under the aegis of Collective Security Treaty in March 2000. Around 10,000 Russian, Tajik, Kazakh, Kyrgyz and Uzbek troops participated in these exercises. These exercises demonstrated the viability of CST as a mechanism to combat drug trafficking, cross-border Islamic militancy and other dangers the Central Asian countries were facing.

During the meeting of the Collective Security Treaty in Minsk in May 2000, the head of the participating countries made a joint declaration in which they pledged to fight jointly against all kinds of terrorism. The meeting also decided to develop a mechanism to coordinate their joint efforts in struggle against international terrorism. Addressing the meeting Russian President Vladimir Putin outlined the need for creating a mechanism which can make the Collective Security Treaty a working instrument capable of reacting to a dynamically changed world. The charter of the Summit also put too much emphasis on joint struggle against international terrorism.[15] The importance of Collective Security Treaty as a mechanism to combat international terrorism can be understood from the fact that the 201st Motorised Division of Russian Armed forces are still playing a crucial role in protecting Tajikistan. On the other hand this also shows the prominence of Russia in protecting the Central Asian security structure.

In a meeting of Collective Security Council which was held in May 2001, in Armenian capital Yerevan, the participating countries such as Russia, Kazakhstan, Kyrgyzstan and Tajikistan decided to establish a Collective Rapid Deployment Force in which each country will contribute army units. The Prime Minister of Kyrgyzstan, Kurmanbek Bakiyev, pointed out to the "importance of officially combating international terrorism and armed extremism, and stressed for creation of regional system of collective security".[16]

Following the Summit, a Collective Rapid Action Force for Central Asia was set up to counter the threat of terrorism. It started functioning from 1 August 2001. The headquarter of the centre was set up in Bishkek. During his meeting with Tajik President Emomali Rakhmanov, President Putin during an informal CIS Summit in Sochi, gave support to Tajik President's fight against terrorism and drug trafficking. The Tajik President also apprised the Russian President regarding various measures being undertaken to face the challenges posed by religious extremist groups, drug traffickers and other insurgent groups who were trying to threaten the security and stability of Central Asia.

In accordance with earlier decision of establishing Central Asian Collective Security Rapid Deployment Force, the forces started military exercises in Kyrgyzstan. According to Collective Force Commander, Sergai Chernomordin, "the exercises testified the fact that these forces had been finally activated, and hence had both practical and significant political meaning".[17]

The 11 September 2001 attack on US by the Al-Qaeda radical groups with the backing of the Taliban in Afghanistan, altered the geo-strategic situation in Central Asia. It also vindicated the long standing problems raised by CIS and Central Asian countries, since 1996, regarding the dangerous role of the Taliban in the whole of Central and South Asia. Soon after the attack, in the focus of political analysis and general public, Central Asia became the prime attention. The US government in order to finish the fundamentalist regime of Taliban and Al-Qaeda asked for Central Asia's help so that the US could station its troops and other military equipments. In this process, the CIS states could not stand aloof. They started consultations among each other and offered full cooperation to the US led multi-national force in their operation in Afghanistan.

On 30 November 2001, all the members of the Commonwealth of Independent States participated in a Moscow summit to sum up the results achieved in last 10 years. The leaders acknowledged that the cooperation among the CIS countries was not as smooth as it was believed to be. The CIS leaders made a joint-statement with a positive estimation of the anti-terrorist operation in Afghanistan. The 12 presidents of the member countries were also unanimous in their view that the "struggle of the world community against international terrorism must be carried out on a comprehensive and long term basis in accordance with the international law and UN statute. "Our people, as the declaration points out, want to see Commonwealth as zone of stability and security, ethnic accord and sustainable scientific, political and economic developments, as these have been mentioned after the meeting".[18]

Similarly, at the meeting of the Collective Security Treaty in May 2002 in Moscow, a decision was made at the end of the meeting to turn the mechanism and structures that exist for cooperation with member states into an international regional organisation to be called the Collective Security Treaty Organisation. Addressing the meeting, Vladimir Putin pointed out that "the meeting provided opportunity to us to discuss whole range of issues, which we called problems of security". Russian Foreign Minister Igor Ivanov while addressing the ministers' meeting of the Collective Security Treaty urged for "joint action within the framework of the international anti-terrorism coalition and a coordinated line of handling Afghan settlement issues testify to the efficiency of Collective Security Treaty and Shanghai Cooperation Organisation".[19]

Apart from Collective Security Treaty, the other important trans-regional organisation is Shanghai Cooperation Organisation (SCO) through which Central Asian republics try to solve their grave problems, which they face. It was previously known as Shanghai Five consisting of four Central Asian republics, Russia and China.

Shanghai Cooperation Organisation

Shanghai Cooperation Organisation initially came into existence in 1996 to solve the complex border problems faced by countries of Central Asia, China and Russia. However, gradually it moved away from solving complex border demarcation to drug trafficking, growth of religious fundamentalism and trafficking of small arms, which all the countries are facing.

The first summit of SCO was held in Shanghai in April 1996. In the first summit, an agreement was signed on confidence building measures in military field. At Moscow Summit in 1997, another agreement was signed on the reduction of military forces in border areas. The two interrelated agreements representing a deepening process have laid a solid legal basis for mutual trust and common security among five neighbouring states.[20]

However, after Moscow Summit, the priority of SCO has been changed. Having more or less solved the boundary disputes, they shifted their focus and started looking on a priority basis to problems which each of the countries are facing. They decided to fight collectively to counter national separatism, political and religious extremism, international terrorism, illicit drug trafficking and small arms. The major factor which compelled the SCO members to shift their aims and objectives was the rise of Taliban to power in Afghanistan. During this period, China was greatly concerned about rise of Islamic fundamentalism in Xinjiang province, which got direct support from Taliban regime to increase their subversive activities in the Uighur dominated region. The Islamic radical groups not only fomented trouble in China, but also participated in many subversive activities in Central Asian republics and Russia. In order to carry out their objectives, the Islamic militants required huge amount of money. The only way to generate such large sums of money was to carry out narcotics business and other corresponding illicit business. Therefore, not only Central Asia but also China's Xinjiang province became the hub of narcotic trade. During 1998, China's border guards detained citizens with drugs on several occasions. Drugs from Osh region of Kyrgyzstan used to flow to China. This led to belief among the foreign policy making circles in these countries that a single country would not be able to face on its own the challenge posed by drug-traffickers and radical Islamic fundamentalist groups. This realisation compelled the participating countries of SCO to put joint efforts in order to check this imminent danger. In this background, the third meeting of Shanghai Five was held at Almaty in 1998. This summit took the developments in this region into consideration and the resolution passed at the summit condemned the growth of religious fundamentalism, narcotics trade and illegal migration.

In between Almaty Conference in 1998 and the Bishkek Conference in 1999, significant developments were witnessed in the Central Asian region. The Batken incident, which took place in 1999, showed that Islamic fundamentalist forces in collusion with foreign countries could wreck havoc and threaten the unity, integrity and solidarity of the nation-state system. The fourth conference of SCO was held in Bishkek in August 1999. The joint declaration which came out after the summit of the five states declared solemnly the determination to jointly fight national separatism, international terrorism and religious extremism which constituted a threat to regional security, stability and development by encouraging weapons trafficking, drug trafficking and illegal migration. For this purpose, the meeting decided that the five participating nations would work out corresponding multinational programme, sign necessary multilateral cooperative treaties and accords and also hold regular meeting of officers from their departments of justice, border, customs etc. According to situation they also decided to hold anti-terrorism and anti-riot manoeuvres.[21]

The countries also expressed determination to prevent the use of their territories from engineering activities detrimental to the sovereignty, security and public law and order of any of the five states. The sides also stressed to observe the following basic principles in relations between themselves and in international affairs:

1. to be guided by mutual respect for sovereignty and territorial integrity, equality and non-interference in domestic affairs of one another.
2. to develop multi-lateral cooperation on the principles of equality and mutual advantage.
3. to help consolidate the role of the United States as the key mechanism for maintaining international peace and security and for ensuring a peaceful settlement of modern international regional problems and oppose the use of threat of force sanctioned by the UN Security Council in international relations.
4. to strictly observe the provisions of the Nuclear non-Proliferation Treaty and the comprehensive Nuclear Test Ban Treaty.[22]

Following the Bishkek Summit in December 1999, the chief of the law enforcement agencies and special services of the Shanghai Cooperation Organisation met in Bishkek and signed an agreement on mutual understanding. The participating countries expressed grave concern about the increasing number of acts of international terrorism, separatism, other manifestations of extremism and the growing organised crime and illegal migrations. The meeting also decided on meeting once a year, of the chiefs of law enforcement agencies. They also reaffirmed their determination to prevent the use of their countries for organising any activity that may damage their sovereignty.[23] At the Bishkek Summit, it was decided to set up an anti-terrorist centre in Bishkek in order to curb trans-border militancy, radical fundamentalism etc.

On 30th March 2000, the defence ministers of Shanghai Five member countries met in Kazakh capital Astana. After an overall analysis of the situation in Central Asia and its surrounding areas, the Defence Minister of the five countries pointed out those positive factors had increased continuously and peace and development remained the mainstream of the situation in the region. However, the destabilising factors still exist and the situation remained complicated due to religious extremism, ethnic separatism, international terrorism etc. The defence ministers, therefore, urged for close cooperation among the member countries for solving the complicated problems, which they continuously faced.[24]

Shortly after the defence ministers meeting in March, the fifth Shanghai Five meeting was held in Dushanbe, the capital of Tajikistan in July 2000. The significance of this summit lied in the fact that Uzbekistan participated in the conference as an observer- an example of the growing impact of Sanghai Five. The participating countries voiced their commitment for human rights. The Dushanbe Declaration also formalised the intention of member countries to fight international terrorism, illicit drug trafficking and illegal arms sale, separatism as well as religious extremism. During this meeting, efforts were also made to change the name "Shanghai Five" into "Shanghai Forum". As Putin stated in the summit meeting, "our discussions have far transcended the boundaries of trans-border cooperation, therefore, the need is to change it from Shanghai Five to Shanghai Forum".[25]

The sixth summit of Shanghai Cooperation Organisation was held at Shanghai in June 2001. In this conference, Uzbekistan became full fledged member of the organisation and the organisation was rechristened. The conference took a common stand with regard to terrorism, extremism and separatism. It was decided at the meeting that Anti-terrorism and Separatism Coordination Centre will be set up in Bishkek to fight against local guerrilla forces, which might be Uzbeki fundamentalists or Xinjiang's Uighur separatists. The countries also agreed that they will not provide shelter to militants of respective countries.[26]

The SCO member countries also decided to kick start consultation and coordination in regional and international affairs, support and cooperate with each other on major international and regional issues, and promote and consolidate regional and world peace and stability.[27] Addressing the gathering, the Kyrgyz President Askar Akayev thanked all parties involved in the SCO, for their valuable assistance and support to Kyrgyzstan in its effort to combat international terrorist forces, and hoped that all SCO member countries would show concern and put efforts to meet the situation in Afghanistan.[28]

The leaders of Shanghai Five states on 5 July 2000 signed the Dushanbe Declaration which reflected the need for coordinating efforts in fighting international terrorism and regional extremism. "The sides are stating their readiness for coordinated actions to prevent these factors and positively assess the results of the meetings between the law enforcement and security chiefs", mentioned the declaration. The five leaders expressed determination not to allow the territory of their countries to be used for activities which would be damaging the security of each of them. The sides pledged to continue proportionate assistance to countries where territories are subject to the danger of being used for adverse purposes by international extremists and terrorist forces.[29]

In the same summit, the foreign ministers of the member states of Shanghai Five signed a joint communiqué which said that the meeting paid special attention to the problems of regional security, the build up of tension in Afghanistan an the struggle against terrorism, drug trafficking and separatism.[30]

Tajik President Rahmanov said "this organisation shows to the world how countries with different civilisations and varied cultural traditions are maintaining good neighbourly relations to carry out effective cooperation in various fields and to achieve mutual respect and trust".[31]

In the post 11 September incidents, the SCO extended its support to US in its fight against Taliban. With the Chinese initiative, the foreign ministers meeting took place in Beijing on 7 January 2002 to discuss the security environment in the region. The joint statement emphasised the leading role of the United Nations in the struggle against international terrorism. The meeting also stressed that the scope of the anti-terrorist struggle may not be extended arbitrarily. The member states also held that fight against terrorism should be carried out at all levels-global, regional and national and with no double standards.[32]

The presidents of six SCO member countries held meeting in June 2002 at St. Petersburg. The final communiqué which was adopted after the end of the summit, showed great concern raised by the member states to regional security. The declaration or SCO charter highlighted joint actions to crack down upon all forms of terrorism, separatism and extremism and other cross border crimes as one of the basic tasks of the organisation. The charter also declared that the participating countries would take essential steps to execute the Shanghai Treaty on cracking down terrorism, separatism and extremism and also would draft documents on multilateral cooperation on the fight against drug trafficking, arms smuggling and other forms of cross border crimes as well as illegal migration, says the charter.

NATO and OSCE

Apart from Collective Security Treaty and Shanghai Cooperation Organisation the Central Asian countries have also sought the cooperation of NATO and OSCE, in their efforts to combat drug trafficking, cross border terrorism, and growth of militancy. In this regard OSCE is playing a crucial role in the Central Asian region.

The Organisation of Security and Cooperation in Europe came into existence during the Cold War to take care of the security of Europe. The organisation came into force in 1975 during the Helsinki Accord. During the Cold War period, the organisation then known as OSCE, Council of Security and Cooperation in Europe (CSCE) basically confined its role to Europe and even the Eastern European countries were not under the CSCE, as these countries were ruled by communist regimes.

However, after the end of the Cold War, CSCE slowly tried to increase its sphere of influence, and former communist countries became member of this organisation. Soon after, the organisation broadened its scope and sphere of influence to Central Asian region and the countries in the region became members of this organisation by the end of 1992.

The Organisation of Security and Cooperation in Europe resorted to a number of mechanisms to resolve conflicts like early warning systems, preventive diplomacy and conflict management, to attenuate sources of discord. Certain institutional mechanisms were also created like the High Commissioner on National Minorities. The High Commissioner on National Minorities was basically created to solve the inter-ethnic rivalries and warning CSCE regarding the volatile ethnic conflict. Besides these objectives, the other objective of OSCE is to promote the spirit of democratic culture and values. In recent years, in order to combat the proliferation of light weapons and drugs it has established a forum called Forum for Security Dialogue (FSD). The FSD will examine the implementation of existing politico-military commitments and particularly agreements related to the code of conduct on politico-military aspects of security and document on small arms and light weapons.

The Central Asian states got admitted to CSCE not by virtue of their geographical location but as a legacy of being parts of the former Soviet Union. The Central Asian states after getting membership of this organisation have been playing a vital role in contributing towards effectiveness and strengthening of this organisation. The OSCE has also tried to bolster the security, sovereignty, territorial integrity, economic and social progress, development of legislative and democratic political institutions, the respect for human rights and rights of national minorities.[33]

In October 1995, OSCE opened a bureau in Tashkent. Mayak Radio on 11 October quoted the bureau chief, Alais Rezmik saying that the bureau's sphere of activity covered regional security, stability and economic cooperation. "Our main task is to promote the development of cooperation between the OSCE and the states of the Central Asian region", he said.[34]

In 1999, at the Istanbul Summit, the CSCE member states vowed to cooperate more actively and closely to meet the intractable challenges of international terrorism, violent extremism, organised crime and drug trafficking. In order to combat the growing menace of drug trafficking and organised crime, under the sponsorship of UN office for Drug Control and Crime Prevention (UNODCCP) and the CSCE chairmanship staged a two day conference in Tashkent on 19-20 October 2000, on "Enhancing Security and Stability in Central Asia: An Integrated Approach to Counter Drugs, Organised Crime and Terrorism". After the conference, the five Central Asian states came out with a declaration outlining measures for "improving cooperation, coordination, exchanging information, enhancing preventive and central measures and strengthening Justice System and rule of law". The conference further emphasised the need for cooperation and coordination of CSCE in the security aspects of Central Asia. The participating countries called for coordination at a national, regional, inter-regional and international level in order to adopt measures to prevent, control and eliminate the inter-related phenomena of drug trafficking, organised crime and terrorism.[35]

On 16 November 1999, at the initiative of European Union and Canada, the OSCE states decided to take effective measures to curb illicit trafficking of small arms. The aim of CSCE Document on Small Arms and Light Weapons which was endorsed by the Vienna Ministerial meeting on 27-28 November 2000 was to "provide a substantial contribution to the process underway in the United Nations on the illicit trade in small arms and light weapons in all aspects". The ministerial meeting highlighted the danger posed by the illicit proliferation of small arms and it mentioned Central Asia as one of the region worst affected by the spread of small arms and light weapons. The OSCE states decided to combat illicit trafficking, reduce excessive accumulation of small arms and control their spread by variety of means which include: exercising restraint as regards their own small arms holdings, ensuring that small arms are produced, transferred and held for only legitimate defence and security need. The conference also decided to develop effective measures to regulate small arms in post-conflict situations.[36] The OSCE also decided to hold a seminar on military doctrine at the level of the experts of the CSCE on 11-13 June 2001.

The Bishkek International Conference of 13-14 December 2001 on Enhancing Security and Stability in Central Asia which was organised under the sponsorship of OSCE played a crucial role in developing mechanism to combat drug trade and small arms in this region. The significance of this conference was the fact that it was first such summit to be organised with the sponsorship of CSCE in the aftermath of 11 September incident. The United Nations Office for Drug Control and Crime Prevention (UNODCCP) also participated in the conference. In the Bishkek conference, representatives from 50 countries and 21 international organisations participated. The conference took the first step in following up the CSCE Bucharest Action Plan for combating terrorism by drawing up the programme of action which this conference adopted. The participants in this conference invited international and regional organisations to strengthen cooperation and coordination to combat the menace of terrorism and drug trafficking. The conference also outlined the need for coordination between various anti-terrorism organisations which were formed to fight the trans-national organised groups and called for checks on accumulation and uncontrolled spread of illicit trafficking of Small Arms and Light Weapons (SALW). The conference further decided to organise a series of workshops in all Central Asian countries, which aimed at training the security forces of these countries to combat small arms and drugs. The conference rejected firmly the identification of terrorism with any particular religion or culture as well as the unacceptable attempts by terrorists and violent extremists to present their case as a struggle in defence of religion and culture. The conference also pointed out that terrorism is a global problem and that there must be no safe haven for the perpetrators of such crimes and their supporters. The conference also noted that, the Central Asian region is exposed to specific challenges and threats to its security. It also outlined that contributions of the states in the region to the global coalition against international terrorism and emphasised the necessity to render political support and financial and technical assistance to the states of Central Asia in this context, including support for sustainable development. This shows how CSCE has been trying to help this region through developing multilateral relations.

NATO

Another international organisation with whom Central Asian countries developed relations and also signed number of treaty is North Atlantic

Treaty Organisation (NATO). NATO, which was established in 1949 as a challenge to the Soviet bloc has reoriented itself after the ignominious end of the Cold War. It soon developed a number of mechanisms to attract the newly independent countries of Eastern Europe and Central Asia. The Central Asian states, particularly the two bigger states i.e. Kazakhstan and Uzbekistan looked up to NATO as a mechanism to fill the vacuum created after the demise of Soviet Union. In this connection, the observations made by Kazakh President Nursultan Nazarbayev are noteworthy:

"The NATO has a suitable goal for our rapprochement to assist the democratic development of the states of central and Eastern Europe and the CIS and to prevent regional conflict as far as possible. NATO member-states, for the purpose of cooperation with these states, have committed themselves to prove their accumulated experiences and considerable expert potential defence policy. Considering all this, we will broaden contacts with NATO, provided their sphere and limits are strictly determined and they are not damaging our military cooperation within the CIS framework or bilateral ties".[37]

NATO for the first time made its presence felt in the Central Asian region through the participation of Central Asian countries in the North Atlantic Cooperation Council and Partnership for Peace (PFP programme). The strategic objectives of the NATO and PFP in this context can be summarised as follows:

- to involve Central Asian countries in the European security architecture based on cooperative process and on mutual consultations in case of threat;
- to increase military cooperation and information exchange;
- to contribute to stability in the region through democratic central over militancy and balanced civil-military relations; and
- to increase inter-operability for inter alia peacekeeping operations on the basis of a common conceptual approach.[38]

In August 1995, military exercises were conducted in Louisiana (USA) which included the participation of some military units of Central Asian states alongside military units of Canada. To deepen this cooperation, NATO headquarters prepared similar exercises in August 1996 in North Carolina. Uzbekistan, Kazakhstan and Kyrgyzstan have established a joint Central Asian peacekeeping battalion (Centrasbat), which is receiving significant backing from the United States and the NATO. Centrasbat exercises held in the Kazakhstan desert near Uzbekistan in September 1997 that also included US, Turkey and Russian troops. Additionally, the

US military held joint exercises with Uzbekistan troops in the Fergana valley, eighty kilometres from the Tajikistan border in June 1997.[39]

To develop further military cooperation and transparency in its relations with the newly independent Central Asian states, NATO Secretary General Javier Solana visited these republics. He arrived in Almaty on 11 March 1997. Both Javier Solana and President Nazarbaev agreed to broaden cooperation with NATO within the Partnership for Peace programme (PFP). Solana expressed NATO's readiness to help in training of Kazakh's military officers.[40] Javier Solana also held talks with Uzbek Defence Minister Rustom Ahmed and Foreign Minister Abdulaziz Komilov in Tashkent on 13 March 1997. Komilov clarified the stand of Uzbekistan to the visiting NATO Secretary General stating that Uzbekistan in accordance with its foreign policy principles would not join and military or military-political blocs.[41]

NATO along with Central Asian states, Russia and other countries started military exercises in Kazakhstan aimed at checkmating radical Islamic forces. The joint military exercises known as Centrasbet 2000, aimed at boosting military relationship and regional security within the framework of NATO's Partnership for Peace programmes. Nazarbayev acknowledged that "peace and security in Central Asia could only be assured through the joint efforts of regional states and with broad international support. The military exercises also aimed at training forces in various fields such as refugee control, patrolling and security operation".[42]

In the post-September 11 phase, NATO got an opportunity to play a bigger role in Central Asia. Most of the NATO member countries also participated in the International Security Assistance Force (ISAF) in their operation against Taliban and Al-Qaeda. Donald Rumsfeld in an interview to journalists in Washington told that the US-NATO-Central Asian countries relationship is good for them, good for US and is good for NATO. Through NATO's cooperation, the Central Asian army equipped themselves with sophisticated arms, and weapons which can help them easily to thwart the militant activities.

GUUAM

Apart from above mentioned organisations, Uzbekistan is the only Central Asian republic which became member of GUUAM. As a regional organisation GUUAM came into existence when the presidents of Azerbaijan, Georgia, Moldova and Ukraine met in Strasburg during summit of the council of Europe and stated their mutual interest in developing bilateral and regional cooperation, European and regional security, political and economic contacts. The joint communiqué issued after the meeting underscores the need for strengthening bilateral cooperation among the member countries based on the principles of respect for the sovereignty, territorial integrity, inviolability of state frontiers, mutual respect, cooperation, democracy, supremacy of law and respect for human rights. Uzbekistan joined the organisation on 24 April 1999 during the NATO/ EAPC Summit in Washington DC. During the April 1999 summit, the GUUAM presidents renewed their plea to develop interaction within the framework of the Euro-Atlantic Partnership Council and NATO's Partnership of Peace programme and deepened political cooperation with the aim to strengthen peacekeeping capability upon the relevant legal basis. They were also pleased to undertake joint actions to strengthen the regime of non-proliferation of nuclear and other types of weapons of mass destruction as well as to prevent arms transfer to the conflict zone. The presidents also noted that cooperation within the GUUAM is not directed against the third country or a group of countries and membership is offered to any country which subscribes to fundamental principles and goals of the GUUAM group. On 4 October 2000, while addressing the United Nations on behalf of GUUAM countries the representatives of Azerbaijan highlighted the problem of illegal drug trafficking. He pointed out that GUUAM states have elaborated the national strategies for drug control particularly on the reduction of drug supply and its consumption. The importance of GUUAM as a body for multi-lateral cooperation can be highlighted from the fact that in June 2000, the then NATO Secretary General George Robertson praised the development of GUUAM and pledged the cooperation of NATO with the new organisation. On 18 May 2000 in Washington DC the ambassadors of GUUAM countries to the United States declared their intention to further strengthen the relationship with the US. The ambassadors described four immediate objectives of GUUAM:

1. to promote east-west trade and transportation corridor.
2. develop interaction within the framework of the Euro-Atlantic Framework Council and NATO's Partnership for Peace programme.
3. to prevent the proliferation of weapons of mass destruction in region.
4. to combat the trafficking in narcotics in their countries.[43]

Following the 11 September 2001 incident, the GUUAM states took a united stand against terrorism and criticised the barbaric acts of terrorism that were committed against the United States. The United States and the GUUAM states acknowledged that terrorism is not identified with any particular religion and culture. The GUUAM started giving unqualified support to the United States in its fight against radical Islam led Al-Qaeda. The GUUAM states also agreed to work closely with US in preventing drug trafficking in illegal-trade and migration. During their meeting, the foreign ministers of GUUAM states and the US Under Secretary of State for political affairs explored possibilities for increased counter terrorism cooperation between the United States and GUUAM as an important regional organisation. In their statement regarding the terrorist attacks of 11 September, the GUUAM states unanimously stressed that a challenge was not only posed to United States of America but to the entire world community. They also pointed out that events of 11 September demonstrated with much clarity the need to establish conditions in the system of international relations which would exclude the possibility of a repetition of such tragedies.[44]

Though only one Central Asian country joined GUUAM, but it is playing a crucial role in coordinating efforts of five countries in combating drug trafficking, checking illegal migration and other such cross-border terrorist activities. Although GUUAM got active support from western countries but it can not play an effective role in combating the problems of the region without the cooperation of the Collective Security Treaty in which Russia is a dominant player.

Conference on Interaction and Confidence-Building Measures in Asia

CICA is another regional institutional mechanism that has developed at the initiative of Central Asian countries, particularly Kazakhstan. Through this organisation, the Central Asian countries have also come together to fight cross-border terrorism, problems of drug and illicit trafficking of small arms. The major objective of Kazakhstan initiating such a forms is to develop effective mechanisms of preventive diplomacy in Asia and development of a new system of relations between the states of the vast Asian region with the aim of ensuring security and stability in the Asian continent. The process of CICA started in 1992 and since then it has been playing a crucial role in developing mutual cooperation and combating problems which today confront the member countries. The participants of CICA agreed to establish a Special Working Group (SWG) with the task of preparing an broad-sheet of organisational and ideological aspects for the CICA meeting at the level of deputy foreign ministers.

In Almaty, the meeting of deputy foreign ministers was held during 1-3 December 1997. In this meeting, the member countries decided to establish the contact group which comprised the representatives of the Embassies accredited in Kazakhstan. The contact group became an instrument for non-formal discussion on CICA and provide the constant work during the inter-sessional period.[45]

The ministers of foreign affairs of the CICA member states, to further reaffirmed their support to the development of the CICA process as a regional forum, signed the declaration on the principles, guiding relations among CICA member states.

The meeting of the Special Working Group on preparing the CICA Summit was held on 12-14 April 2000. The participants fully supported the measures undertaken to combat terrorism, extremism, drug trade, international criminality and environmental problems.[46]

Another important International Symposium on "Asian Security in the Context of the Development of CICA" was organised in Kazakhstan in June 2000. The participating countries agreed that only through regional cooperation they would be able to resolve common problems like cross border, terrorism, economic development and confidence building measures.[47]

Another important landmark in the development of CICA was the CICA Summit held in June 2002 in the Kazakh capital Almaty. In this conference, 16 countries participated. The importance of this conference lies in the fact that, this was the first such conference organised in the aftermath of 11 September 2001. The participants in the conference expressed deep concern over the spread of terrorist activities all over the world, including the CICA member states. The declaration on elimination of terrorism and assisting dialogue between civilisations pointed out that the heads of state and government from the CICA member countries are resolved to fight terrorism and boast bilateral, regional and international cooperation in line with the UN Charter to meet the challenge.

The conference also outlined that member states unconditionally and unequivocally condemn terrorism in all its forms and manifestations as well as any support or acquiescence to it and failure to directly condemn it. The menace of terrorism has been magnified by its close links with drug-trafficking, illicit trafficking of small arms and light weapons. The declaration of CICA also underlined the fact that illicit trafficking in small arms and light weapons posed a threat to peace and security and it was directly linked with terrorist activity, separatist movements, drug trafficking and armed conflicts.

In order to checkmate religious fundamentalism, illicit trafficking of drugs and small arms various mechanisms were developed in this conference to check these negative tendencies.

Finally, the declaration urged all participating countries to resolve their dispute peacefully through negotiations in accordance with the principles enshrined in the UN Charter and international law. The meeting also decided to follow institutional building measures to follow the declarations.

Organisation of Islamic Conferences (OIC)

The Central Asian republics soon after attaining independence became focus of attraction for the Islamic countries particularly Saudi Arabia, Iran and Pakistan. The main objective of these countries in the beginning of 1990s was to bring these Central Asian republics into same regional forum, through which they can influence this region. In this process, they found Organisation of Islamic Countries a good forum for them to bring these countries into their fold. The vast natural resources and close religious ties also motivated them to share close contacts with them. The Central Asian countries on their part found a suitable regional ally. They also participated actively in this organisation and discussed a number of problems which they confronted after attaining independence. Among the most important problems that challenged them is the growth of radical Islamic fundamentalism, partly aided and abetted by many Islamic countries and some of them are members of OIC. The main objective of OIC is to promote Islamic solidarity among member states, to consolidate among member states in the economic, social, cultural, scientific, and other vital fields of activities and to carry out consultations among member states in international organisations. The other major objective is to create a suitable atmosphere for the promotion of cooperation and understanding among member states. During its Tehran Declarations of 1997, the OIC vehemently condemned terrorism in all its forms and manifestations and distinguished terrorism from the struggle of people against colonial domination or foreign occupation and their right to self-determination. The conference also noted that killing of innocent people is forbidden in Islam and reiterated their commitment to the provisions of the OIC code of conduct for combating international terrorism and their resolve to intensify their efforts to conclude a treaty on this issue and called on the international community to take all necessary measures for combating terrorism. It also supported combating illicit trafficking of narcotics in conformity with international law and the United Nations Charter and without prejudice to sovereignty.[48] In an extra-ordinary Foreign Ministers Conference which was held at Kuala Lumpur in the aftermath of 11 September, it condemned the barbaric act committed by radical Islamic forces in the United States. The conference urged the need to convene an international conference on terrorism in order to adopt a balanced international definition of terrorism so as not to leave it in the hands of superpowers to lay down a definition which serves their interests and jeopardises others. The conference also noted that the issue of fighting terrorism should be assigned an international role entrusted to it in order to maintain international peace and security.

The Central Asian countries also played a significant role in this conference in passing resolutions which aimed at condemning terrorism and fostering international peace and security.

A close analysis of the efforts of the Central Asian states in post-independence phase basically shows that they tried to use multilateral forum for regional cooperation as an effective means to put up a joint effort in facing the problem. If we make a balance sheet regarding Central Asian states with multilateral forum, it can be observed that they gained much in terms of international recognition, obtained large-scale financial assistance which they needed to rebuild their national economy and also received aid to develop and restructure their armed forces. This helped Central Asian states to a great extent in their combat against narcotics trade, illegal proliferation of small arms and radical Islamic forces.

In order to combat drug trade and Islamic fundamentalism, the Central Asian States operating through regional security mechanisms like Collective Security Treaty, Shanghai Cooperation Organisation, NATO, OCSE, CICA, developed economic relations with other major regional organisations like Economic Cooperation Organisation and Eurasian Economic Community. Their major objectives behind their cooperation with these organisations are as follows:

- To get an opportunity to participate in regional economic organisations so that they can develop their economy through regional trade and getting financial assistance from the regional organisations.
- To exploit their own vast natural resources through technical assistance from the regional organisations.
- The Central Asian states have never had the experience of managing an independent national economy.So through participation in regional organisations they hoped to get a first hand experience of managing an independent economy.
- The Central Asian countries realised that through regional organisations, they would be able to handle the transitional nature of the Central Asian economy, and solve other important problems like, poverty, drug trafficking, unemployment, which are thought to be responsible for growth of religious extremism and cross border terrorism.

Among such regional organisations, the two major economic grouping that need mention are the Economic Cooperation Organisation (ECO) and Eurasian Economic Community (EEC), formerly known as Customs Union.

Economic Cooperation Organisation

Economic Cooperation Organisation came into force in 1985, with the three Islamic republics - Iran, Pakistan and Turkey, for the purpose of promoting economic, technical and cultural cooperation among member state. Soon after attaining independence the newly established Central Asian states took initiative in joining Economic Cooperation Organisations. Turkmenistan and Uzbekistan were the first Central Asian states to join Economic Cooperation Organisations. Later, the other three Central Asian states Kazakhstan, Kyrgyzstan and Tajikistan joined the ECO. Initially they joined, as observers and later, got full member status after their formal accession to the Treaty of Izmir at a special meeting which was held at Islamabad on 28 May 1992.

After having the Central Asian member states, the member countries felt the need for restructuring the organisational and institutional structure of the Economic Cooperation Organisations in order to be effective with the changing times.

When it was formed, the objectives of ECO were mainly to deal with initiating economic liberalisation and effective utilisation of natural resources in their respective countries, to ensure that they cooperate each other in checking trafficking of drugs within their respective countries. The member countries also decided that they will be forming ECO mechanism to solve problems which confront the member countries. The ECO proposed a new "plan of action" in its ministerial meeting in February 1993 in Pakistan. The "plan of action" called for the mobilisation of resources to create a market-oriented economy for the benefit of the population of the member countries. A special fund with an initial capital of $3,00,000 was set up to conduct feasibility studies of the goal outlined in the May 1990 meeting.[49]

The other important objectives outlined in Islamabad ministerial conference were improvement of regional transportation and communication, removal of trade barriers and the improvement of the preferential tariff system in the region, and to develop proper mechanism to exploit the vast oil resources which these countries are having.[50]

Some major decisions were taken in the third ECO summit which was held at Islamabad on 14-15 May 1995. It also witnessed the signing of ECO Transit Trade Agreement, Articles of the Agreement of the ECO Trade and Development, Charter of the ECO cultural institute and charter of the ECO Foundation. They have also signed MoU for cooperation between ECO and UNDCP.

A meeting of the Economic Cooperation Organisation's committee on fighting drugs trade opened in Ashgabat on 5 December 1995. The main purpose of the meeting was to work out a joint action plan for creating a barrier against the entry of drugs into the ECO member countries.[51]

Another summit meeting of the ECO was held on 14 May 1996 in Ashgabat. The summit meeting was a landmark meeting from the point of view that in this summit meeting strong resentment was expressed by the members against the political role of the organisation. The opinion was headed by Islam Karimov who even threatened to withdraw from the organisation if that continued. He was endorsed by Tajikistan and Kazakhstan. Nevertheless, the leaders stressed the role of the ECO in combating drug trafficking and mediating in regional conflicts.[52]

A one-day meeting of the foreign ministers of the economic cooperation organisation in the city of Alma Ata on 9 May ended with the endorsement of three cooperation agreements. The three main areas o cooperation approved by ECO foreign ministers were transport, dru; trafficking and customs regulation. The Uzbek leader refused to sign o any of these agreements saying that his country needed sometime t study them.[53] After 1996, this was the second time when strong opinio regarding the functioning of ECO was expressed by Uzbekistan. In 199 the Uzbek President had expressed his resentment over the political role (ECO but this time the Uzbek Foreign Minister even refused to sign th document which was mutually agreed upon in the meeting.

The 11th meeting of the council of ministers was held in Tajikistan. ! the communiqué the signatories decided early construction of the missi roads and rail links, the need for enhanced interaction of the priva business communities of ECO, cooperation in the protection of t environment.[54]

Despite achieving some degree of economic success like, developi infrastructure projects cooperatives, laying down rail lines like t completion of the Tejan-Sarraks-Meshad-Bandar Abbas railway line tl links Central Asia with the Persian Gulf and helps in transportation of and gas, and a broad consensus on major political issues there has b wide discrepancies among the ECO members on various political issue was reported that once Uzbek President Islam Karimov criticised the r played by Pakistan in sponsoring terrorism in Uzbekistan in the name Islam. Similarly, all the three founding members of ECO - Iran, Pakistan : Turkey want to dominate Central Asia and want to keep it under tl sphere of influence rather than genuinely develop of Central Asi Despite these drawbacks, ECO has provided opportunity to Central A: states to come out of their Soviet legacy and to reshape their iden

Their emphasis on fighting drug trafficking in the region has been visible. Their limited approach to the issue can be understood from the fact that terrorism for them is more a political issue than drug trafficking which has economic implications. Therefore, in order to avoid any kind of embarrassment the member states, some of which are alleged by the others to have encouraged terrorism in other states, they have dealt with the issue of drugs rather than terrorism. The second reason, the issue of human rights violations under the garb of anti-terrorism crackdown also prompted Islam Karimov, in 1996, to criticise ECO for meddling in political issues rather than economic ones. Despite its lacunas and shortcomings, ECO has gone a certain way in dealing with the situation in Central Asia. Some of its efforts to control drug trafficking can be studied from the table given below:

Table 2

Drug Control

No.	*Title of Meeting*	*Venue*	*Date*
1.	Initial Joint Meeting of National Focal Points of ECO to discuss the Plan of Actions.	ECO Sectt.	1999
2.	Two semi-Annual Meetings of the Focal Points in ECO Member States to review the progress made with regard to UNDCP Project.	Any ECO Member State	1999
3.	ECO-UNDCP Legal Training Workshop on Judicial Cooperation in drug-related casework for the ECO Region	Tehran	March 1-5, 1999
4.	Ministerial Conference on "Civilizations Countering the World Drug Problem.	Tehran	April 12-13, 1999
5.	35th Session of the Subcommission on Illicit Drug Traffic and Related Matters in the Near and Middle East		February 2000

Source: http://www.ecosecretariat.org/

Apart from the ECO, the Central Asian states also in recent years have developed multi-lateral trade relationships involving some CIS states. In December 1995, four CIS states decided to set up Customs Union. Later, in February 1999, Tajikistan joined it. Finally, the grouping culminated in Eurasian Economic Community. The Eurasian Economic Community came into existence on 10 October 2000, when the presidents of Russia, Kazakhstan, Belarus, Kyrgyzstan and Tajikistan signed a treaty in the

Kazak capital Astana. The basic objectives outlined in the summit are to out a coordinated restructuring of economies, devising and implementing joint programmes, forming a common energy market, conducting joint research and development in priority areas of science and technology. In the field of trade and commerce, the basic objective of EEC was to form a single customs tariff and a single system of non-tariff regulatory resources.[56] The EEC agreements included a weighted voting and financing scheme. In the scheme Russia will exercise 40 per cent of voting rights and will be responsible for meeting 40 per cent of organisation's expenses. Belarus and Kazakhstan have 20 per cent of the shares, Kyrgyzstan and Tajikistan each have 10 per cent. The EEC Charter specified that a vote on a major policy issue will require 2/3 support. This, to some extent, curtails the dominance of Russian in the voting pattern.[57]

In their fight against terrorism and militancy the Central Asian states are devising a sort of dual strategy of both military regional cooperation and economic regional cooperation with external powers to improve their economy, enhance security and stability, combat drug and small arms trafficking. However, the regional cooperation mechanisms involving outside powers have not achieved the desired objectives so far. It requires pragmatic approach on part of both leaders of Central Asia countries and other outside powers to develop a comprehensive framework of regional security which will enhance security and stability of Central Asia.

References

1. Adam Roberts, "A New Age in *International Relations*", International Affairs, Vol. 67, No. 3, July 1991, pp. 513-14.
2. R. Stubbes, and G. Underfill (eds.), *Political Economy and Changing Global Order*, London, Macmillan, 1994.
3. CIS, *Treaty on Collective Security Russia, and the CIS: Documents Data and Analysis*, Zbigniew Breziziseki and Page Sullivan (eds.), London, M.E. Sharpe, 1997, p. 539.
4. *ITAR-TASS*, Moscow, 16 July 1992, rep. in *SWB/SU*/1436/B/1, 18 July 1992.
5. Mayak Radio, Moscow, 27 September 1993, rep. in SWB/SU/ 1806/G/4, 29 September 1993.
6. *Ibid.*, 1594/C/2, 3 January 1993.
7. Oumireserik Kasenov, "Central Asia: National, Regional and Global Aspects of Security", *Himalayan and Central Asian Studies*, Vol. 1, No. 1, April-June, 1997, pp. 30-31.
8. *Ibid.*, p. 31.

9. *ITAR-TASS*, Moscow, 25 October 1995, rep. in SWB/SU/2446/A/1, 28 October 1995.
10. *Interfax*, Moscow, 22 December 1995, rep. in SWB/SU/2495/G/1, 28 December 1995.
11. *ITAR-TASS*, Moscow, 3 September 1996, rep. in SWB/SU/2709/G 1, 5 September 1996.
12. *Interfax*, Moscow, 6 January 1998, rep. in SWBN/SU/3118/G/1, 7 January 1998.
13. *Interfax*, Moscow, 2 October 1999, rep. in SWB/SU/3657/G/2, 5 October 1999.
14. Kyrgyz Radio, Bishkek, 5 November 1999, rep. in SWB/SU/3686/G/1, 8 November 1999.
15. *Vremaya*, MN, 25 May 2000.
16. *News from Russia*, Vol. IV, No. 22, 1 June 2001, pp. 8-9.
17. *Ibid.*, Vol. IV, No. 34, 24 August 2001.
18. *The Times of Central Asia*, 6 December 2001.
19. *Ibid.*, 16 May 2002.
20. Cheng Mingshen and He Xiguan, "The 'Shanghai Five' Mechanism for Regional Security", *Contemporary International Relations*, Vol. 10, No. 8, August 2000, pp. 1-2.
21. Chen Mingshen and He Xiguan, *op.cit.*, pp. 5-6.
22. *ITAR-TASS*, Moscow, 25 August 1999, rep. in SWB/SU3623/G/1, 26 August 1999.
23. *Interfax*, Moscow, 2 December 1999 rep. in SWB/SU/3708/G/3, 3 December 1999.
24. *Xinhua*, Beijing, 30 March 2000 rep. in SWB/SU/3804/G/1, 1 April 2000.
25. *Rossiskaya Gazetta*, 6 July 2000.
26. *The Times of Central Asia*, 28 June 2001, p. 3.
27. *News from China*, 15 August 2001, p. 5.
28. *Ibid.*, p. 3.
29. *ITAR-TASS*, Moscow, July 2000, rep. in SWB/SU/3885/G/1, 6 July 2000.
30. *Interfax*, Moscow, 4 July 2000, rep. in SWB/SU/3885/G/1, 6 July 2000.
31. *Ibid.*, p. 3.
32. *The Times of Central Asia*, 10 January 2002.
33. Oumirserik Kasenov, *op.cit.*, pp. 44-45.
34. Ostan Kino Radio Mayak, Moscow, 11 October 1995, rep. in SWB/SU/2033/G/2, 13 October 1995.

35. http://www.my/20documents/osce/203htm.
36. "Non-Proliferation, Arms Control, Disarmament, 2000", *SIPRI Year Book*, 2001, pp. 560-561.
37. Tabasum Firdous, *Central Asia: Security and Strategic Imperatives*, New Delhi, Kalpaz Publications, 2002, pp. 146-147.
38. Burno Coppieters et al., "The Central Asian Region in a New International Environment", *NATO Review*, Vol. 4, No. 5, September 1996, pp. 28-29.
39. Sam Nunn, Bernett R. Rubin and Nancy Lubin, *Calming the Fergana Valley*, New York, The Century Foundation Press, 1999, p. 116.
40. *Interfax,* Moscow, 14 March 1997 rep. in SWB/SU/2867/G/2, 15 March 1997.
41. *Ibid.*
42. *Reuter*, Almaty, 13 September 2000.
43. www.guuam.org
44. *Ibid.*
45. At the Dawn of the 21st Century, Kazakhstan, Embassy of Kazakhstan, New Delhi, p. 17.
46. *Ibid.*
47. *Ibid.*
48. http://www.oic-oci.org
49. Mehrdad Haghayeghi, "Economic Cooperation Organisations: A Preliminary Assessment", *Central Asia Monitor*, No. 1, 1995, pp. 16-17.
50. *Ibid.*
51. Turkmen Radio, Ashgabat, 5 December 1995, rep. in SWB/SU/2480/G/3, 7 December 1995.
52. *Interfax*, Moscow, 14 May 1996, rep. in SWB/SU/2613/G/1, 16 May 1996.
53. *IRNA*, Tehran, 9 May 19998, rep. in SWB/SU/3223/G/1, 11 May 1998.
54. http: //www.ecosecretariat.org
55. Devendra Kaushik, "Regional Cooperation: The Central Asian Experience", *Contemporary Central Asia*, Vol. IV, No. 122, 2000, pp. 35-36.
56. *ITAR-TASS*, Moscow, 10 October 2000.
57. Devendra Kaushik, *op.cit.*, p. 36.

Conclusion

After seven decades of communist system under Soviet Union, five new republics in Central Asia that became independent are today facing the difficult and potentially destabilising tasks of political and economic restructuring-urgently needed to cope with the changing domestic and international environments. This process has unleashed new social and political forces with various objectives, capable of having a definite qualitative impact on the structure and functions of the post-communist governments.

In the post-World War II period, the world security scenario has undergone a massive change where not only the state actors but also non-state actors have played a determining role. Due to ideological rivalry, terrorism, especially during the Cold War period, has received a tacit legitimacy as an instrument of foreign policy in international relations, and divisions. The lack of a commonly accepted definition of 'terrorism' has provided it the much needed fillip to grow. As a result, the world has been witnessing increasing number of countries spread across the globe coming under the fold of this menace.

Central Asia, the cradle of many civilisations in the past, due to its geographical location, has always been host to many religions. It not only embraced them but also has contributed to their growth and intellectual and cultural enrichment. One such religion is 'Islam', which is the latest entrant to the region, coming as late as the eighth century AD and has stayed there as a popular religion, patronised by the local rulers and people. This region has also contributed to the enrichment of Islam. People then mostly nomadic in nature,without any settled agrarian base, adopted this monotheistic religion quickly. However, with the state patronage and settled life style, Islam got great intellectual boost and produced eminent Islamic scholars through the ages. 'Sufism' found its patronage and enrichment in this region. The Islamic culture, literature, intellect and practice had its inputs from Central Asia that took it to great heights.

Tsarist occupation of the region brought these activities to a grinding halt as the region once again relapsed to chaos and confusion with its polity and economy largely controlled from outside rather than locally. But qualitative changes took place when socialism was established in Soviet Russia followed by Stalin's handling of religious and nationality questions. For the first time in its history Central Asia was confronted with a kind of state atheism that made religion and religious practices a taboo. Mosques were closed down, religious schools, madrassahs outlawed, Islamic *shariah* and *sunnat* declared illegal, religious practices like *Nikkah* (marriage) and circumcision banned. The central crackdown on such activities was ferocious and severe. Stalin, later realising the impossibility of the total separation of the people from religion, had created a system of state-sponsored and controlled, religious activities in order to ventilate people's urges for religion in Central Asia. These government-sponsored institutions were inadequate to satisfy the people and mainly propagated the programmes and policies of the government through their *muftis*. This policy continued through Khrushchev, Brezhnev and his successors with minor changes from time to time depending upon the understandings of the leaders.

With the advent of Gorbachev, the scenario changed drastically. He inherited a state that was infested with the lacunae of the old system and which had alienated the religious population of Central Asia, who in spite of the restrictions imposed by the Soviet government maintained their religious traditions. There were secret and clandestine observances of religious rites and practices. Religious teachings were going on, though at a very small scale, secretly.

In the seventies, the world witnessed several radical developments in the Islamic world, Arab-Israel war, Iranian Revolution, Pakistan's religious and military dictatorship and Moscow's intervention in Afghanistan. All these developments someway or the other, played into the hands of the two rival superpowers. USSR's repressive attitude towards Islam had already alienated it from the hardcore Islamic world and the US had put them on its side with few exceptions. The various determinants of world politics including that of Islam were encouraged by one or the other. As a matter of policy, America, through Saudi Arabia and Pakistan, extended its support to the Mujahideen in Afghanistan fighting against Moscow. Arms, ammunitions, finances and all other requirements were generously supplied to them.

While this ideological rivalry and mutual antagonism was going on between the then two superpowers, another major development was taking place as an offshoot of this phenomenon. Inspired by the developments and triumphant of the successes in Iran, Pakistan, Egypt; with resources from abroad and allured by the booming drugs money, and backed by countries from the gulf region, Islamic radical forces were all out to take over the whole world in their venture to establish the Islamic umma. In their effort, they not only enjoyed men and material support but also the spiritual and ethical justification from the religious interpretations of Islam. Thus, 'jihad' became a divine mission for them.

To add to it, there was an upsurge in 'Wahhabism' and 'Deoband' school of thought in the Islamic world, promoted by Saudi Arabia and Pakistan respectively. Both believed in puritanical and conservative restoration of Islamic society as per the *sharia* and *hadith* of Islam. For them, every aspect of human life was addressed to by these two religious commandments. Therefore, anybody who disbelieved it, or who opposed it are 'Kafirs'- worthy of prosecution.

This agenda could not have found more suitable conditions other than that of Afghanistan with the Russian intervention in 1979. As mentioned earlier, supported and aided by US, the Mujahideen forces in the 1980's set out to liberate Afghanistan and establish the Islamic *umma.*

Realising the impossibility to carry on the Cold War and pressed with various internal compulsions like sagging economy, the social discontent, rise of ethnic nationalism and strong resentment in some parts of the USSR, Gorbachev initiated the processes of *Glasnost* and *Perestroika*. In the initial years of *Glasnost* and *Perestroika*, there was hardly any impact on the socio-religious dimensions. However, Gorbachev pushed it through with indomitable zeal and fervour. The first major global political impact was visible when USSR decided to withdraw from Afghanistan. It not only brought the 'Cold War' almost to an end but also created rippples all over world.

Soviets left the entire nation of Afghanistan in quandary. It withdrew so fast that there was no time for installing a proper representative government there. As a result, Afghanistan which was already divided vertically and horizontally along ethnic and clan lines relapsed into a civil war. This development not only was disastrous for Afghanistan but jeopardised the security of the region. As the fighting between the warlords- who had taken over the country immediately after the departure of Russian forces, continued year after year. America, which had no stakes in the region did not show much interest to ensure stability in the region. In 1995, finally, there emerged a new force later known as 'Taliban', created, equipped and trained by Pakistan which took over Kabul and began a phase of radical Islamism based on Deoband school of thought. Mullah Omar not only became the undisputed leader but also turned the clock of Afghanistan back into the medieval ages with the imposition of *sharia* and *hadith.*

Only a few countries like Pakistan and Saudi Arabia recognised the Taliban which remained completely isolated from the rest of the world. No press, no freedom, no communication, no liberty of any kind was granted. This success of Taliban in Afghanistan further skyrocketed the fervour of the Islamic radical forces who turned their attention further north where they could see greener pastures.

Lack of any real political rival, total international isolation and availability of resources made Taliban spread its tentacles towards its neighbouring Central Asian countries. Two other developments fuelled its urge further. The first was the outbreak of Tajik civil war and the second was the arrival of Osama bin Laden, the Saudi born terrorist, who inspired by Wahhabism of Saudi model, turned his guns towards America. Flushed with funds from large-scale narcotics trafficking and small arms trade, Taliban started supporting the opposition group led by IRP-one of the radical fundamentalist Islamist parties in Central Asia. Later, it also supported all other like-minded parties like Islamic Movement of Uzbekistan and Hizb-ut-Tahrir. This brought radical religious fundamentalism to the Central Asian region which was otherwise a region with tolerant and liberal Sufi traditions. The advent of this ideological variant with the aim and objective to install Islamic government in these states turned more and more into a political phenomenon.

Soon after independence, the Islamist forces in the region strongly endeavoured to revive the old Islamic traditions in a radical mould. As a result, thousands of mosques were built, and *madrassahs* proliferated in large numbers. People were encouraged to take *haj* in large numbers, religious teachings were encouraged, and students migrated to other countries like Egypt and Pakistan to get religious teachings. In Pakistan, madrassahs were opened to accommodate students from Central Asia. Countries like Iran, Saudi Arabia and Pakistan sent thousands of copies of 'Holy Koran' and a number of Islamic clerics to impart Islamic teaching in the region. People celebrated Islamic rituals in open and in grandiose manner. Islamic *shariah* was venerated with utmost commitment. All these activities took place outside the state sponsored religious establishments, which were opened for the public to carry on their religious activities.

Tajikistan felt the impact of these developments when civil war broke out and within five years around 50,000 people were killed and nearly 2, 00,000 people became homeless refugees. Incidentally, one of the parties in the whole episode was the government itself, opposed by radical Islamic forces organised on ethnic and regional lines. Tajik events were followed by Tashkent bombing in Uzbekistan and the Batken incursion in Kyrgyzstan. The governments largely initially chose to meet this challenge using repressive measures and cracked down heavily on the suspected radical forces. Press freedom was curtailed, human rights squeezed, freedom of any kind negated and all kinds of religious activities was banned. As the government crackdowns increased, the terrorist incidents also increased with greater ferocity and magnitude. Bomb blasts, shootings, hostage takings and all other methods of terrorism were employed by them.

Observers differ from each other regarding the causes of the growth of religious extremism and terrorism in the region. While some are of the view that this was because of the government's repressive policies, others say that it is inherent in the nature of Islamic radicalism.

At the same time, it is a fact that there are considerable variations at both inter and intra-republican levels as far as propensity towards Islam is concerned. Classified on the lines of sedentary/tribal life-styles, Uzbekistan and Tajikistan go to the top of the list followed by Kyrgyzstan, Kazakhstan and Turkmenistan. At the intra-republican level, the propensity towards Islam seems to have its centre in the Fergana Valley, which has been divided among three republics-Uzbekistan, Tajikistan and Kyrgyzstan. There are of course other regions with similar Islamic orientation such as Kara Kalpak- part of eastern Turkmenistan bordering Uzbekistan and several regions in Tajikistan. The most significant pattern among all these is that the Uzbeks are found every where in large numbers. As anticipated, the organisational strength and the mobilisation capacity of Islamic forces have been more advanced in Uzbekistan and Tajikistan as compared to the other republics.

The Islamic proclivity has been only one of the four parameters influencing the nature, scope and intensity and speed of Islamic revival in Central Asia. The others being, the strengths and weaknesses of the democratic drive, the governments' policies towards Islam, their willingness to institute socially inclusive political reforms, and the ethnic orientation and make up of each republic. Out of these, the political context has the potential to move Islam in a sharply radical direction.

The repressive policy of the state has been carried out to the extreme in Uzbekistan and Tajikistan. While, Uzbekistan has banned all the Islamic parties and organisations, Tajikistan till the end of the civil war, followed the same and in the civil war settlement recognised them and made them partners in the government. In Uzbekistan and in the pre- civil war settlement period in Tajikistan, the Islamic leaders were jailed, given death sentences or forced to exile for advocating a particular set of ideas. Gradually, and especially after 1999, even the other regimes in Central Asia have been responding to terrorism with increased repression, viewing not just Islamic militancy but all Islamic practice as a threat to their grip on power. Such steps, according to some, have only fuelled the support for the radical Islamic groups. The experts underline that any further repression is bound to strengthen the resolve of the Islamic forces and further radicalise their agenda. To substantiate their opinion, they cite the example of Kazakhstan and Turkmenistan, where due to the absence of sharp governmental repression, less radicalisation of Islam has taken place in comparison to Uzbekistan or Tajikistan. Secondly, experience from all over the world shows that authoritarian policies like that of banning of Islamic parties and movements, almost invariably, strengthens the legitimacy of such organisations and adversely affects the legitimacy of the government.

Another set of opinion sees the answer to Islamic radicalism in the democratic drive in Central Asia. According to it, if democracy is given a chance to flourish, it would weaken the radical tendencies of religion, for it offers an ideological paradigm with popular political objectives. Much like the Islamic drive, the democratic drive has not been a phenomenon with uniform inter-republican patterns. On the contrary, the propensity towards democracy varies considerably from republic to republic with Kyrgyzstan and Kazakhstan having the strongest and Uzbekistan, Tajikistan and Turkmenistan with weakest tendencies.

Given its mild Islamic proclivity and unique ethnic composition, Islam has played a secondary role in Kazakhstan and will continue to do so in the foreseeable future. This is in part due to the presence of a large non-Muslim population, which almost equals its Muslim population. The ethnic composition has changed in the recent years because of the departure of the Russians and higher birth rates among the Kazakh population. But the rate of change is not enough to fundamentally alter the present ethnic picture. This is also to some extent similar in Kyrgyzstan, where the Slavic population is sizeable, making the success of the radical Islamic forces a lesser possibility. On the other hand, the picture is substantially different in Uzbekistan and Tajikistan, where the ratio of non-Muslim population to that of the Muslim population is substantially smaller.

Ethnic make up, as a factor, however, is counterpoised by the ongoing ethnic separatism. Reinforced by tribal, regional, sub-regional and local exclusivist tendencies, ethnic separatism has been on the rise in the region.

Another important factor which plays a crucial role in the entire scenario is the economy of the republics and the living standards of the people. As has been discussed in chapter 2 and chapter 3, the withdrawal of Soviet economic support has created a financial havoc in the Central Asian republics. The economic policies which were followed during the USSR had made these republics totally dependent on Moscow. In the post-independence period, the issue of deteriorating economic standards, grinding poverty and unemployment has been raked up by the Islamists.

There also has been a tremendous shift in the security paradigm of Central Asia in the recent past. In the pre - 11 September 2001 period, Afghanistan's civil war was the biggest threat to Central Asian security. This scenario was further exacerbated by the growth of Islamic extremism and terrorism associated with Osama bin Laden and his Arab Afghans who had considerable influence over the Taliban, the IMU and Islamic Jehadi groups in Pakistan. Osama encouraged the Taliban leaders to embrace an internationalist pan-Islamic ideology. In addition to funding IMU operations, he enlisted other Central Asian militants into his own group, Al-Qaeda. The latter's global network, which according to the US intelligence had operatives and cells in 34 countries, linked the Central Asian radicals to the politics of global radical Islam. All these groups profited from the drug trade based in Afghanistan in which Taliban and Laden were heavily involved. In the 1980s, the drug export routes ran solely through Pakistan. Now they extend through Iran, China and the Central Asian states and the Gulf and are controlled by Pakistani, Afghan, Arab, Chechen and Central Asian crime organisations. Drugs fund political activism and weapons. It is als the financial mainstay of IMU and other radical Islamic movements.

The sovereignty and stability of the nascent Central Asian republics are now poised against militancy and cross-border terrorism. The collapse of the Soviet Union left these republics in a state of confusion. As there was no real freedom movement to precede their independence, social and political institutions in these republics were hardly developed to carry the stupendous task of independent existence. Secondly, the lack of such a movement also had its impact on the social cohesion (ethnic, clan and tribal) and resulted in minimum democratic awareness. The rulers of these republics are all ex-communists with slightly lighter shade. Their reluctance to generate democratic awareness and spirit has meant the continuation of the old political methods which the religious forces are vehemently opposed to. The worst casualty out of this coflict is the aspirations of the people, which has further widened the social gulf and has been threatening the stability of the nations. For example, civil war in Tajikistan from 1992-97 not only harmed the social unity and stability of the republic but also hindered the process of socio-economic development.

Militancy and terrorism in Central Asia is the result of an unholy nexus between religious fundamentalism, narcotics trafficking and small arms trading. This region, being a traditionally drug cultivating one, has found new patrons in the form of the Islamic radical forces there. Afghanistan has always been the hub of drug trade in the region. It not only produced the highest amount of poppy in the region but also contributed to 16 per cent of the total world consumption. This illegal drug trade has sustained militancy and terrorism in the region. The huge amount of fund which these groups require is largely met through such trade. For example, Osama bin Laden who headed Al-Qaeda, financed the entire activity from the drugs trade which he carried on in consonance with Taliban. Being agrarian economies with over dependence on cotton cultivation, the region finds it difficult to progress economically and finance the huge social development costs. In the post-independence period, the withdrawal of central subsidy from Moscow has aggravated the situation further. Lack of industrial development and other means of employment have pushed the region into poverty which in a vicious circle has lead to an upsurge in religious fundamentalism and crime.

The proliferation of the small arms in the region has also worsened the situation further. The illegal money which comes from the large scale drug trade is ainly routed to arms procurement by the terrorist and criminal groups. These arms are sophisticated, small and largely used by the terrorists to counter security forces.

The growth of Islamic fundamentalism in the form of Wahhabism and Deobandism has contributed tremendously to the growth of militancy and terrorism in the region. Seven decades of restrictions on religious matters were lifted suddenly in 1991. The civil society which had preserved the ethos of Islam in the previous decades, enthusiastically came out in open and practised religion. In the absence of any democratic mechanism to absorb this resurgence of religious spirit, the religious fundamentalist groups, largely aided and abetted by the neighbouring countries, have exploited the situation and tried to change the mode of religious expressions. At the same time, the situation in Afghanistan - the establishment of Taliban rule that received support from Pakistan and Saudi Arabia, added fuel to fire. Fundamentalist groups like Islamic Renaissance Party, Hizb-ut-Tahrir and Islamic Movement of Uzbekistan resorted to terrorist methods to establish their authority and express their opposition to the government's repression. While these were the immediate reasons, the greater objectives of these groups lay in the establishment of theistic Islamic states replacing the present secular ones.

Weak economies and large scale unemployment are other factors for the growth of fundamentalist terrorism. As experts suggest, a developed and self-contended population in the region would have been more tolerant than radical. The region had been a seat of tolerant and liberal Islamic culture which is manifested in the form of 'Sufism', which has been denounced by the other radical Muslims as *kafirs* - the non-believers. The post-independece economy of the region resulted in poverty and unemployment which has been thoroughly exploited by the radical forces to consolidate their support and legitimacy among the common masses.

The local governments have also not been able to address the situation with dexterity and prudence. They have relied more on repressive methods instead of addressing the problem democratically. The growth of democratic process in the region has been negligible. On the other hand, these rulers are becoming increasingly arbitrary and despotic violating all the norms of democracy. This lack of political and democratic development has provided the radical forces a greater legitimacy among the public and has projected them as martyrs. Human rights have been grossly violated, and all other civil and political rights have been drastically curtailed. Such reactionary policies have created a great resentment among the masses, providing a ground for the radical extremism. Multi-party democracy is still a far-cry in Central Asia. Instead, the present governments have resorted to illegal methods like electoral malpractices to perpetuate their rule, further weakening democratic development in these states. Tajikistan is a classic example of how democratic development can go a long way in winning the confidence of people. The government not only brought the civil war to an end, but also made a section of the radical fundamentalist forces a part of the government. It is a fact that the more the repression by the government, the greater is the reaction by the radical forces and this creates a vicious circle. Secondly, the lack of stability and security leads to greater negligence by the government of the socio-economic development initiatives providing opportunity to the radical forces criticise the establishment.

In the post-Cold War period, in the light of the new security scenario in world politics, there is a realisation all over the world that no state can defend itself or mitigate the problems of its security unilaterally and in isolation. Therefore, international cooperation is a veritable need in fighting not only traditional but also non-traditional forces which threaten the security and stability of a nation. This realisation has gained more relevance with the growth of militancy and terrorism in Central Asia. In spite of harsh repressive methods adopted by the governments in the region, militancy and terrorism has been surviving, forcing the countries to enter into bilateral and multi-lateral cooperation with other powers for a coordinated approach to fight this menace. As terrorism in Central Asia is cross-border in nature, the involvement of several states with a strong, coordinated and cooperative approach in tandem with other world organisations, can ensure their victory against the problem.

Since 1992, there have been a number of endeavours in this direction. Soon after independence, the nascent republics in the Central Asian region in their quest for security entered into the Collective Security Treaty, with Russia as the main guarantor of their security imperatives. It was followed by multilateral organisations of both security and economic orientation like Shanghai Cooperation Organisation, GUUAM which has Uzbekistan in it, the Economic Cooperation Organisations, Eurasian Economic Community, Six Plus Two, the Conference on Interaction and Confidence-building in Asia. Besides these efforts, the Central Asian countries also joined other international bodies viz. Organisation for Security and Cooperation in Europe, the Organisation of Islamic Conference, Economic Cooperation Organisation and North Atlantic Treaty Organisation's Partnership for Peace (PFP) programme.

All these organisations in spite of their specific purposes and functions have unambiguously expressed their rejection of terrorism and militancy in the region through their various resolutions and actions. Some have also engaged themselves directly in these efforts by cooperating militarily and economically. However, despite such united opinion against terrorism these organisations have been successful only to a limited extent. The economic condition of not only the Central Asian states but also other regional powers has hampered the efforts of the regional organisations. Secondly, stiff competition between the two countries involved for the oil resources in the region makes their cooperation against terrorism a half-hearted effort. For example, the Shanghai Anti-Terrorist Centre in Bishkek has been suffering from shortage of funds from the very beginning. Thirdly, among the regional cooperation organisations, there are also countries which are directly or indirectly have supported terrorism for their own limited geopolitical objectives. Therefore, when they come out against terrorism, they are hardly taken with ease by others. Another factor is the strong mutual suspicion, which prevails, for example, between Iran and Pakistan, Pakistan and Turkey, Afghanistan and Iran has hindered the progress of these organisations.

Besides the shorcomings in the fight against the problem, since September 11 terrorist attack in the US, the world has become increasingly sensitive and aware of the dangers of global terrorism. There is greater coordination at the international level to weaken the base of terrorism and eliminate their global network. This would certainly make the task of the Central Asian states a lot easier. The removal of the Taliban in Afghanistan which has further eroded the support system of the terrorists is one of the most recent outcomes of this international effort. At the same time, it should be underlined that ultimately suitable internal environment has also to be created in the Central Asian republics to discourage people away from militancy, terrorism and religious fundamentalism.

Appendix

The Call to JIHAD by the Islamic Movement of Uzbekistan

The following document was issued in August 1999 by the Islamic Movement of Uzbekistan as a declaration of jihad against the government of Uzbekistan. Originally written in Uzbek, it has appeared on the Internet in English.

In the name of Allah the Most Compassionate the Most Merciful A Message from the General Command of Islamic Movement Uzbekistan "and fight them until there is no more fitnah and the religion is all for Allah" Al Anfaal: 39

The Amir (Commander) of the Harakatul Islamiyyah (Islamic Movement) of Uzbekistan, Muhammad Tahir Farooq, has announced the start of the jihad against the tyrannical government of Uzbekistan and the puppet Islam Karimov and his henchmen. The leadership of the Islamic Movement confirm the following points in the declaration:

- This declaration comes after agreement by the major ulema and the leadership of the Islamic Movement.
- This agreement comes based on clear evidence on the obligation of Jihad against the *tawagheet* as well as to liberate the land and the people.
- The primary objective for this declaration of Jihad is the establishment of an Islamic state with the application of the Sharia, founded upon the Koran and the Noble Prophetic sunnah.

Also from amongst the goals of the declaration of Jihad is:

- The defence of our religion of Islam in our land against those who oppose Islam.
- The defence of Muslims in our land from those who humiliate them and spill their blood.

The defence of scholars and Muslim youth who are being assassinated, imprisoned and tortured in extreme manners-with no rights given them at all.

And almighty says:

"And they had no fault except that they believed in Allah, the All Mighty, Worthy of all praise!" Al Buruj: 8

Also to secure the release of the weak and oppressed who number some 5,000 in prison, held by the transgressors. The Almighty says:

"And what is the matter with you that you do not fight in the way of Allah and the weak and oppressed amongst men, women and children" An Nissa: 75

And to reopen the thousands of mosques and Islamic schools that have been closed by the evil government.

The Mujahideen of the Islamic Movement, after their experience in warfare, have completed their training and are ready to establish the blessed Jihad.

The Islamic Movement warns the Uzbek government in Tashkent from propping up or supporting the fight against Muslims.

The Islamic Movement warns tourists coming to this land that they should keep away, lest they be struck down by the Mujahideen.

The reason for the start of the Jihad in Kyrgyzstan is due to the stance of the ruler Askar Akayev Bishkek, in arresting thousands of Muslim Uzbeks who had migrated as refugees to Kyrgyzstan and were handed over to Karimov's henchmen (i.e. Uzbek regime).

The Most High says:

"Verily the oppressors are friends and protectors to one another."

The Islamic Movement shall, by the will of Allah, make Jihad in the cause of Allah to reach all its aims and objectives.

It is with regret that Foreign Mujahideen (Al Ansar) as of yet have not entered our ranks.

The Islamic Movement invites the ruling government and Karimov leadership in Tashkent to remove itself from office-unconditionally, before the country enters into a state of war and destruction of the land and the people. The responsibility for this will lie totally on the shoulders of the government, for which it shall be punished.

Allah is great and The Honour is for Islam.

Head of the Religious Leadership of the Islamic Movement of Uzbekistan
Az Zubayr Ibn' Abdur Raheem 4th Jumadi Al Awwal (ah) 25 August 1999

Cited in Rashid,' Ahmed, *Jihad: The Rise of Militant Islam in Central Asia*, Hyderabad, India, Orient Longman, 2002.

We will be one in the Struggle with Terrorism
Appeal of the Olly Majlis to the People of Uzbekistan

Dear fellow citizens,

The struggle of world society against terrorism, which is a threat to all mankind, is taking ever more urgent forms.

The threat of terrorism, called the plague of the 21st century, cannot leave people with clean thoughts indifferent, including our people.

We Olly Majlis deputies express our full support for the firm and focused efforts of the international coalition and all progressive forces, directed to wiping out terrorism.

We support unanimously the declaration of President Islam Karimov of October 5, which was a clear expression of our position in the struggle with international terrorism, as stated in an interview with the Uzbek national press agency.

It is well known, and Uzbekistan may times warned, that precisely international terrorism, like a monster, raises its head in various regions of the earth these days, and is a threat to all world civilisation.

President Islam Karimov, in his speech to the 48th session of the UN General Assembly in 1993, in his book "Uzbekistan on the threshold of 21st century: threats to security, conditions and guarantees of progress", published in 1997 and reissued in many countries, at the Istanbul summit of the OSCE in 1999, at the 1999 millennium summit of the UN General Assembly in 2000, and in many of his speeches to international forums, repeatedly warned the world that the territory of Afghanistan has turned into a source of terrorism, and has made concrete proposals on the joint struggle with this danger.

In August 2000, the Olly Majlis issued an appeal to all nations to untie in the struggle with international terrorism.

Unfortunately, international society did not pay enough attention to all these appeals concerning the threat to terrorism.

Only after the inhuman terrorist acts of September 11 in New York and Washington did the leading countries of the world, headed by the US, unite in a broad struggle against this evil.

Our people have suffered from this tragedy, which feeds on the drug trade, and cannot stand aside in this struggle.

Thus our people, united with all progress forces, shows resolution and firmness in making its contribution to the efforts of international society in the fight against terrorism.

The independent policies of Uzbekistan and its President in the struggle against this plague of the 21st century serve to raise the authority of our state in the world arena.

We openly declare that Uzbekistan is interested in the full liquidation of the sources of terrorism, not only in Afghanistan, but also in the whole world. This serves the interest of peace, progress, and a future for our children.

Let those who have chosen the path of violence and betrayal know that no force can turn our people from their chosen path, the path of building a free democratic society.

Dear citizens!

The events in Afghanistan today clearly show that the struggle with terrorism is not the work of one day or even one month. At this complex time, each of us should fully do his duty, protect his children and close ones from this pernicious and dangerous phenomenon, and be on guard. Only then can he consider that he is doing his duty to contribute to peace here and in the world, for our great future. Now more than ever, the slogan, "Protect your home yourself" is relevant.

We want our neighbours, the Afghan people, to live in peace and stability.

The future of Afghanistan is in the hands of the Afghan people. The kind of state and path of development will be chosen by the country, by its peoples and tribes. It is important that this process take place with the help of the UN. To straighten out the economy, destroyed by 22 years war, requires the help of international society.

Most of the humanitarian aid for Afghanistan now goes through Uzbekistan. We repeat that for humanitarian aims, our ground, water and air space is open.

Dear friends!

Appealing to our citizens and people, we declare:

The defence of independence, the age-old dream of our ancestors, depends on the will and determination of each of us.

This wonderful land is our common motherland, and the duty of each of us is to confidently work and struggle in the name of peace and prosperity.

At this vital time of historical suffering, we, Olly Majlis deputies, express the will of our people, and once again show all round support to the responsible policies of President Islam Karimov in the struggle with international terrorism, calling on all to unite in this struggle and be vigilant.

We express the hope that our appeal will find response in the hearts of all who live on our earth, regardless of nationality, language and faith.

Olly Majlis of the Republic of Uzbekistan

Downloaded from http: //www.press.service.uz/eng/pressa eng/ pressa_eng4.htm

Declaration Adopted by Uzbek Forum on Security in Central Asia Tashkent, Uzbekistan 19-20 October 2000

Text

In the spirit of the security platform based on cooperation which was adopted at the OSCE summit in Istanbul, the participating Central Asian countries hereby specify the following areas of activity which will create a basis for reinforcing cooperation between Kazakhstan, Kyrgyzstan, Tajikistan, Turkmenistan and Uzbekistan:

(a) sharing the concern of the participating Central Asian countries over international terrorism, extremism that involves violence, organised crime and the illegal circulation of drugs and arms;

(b) recognising that international terrorism, extremism that involves violence, organised crime and the circulation of drugs pose an increasingly greater threat to security;

(c) supporting the Political Declaration adopted by the 20th special session of the UN General Assembly, which notes that drugs ruin people's lives, destroy communities, undermine a person's stable development and general crime. Drugs pose a serious threat to tne health and wellbeing of all mankind, the independence of states, democracy, the stability of nations and the structures of all societies, as well as the dignity and hopes of millions of people and their families;

(d) being convinced that the world drugs problem must be resolved multi-nationally;

(e) being anxious about the affect on our society of serious crimes which are global in nature, and being convinced of the need for bilateral, regional, and international cooperation in the field of crime prevention and criminal law;

(f) displaying our anxiety in connection with the problem of trans-national organised crime and the interrelationship between its various forms;

(g) stressing that strengthening regional cooperation will promote stability and security in Central Asia;

(h) expressing deep anxiety over the link between the illegal production and circulation of drugs, and over the involvement of terrorist groups, criminals and trans-national organised crime, and announcing our firm decision to reinforce our cooperation in response to these threats;

(i) maintaining that national, regional and joint action by the international community is essential for resisting these challenges, including those which come from areas that are very close to OSCE countries;

(j) noting with gratitude the initiative of the OSCE and the UNPDCCP chairmanship on holding the international conference on strengthening security and stability in Central Asia and jointly fighting against drugs, organised crime and terrorism (city of Tashkent, 19-20 October 2000) and expressing our gratitude for the hospitality of the Republic of Uzbekistan, we:

1. reaffirm that action directed against drugs, organised crime and terrorism is the responsibility of each interested state, as well as being a common and joint responsibility which requires an adequate, integrated and balanced approach in full accordance with the purposes and principles of the UN Charter, the OSCE's Helsinki Final Act, the OSCE Copenhagen document, the OSCE Paris Charter for a new Europe, the declarations of the OSCE summit meetings in Budapest, Lisbon and Istanbul, as well as with the conclusions formulated in the OSCE charter on security in Europe, adopted in Istanbul in November 1999;
2. recognise the existing links between drugs and terrorism, as well as the varied nature of organised crime, and understand that each of them requires and adequate, differentiated political and legal approach;
3. express our support for UN objectives in the field of crime prevention and criminal law, in particular in the field of reducing the level of crime, more effective and active ways of establishing law and order and exercising justice, respecting human rights and fundamental freedoms, as well as guaranteeing justice, humanity and professional behaviour;
4. maintain the need to study the roots of the problem of drugs, organised crime and terrorism by means of reinforcing human development, guaranteeing economic growth, improving the effective system of administration

and applying democratic principles;

5. stress the responsibility of each state for creating and strengthening a fair, responsible and effective system of criminal law in accordance with UN Charter and international law;
6. stress the importance of fully observing the three international conventions on drugs control, as well as adopting and improving comprehensive national legislation and a strategy for implementing the stipulations of these conventions;
7. attach prime importance to the urgent adoption and implementation of the UN convention against transnational organised crime, as well as the relevant protocols on it;
8. think it is necessary to prevent and fight all signs and forms of terrorism by means of optimising relevant national legislation and strategies, as well as by means of acceding to existing international conventions and implementing them;
9. recognise the significance and role of civil society and the development of democratic institutions in the fight against drugs, organised crime and terrorism, as well as the need for full observance of the principles of the primacy of law;
10. reaffirm the importance of the OSCE principle of comprehensive security, which combines respect for human rights and fundamental freedoms, as well as democracy and the primacy of law. We commit ourselves to fighting threats to security by not violating human rights and people's fundamental freedoms, and not creating obstacles for people who wish to travel;
11. stress that an effective fight against drugs, organised crime and terrorism is impossible without guaranteeing economic growth and developing infrastructure and social programmes. In this connection, we note the particular significance of the economic dimensions as an equally important component of the OSCE blueprint for comprehensive security in the region;
12. welcome the initiative of the Central Asian countries aimed at strengthening cooperation and trust in the region;

13. declare our intention to deepen our cooperation with regard to strengthening security and stability in Central Asia on the basis of a joint approach in the fight against drugs, organised crime and terrorism in line with the document entitled, "priorities of cooperation in the fight against the illegal circulation of drugs, organised crime and terrorism in Central Asia".

Signed by the Presidents of
Kazakhstan
Kyrgyzstan
Tajikistan.
Uzbekistan
Source: SWB/SU/3982/G/1, 27 October 2000

The Joint Statement of the Central Asian Leaders Following the Central Asian Security Summit, Bishkek, Kyrgyzstan, 20 August 2000

Text

We participants of the Bishkek meeting, having discussed the situation in Central Asia following the terrorist actions of international bandit formations, express our serious concern about the widening dimensions of their armed sorties, which we assess unambiguously as blatant acts of aggression, terrorism and extremism.

The fact that actions by international terrorists are assuming a permanent and chronic nature is a special cause for concern. This indicates their aim to undermine security and stability in Central Asia and destabilise the regional and international situation in the long term. This is also shows that Central Asia is becoming one of the main targets of hostile actions of international terrorism and extremism.

On the basis of the provisions of the treaty on joint action in the fight against terrorism, political and religious extremism and trans-national organised crime and other threats to the stability and security of the sides, and of the Collective Security Treaty and bilateral political and legal documents; and recognising that actions of terrorism and banditism in Central Asia and Chechnya, and the military and political confrontation in Afghanistan are links of one chain, the participants of the meeting confirmed their unity in making a legitimate assessment of the ongoing events and concluding that international terrorism is encroaching upon the constitutional and democratic foundations of our societies.

Proceeding from this we confirm our firm determination to give a commensurate response and to put end to brazen bandit sorties.

We firmly state that terrorist actions will be crushed using the most decisive measures in accordance with the norms of international law.

The heads of state signatory to the treaty on joint actions against terrorism, political and religious extremism, trans-national organised crime and other threats to the stability and security of the sides of 21 April of the current year stressed the necessity for the sides strictly to observe all obligations undertaken within the framework of the treaty.

We deem it necessary to consider the situation emerging in Central Asia at a session of the Collective Security Council and to outline urgent measures to settle it, including radical reinforcement of the border on the southern flank of Central Asia and wiping out terrorists where they are located.

Taking into consideration the tense situation emerging on the Tajik-Afghan border, we are convinced that it is expedient to take additional measures to reinforce this, as the southern border of the CIS.

We again turn to the UN Security Council, the OSCE, the OIC (Organisation of Islamic Conference) and all states of the world not only decisively to condemn international terrorism and extremism but also to move from mere declarations to working out coordinated practical measures aimed at rooting out this global threat.

Signed by Leaders of
Kazakhstan
Kyrgyzstan
Tajikistan.
Uzbekistan
Source: SWB/SU/3925/G/1, 22 August 2000.

Multilateral Efforts outside CIS without Concrete Outcome

Date	*Countries*	*Result*
25 April 1993	Tajikistan-Afghanistan	refugee and border problem discussed.
25 May 1993	India-Kazakhstan	Among other things discussed fundamentalism, terrorism.
8 Sep. 1993	Russia-Tajikistan-Afghanistan	Russian foreign ministers visited both the countries, discussed regional security
27 Sep. 1993	UN symposium on CIS Security	symposium organised on security in CIS
3 Dec. 1993	India-Uzbekistan	expressed their total opposition fundamentalism and terrorism.
17 Dec. 1993	Russian border troops chief and Turkish President	agreed on a draft for joint patrolling of Turkey's southern border.
23 March 1994	Russian FM visited Tajikistan	Russian FM observed joint military exercise and discussed security.
20 April 1994	China-Turkmenistan	Chinese President visited, China-Turkmenistan regional security issues.
21 April 1994	China-Uzbekistan	Chinese President visited, China-Uzbekistan regional security issues.
25 April 1994	China-Kazakhstan	discussed ways of furthering bilateral relations as well as regional and international issues.
1 June 1994	Kyrgyzstan-NATO	Kyrgyzstan joined the NATO Partnership for Peace.
3 July 1994	Turkmenistan-Iran	discussed cooperation between the two on illegal drug trafficking.
11 Sep. 1995	China-Kazakhstan	increasing bilateral relations including defence cooperation.

15 Sep. 1995	All CARs, UN, CSCE, OIC	seminar on integrated regional security.
23 Nov. 1995	Iran-Turkmenistan	Iranian military delegation visited Turkmenistan and discussed probable cooperation.
17 July1996	Turkmenistan-Iran	discussed border situation.
10 May 1997	Tajikistan, Afghanistan, Iran	discussed regional scene and agreed for greater regional cooperation.
1 July 1997	Tajikistan-Saudi Arabia	condemned the attempt to use Islam in mercenary political goals in Central Asia.
16 July 1997	OSCE-Uzbekistan	discussed regional and world security and prospects of cooperation.
5 Oct. 1997	Kazakhstan-China	Defence Minister (Kazakhstan)discussed bilateral cooperation and border security with Chinese head of the state and Chinese Defence Minister.
13 Jan. 1998	Tajikistan-China	Tajikistan Defence Minister and Chinese Defence Minister discussed bilateral military cooperation and Chinese help.
11 Feb. 1998	Kyrgyzstan-China	Kyrgyzstan Defence Minister called for greater cooperation between the two.
27 Feb. 1998	US-Uzbekistan	The joint commission signed a document on a plan of cooperation between the US Defence Department & Uzbek Defence Ministry discussed the question of regional security.

5 March 1998	Kazakhstan-Turkmenistan	Kazakhstan Defence Minister and General Staff Chief of Turkmenistan, discussed cooperation between Kazakhstan and Turkmenistan defence ministers.
9 April 1998	Kyrgyzstan-China	China Defence Minister and Kyrgyzstan Chief of Staff agreed to increase the ties between both the countries' defence ministers.
13 April 1998	Turkey-Uzbekistan	Turkish PM, Uzbekistan's President signed a package of agreements and discussed regional problem and bilateral relations.
20 April 1998	Uzbekistan-OSCE	OSCE Chairman, Uzbekistan President discussed regional security and ways of improving relations, OSCE Chairman expressed concern over drug smuggling from CIS countries.
7 May 1998	China-Kazakhstan	Discussed the issue of national splittists.
30 June 1998	Uzbekistan-Israel	discussed struggle against terrorism and Islamic fundamentalism.
31Aug. 1998	Turkmenistan-China	discussed bilateral co-operation and steps to fight against terrorism.
1Oct. 1999	OSCE-Kyrgyzstan	OSCE denounced terrorism both discussed the terrorism in Kyrgyzstan.
4 Oct. 1999	Un-Kyrgyzstan	both discussed problem of fighting drug trafficking.
7 Oct. 1999	Kazakhstan-Iran	Presidents discussed joint steps on drugs trafficking.

18 Dec. 1999	US-Kazakhstan	Kazakhstan Defence Minster discussed with his counterpart regarding military cooperation and fighting international terror.
20 Dec. 1999	UN-Kazakhstan	discussed growing extremism, combating drug dealing.
30 March 2000	Tajikistan-China	Both Defence ministers discussed regional security and separatism.
10 April 2000	Uzbekistan-Russia	Russia presidential envoy and Uzbekistan President discussed plans to fight international terrorism, drugs, and crime and an anti-terrorist centre in Uzbekistan.
12 April 2000	Russia-Kyrgyzstan	The Russian presidential envoy visits Kyrgyzstan and discusses possible bilateral cooperation fighting terrorism extremism, drug trafficking, promised Russian military help on demand.
2 Oct. 2000	Turkey-Uzbekistan	Turkey offered its expertise in dealing with terrorism in Uzbekistan, both discussed the fight against terrorism illegal drug and arms trade.
19 Oct. 2000	Uzbekistan-OSCE	discussed fighting drug-addiction, religious extremism and terrorism, OSCE pledged support.
20 Oct. 2000	Tajikistan-UN	discussed measures to fight drug trafficking.
2 Dec. 2000	NATO	NATO organised a seminar on the situation in Central Asia and discussed

		terrorism and drugs trafficking in CA.
20 Dec. 2000	Kazakhstan-NATO	discussed Afghan problem and Central Asia security.
12 March 2001	Tajikistan-Iran	Tajikistan President and Iran Defence Minister discussed military cooperation.

Bilateral Eforts Outside

Date	*Countries*	*Result*
11 Sep. 1992	Tajikistan-CIS/Russia	economic cooperation, defence and banking alliances economic court.
21 Oct. 1992	Tajikistan-Uzbekistan	deployment of CIS peace peacekeeping forces.
2 Nov. 1992	Tajikistan-Uzbekistan	assistance for stability in Tajikistan.
31 May 1993	Kazakhstan-Uzbekistan	economic, spiritual life and culture, stress importance of economic integration.
11 June 1993	Kyrgyzstan-Kazakhstan	bilateral cooperation
16 June 1993	Kyrgyzstan-Russia	dual citizenship, ethnic Russians in Kyrgyzstan.
17 July 1993	Kazakhstan-Kyrgyzstan-Turkmenistan-Uzbekistan	fighting drugs related crime.
27 Jan. 1994	Russia-Kyrgyzstan	support for reform programme in Kyrgyzstan.
17 Feb. 1994	Russia-Kazakhstan	dismantling nuclear arsenal, dual citizenship.
17 Feb. 1994	Russia-Uzbekistan	Russian communities in Uzbekistan discussed.
4 Nov. 1994	Turkmenistan-Russia	on ensuring regional security.
27 March 1995	Kyrgyzstan-Russia	economic cooperation.
22 July1995	Turkmenistan-Tajikistan	talks on inter-Tajik settlement.
19 Sep. 1995	Russia-Kazakhstan	informal consultations on problems regarding Russia-Kazakhstan relations and CIS.

27 Oct. 1995	Tajikistan-Uzbekistan	UN peace steps in Afghanistan
25 Nov. 1995	Kazakhstan-Tajikistan	regional security, CBMs.
28 Dec. 1995	Tajikistan-Uzbekistan	discuss bilateral cooperation.
23 Feb. 1996	Russia-Uzbekistan	Bilateral ties and regional issues.
29 March 1996	Turkmenistan-Kazakhstan	CIS integration with Kazakhstan counterpart.
10 July 1996	Russia-Turkmenistan	bilateral issues including Caspian Sea.
27 July 1996	Russia-Kyrgyzstan	discuss cooperation between secret services.

Discussions, Talks without Treaties

Date	*Countries*	*Topic*
26 May 1993	Kazakhstan-Uzbekistan	discussed the prospects for development cooperation.
28 April 1997	Uzbekistan-Kazakhstan-Kyrgyzstan	trilateral military cooperation and partnership with NATO.
24 July 1997	Kyrgyzstan-Uzbekistan-Kazakhstan	economic integration, afghanistan and Tajikistan situation.
6 Jan. 1998	five CARs	statement issued for individual approach to CIS.
26 Jan. 1998	Russia	approved draft accord with Uzbekistan, money laundering
26 Feb. 1998	customs, border and law enforcement agencies of all the five CARs	to stop Afghanistan drug trafficking.
3 March 1998	Kyrgyzstan, Tajikistan and Uzbekistan	threat of Islamic extremism in the region.
26 March 1998	Kazakhstan-Tajikistan-Uzbekistan-Kyrgyzstan	admitted Tajik to economic union, adopted a declaration on following regional integration.

26 June 1998	Kazakhstan-Tajikistan-Uzbekistan-Kyrgyzstan	discussed ways of developing cooperation also a draft interstate treaty.
16 July 1999	Russia-Tajikistan	discussed extremism and drug-Uzbekistan trafficking in Central Asia.
29 Sep. 1999	Kazakhstan-Tajikistan-Uzbekistan-Kyrgyzstan	international meeting of prominent figures with sphere of culture and science from four CARs except Turkmenistan. Nazarbayev called for CAR integration, called for strengthening CIS.
17 Nov. 1999	Russia-Tajikistan	discussed boosting up bilateral cooperation.
2 April 2000	Russia-Tajikistan	called for CIS effort to fight international terrorism.
14 June 2000	Kazakhstan-Tajikistan-Uzbekistan-Kyrgyzstan	Central Asian Economic Community meeting discussed among other things expanding economic cooperation, setting-up joint ventures fighting drug trafficking and terrorism.
19 Aug. 2000	Kazakhstan-Uzbekistan	both sides talked on Islamic unrest.
23 Aug. 2000	Kazakhstan-Uzbekistan	considered pooling of forces (Bishkek) for fighting terrorism.
16 Sep. 2000	Tajikistan	called for pooling efforts by CARs against terrorism.
17 Feb. 2000	Tajikistan	supported setting up of a Shanghai Five anti-terrorist centre.
19 March 2001	CIS representatives meeting	criticised Uzbekistan for unilateral and excessive use of force against militancy.

CICA Declaration on Eliminating Terrorism and Promoting Dialogue among Civilizations:

We, the Heads of State or Government of the Member States of the Conference on Interaction and Confidence Building Measures in Asia (CICA), gathered in Almaty for the First CICA Summit, do hereby declare the following:

We are deeply concerned by the increase in all acts of terrorism worldwide, including in CICA Member States. We are fully committed to fighting terrorism and strengthening bilateral, regional and international cooperation, in accordance with the UN Charter, required to meet this challenge. We emphasize the central role of the United Nations, its General Assembly and Security Council, in developing the framework for this.

We express our deepest sorrow over the loss of innocent lives in all acts, methods or practices of terrorism and convey our sympathies and condolences to the families of the victims.

We condemn all forms and manifestations of terrorism, committed no matter when, where or by whom, as barbaric offences and criminal acts indiscriminately directed at the life and well-being of innocent individuals and peoples as well as threatening the peaceful coexistence among nations. No considerations whatsoever can be invoked to justify terrorism.

We are convinced that terrorism constitutes a direct violation of human rights and, in particular, the right to life, freedom, security and development.

We emphasize that eliminating terrorism is the common goal of all cultures and civilizations. We believe that all religions of the world reject violence and terrorism and advocate the protection of human rights.

We underline that terrorism cannot be attributed to religion, nationality, or civilization. We believe that it is essential not to allow terrorists to lure us into a conflict of religions, cultures or civilizations. We also pledge to be particularly vigilant, in order to ensure that the global fight against terrorism does not become a war targeting particular cultures, religions or nations. We all stand united in this fight.

We reaffirm our strong commitment to all norms and principles of international law, the purposes and principles of the UN Charter, including the right to self-determination, and the CICA Almaty Act concerning the maintenance of international peace and security and the promotion of good-neighbourly and friendly relations and cooperation among countries.* (The Republic of Azerbaijan reserves its special position on this paragraph).

We actively support efforts undertaken by the international community, in accordance with UN Charter, to combat terrorism. The fight against terrorism should be global, comprehensive and sustained, and not selective or discriminatory and should avoid applying double standards.

We are also against using the fight against terrorism as a pretext for interference in the internal affairs of sovereign States. We reject the use of force not in compliance with the UN Charter against sovereign States.

We reaffirm the key significance of, and pledge to fully support implementation of, UN Security Council Resolution 1373 and other relevant UN resolutions on combating terrorism which provide the basic framework for national, regional and international obligations and efforts to combat this universal evil.

We underscore the need to respect human rights and rule of law in combating terrorism.

We encourage States Parties to the various UN anti-terrorism Conventions to consult and cooperate, in accordance with the provisions of these Conventions, to ensure their effective implementation. We will contribute to the early elaboration and adoption by the UN of other appropriate instruments, such as the Comprehensive Convention on International Terrorism and the International Convention for the Suppression of Acts of Nuclear Terrorism.

We are open for cooperation in combating terrorism with all other states, regional and international organizations and forums. Taking into account the trans-national character of terrorism, as well as its close links with other challenges and threats to security such as organized crime, narcotics and human trafficking as well as illicit arms trafficking, we will seek to foster cooperation between our relevant authorities and to maintain regular exchange of information in order to enhance international capacity to stop financing of terrorism and eliminate it.

We consider as one of the primary tasks of the international community to strengthen efforts to eliminate poverty, unemployment, illiteracy, extremism, intolerance, entrenched hatred and all forms of discrimination. We believe that it is necessary to ensure sustainable development of all regions of the world and to pay more attention to the socio-economic impact of globalization. It will also be of high importance for our cause to encourage the peaceful settlement of regional and international crises and conflicts.

We support international efforts for the rehabilitation and reconstruction of Afghanistan in order to help revive this country as a stable and prosperous member of the international community.

The CICA Member States intend to strengthen cooperation and dialogue among them in order to promote common values, mutual understanding and confidence for the benefit of the joint fight against terrorism.

We consider CICA as a unique Asian forum which comprises states of different cultures and traditions making it one of the most important mechanisms to promote dialogue among civilizations and cultures. In this context, we reconfirm our full support for the United Nations General Assembly Resolution A/RES/56/6 on Dialogue among Civilizations and are convinced that implementation of its Programme of Action positively contributes to international efforts to attain universal peace, welfare and stability. The CICA Member States intend to comprehensively and actively promote such a dialogue taking into account that Eurasia has not only been a cradle of some of the world's largest civilizations but has also served as a bridge between them.

Almaty, June 4, 2002

Available at: http://www.homestead.com/prosites-kazakhembus/cica.html downloaded on 25 June 2002.

Table 3
Basic Macroeconomic Indicators (1999)

	GDP Growth	*Inflation*	*Fiscal Balance*	*Current Account*	*Foreign Direct Invest-ment*	*Exchange rate*
	(%)	(%)	(% of GDP)	(% of GDP)	(Million US$)	(Na.cur/$)
Kazakhstan	2.7	17.8	-5.4	-1.0	1587	109.6
Kyrgyzstan	3.7	35.9	-13.0	-14.8	35	39.0
Tajikistan	3.7	30.1	-3.1	6.2	29	1,237.2
Turkmenistan	14.9	19.5	-1.8	-17.3	80	*5,200
Uzbekistan	4.1	-0.02	29.0	-	-2.6	-
ECO region	-0.1	-	113	3934	*125	-

Note: (*) Official exchange rate.
Source: http://www.ecosecretariat.org/

Glossary

Abu Hanifeh-al-Numan-ibn-Thabit-ibn-Zuta Founder of Han'afi school of thought in Islam.

Adolat (Justice) Radical Islamic group in the Fergana Valley. A precursor of the IMU.

Aksakals (From Turkic white bearded old man) An elected village elder as well as any respected old man.

Al-Qaeda (The Base) Global terrorist network headed by Osama bin Laden.

Al-Wadah The newspaper which was brought out by IRP.

An-Nabhani, Sheikh Taqiuddin Filastyni (the Palestinian) Founder of the HT.

Basmachi A Turkic term that means "bandit" used by Soviets to describe both the revolt and Islamic Mujahideen who opposed the Communist system in Central Asia after 1917.

Beys A rich man, major landowner, livestock owner or money lender in Central Asia, before the October Revolution.

Birlik (Unity) Opposition Party in Uzbekistan. Founded in 1988 and banned in 1992, Birlik subsequently established the Human Rights Society of Uzbekistan.

Commonwealth of Independent States (CIS) A post-independence Commonwealth that in 2001 consisted of Armenian, Azerbaijan, Belarus, Georgia, Kazakhstan, Kyrgyzstan, Moldova, Russia, Tajikistan, Turkmenistan, Ukraine, Uzbekistan.

Dekhkans Peasants

Dostum, Gen. Rashid Leader of the anti-Taliban United Front (also called the Northern Alliance) after the assassination of Ahmad Shah Masood and a leader of the Uzbek minority in the northern Afghanistan.

Erk (Freedom) Opposition party in Uzbekistan. A splinter group of Birlik, Erk was founded in 1990 and banned in 1992; it subsequently established the Independent Human Rights Organisation of Uzbekistan.

Hadith The body of traditions about the sayings and acts of the Prophet Muhammad that delineate proper Muslim behaviour and from along with the Koran, the basis for Sharia (Islamic law).

Haj The annual pilgrimage to Mecca, a religious rite every Muslim is required to perform at least once.

Hejab Head scarf that covers the hair and neck.

Hekmatyar, Gulbuddin Afghanistan warlord who founded the Hizb-i-Islami.

Himmatzada, Muhammad Sharif Leader of the military wing of the IRP.

Hindustani, Muhammad Rustamov Deobandi Muslim leader of an underground Islamic movement in Tajikistan during the Soviet era.

Hizb-i-Islami (Party of Islam) Most extreme party of Afghan Mujahideens formed to resist the Soviet invasion of Afghanistan; founded by Gulbuddin Hekmatyar.

Hizb-i-Islami-Turkistan (Islamic Party of Turkistan) reputed name change of the IMU, signifying a new mission to bring Islamic revolution to the whole of Central Asia and Xinjiang Province.

Hizb-ut-Tahrir al-Islami (HT; Party of Islamic Liberation) Fundamentalist Islamic movement that seeks, through non-violent means, to restore the caliphate and institute Sharia through out the Muslim world.

Ibrahim, Veli First Secretary of Tatar Communist Party; executed in Crimea by Soviet authorities.

Ikhwan-ul-Muslimeen (Muslim Brotherhood) Group established in the 1930s in Egypt that advocated that colonies seek independence from their colonisers try to form Islamic states.

Imam Prayer leader at a mosque who has also acquired some religious learning and has respect and support of the community.

Inter Services Intelligence (ISI) Pakistan's secret service.

Islam Lashkarlry (Fighters for Islam) Radical Islamic group in the Fergana Valley.

Islamic Movement of Uzbekistan (IMU) Militant Islamic group founded in 1999 by Tohrir Yuldeshev and Juma Namangani that has declared a jihad against the government of Uzbekistan.

Islamic Renaissance Party (IRP) Islamic political organisation founded in the Soviet Union in 1990, with independent branches in the Central Asian republics. The IRP is the only legal party in Tajikistan.

Jamiat-i-Islami (Islamic Party) Largest religious party in Pakistan.

Jamiat-i-Ulema Islami (JUI; Islamic Ulema Party) Pakistani organisation that supports the IMU and the Taliban.

Jihad The way an individual can become a better Muslim and be service to society; can also be a call to holy war against non-Muslims.

Jima Public consensus.

Kalym Bride price.

Khilafat (Caliphate) The Islamic state established by the successors to The Prophet Muhammad that in the early Islamic period after His death united all Muslim lands under a single Caliph (Khalifa), literally "successor to The Prophet".

Kulaks Russian rich peasant bourgeois who became rich by predatory exploitation, loan sharking and speculation.

Kurultay Congress of Muslims of Central Asia.

Laden, Osama bin Exiled Saudi Arabian militant, head of Al-Qaeda.

Lali Badakhshan Party of the Pamiri Tajiks who sought greater autonomy during the Tajik civil war.

Lashkar-i-Jhangvi Extremist Pakistani anti-Shia group.

Madrassa School where students study Islamic subjects, Islamic law, and the Koran.

Masood, Ahmad Shah, Defence Minister of Afghanistan until the Taliban takeover; leader of the anti-Taliban forces (the United Front) after 1997; assassinated in September 2001.

Mujahideen Fighter who undertakes jihad for Islam.

Mullah Traditional Islamic prayer leader at a mosque.

Nabiev, Rakhmon, President of Tajikistan, 1991-92; although Tajikistan now has a coalition government, the United Nations still recognises Nabiev as President.

Nahzar-i-Islami (Islamic Knowledge) Illegal Tajik Islamic educational organisation, founded by Sayed Abdullah Nuri.

Namangani, Juma Founder and military leader of the IMU.

NGO Nongovernmental Organisation.

Nomenklatura Ruling Soviet Communist elite.

Nuri, Sayed Abdullah Founder of Nahzar-i-Islami and founding member and leader of a Sufi order.

Pir Title given to the head of a Sufi order.

Quatra-ibn-Muslim the Arab invader who was responsible for the successful infiltration of Islam into Central Asia.

Qyias Analogy.

Ra'y Private opinion.

Rabbani, Burhanuddin President of Afghanistan, 1992-96.

Shanghai Five Group of five countries (China, Russia, Tajikistan, Kazakhstan, and Kyrgyzstan) that share common borders and are pledged to meet at summit level annually. In 2000 renamed the Shanghai Forum, with Uzbekistan added as a country with observer status. In 2001, renamed Shanghai Cooperation Organisation; Uzbekistan was made a member, and various other countries were given observer status.

Sharia The Islamic legal system and code based on the Koran and the hadith of the Prophet Muhammad.

Shia Islam The sect of Islam found mainly in Iran and other Arab countries.

Shura Religious (Islamic) or political council.

Shura-i-Islam Counter-revolutionary organisation who led Basmachi revolt.

Shura-i-Ulema Counter-revolutionary organisation who led Basmachi revolt.

Sipahi-i-Sahaba Extremist Pakistani anti-Shia group.

Solih, Muhammad (pseudonym of Salay Madaminov) Poet and exiled leader of Erk.

Sufi Islam Islamic mysticism or the practioner of mysticism.

Sunni Islam The majority sect of Islam.

Tariqa A Sufi religious order.

Tauba (Repentance) Radical Islamic group in the Fergana Valley.

Turajonzada, Akbar Grand Mufi (Qazi) of Tajikistan's Muslims during the last year of Soviet period; IRP leader (expelled 1998); member of the coalition government of Tajikistan since 1998.

Ulema Body of scholars of Islamic theology.

Umma Islamic world community.

United Tajik Opposition (UTO) Coalition of the IRP and the nationalist Tajik parties during the Tajikistan civil war.

Volost An administrative and territorial unit in Russian from 11th through the 20th century

Wahhabi Extremist sect of Islam that originated in Saudi Arabia.

Yashmiak Veil.

Yuldeshev, Tohrir Abdouhalilovitch Founding member and leader of the IMU.

Zaloom, Sheikh Abdul Qadeem Leader and prolific author of the HT.

Zia ul Haq, Muhammad President of Pakistan, 1978-88.

Ziyoyev, Mirzo Minister in the Tajikistan government; friend of IMU leader Juma Namangani.

Bibliography

Primary Sources

"Uzbek Popular Front", *Central Asia and Caucasus Chronicle*, Vol. 8, No. 6, Dec-Jan, 1989-90.

Agreement to set up a Commonwealth by Central Asian states, 2 January 1993.

Agreements of Central Asian States Mutual Security Treaty, 19 November 1993.

Almaty Act, June 2002.

Ashgabat Summit of Central Asian Presidents, 6 January 1998.

CICA Declaration on Eliminating Terrorism and Promoting Dialogue among Civilisations, 4 June 2002, Almaty, Kazakhstan, http://www.homestead.com/prosites-kazakhembus/cica/html.

Constitution of the Republic of Kazakhstan, 1994. http://www.geocities.com/capitolhill/lobby/2171/kzconst.html-7k

Constitution of the Republic of Kyrgyzstan http://www.kyrgyzstan.org/law/constitution.htm-87k

Constitution of the Republic of Tajikistan http://www.geocities.com/paris/9305/constitution.html.43k

Constitution of the Republic of Uzbekistan, Tashkent, 1992 www.geocities.com/Paris/9305/constitution.html.43k

CPSU 19th All Union Conference: Documents and Materials, Moscow, Novosti Press Agency Publishing House, 1988.

Declaration Adopted by Uzbek Forum on Security in Central Asia, Tashkent, Uzbekistan, 19-20 October 2000.

Documents and Materials of 27th CPSU Congress, February 25 1986, Moscow, Novosti Press Agency, 1986.

Gorbachev, Mikhail, *Perestroika: New Thinking for our Country and the World*, New York, 1987.

Karimov, Islam, *Uzbekistan along the Road of Deepening Economic Reform*, Tashkent, Uzbekistan, 1995.

Uzbekistan on the Threshold of the 21th Century, Tashkent, Uzbekistan, 1997.

Uzbekistan: The Road of Independence and Progress, Tashkent, 1993.

Moscow Summit of CIS Council of Heads of States, 29 April 1998.

Nazarbaev, Nursultan, *Without Right or Left*, London, 1992.

On VI Session of the Second Convocation of Olly Majlis of the Republic of Uzbekistan, Press Release, Uzbek Embassy, New Delhi.

Russia Demands its Army as CIS Peacekeeper, 8 March 1993.

Shanghai Declaration, 15 April 1995.

The Agreement on Collective Security, 15 May 1992.

The Joint Statement of the Central Asian Leaders Following the Central Asian Security Summit, Bishkek, Kyrgyzstan, 20 August 2000.

The Treaty on Collective Security, Tashkent, 15 May 1992.

Books

Ahmar, Moonis, Siddiqui Farhan Hanif, *The Challenges of Conflict Resolution and Security in 21th Century: Problems and Prospects*, Programme on Peace Studies and Conflict Resolution, Department of International Relations, University of Karachi, 2001.

Akiner, Shirin (ed.), *Politics and Economic Trends in Central Asia*, London, I.B. Tauris & Co. Ltd., 1992.

The Islamic Peoples of the Soviet Union, London, Keagan Paul International, 1983.

Allworth, E. (ed.), *Central Asia: A Century of Russian Rule*, New York, Columbia University Press, 1967.

Nationality Group Survival in Multiethnic States: Shifting Support Patterns in the Soviet Baltic Region, New York, Praeger Publishers, 1977.

The Nationality Question in Soviet Central Asia, New York and London, Praeger Publishers, 1973.

Allworth, E. *Ethnic Russia in the USSR: The Dilemma of Dominance*, New York, Pergamon, 1973.

Amin, Tahir, "Pakistan, Afghanistan and Central Asian States" in Ali Bannuazizi and Myron Weiner (eds.) *New Geo Politics*, London, I.B. Tauri, 1994.

Anderson, John, *Kyrgyzstan: Central Asian Island at Democracy*, Hardwood Academic Publishers, Amsterdam, 1999.

The International Politics of Central Asia, London, Manchester University Press, 1997.

Anderson, Walter K., Shridhar D. Damle, *The Brotherhood in Saffron, The RSS and Hindu Revivalism*, Boulder, CO, West View, 1987.

Babakhanov, Mufti Ziauddin Khan, *Islam and the Muslims in the Land of the Soviets*, Moscow, Progress Publishers, 1980.

Bacon, Elizabeth E., *Central Asia under Russian Rule: A Study in Cultural Change*, New York, Cornell University Press, 1966.

Ballance, O'Edgar, *Islamic Fundamentalist Terrorism 1979-95, The Iranian Connection,* London, Macmillan *Press*, 1997.

Bannuazizi, Ali and Weiner, Myron (eds.), *The New Geopolitics of Central Asia and its Borderlands*, London, I. B. Tauris and Co. Ltd, 1994.

Barth, Frederick (ed.), *Ethnic Groups and Boundaries: The Social Organisation of Culture Difference*, London, Allen and Unwin, 1969.

Bennigsen, A & Quelquejay, C. L., *Islam in the Soviet Union*, London, Pall Mall Press, 1967.

Bennigsen, Alexandre and Marie Broxup, *The Islamic Threat to the Soviet State*, London, Croom Helm Ltd, 1983.

Bialer, Seweryn (ed.), *Politics, Society and Nationality inside Gorbachev's Russia*, Boulder Colo, 1989.

Bordeaux, Michael (ed.), *The Politics of Religion in Russia and the New States of Eurasia,* Armonk, New York, M. E. Sharpe, 1995.

Carr, E. H., *Nationalism and After*, London, Macmillan Ltd., 1945.

Chopra, V. D. (ed.), *Religious Fundamentalism in Asia*, New Delhi, Vikas Publishing House, 1994.

Cline, Ray S. and Yonah Alexander, *Terrorism, the Soviet Connection,* New York, Centre for Strategic Studies and International Studies, George Town University, 1984.

Clutterback, Richard, *Living with Terrorism*, New York, Arlingdon House Publishers, 1975.

D'Encauese, Helene Carrere, *The End of Soviet Empire, the Triumph of the Nations*, New York /London: Harper Collins, 1993.

The Great Challenge: Nationalities on the Bolshevik, 1917-30, New York and London, Holmes and Meir, 1992.

Dani, A. H., *New light on Central Asia*, Lahore, Sang-e-Mell Publication, 1993.

Dawisha, Karen and Bruce Parrots (eds.), *Conflicts, Cleavage and Changes in Central Asia and the Caucasus*, Cambridge, Cambridge University Press, 1997.

Dobson, Christopher & Ronald Payne, *The Weapons of Terror*, London, Macmillan Press, 1979.

Dror, Y., *Crazy States*, New York, Millwood, 1980.

Eickelman, Dale (ed.), *Russia's Muslim Frontiers: New Direction in Cross-Cultural Analysis*, Indianapolis, Indiana University Press, 1994.

Esposito, John L., *The Islamic Threat: Myth or Reality*? New York, Oxford University Press, 1995.

Fierman, William, *Soviet Central Asia: The Failed Transformation*, Oxford, Westview Press, 1991.

Fuller, Graham, *Central Asia: The New Geo-Politics*, Santa Monica, RAND Corporation, 1992.

Gearty, Conor, *Terrorism*, Aldershot, England, Dartmouth, 1996.

Gross, Jo-Ann (ed.), *Muslims in Central Asia: Expressions of Identity and Change*, Durham, NZ, Duke University Press, 1992.

Guibernau, Montserrat and John Rex (eds.), *The Ethnicity Reader Nationalism, Multiculturalism and Migration*", Cambridge Polity Press, 1997.

Gurr, Ted Robert, *Why Men Rebel?,* Princeton, Princeton University Press, 1970.

Haghayeghi, Mehrded, *Islam and Politics in Central Asia*, London, Macmillan press, 1995.

Hajda, Lambomyr & Mark Beissinger (eds.), *The Nationalities Factor in Soviet Politics and Society,* San Francisco, West View Press, 1990.

Hiro, Dilip, *Between Marx and Muhammed, The Changing Face of Central Asia,* London, Harper Collins Publishers, 1994.

__________, *Islamic Fundamentalism*, London, Paladin Grafton Books, 1988.

Hunter, Shireen T., *Central Asia since Independence*, The Washington Papers, 168, Centre for Strategic and International Studies, Washington D.C., 1996.

Ibrahim, Diloram, *The Islamisation of Central Asia: A Case Study of Uzbekistan*, Leicester, the Islam foundation, 1993.

Kaser, Michael and Santosh Mehrotra, *The Central Asian Economies after Independence*, London, RIIA, 1992.

Kaufman, Richard and Hardt, John, *The former Soviet Union in Transition*, Armonk, New York, M. E. Sharpe, 1993.

Kaushik, Devendra, *Central Asia in Modern Times: A History From Early 19th Century,* Moscow: Progress Publishers, 1970.

Kellas, James G., *The Politics of Nationalism and Ethnicity*, London, Mcmillan Press Ltd., 1991.

Kolarz, Walter, *Russia and Her Colonies*, New York, Frederick A Praeger, 1952.

Kredar, *Peoples of Central Asia, Uralic and Altaic Series*, Bloomington, Indiana University Press, 1966.

Lacquer, Walter, *The Age of Terror*, London, Widenfield and Nicolson, 1987.

Lapidus, G. W., Victorizalavsky and Phillip Goldman (eds.), *From Union to Commonwealth: Nationalism and Separatism in Soviet Republics*, Cambridge University Press, New York 1992.

Livingstone, Neil C., *The War against Terrorism*, Lexington, Massachusetts, Toronto, Lexington Books, 1982.

Malik, Hafeez (ed.), *Central Asia: Its Strategic Importance and Future Prospects*, St. Martin Press, New York, 1994.

Mandelbaum, Michael, *Central Asia and the World*: *Kazakhstan, Uzbekistan, Tajikistan, Kyrgyzstan, Turkmenistan*, New York, Council on Foreign Relations Press, 1994.

Mann, Poonam, "Central Asia and US: After September 11", *World Focus,* Vol. 23, No. 6, June 2002.

Manz, Beatrice F, (ed.), *Central Asia in Historical Perspective*, Boulder, Colorado and Oxford, UK, Westview Press, 1994.

Martimer, Edward, *Faith and Power: The Politics of Islam*, London, Faber, 1982.

Marwah, Ved, *Uncivil Wars, Pathology of Terrorism in India,* New Delhi, Indus, Harper Collins Publishers, 1995.

Mesamed, Vladimir, "Inter-Ethnic Relations in the Republic of Uzbekistan", *Central Asia Monitor*, No. 6, 1996.

Neill, Bard, E.O' et al, *Insurgency in the Modern World,* Colorado, West View Press, 1980.

Neill, Bard, E.O', *Insurgency and Terrorism*, Brassey's (US), Inc, Maxwell Macmillan Pergamon Publishers Corporation, 1990.

Netanyahu, Benjamin (ed.), *International Terrorism, Challenge and Response*, Jerusalem, The Jonathan Institute, Transaction Books, New Brunswick, USA, 1981.

Paget, Julien, *Counter Insurgency Campaign*, London, Faber and Faber, 1967.

Panarin, Sergei A. Nlavmkin, Vitaly, *State Religion and Society in Central Asia: A post-Soviet Critique*, Reading, Ithaca Press, 1993.

Park, A.G., *Bolshevism in Turkestan, 1917-27*, New York, Columbia University Press, 1957.

Patnaik, Ajay (ed.), *Commonwealth of Independent States- Problems and Prospects*, Konark Publishers, New Delhi, 1995.

Patnaik, Ajay, *Central Asia*: *Between Modernity and Tradition*, New Delhi, Konark Publishers, 1996.

Perestroika and Women Labour Force in Soviet Central Asia, New Literature, New Delhi, 1989.

State Building in Tajikistan, Research Monograph, Maulana Abul Kalam Azad Institute of Asian Studies, Calcutta, 2000.

Prabha, Kshitij, *Terrorism: An Instrument of Foreign Policy*, New Delhi, South Asian Publishers, 2000.

Rapopart, David C. (ed.) *Inside Terrorist Organisations,* London, Frank Cass, 2001.

Rashid, Ahmed, *Jihad: The Rise of Militant Islam in Central Asia*, Hyderabad, India, Orient Longman, 2002.

The Resurgence of Central Asia: Islam or Nationalism, Karachi: Oxford University Press, 1994.

Reich, Walter, *Origins of Terrorism, Psychologies, Ideologies, Theologies, States of Mind*, Cambridge, Woodrow Wilson International Centre for Scholars and Cambridge University Press, 1990.

Roi, Yaacov (ed.), *Muslim Eurasia Conflicting Legacies*, London, Frank Cass, 1995.

Roi, Yaacov, *Islam in the Soviet Union: From World War II to Perestroika*, Hurst and Company, London, 2000.

Sacks, Michael Paul and Jerry G. Pankhurst (eds.), *Understanding Soviet Society,* London, Unwin Hyman Ltd., 1988.

Saksena, N. S., *Terrorism, History and Facts in the World and India*, New Delhi, Abhinav Publications, 1985.

Schmid, Alex P., Albert J. Jongman et al, *Political Terrorism*, Amsterdam/Oxford/New York, North Holland Publishing Company, 1988.

Seger, Karl A., *The Anti-Terrorism Hand Book, A Practical Guide to Counter-action Planning and Operations for Individual, Business and Government,* New Delhi, Lancer International, 1990.

Singh, Sangat, *Pakistan's Foreign Policy: An Appraisal,* Bombay, Asian Publishing House, 1970.

Slann, Martin, & Bernard Schechterman, *Multi-dimensional Terrorism*, London, Lynne Reinner Publishers, 1987.

Smith, Anthony, *Against Every Human Law, Terrorist Threat to Diplomacy*, Sydney, Australian National University, 1988.

Smith, Graham, *The Nationalities Question in the post-Soviet States*, New York, London, Longman Group, 1996.

Snyder, Jedc (ed.), *After Empire: The Emerging Geopolitics of Central Asia*, Washington D.C., Ft, McNair, National Defence University Press, 1996.

Sterling, Claira, *The Terror Network, The Secret War of International Terrorism*, London, Widenfield and Nicholson, 1981.

Teresa Rakowska-Harmstone, *Russia and Nationalism in Central Asia: The Case Study of Tadjhikistan,* Baltimore, Md and London, John Hopkins University, 1970.

Thackrah, John Richard, *Encyclopaedia of Terrorism and Political Violence*, London and New York, Routledge and Kegan Paul, 1987.

Tishkov, Vallery, *Ethnicity and Nationalism and Conflict in and after the Soviet Union*, London, Sage Publications, 1997.

Tornavist, Olle, *Politics and Development: A Critical Introduction*, New Delhi, Sage Publications, 1999.

Vassiliev, Alexi (ed.), *Central Asia: Political and Economic Challenges in the Post-Soviet Era*, London, Saqui Book, 2001.

Warikoo, K (ed.), Central Asia: Emerging New Order, New Delhi, Har Anand Publisher, 1995.

Warikoo, K and Norbu, D (eds.), *Ethnicity and Politics in Central Asia*, New Delhi, South Asia Publishers Pvt. Limited, 1992.

Wheeler, G., *The Modern History of Soviet Central Asia*, London, Weidenfield and Nicholson, 1964.

White, Brian, Richard Little and Michael Smith (eds.), *Issues in World Politics*, New York, Palgrave, 2001.

Wielkinson, Paul, *Political Terrorism*, New York, Johnwiley and Sons, 1977.

Terrorism: British Perspectives, Hong Kong, Dartmouth, 1993.

Zenkovsky, S, *Pan-Turkism and Islam in Russia*, Cambridge Mass., Harvard University Press, 1960.

Articles

Abazov, Rafis, "Central Asia's Conflicting Legacy", *Nationalism and Ethnic Politics*, Vol. 5, No. 2, Summer 1999.

Abidl, A. H. H., "Iran and Central Asian Republics, Interests and Approaches", *Strategic Analysis*, Vol. 18, No. 3, June 1995.

Adam, Sunil, "Philosophy of Terrorism: A Historical Perspective", *Strategic Analysis*, Vol. 11, No. 9, December 1986.

Ahmar, Moonis, "Conflict Resolution and Confidence Building in Central Asia", *Strategic Studies*, Vol. 16, No. 3, Spring, 1994.

Ahmed, Dr. Shamina, "The Political Implications of Ethnicity in Central Asia", *Regional Studies*, Vol. 13, No. 2, Spring, 1995.

Ahmed, Rashid, "The Fires of Faith in Central Asia", *World Policy Journal*, Spring, 2001.

Ahrari, M. E., "Dynamics of New Great Game in Muslim Central Asia", *Central Asian Survey*, Vol. 13, No. 2, 1994.

Akbarzadeh, Shahram, "Islamic Clerical Establishment in Central Asia", *South Asia*, Vol. XX, No. 2, 1997.

"Nation Building in Uzbekistan", *Central Asian Survey*, Vol. 15, No. 1, 1996.

"Political Islam in Kyrgyzstan and Turkmenistan", *Central Asian Survey*, Vol. 20, No. 4, 2001.

"The Political Shape of Central Asia", *Central Asian Survey*, Vol. 16, No. 4, 1997.

Akcali, Pinar, "Islam as a 'Common Bond' in Central Asia: Islamic Renaissance Party and the Afghan Mujahideen", *Central Asian Survey*, Vol. 17, No. 2, 1998.

Akcalt, Pivar, "Islam as a 'Common Bond' in Central Asia: Islamic Renaissance Party and the Afghan Mujahideen", *Central Asian Survey*, Vol. 17, No. 2, June 1998.

Akhtar, Naseema, "Pakistan and Central Asian Republics", *Foreign Affairs Reporter*, Vol. 44, No. 9-10, September-October 1995.

Akhtar, Shameem, "Implications of Current Developments in Afghanistan", *Pakistan Horizon*, Vol.45, No. 3, July 1992.

Akzali, Pinar, "Islam as a Common Bond in Central Asia: Islamic Renaissance Party and the Afghan Mujahideen", *Central Asian Survey*, Vol.17, No.2, 1998.

Akzali, Pinar, "Islam as a Common Bond in Central Asia: Islamic Renaissance Party and the Afghan Mujahideen", *Central Asian Survey*, Vol.17, No.2, 1998.

Ali, Farz, "Ethnic Conflicts in Afghanistan, Tajikistan and Uzbekistan", *Link*, No. 4 October 1994.

Allison, Roy, "The Security Priorities and Military Ties of the CIS Central Asian States", *Amu Darya*, Vol. 1, No. 2, Summer and Fall, 1996.

Allworth, E., "The Disarming of Islamic Central Asia: Technology in Relations with Russia before Full Sovietisation (Part I)", *Central Asia Monitor*, No. 3, 1995.

Amin, Tahir, "Pakistan and the Central Asian States", *Strategic Studies*, Vol. 16, No. 4, Summer, 1994.

Anderson, John, "Constitutional Development in Central Asia", *Central Asian Survey*, Vol. 16, No. 3, 1997.

"Authoritarian Political Development in Central Asia: The Case of Turkmenistan", *Central Asian Survey*, Vol. 14, No. 4, 1995.

Arapov, Aleksai, and Umanskit. T, "Asianism, the External and Internal Manifestation of Ethno-politics in Central Asia: A View from Uzbekistan", *Russian Social Science Review*, Vol. 35, No. 4, July-August 1994.

Aripov, Elder T., "Central Asia in the Post-Soviet Period: Myths and Realities", *Central Asia Monitor*, No. 3, 1999.

Ataov, Turkkaya, "Central Asia on the Threshold of the 21st Century", *Himalayan and Central Asian Studies*, Vol. 1, No. 3, October-December 1997.

Aydin, Mustafa, "Turkey and Central Asia, Challenges of Change", *Central Asian Survey*, Vol. 15, No. 2, June 1996.

Aytmatov, Askar, "The Shade of Extremism over Central Asia", *Perceptions*, December 2000-February 2001.

Babadzhanov, Bakhtiyar, "Radicalisation of Islam in Uzbekistan: A Study of Hizb-ut-Tahir-al-Islami", *Contemporary Central Asia*, Vol. IV, No. 1 & 2, 2000.

Badley, Thomas, J., "Defining International Terrorism: A Pragmatic Approach", *Terrorism and Political Violence*, Vol. 10, No. 1, Spring, 1998.

Bakshi, G. D., "Central Asian Cauldron: Conflict Prognostication", *Strategic Analysis*, Vol. 19, No. 3, June 1996.

Bakshi, Jyotsna, "No Single Power or Power Centre can have Exclusive Sway over Central Asia, A Geopolitical Analysis", *Strategic Analysis*, Vol. 22, No. 1, April 1998.

"Russia's Policy towards Central Asia, Part- I", *Strategic Analysis,* Vol. 22, No. 10, January 1999.

"Russia's Policy towards Central Asia, Part- II", *Strategic Analysis,* 22 (11), February 1999.

Bal, Idris, "Instruments of Soviet Control in Central Asia", *Eurasian Studies*, Vol. 3, No. 2, Summer 1996.

Bannerjee, D and P. Stobdan, "Central Asia: Current Situations and Future Prospects" A Study by IDSA, New Delhi and Russian Academy of Sciences, Moscow, *Strategic Studies,* Vol. 23, No. 8, August 1993.

Bannerjee, D., "Central Asian Republics Today", *Strategic Analysis*, Vol. 17, No. 5, August 1994.

"Emergence of Central Asia", *Asian Strategic Review*, IDSA, 1991-92.

"Recent Development in Central Asia and Their Security Implications", *Strategic Analysis*, Vol. 15, No. 5, August 1992.

"Security and the Nuclear Issue", *World Focus,* Vol. 14, No. 3-4, March-April, 1993.

"Security Issues in Central Asia", *USI Journal*, Vol. 123, No. 511, January-March 1993.

Belokrenitsky, Vyacheslav Ya, "Central Asia in the New Eurasian Geopolitics: Implications for Pakistan and Russia", *Pakistan Horizon*, Vol. 48, No. 3, July 1995.

"Russia and Greater Central Asia", *Asian Survey*, Vol. 34, No. 12, December 1994.

Bhatty, Maqbool A., "Pakistan's Perspectives on Central Asia", *Strategic Studies,* Vol. 16, No. 3, Spring, 1994.

Bialer, Serneya, "The Passing of Soviet Order", *Survival*, No. 2, 1990.

Bingol, Yilmoz, "Turkey Policy towards Post-Soviet Central Asia: Opportunities and Challenges", *Eurasian Studies*, No.14, Summer/Autumn, 1998.

Blank, Stephen, "Central Asia, South Asia and Asian Security", *Eurasian Studies*, Vol. 2, No. 3, Fall, 1995.

"Ethnic and Party Politics in Soviet Kazakhstan, 1920-24", *Central Asian Survey*, Vol. 10, No. 3, 1991.

Bondarevsky, G. L., "Tajikistan-Afghanistan: Two Hot Beds of War", *World Affairs*, June 1993.

Bonner, Arthur, "Islam and the States in Central Asia: A Comparative Essay", *Central Asia Monitor*, No. 6, 1995.

Bremer, I. Paul, "Terrorism: It's Evolving Nature", *Department of State Bulletin,* 89 (2146), May 1989.

Brenninkhmeijer, Olivier, "Tajikistan's Elusive Peace", *World Today,* Vol. 52, No. 2, February 1996.

Broxup, Marie, "Islam in Central Asia since Gorbachev", *Asian Affairs*, Vol.18, No. 3, 1987.

Buren, Jhang, "Theme of the 'Shanghai Five' Mechanism", *Contemporary International Relations*, Vol. 11, No. 3, March 2001.

Calabrese, John, "China's Policy towards Central Asia: Renewal and Accommodation", *Eurasian Studies*, Vol. 16, Autumn-Winter, 1999.

Canfield, Robert C., "Restructuring in Greater Central Asia: Changing Political Configurations", *Asian Survey*, Vol. 32, No. 10, October 1992.

Chalk, Peter, "Evolving Dynamics of Terrorism in the 1990s", *Australian Journal of International Affairs*, 53 (2), July 1999.

Chang, Felix K., "China's Central Asian Power and Problems", *Orbis*, Vol. 41, No. 3, Summer, 1997.

Chenoy, Anuradha M., "Political and Economic Processes in Central Asian Republics", *International Studies*, Vol. 34, No. 3, 1997.

Choudhury, Sushil, "The New Order in Central Asia and its Impact on India", *Link,* 21 June 1992.

Cooper, Robert and Mats Berdal, "Outside Intervention in Ethnic Conflicts", *Survival*, Spring, 1993.

Coppietaer, Bruno et al., "Central Asian Region in a New International Environment", *NATO Review*, 44 (5), September 1996.

Coriey, Felix, "Turkmenistan Crushes Religious Minorities", *Central Asia Monitor*, No. 1, 2001.

Cronier, Bruno De, "Economic Cooperation Organisation, Towards a New Silk Road on the Ruins of the Cold War", *Central Asian Survey,* Vol.15, No. 1, March 1996.

Cutler, Robert M., "Islamic Militancy in Central Asia: What is to be Done", *Global Affairs Commentary*, 19 October 2001.

Daanvander, Schriek, "The Central Asian Taliban", *The Times of Central Asia*, 18 October 2001.

Dannervther, Roland, "Creating New States in Central Asia", *Adelphi Papers*, 288, March 1994.

Das, Dilip K., "Impact of Anti-terrorist Measures on democratic Law Enforcement: The Italian Experience", *Terrorism*, Vol. 13, 1990.

Das, Rahul Peter, "Great Game Continued", *World Affairs*, Vol. 4, No. 3, July-September 2000.

Davis, Anthony, "Pakistan in Quandary over New Sanctions against the Taliban", *Jane's Intelligence Review*, Vol. 13, No. 2, February 2001.

Delvoil, Lovis A., "Islamisation of Pakistan's Foreign Policy", *International Journal,* 51, Winter, 1995-96.

Deutch, John, "Terrorism", *Foreign Policy*, No. 108, Fall, 1997.

Dikshit, Prashant, "Small Arms, Drugs, and International Terrorism", *International Studies*, Vol. 32, No. 2, 1995.

Dixit, Abha, "Islamabad's Central Asian Strategy Runs into Rough Weather", *Strategic Analysis*, Vol. 15, No. 3, June 1992.

Djalili, Mohammad Reza, "Experiments in Regional Cooperation in Third World- ECO in search of Synergy between Western and Central Asia", *World Affairs*, Vol. 1, No. 3, July-September 1997.

"In Search of New Friends: Iran and Central Asia", *World Affairs*, Vol. 1, No. 1, January-March 1997.

Dobson, Richard B., "Kyrgyzstan in a Time of Change", *Central Asia Monitor*, No. 1, 1995.

Dorian, James P. et al., "Central Asia and Xinjiang, China: Emerging Energy, Economic and Ethnic Relations", *Central Asian Survey*, Vol. 16, No. 4, December 1997.

Emadi, H., "State, Ideology and Islamic Resurgence in Tajikistan", *Central Asian Survey,* Vol. 13, No. 4, 1994.

Enders, Walter and Sandler, Todd, "Transnational Terrorism in the post-Cold War Era", *International Studies Quarterly,* Vol. 43, No. 1, March 1999.

Fierman, William, "Religion and Nationalism in Soviet Central Asia", *Problems of Communism*, Vol. 38, No. 4, July-August 1989.

Firdous, Tabassum, "Central Asia Security Stakes and Strategies", *World Affairs*, 4 (1), June 1995.

Foltz, Richard, "Uzbekistan's Tajiks: A Case of Repressed Identity?", *Central Asia Monitor*, No. 6, 1996

Freedman, Robert, "Russia and Central Asia under Yeltsin", *Central Asia Monitor*, No. 4, 1996.

Freij, Hanna Yousif, "State Interests Vs. Umma: Iranian Policy in Central Asia", *Middle East Journal*, Vol. 50, No. 1, Winter 1996.

Fuller, Graham, "The Future of Political Islam", *Foreign Affairs,* Vol. 81, No. 2, March-April 2002.

Gankovsky, YU. V., "Ruling Elite of Central Asian Yesterday and Today", *Defence Journal*, Vol. 21, No. 5-6, May-June 1996.

Gerner, Kristian, "From the Black Sea to the Adriatic Ethnicity, Territory and International Security", *Security Dialogue*, Vol. 24, No. 1, March 1993.

Gibbs, Jack P., "Conceptualisation of Terrorism", *American Sociological Review,* Vol. 54, No. 30, June 1989.

Gleason, Gregory, "Politics of Counter-Insurgency in Central Asia", *Problems of Post-Communism*, Vol. 49, No. 2, March-April 2002.

Glenn, John, "Contemporary Central Asia: Ethnic Identity and Problems of State Legitimacy", *European Security*, Vol. 6, No. 3, Autumn, 1997.

Goldberg, Joseph E., "Understanding the Dimensions of Terrorism", *Perspectives on Political Science*, Vol. 20, No. 2, Spring, 1991.

Goodhand, Jonathan, "From Holy War to Opium War: A Case Study of the Opium Economy in North Eastern Afghanistan", *Central Asian Survey*, 19 (2), June 2000.

Goyal, D. R., "Islamic Terrorism", *World Focus*, 20, 1 (241), January 2000.

Grant, J., "Decolonisation by Default: Independence in Soviet Central Asia", *Central Asian Survey*, Vol. 13, No. 1, 1994.

Guangcheng, Xing, "An Analysis of Internal and Foreign Policies, Newly Independent Countries in Central Asian Region", *Foreign Affairs Journal*, No. 26, December 1992.

Gumpel, Werner, "Economic Development and Integration in Central Asian Republics", *Eurasian Studies*, No. 13, Spring, 1998.

Gupta, Rakesh, "Tajikistan: Locked Horns for Power", *Strategic Analysis*, Vol. 15, No. 5, September1992.

Guthbertson, Ian, "New 'Great Game'", *World Policy Journal*, Vol. 11, No. 4, Winter 1994-95.

Halbach, Uwe, "Islam in the CIS, a Rebirth", *Aussen Politik*, Vol. 47, No. 2, 1996.

Halbach, Uwe, "Russia and its Southern Flank", *Strategic Digest*, Vol. 24, No. 9, September 1994.

Haghayeghi, Mehrdad, "Economic Cooperation Organisations: A

Preliminary Assessment", *Central Asia Monitor*, No. 1, 1995

"Islamic Revival in the Central Asian Republics", *Central Asian Survey*, Vol. 13, No. 2, 1994.

Haider, Ejaz, "Pakistan's Afghan Policy and its Fall Out", *Central Asia Monitor*, No. 5, 1998.

Haq, Ikramul, "Pak-Afghan Drug Trade in Historical Perspective", *Asian Survey,* Vol. 36, No. 10, October 1996.

Hetmanek, A., "The Political Face of Islam in Tajikistan: A Review of Mureil Atkin's the Subtlest Battle", *Central Asian Survey*, Vol. 9, No. 3, 1990.

"Islamic Revolution and Jihad Come to the Former Soviet Central Asia, The Case of Tajikistan", *Central Asian Survey*, Vol. 12, No. 3, 1993.

Horsman, Stuart, "Uzbekistan's Involvement in Tajik Civil War, 1992-97: Domestic Considerations", *Central Asian Survey*, Vol. 18, No. 1, March 1999.

Howell, Jude, "Coping with Transition: Insights from Kyrgyzstan", *Third World Quarterly,* Vol. 17, No. 1, March 1996.

Hyman, Anthony, "Central Asian Republics: Independence and After", *The Commonwealth Journal of International Affairs*, 341, January 1997.

"Moving out of Moscow's Orbit: The Outlook for Central Asia", *International Affairs*, Vol. 69, No. 2, 1993.

"Power Politics in Central Asia's New Republics", *Conflict Studies*, 273, August 1994.

Imam, Jafar, "How and Why the Soviet Union Disintegrated", *International Studies*, Vol. 29, No. 4, 1992.

Ivanov, Igor V., "Common Concerns, Common Interests, Building Regional Stability Peace and Prosperity", *Disarmament*, Vol. 20, No. 1, 1997.

Jacob, JFR, "New Great Game-Rivalries in Central Asia", *Indian Defence Review*, Vol. 10, No. 4, October-December 1995.

Jalali, Ali A., "Reminiscing the Past and Looking to the Future", *Central Asia Monitor*, No. 4, 2000.

Janabel, Jiger, "When National Ambition Conflicts with Reality: Studies on Kazakhstan's Ethnic Relations", *Central Asian Survey*, Vol. 15, No. 1, March 1996.

Jenkins, Brian, "International Terrorism: Trends and Potentialities", *Journal of International Affairs*, Vol. 32, No. 1, Spring/Summer, 1978.

Jha, Manish, "Islam and Central Asia: A Case Study of Kazakhstan", *BLISS Journal,* Vol. 20, No. 2, April 1999.

Kamilov, Abdulaziz, "Step Towards Regional Peace Development", *Disarmament*, Vol. 20, No. 1, 1997.

Karimov, Islam, "Uzbekistan on the Threshold of the 21st Century: Threats to Security and Stability", *Himalayan and Central Asian Studies*, Vol. 1, No. 3, October- December 1997.

Karin, Erlan, "Terrorism is Deadly Virus Plaguing Society", *The Times of Central Asia*, 9 May 2002.

Kartha, Tara, "Countering Trans-national Terrorism", *Strategic Analysis,* Vol. 23, No. 11, February 2000.

"Light Weapon Proliferation and Regional Instability in Central Asia", *Strategic Analysis,* Vol. 19, No. 9, December 1996.

"Trans-national Terrorism and Radical Extremism", *Aakrosh,* Vol. 2, No. 5, October 1999.

Kasagarli, Sultan Mahmut, "The Uighur Turks of Central Asia", *Central Asian Monitor*, No. 4, 1999.

Kaseno, Oumerseric, "Military Aspects of Security in Central Asia: National and Regional Security Strategies", *Amu Darya*, Vol. 1, No. 2, Summer/Fall 1996.

Kasenov, Oumirserik, "Central Asia: National, Regional and Global Aspects of Security", *Himalayan and Central Asian Studies*, Vol. 1, No. 3, April-June 1997.

Katz, Mark N., "The Decline of Soviet Power", *Survival,* No. 2, 1990.

Kaushik, Devendra, "Central Asia: Changing Geo-Political Alignment in the Aftermath of 11 September", *Dialogue*, Vol. 3, No. 4, 2002.

"India to Take Active Interest in the Central Asian Region –An Overview", *EIR*, Vol. 26, No. 35, 3 September 1999.

"Islamic Fundamentalism in Central Asia", *Himalayan and Central Asian Studies*, Vol. 4, No. 3-4, July-Dec., 2000.

"The Balance Sheet of 'OZODI'", *World Focus*, Vol. 19, No. 3, March 1998.

Keller, Shoshana, "Islam in Soviet Central Asia, 1917-1930, Soviet Policy and the Struggle for Control", *Central Asian Survey*, Vol. 11, No. 1, 1992.

Khaled, Adeeb, "Tashkent 1917, Muslim Politics in Revolutionary Turkestan", *Slavic Review*, Vol. 55, No. 2, Summer, 1996.

Khan, Hina, "Russian Expansionism in Central Asia and the Region's Response", *Pakistan Horizon,* Vol. 49, No. 2, April 1996.

Khan, Ijaz, "The Taliban, Iran and Central Asia: A View from Peshawar", *Central Asia Monitor*, No. 2, 1999.

Khan, Rasheedudin, "Central Asia's Geopolitical Importance", *World Focus,* Vol. 13, No. 11-12, November-December 1992.

Khan, Rashid Ahmed, "Pakistan's Relations with the Central Asian

Republics: Problems and Prospects", *BLISS Journal,* Vol. 15, No. 3, July 1994.

Khazanov, Anatoly M., "Ethnic Problems of Contemporary Kazakhstan", *Central Asian Survey,* Vol. 14, No. 2, 1995.

Khodjibaev, Karim, "Small Arms Proliferation and Social Militarisation in Tajikistan", *Central Asian Monitor*, No. 3, 1999.

Kidwai, Saleem, "Islam and Terrorism", *Journal of Peace Studies*, Vol. 7, No. 1, January-February 1999.

"US Strategy in Central Asia", *Journal of Peace Studies*, Vol. 6, No. 2, March-April 1999.

Kirimli, Meryan, "Uzbekistan in the New World Order", *Central Asian Survey*, Vol. 16, No. 1, March 1997.

Knyazev, Alexander, "International Terrorism in Central Asia, Part II", *Aakrosh*, Vol. 4, No. 12, July 2001.

Kubicek, Paul, "Regionalism, Nationalism and Realpolitik in Central Asia", *Europe-Asia Studies*, Vol. 49, No. 4, June 1997.

Kumar, Sumita, "Narcotics Trafficking in Central Asia", *Asian Strategic Review*, IDSA, 1996-1997.

Lal, Chaman, "Terrorism and Insurgency", *Seminar,* 483, November 1999.

Lamballe, Alain, "Xinjiang, a Developing Region of China", *Aakrosh*, Vol. 4, No. 11, April 2001.

Leader, Stefan, "Drug Money: The Fuel for Global Terrorism", *Jane's Intelligence Review*, February 2000.

Lipovsky, Igor, "Awakening of Central Asian Islam", *Middle Eastern Studies,* Vol. 32, No. 3, July 1996.

"In search of a New Political Identity", *Middle East Journal*, Vol. 50, No. 2, Spring, 1996.

Mackerras, Colin, "Xinjiang at the Turn of the Century: The Causes of Separatism", *Central Asian Survey,* Vol. 20, No. 3, 2001.

Magnus, Ralph H. and Eden Naby, Afghanistan and Central Asia, Mirrors and Models, *Asian Survey*, Vol. 35, No. 7, July 1995.

Mahmood, Annice, "Collapse of the Soviet Union and its Implications for Central Asia", *Strategic Studies,* Vol. 16, No. 3, Spring 1994.

Mahmood, Tehmina, "Pakistan and Central Asia", *Eurasian Studies*, Vol. 3, No. 4, Winter, 1996-97.

Maitra, Ramatanu, "Foreign Backed Taliban Armies Threaten Central Asia", *EIR*, Vol. 27, No. 35, 8 September 2000.

Makarenko, Tamara, "Central Asia Commits to Military Reforms", *Jane's Intelligence Review*, Vol. 12, No. 9, September 2000.

"Crime and Terrorism in Central Asia", *Jane's Intelligence Review,* July 2000.

"Seeking Security in Central Asia", *Jane's Intelligence Review*, Vol. 13, No. 1, January 2001.

"The Changing Dynamics of Central Asian Terrorism", *Jane's Intelligence Review*, February 2002.

Maley, William, "The Dynamics of Regime Transition in Afghanistan", *Central Asian Survey*, Vol. 16, No. 2, June 1997.

Malik, Iftikar H., "Issues in Contemporary South and Central Asian Politics, slam, Ethnicity, and the State", *Asian Survey,* Vol. 32, No. 10, October 1992.

Mann, Poonam, "Taliban at the Doorstep of Central Asia", *Strategic Analysis*, Vol. 25, No. 1, April 2001.

Mehrotra, O. N., "Commonwealth of the Former Soviet Republics", *Strategic Analysis*, Vol. 14, No. 11, February 1992.

"Light Weapons Proliferation and Regional Instability in Central Asia", *Strategic Analysis*, Vol. 19, No. 9, December 1996.

Melet, Yasmin, "China's Political and Economic Relations with Kazakhstan and Kyrgyzstan", *Central Asian Survey*, Vo. 17, No. 2, June 1998.

Menon, Rajan, and Henri J. Barkey, "The Transformation of Central Asia: Implications for Regional and International Security", *Survival*, Vol. 34, No. 4, Winter, 1992-93

Mesbani, Mohiaddin, "Tajikistan, Iran and the International Politics of the 'Islamic Factor'", *Central Asian Survey*, Vol. 16, No. 2, June 1997.

"Russian Foreign Policy and Security in Central Asia and the Caucasus", *Central Asian Survey*, Vol. 12, No. 2, 1993.

Mingde, Liu, "Changes of the Strategic Positions of Central Asia and the Contest among Outside Forces", *International Strategic Studies*, No. 3, July 1998.

Minshan, Chen and Xinguan, He, "Central Asia: Today and Tomorrow", *Contemporary International Relations*, Vol. 5, No. 8, August 1995

Mirsky, George I, "Central Asia's Emergence", *Current History*, Vol. 91, No. 567, October 1992.

Mishra, S. S., "Chinese Perspectives on Central Asia, Threat of Uighur Separatism", *Journal of Peace Studies*, Vol. 8, No. 3, May-June 2001.

Mohapatra, Aswini K., "Turkey's Quest for a Regional Role in Central Asia", *International Relations*, Vol. 38, No. 1, January-March 2000.

Mohapatra, Nalin Kumar, "Drugs and Small Arms, Its Impact on Regional Security in Central Asia".

Mohsenin, Mehrdad, "Iran's Relations with Central Asia and Caucasus", *Iranian Journal of International Affairs*, Vol. 7, No. 4, Winter, 1996.

Moimaddinin, Javed, "Iran and Central Asian Republics: Opportunities and Challenges", *Pakistan Horizon*, Vol. 48, No. 1, January 1995.

Moldasheva, Gulnara, "International Competition, the View from Central Asia", *Central Asia Monitor*, No. 3, 2001.

Murarka, Dev., "Pak-Soviet Relations, US Concern", *Mainstream*, Vol. 19, No. 51, 22 August 1981.

Naby, Eden, "Ethnicity and Islam in Central Asia", *Central Asian Survey*, Vol. 12, No. 2, 1993.

Nath, Rajendra, "New Realities of Central Asia", *Defence Today*, Vol. 4, No. 2, April- June 1996.

Nourzhanov, Kirill, "Turkmenistan: Half Way through the Golden Age?", *Central Asia Monitor*, No. 1, 1995.

Olcott, Martha Brill, 'The Myth of "Tsentral'naia Aziia', *Orbis*, Vol. 38, No. 4, Fall 1994.

"Central Asia's Islamic Awakening", *Current History*, Vol. 93, No. 589, April, 1994.

"Central Asia on Its Own", *Journal of Democracy*, Vol. 4, No. 1, January 1993.

"Central Asia: The Calculus of Independence", *Current History*, Vol. 94, No. 594, October 1995.

"Central Asia's Catapult to Independence", *Foreign Affairs*, Vol. 71, No. 3, Summer, 1992.

"Central Asia's Post-Empire Politics", *Orbis*, No. 2, Spring, 1992.

"Demographic Upheaval in Central Asia", *Orbis,* Vol. 40, No. 4, Fall 1996.

"Perestroika in Kazakhstan", *Problems of Communism*, Vol. 39, No. 4, July-August 1990.

"The Soviet (dis)union", *Foreign Policy*, No. 82, Spring, 1991.

Palat, K. Madhavan, "Emergence of Central Asia", *Indian Historical Review*, Vol. 18, No. 1-2, July 1991 and January 1992.

Palat, Madhavan K., "Emergence of Central Asia", *World Affairs*, Vol. 2, No. 1, June 1993.

Pande, M. C., "Mechanics of International Terrorism", *Strategic Analysis*, Vol. 13, No. 10, January 1990.

Panjavi, Riyaz, "Conflict in Afghanistan: Implications for Central South Asia", *Journal of Peace Studies*, Vol. 6, No. 2, March 1999.

Pasha, S. A. M., "The Islamic Phenomenon Central Asia", *Strategic Bulletin*, Vol. III, No. 1, July 1998.

"Turkey and the Republics of Central Asia, Emerging Relations and Dilemma", *International Studies*, Vol. 34, No. 3, 1997.

Patil, V., "Soviet Policy towards Pakistan", *Indian Journal of Political Science*, Vol. 38, No. 4, October-December 1977.

Patnaik, Ajay, "Central Asia since Soviet Disintegration", *World Focus*, Vol. 28, No. 8, February 2000.

Patterson, Mervyn, "Soviet Central Asia: A Time for Reflection", *Middle Eastern International*, 25 September 1992.

Peker, Gunden, "Islam: Myth or Reality in Central Asia", *Eurasian Studies*, Vol. 3, No. 3, Fall 1996.

Peters, William, "Centenary Conference of Central Asia: Past, Present and Future", *Asian Affairs*, Vol. 33, No. 1, February 2002.

"Central Asia and the Minority Question Part-II", *Link*, June 1991.

Pluchinsky, Dennis A., "Terrorism in the former Soviet Union, A Primer, A Puzzle, A Prognosis", *Studies in Conflict and Terrorism*, No. 21, 1998.

Primoratz, Igor, "What is Terrorism", *Journal of Applied Philosophy*, Vol. 7, No. 2, 1990.

Puri, Madan Mohan, "Central Asian Geo-Politics, the Indian View", *Central Asian Survey*, Vol. 16, No. 2, June 1997.

Qing, Chang, "Brief Analysis on China's Relations with the Five Central Asian Nations", *Foreign Affairs*, No. 33, September 1994.

Rahman, F., "Evolution of Soviet Policy towards Muslims in Russia: 1917-1965", *Institute of Muslim Minority Affairs*, Jeddah, King Abdul Aziz University, Vol. 1, No. 2, 1980.

Rahmani, Mansur, "NATO and OSCE: New Security Roles in Central Asia and the Caucasus", *Amu Darya*, Vol. 4, No. 9, Spring 1999.

Ramachandra, G. P., "Understanding Terrorism", *Asian Studies*, Vol. 5, No. 1, January-March 1987.

Ranstrop, Magnus, "Terrorism in the name of Religion", *Journal of International Affairs*, Vol. 50, No. 1, Summer 1996.

Rashid, Ahmed, "Islam and Nationalism in Pakistan and Central Asia", *South Asia*, An Address, Vol. 18, No. 2, December 1996.

"New Struggle in Central Asia", *World Policy Journal*, Vol. 17, No. 4, Winter, 2000-2001.

"The Taliban: Exporting Extremism", *Foreign Affairs*, Vol. 78, No.6, November-December 1999.

Rizvi, Ali Abbas, "Pakistan and Security of Central Asian States", *Asian Defence Journal*, No. 5, May 1994.

Robbins, Phillip, "Between Sentiment and Self-Interest: Turkey's Policy towards Azerbaijan and the Central Asian States", *Middle East Journal*, Vol. 48, No. 4, Autumn, 1993.

Roi, Yaacov, "Central Asian Riots and Disturbances, 1989-1990: Causes and Context", *Central Asian Survey*, Vol. 10, No. 3, 1991.

"The Islamic Influence on Nationalism in Soviet Central Asia", *Problems of Communism*, Vol. 39, No. 4, July-August 1990.

Rowson, Elizabeth, "Uzbekistan Diary, Part-II", *Link*, June 1995.

Roy, Alison, "The Security Priorities and Military Ties of the CIS Central Asian States", *Amu Darya*, Vol. 1, No. 2, Summer and Fall, 1996.

Roy, Olivier, "Islam and Central Asia", *Seminar*, Vol. 393, May 1992.

Rubin, Barnett, "The Fragmentation of Tajikistan", *Survival*, Vol. 35, No. 4, Winter, 1993-94.

Rubinstein, Alvin Z, "Geopolitical Pull on Russia", *Orbis*, Vol. 38, No. 4, Fall 1994.

Rumer, Boris, "Central Asia's Gathering Storm", *Orbis*, Vol. 37, No. 1, Winter 1993.

Rustamji, "Assassination, Terrorism and Security", Mainstream, Vol. 34, No. 6, 13 January 1996.

Sabal, Steven, "The Creation of Soviet Central Asia: The 1924 National Delimitation", *Central Asian Survey*, Vol. 14, No. 2, 1995.

Salahuddin, Ahmed (Abu Taher), "Nature and Outcome of States' Response to International Terrorism", *BLISS Journal*, Vol. 12, No. 2, April 1991.

Scarr, G. B., "Possible Ways to Diffuse Inter-Ethnic Tensions in the USSR", *Central Asian Survey*, Vol. 9, No. 3, 1990.

Sebastian, P. A., "Terrorism and the State", *Economic and Political Weekly*, Vol. 31, No. 25, 22 June 1996.

Sengupta, Anita, "Minorities and Nationalising States in Central Asia", *International Studies*, Vol. 34, No. 3, 1997.

Shafiee, Ismail, "Islamic Republic of Iran and Central Asia and Caucasian Republics", *Strategic Analysis*, Vol. 16, No. 2, May 1993.

Shams-ud-din, "Geopolitics of Central Asia", *Indian Journal of Politics*, Vol. XXIX, No. 12, 1995.

"Scramble for Influence in Central Asia", *Strategic Studies Journal*, No. 7, 1994.

"The New Great Game in Central Asia", *International Studies*, Vol. 34, No. 3, 1997.

Sharma, Jagadish, "Central Asia: Iranian and Turkish Perspectives", *Journal of Peace Studies*, Vol. 6, No. 2, March-April 1999.

Sharma, R. R., "Russia and Central Asia", *World Focus*, Vol. 16, No. 4, April 1995.

Sheif-Jadeh, Hossein S., "National Identity Crisis in Central Asia and the Caucasus", *Iranian Journal of International Affairs*, Vol. 6, No. 3-4, Fall/Winter, 1994-95.

Shevstova, Lilin, "The August Coup and Soviet Collapse", *Survival*, Spring, 1992,

Shiraji, Habibullah Abdlhasan, "Political Forces and Their Structures in Tajikistan", *Central Asian Survey*, Vol. 16, No. 4, December 1997.

Singh, K. R. "International Terrorism as an Instrument of State Policy", *International Studies,* Vol. 32, No. 2, April-June 1995.

"Central Asia in the Post-Cold War Era: The Strategic Dimensions", *USI Journal*, 1992.

Singh, Swaran, "Sino-Central Asian Engagement", *World Focus*, Vol. 28, No. 8, August 2000.

"Sino-Central Asian Ties: Problems and Prospects", *Strategic Analysis*, Vol. 24, No. 6, September 2000.

Sinha, P. B., "Pakistan - The Chief Patron - Promoter of Islamic Militancy and Terrorism", *Strategic Analysis*, Vol. XXI, No. 7, October 1997.

Slipchenko, V. I., "Russia's Political and Military Problems in Central Asia", *European Security*, Vol. 6, No. 1, Spring, 1997.

Smith, R. Grant, "Tajikistan: The Rocky Road to Peace", *Central Asian Survey,* Vol. 18, No. 2, 1999.

Snyder, Jack, "Nationalism and the Crisis of the Post-Soviet State", *Survival,* Vol. 35, No.1, Spring, 1993.

Snyder, Jeb, "Security Interests in Russia's Southern Periphery", Jane's Intelligence Review, Vol. 6, No. 12, December 1994.

Sosper, J., "Unofficial Islam: A Muslim Minority in the USSR", *Religion in Communist Lands*, Keston, Keston College, Vol. 7, No. 4, 1979.

Sreedhar, "Islamic Radicalism: Central Asia and Beyond", *World Focus*, Vol. 28, No. 8, August 2000.

Stephen, "Creation of Sphere of Influence Russia and Central Asia", *International Journal*, Vol. 49, No. 4, Autumn, 1999.

Stobdan, P., "Emergence of Central Asia: Strategic Implications", *Strategic Analysis*, Vol. 18, No. 3, June 1995.

"Taliban Raises Anxiety in CIS", *Strategic Analysis*, Vol.19, No. 12, March 1997.

"Central Asia in Geopolitical Transition", *Strategic Analysis*, Vol. 22, No. 1, April 1998.

"Central Asia: Change and Stability", *Strategic Analysis,* Vol. 17, No. 2, May 1994.

"Central Asia: Emerging Strategic Equations", *Aakrosh*, Vol. 2, No. 4, July 1999.

"Central Asian Regional Security", *Strategic Analysis*, Vol. 15, No. 5, August 1992.

"China's Central Asian Dilemma", *Strategic Analysis,* Vol. 22, No. 3, June 1998.

"International Aspects of the Conflict Situation in Central Asia, An Indian Perspective", *Strategic Analysis*, June 1992.

"Islamic Reawakening in Central Asia: Towards Stability or Conflict?", *Strategic Analysis*, Vol. 15, No. 5, August 1992.

"On the Central Asian Chessboard", *Strategic Analysis*, Vol. 22, No. 16, January 1998.

"Regional Security Issues in Central/South Asia and Potential for Cooperation", *Strategic Analysis,* Vol. 22, No. 10, January 1999.

"The Question of Central Asian Identity", *Strategic Analysis*, Vol. 21, No. 6, September 1997.

"US Interests in Central Asia: New Agenda for Pakistan", *Strategic Analysis,* Vol. 19, No. 5, August 1996.

Sudarshan, V., "Mad Mullah on a Leash", *Outlook*, Vol. 49, No. 41, 27 October 2000.

Sukhov, Alexey, "Hizb-ut-Tahrir in Kyrgyzstan", *The Times of Central Asia*, 25 October 2001.

Tal, Laurence, "Dealing with Radical Islam: The Case of Jordan", *Survival*, No. 3,

Tarock, Adam, "Iran's Policy in Central Asia", *Central Asian Survey*, Vol. 16, No. 2, June 1997.

Tazmini, Ghoneheh, "The Islamic Revival in Central Asia", *Central Asian Survey*, Vol. 20, No. 1, 2001.

Thurman, Michael, "Leaders of the Communist Party of Uzbekistan in Historical Retrospect", Part-I, *Central Asia Monitor*, No. 6, 1995.

Tishkov, Valery, "Ethnic Conflicts in former USSR, the Rise and Misuse of Typologies and Data", *Journal of Peace Research*, Vol. 36, No. 5, 1999.

Tyson, David, "Shrine Pilgrimage in Turkmenistan as a Means to Understand Islam among the Turkmen", *Central Asia Monitor*, No. 1, 1997.

Vas, E. A., "Central Asia - A Strategic Appraisal", Part- II, *USI Journal*, October-December 1997.

"Central Asia: A Historical Perspective", *USI Journal*, Vol. 127, No. 129, September 1997.

"Central Asia-A Strategic Appraisal, Part- II", *USI Journal*, Vol. 127, No. 530, October-December 1997.

Ved, Mahendra, "Silk Route Turns Destructive Drug Route", *World Focus*, Vol. 28, No. 8, August 2000.

Velayati, Ali Akbar, "The Constructive Role of Islamic Republic of Iran in Maintaining Regional Security", *Amu Darya,* Vol. 1, No. 2, Summer and Fall, 1996.

Walsh, Richard J., "China and the New Geopolitics of Central Asia", *Asian Survey,* Vol. 33, No. 3, March 1993.

Ware, Robert Bruce, "Islamic Factors in Dagestan", *Central Asian Survey*, Vol.19, No. 2, June 2000.

Warikoo, K., "Dynamics of Change in Soviet Central Asia", *World Affairs*, No. 3, December 1991.

"The Resurgence of Central Asia", *Strategic Analysis*, Vol. 15, No. 5, August 1992.

Weiderman, Dethelm, "Asian Dimension of the Dissolution of the USSR Central Asian Conflict Constellation- Origin, Structure, Complexity and Specificity", *Strategic Studies,* Vol. 16, No. 3, Spring, 1994.

Wen, Chai Cheng, "The Disintegration of Soviet Union and its Implication", *USI Journal*, 1993.

Widemann, Diethein, "Asian Dimensions of Dissolutions of the USSR, the Central Asian Conflict - Constellation, Origin, Structure, Complexity and Specificity", *Strategic Studies*, Vol. 16, No. 3, Spring, 1994.

Winrow, Gareth M., "Region at the Crossroads: Security Issues in Post-Soviet Asia", *Journal of South Asian and Middle Eastern Studies*, Vol. 18, No. 1, Fall, 1994.

Winrow, Gareth M., "Turkey and Former Soviet Central Asia: National and Ethnic Identity", *Central Asian Survey*, Vol. 11, No. 3, September1992.

Zhukov, S., and Reznikova, O, "Central Asia in World Politics and Economics", *Problems of Economic Transition*, Vol. 38, No. 8, December 1995.

Report

"Central Asia: Drugs and Conflict", *International Crisis Group Asia Report*, No. 25, 26 November 2001.

"Central Asia: Fault lines in the New Security Map", *International Crisis Group Asia Report*, No. 20, 4 July 2001.

"Central Asia: Islamist Mobilisation and Regional Security", *International Crisis Group Asia Report*, No. 14, 1 March 2001.

"Central Asia: Uzbekistan at 10 - Repression and Instability", *International Crisis Group Asia Report*, No. 21, August 2001.

"Central Asia: Water and Conflict", *International Crisis Group Asia Report*, No. 34, 30 May 2002.

"Tajikistan: An Uncertain Peace", *International Crisis Group Asia Report*, No. 30, 24 December 2001.

"The IMU and the Hizb-ut-Tahrir: Implications of the Afghan Camp", *International Crisis Group Briefing Paper,* 30 January 2001.

Report by the International Helsinki Federation for Human Rights (IHF) on *Human Rights and Terrorism in the Centŕal Asian OSCE Member States*, 10 December 2001.

Uzbekistan 10 years of Independence, Embassy of Uzbekistan, New Delhi, India, July 2001.

Website

http: //www.keston.org
http: //www.guuam.org
http://www.oic-oci.org
http: //www.crisisweb.org
http://www.eurasianet.org
http://www.ecosecretariat.org
http://www.ppc.pims.org/csrc
http://socrates.berkeley.edu/~issues
http://www.faith.edu/pulpits/94-05.htm
http: //www.terrorism/aghai/tcc/us/html
http://www.my/20documents/osce/203htm.
http: //www.uta.edu/pols/psees/turkcon.htm
http: //www.ferghana.ru/news/kirghiz46.html
http://www.usembassy.org.uk/terror 121.html
http://www.bu.edu/iscip/digest/vol2/ed11.html
http://www.undcp.org/terrorism_definitions.htm
http://www.state.gov/g/drl/rls/inf/2000/5724.htm
http://www.kyrgyzstan.org/law/constitution.htm-87k
http://preventgenocide.org/law/domestic/tajikistan.html.
http://www.int.org/external/pubs/ft/scr/2000/cr0027.pdf
http://www.undcp.org/uzbekistan/countryprofilekyr.html
http://hrw.org/backgrounder/eca/uzbekistan 605-bck.htm
http://www.ecostan.org/laws/uzb/uzbekistan con.html.54k
http://www.geocities.com/paris/9305/constitution.html.43k
http://www.homestead.com/prosites-kazakhembus/cica.html.
http: //www.press.service.uz/eng/pressa_eng/pressa_eng4.htm
http://www.iwpr.net/index.pl?archiev/rca/rca-2001/09-70-eng.txt
http:// www.geocities.com/capitolhill/lobby/2171/kzconst.html-7k
http://www.iwpr.net/index.pl?archieve/rca/rca-2000/09-71-2-eng.tat
http://www.eurasianet.org/departments/insight/articles/eav03050/shtmli
http://www.eurasianet.org/departments/insight/articles/eav120899.shtml

Index

D

E

I

O

P

R